The German Reformation

Blackwell Essential Readings in History

This series comprises concise collections of key articles on important historical topics. Designed as a complement to standard survey histories, the volumes are intended to help introduce students to the range of scholarly debate in a subject area. Each collection includes a general introduction and brief contextual headnotes to each article, offering a coherent, critical framework for study.

Published

The German Reformation: The Essential Readings
C. Scott Dixon

The Third Reich: The Essential Readings
Christian Leitz

The Counter-Reformation: The Essential Readings
David M. Luebke

In Preparation

The Enlightenment: The Essential Readings
Martin Fitzpatrick

The English Civil War: The Essential Readings
Peter Gaunt

The Cold War: The Essential Readings
Klaus Larres and Ann Lane

The Russian Revolution: The Essential Readings
Martin Miller

The French Revolution: The Essential Readings
Ronald Schechter

The German Reformation

The Essential Readings

Edited by C. Scott Dixon

Advisory editors:
Carter Lindberg, Boston University and
Euan Cameron, Newcastle University

Copyright © Blackwell Publishers Ltd 1999. Editorial arrangement and introduction copyright © C. Scott Dixon 1999.

First published 1999

2 4 6 8 10 9 7 5 3 1

Blackwell Publishers Ltd
108 Cowley Road
Oxford OX4 1JF
UK

Blackwell Publishers Inc.
350 Main Street
Malden, Massachusetts 02148
USA

British Library Cataloguing in Publication Data

A CIP catalogue record for this book is available from the British Library.

Library of Congress Cataloging-in-Publication Data

The German Reformation : the essential readings / edited by C. Scott Dixon.
    p.   cm. — (Blackwell essential readings in history)
    Includes five essays translated from German.
    Includes bibliographical references and index.
    ISBN 0–631-20810-0 (alk. paper). — ISBN 0–631-20811-9 (pbk.: alk. paper)
      1. Reformation—Germany. 2. Germany—Church history—16th century.
  3. Germany—History—1517-1648. I. Scott Dixon, C. II. Series.
    BR305.2.G45 1999
    274.3′06—dc21

Typeset in 10$^{1}/_{2}$ on 12 pt Photina
by Best-set Typesetter Ltd., Hong Kong
Printed in Great Britain by MPG Books Ltd, Bodmin, Cornwall

This book is printed on acid-free paper

Contents

Acknowledgements

The editor and publishers wish to thank the following for permission to use copyright material:

Thomas A. Brady, Jr., for 'The Reformation of the Common Man, 1521–24' in *Turning Swiss: Cities and Empire, 1450–1550*, Cambridge University Press (1985), pp. 151–83;

Duncker and Humblot GmbH for Richard van Dülmen, 'Reformation und Neuzeit. Ein Versuch', *Zeitschrift für Historische Forschung*, 14 (1987), pp. 1–25; and Wolfgang Reinhard, 'Zwang zur Konfessionalisierung? Prolegomena zu einer Theorie des konfessionellen Zeitalters', *Zeitschrift für Historische Forschung*, 10 (1983), pp. 257–77;

Berndt Hamm for 'Was ist reformatorische Rechtfertigungslehre?', *Zeitschrift für Theologie und Kirche*, 83 (1986), pp. 1–38;

The Editors of *The Journal of Interdisciplinary History* and the MIT Press for Robert W. Scribner, 'The Reformation, Popular Magic, and the "Disenchantment of the World"', *Journal of Interdisciplinary History*, 23 (1993), pp. 475–94. Copyright © 1993 by the Massachusetts Institute of Technology and the editors of *The Journal of Interdisciplinary History*;

Bernd Moeller for 'Was wurde in der Frühzeit der Reformation in den deutschen Städten gepredigt', *Archiv für Reformationsgeschichte*, 75 (1984), pp. 176–93;

Oxford University Press for Gerald Strauss, 'Success and Failure in the German Reformation', *Past and Present*, 67 (1975), pp. 30–63;

Stiftung Historisches Kolleg for Peter Blickle, 'Reformation und kommunaler Geist: Die Antwort der Theologen auf den Verfassungswandel im Spätmittelalter', *Schriften des Historischen Kollegs*, 44 (1996), pp. 1–42.

Every effort has been made to trace the copyright holders but if any have been inadvertently overlooked the publishers will be pleased to make the necessary arrangement at the first opportunity.

1

Introduction: Narratives of the German Reformation

C. Scott Dixon

Centuries have passed since Martin Luther fixed ninety-five theses against indulgences to the door of the castle church in Wittenberg. Few gestures in history, especially one born of so personal a struggle, have had such a profound affect on the course of European history. And few figures in the past, especially one so unlikely or unwilling to be the leader of a public movement as Martin Luther, have shaped the destiny of so many human lives. The posting of the ninety-five theses on 31 October 1517 is now held to be one of the defining moments of European history, just as the Reformation movement which developed out of Luther's initial protest is thought to be one of the crucial stages in the evolution of western culture and society. Historians often refer to the Reformation movement as the start of a new era, a turn from Europe's medieval past to the modern age. The Reformation marks a juncture, a divide, between one period of historical development and another.

And yet, although scholars generally agree that the Reformation has been profoundly important for the evolution of Europe, there is no standard or widely-held estimation of its place in history. We still have much to learn about the nature and the meaning of this event. Centuries have passed, but we are still asking the most basic and elemental of questions. In essence, scholars today have the same agenda as the seventeenth-century church historian Veit Ludwig von Seckendorff, who promised in the preface to his *History of Lutheranism* (1692) 'to bring to light, from material in the archives of the principalities and cities, and those in private ownership, why the reformation of religion took place and with what success, and how from small beginnings it achieved its present state, at which the world never ceases to wonder'.[1] Why the reformation of religion took place and with what success are questions which have

---

1 Cited in A. G. Dickens and John M. Tonkin, *The Reformation in Historical Thought* (Oxford, 1985), p. 116

preoccupied generations of thinkers, and they are questions at the fore-front of the historical enterprise today. This ongoing quest for the meaning and the importance of the Reformation is the subject of this volume.

A traditional narrative account of the origins of the Reformation in Germany has passed into history. Some doubts have been raised whether the ninety-five theses were ever actually posted on the church door, but it seems beyond dispute that on 31 October 1517 Martin Luther, pro-fessor of theology at the University of Wittenberg, circulated a list of criticisms against the practice of indulgences which found a wide read-ership in the German lands. Called to account by the authorities, first by his Augustinian order, then by the Catholic church, and then finally, famously, by the secular authorities at the Diet of Worms in 1521, Luther soon found himself the leader of a movement which would change the face of western Christendom.

Contemporaries termed it the 'Luther Affair,' and it quickly over-whelmed Europe. As early as 1521 the papal nuncio declared that 'All of Germany is in open revolt. Nine-tenths cry out 'Luther!'. And as for the remaining tenth, in so far as they are not bothered about Luther, they see the solution in the slogan "death to the Roman [papal] court'".[2] As tensions mounted and support grew, Luther spent the early 1520s bringing his theological insights to light in a flood of publica-tions. By 1522, the year his German translation of the New Testament was published, Luther had been excommunicated by the Catholic church, placed under ban in the Holy Roman Empire, and cited as a heretic by Rome's leading theologians. He now stood in clear opposition to the Catholic church, and still the reform movement which had emerged in his name continued to gather momentum.

Reformers of all stamps and nationalities appeared, some of whom claimed to speak for Martin Luther, some of whom developed their own understanding of Scripture and their own inspired theology, all of whom claimed to speak for the Word of God. In the Swiss-German lands to the south, for instance, the reform movement led by Huldrych Zwingli projected an image of the Christian community unique to its own tra-ditions and circumstances, while the model of Reformation developed in mid-century by Geneva's John Calvin proved applicable in lands as far afield as Scotland and the Dutch Republic. The Reformation transformed the culture and society of Europe; as it unfolded over the course of the century it proved a revolutionary force. But for many the real revolution occurred the year the German Martin Luther challenged the authority

2   Cited in Luise Schorn-Schütte, *Die Reformation. Vorgeschichte – Verlauf – Wirkung* (Munich, 1996), p. 34.

of Rome. It was a conflict over religious truth, and it would not end until the Protestant faith had survived the threat presented by the Catholic church (or the Antichrist, as Luther saw it) and the new church had been secured in Europe. This is the traditional narrative structure behind the history of the Reformation – the struggle with and ultimate rejection of the Catholic church and the subsequent emergence of the Protestant confession. Not unlike a myth of origins, it pits a heroic figure against an adversary and tells the story as a sequence of events building up to final outcome (or victory). Even today, this is the most familiar narrative account of the event in the German lands.

But there are other ways of conceptualizing the Reformation – there always have been – and that is what the contributions in this volume set out to demonstrate. Without necessarily denying the importance of Martin Luther, or indeed any of the other leading reformers, and without setting out to eclipse the role played by faith or the power of theological ideas, the essays in this collection assume a broad perspective to assess how the Reformation worked as a catalyst for change. They describe how the movement was bound and shaped by the culture in which it was broadcast, as well as how the forces of religious reform came to affect both German and European society in the sixteenth and seventeenth centuries. This approach to the Reformation is primarily concerned with how the reform movement was perceived and expressed by its participants, how it interacted with the trends and tensions of the period, and how Protestant doctrine was translated into social and cultural reality. The central concern still remains the questions posed in the *History of Lutheranism* – 'Why the reformation of religion took place and with what success' – but the analysis is not confined to the study of a static theological corpus or the heroic gestures of an inspired few. Nor is this collection a sampling of the classic Reformations in their national settings, followed by a historical account of the main Protestant churches (Lutheran, Zwinglian, Calvinist, Anglican). The analyses which follow are concerned first and foremost with the Reformation as it occurred in the German lands. Even where the range of investigation strays beyond the Empire, the thoughts and concerns at the heart of the volume are those which have most profoundly informed the scholarship of the German Reformation. But the contributions offer more than just a history of confessional change in a single land. The Reformation caught up in the dynamism of its age is the subject of study in this collection. It is the story of an event whose importance cannot be revealed by way of a single linear narrative. Indeed, it is the sheer range of perspectives, the sheer number of ways in which the story might be told, that makes the Reformation one of the most significant events in European history. Only by acknowledging the total context can we come to terms with the character and meaning of the 'Luther Affair'. This is the conviction behind the selection of articles in this volume.

I

The Reformation has always been perceived in different ways, as have its leaders. This was true at the very outset, when the movement was strongly associated with individuals. Luther's first fame was literary fame, and both his character and his cause fell prey to different interpretations once they were cast in the public medium of print. As an author, Luther worked in two languages, and he thought of two different audiences as he wrote. The learned Latin tracts were written with a readership of Humanists and theologians in mind, while the less demanding and less polemical German works dealt primarily with pastoral and devotional themes and were written with a view to a wider audience. In practice, however, this division could not sustain itself, and by the early 1520s Luther's name was not necessarily associated with a particular theme but rather with a massive (and contentious) literary corpus and an entire reform movement.[3] Humanists and like-minded clergy may have thought of him as an author of religious works, but in the popular mind Luther had become a symbol for much more. This is why it is difficult to speak of *the* reformer Martin Luther or *the* Reformation of the sixteenth century.

The Reformation meant many different things to many different people, even if they made use of the same symbols and shared the same references. Some saw Luther as a preacher and a pastor, a shepherd for lost souls; some saw him as the champion of the German peoples and the defender of truth; and others saw him as a messiah, spreading God's word like a prophet. In portraits and popular woodcuts, he appeared, *inter alia*, as a doctor of theology, a monk inspired by the holy spirit, a nobleman, the German Hercules, and even the seven-headed beast of the apocalypse.[4] And this is just to speak of the Reformation in its association with Martin Luther. To the followers of the reform movement in

---

3   Bernd Moeller, 'Das Berühmtwerden Luthers', *Zeitschrift für Historische Forschung*, 15 (1988), pp. 65–91; Bernd Moeller, 'Die Rezeption Luthers in der frühen Reformation', *Reformations-Theorien. Ein kirchenhistorischer Disput über Einheit und Vielfalt der Reformation*, ed. Berndt Hamm, Bernd Moeller and Dorothea Wendebourg (Göttingen, 1995), pp. 9–19.

4   Thomas Fuchs, 'Martin Luther. Führungsgestalt in der Reformation der Reformatoren', in *Luther in seiner Zeit*, ed. Martin Greschat and Günther Lottes (Stuttgart, 1997), pp. 69–87; Robert Scribner, *For the Sake of Simple Folk* (Oxford, 1994), pp. 14–36; Martin Warnke, *Cranachs Luther* (Frankfurt, 1984).

south Germany or the Swiss lands, the figure of Huldrych Zwingli con-
jured up a set of symbols and a history of the Reformation all its own.
In the opinion of Abraham Scultetus, a court preacher in Heidelberg
who published his views in 1618, the Reformation began with the
preaching of the Gospel, but its success did not come about through
Luther's efforts alone. Zwingli's preaching in Glarus in 1516 was as
crucial to the course of the movement as any initiatives in Wittenberg.[5]
The same claim might have been made for any of the leading reformers. It is unlikely, for instance, that the followers of the radical reformer
Thomas Müntzer perceived of the Reformation in the same way as the
followers of the Wittenberg reformers. Although he was convinced of
the need for church reform as early as 1521, Müntzer did not use the
term Reformation until the year 1524, and then with reference to a
theological vision born of apocalypticism and social meliorism. If his
supporters shared the same vision, even in part, then this notion of
Reformation is of an entirely different nature from that shared by the
early Lutherans.[6]

Even in the age of reform, it would seem, there was no single notion
of what was meant by the term Reformation. Can we then hope to
capture the essence of the movement standing, as we are, so many centuries removed from the event? Can we speak of the essential readings
of the Reformation? Is there any hope of reducing the complexity to a
series of central or essential narratives? The solution, as one recent
analysis suggests, is to abandon the quest for a single explanatory model
and pay heed to the many dimensions of the movement.[7] The full weight
of the Reformation, along with its essential characteristics, is revealed
in its variety.

One way to get at the heart of the Reformation is to look at the religious ideas which made up the early evangelical message. Given the profound social and cultural consequences of the movement (consequences
which will be discussed in later contributions to this volume), it is often
easy to overlook the fact that the Reformation began as an attempt to
reform certain aspects of the late-medieval Catholic church. It was, in
essence, a rethinking of religious ideas, a questioning of traditional

5   Rainer Wohlfeil, *Einführung in die Geschichte der deutschen Reformation* (Munich,
1982), p. 48.
6   Günter Vogler, 'Reformation als Alternative – Alternativen der Reformation', in
Wegscheiden der Reformation. Alternatives Denken vom 16. bis zum 18. Jahrhundert, ed.
Günter Vogler (Weimar, 1994), pp. 11–21.
7   Hans-Christoph Rublack, 'Reformation und Moderne. Soziologische, theologische und historische Ansichten', *Die Reformation in Deutschland und Europa: Interpretationen und Debatten*, eds. Hans R. Guggisberg and Gottfried G. Krodel (Gütersloh,
1993), pp. 28; 17–38.

religious culture, and it first took shape as an intellectual dialogue between antagonistic clergymen over the fate of the Christian church. Clearly, it did not remain a clerical dispute for very long. Through the recently invented medium of the printing press (which was spreading the reform message in cheap and accessible pamphlet publications) and the traditional methods of oral culture (sermons, open-air talks, alehouse banter) Luther's stand against the Catholic church soon found huge numbers of lay supporters in the German lands. But even after it had become a public event, religious ideas remained at its heart. Throughout the first decade or so after Luther and other reformers began to challenge the legitimacy of the Catholic church, it was the force of religious ideas that gave the movement its basic energy. What then was the essential content of the early Reformation message? What was being preached in the German cities in the early years of the Reformation?

The nature of this message is the subject of the contribution by Bernd Moeller (chapter 2). Using the sermons preached and published in the German cities in the 1520s, Moeller offers a profile of the early evangelical message. He does this by looking at the reform movement as it was experienced in the urban setting, where the reformers first delivered their sermons and the printers first sold their books. Moeller tries to abstract a core of essential religious (or Reformation) ideas from the intellectual agitation of the early years. It is a difficult theme, and it requires more than just the projection of Luther's ideas into the public realm. For the early reform movement was marked above all by its trust in the power of the Word. By this, the reformers meant Scripture, the Word of God, and even the most vocal and prolific of the Reformation leaders thought of themselves first and foremost as spokesmen for God's Word, rather than authors set on innovation. Luther himself claimed that it was not his work but God's Word that had brought about the fall of the papacy. But empowering the Word with this type of authority meant that its meaning could not be easily controlled. Never before in Europe's history had so much weight and authority been invested in a text so susceptible to mass expectation and so open to public interpretation. The dynamic of the early Reformation was generated by this sense of immediacy, this conviction that the Word of God was open to all. 'Every man is bound to preach God's Word in house or at table, morning or evening, in field or barn, whether at leisure or at work,' wrote the reformer Andreas Karlstadt, 'and he is to study God's Word and treat of it to those who are round him, or who belong to him.'[8]

In such a climate, it is easy to understand why the early Reformation has been perceived in so many different ways. It is also easy to see how

8   Cited in Felipe Fernández-Armesto and Derek Wilson, *Reformation. Christianity and the World 1500–2000* (London, 1996), p. 148.

the study of a static theological corpus would fail to capture the true quality of the event. Ideas were in flux, caught up in the energy of urban culture. And yet, despite the heterogeneity, Moeller sees an essential and consistent religious message at the heart of the movement. The Reformation did not dissolve into a confusion of voices, Moeller suggests, but took form around a nucleus of leading ideas. A survey of the sermons published in the 1520s reveals a group of theological themes which, taken together, best represent the message of the early Reformation. Moreover, according to Moeller, the religious ideas that predominated have a direct (and essential) affinity with the teaching of Martin Luther. All of the main evangelical authors thought of themselves as members of a Christian community preaching the same fundamental religious truths. Thus it was not a 'confusion of voices' which characterized the early Reformation movement but a 'relatively unified picture' of Luther's ideas which held sway in the cities. 'In its basic outlines and main arguments it was a thoroughly unified and relatively circumscribed theological declaration', concludes Moeller (with co-author Karl Stackmann) in his latest look at this theme, adding that the message was clearly perceived as doctrine, the voice of truth, and a message of salvation all in one 'bound by theological consensus'.[9]

Not all scholars agree with this assessment. A long tradition of research sees more variety than unity in the early reform message. As historians of this school point out, preachers and publishers were not yet subject to the type of supervision that would direct the growth of confessions later in the century, so there were no guidelines or conditions for what might be declared in the name of reform. Nor was there yet a canon of ideas recognized as normative. Luther had set out an agenda, but this was far from the final word or even the final frame for discussion. The Word of God alone was authoritative, but this licensed a freedom of interpretation far removed from a 'relatively circumscribed theological declaration'.[10] Nevertheless, we should not let the lack of

9   Bernd Moeller and Karl Stackmann, *Städtische Predigt in der Frühzeit der Reformation. Eine Untersuchung deutscher Flugschriften der Jahre 1522 bis 1529.* (Göttingen, 1996), pp. 358; 202–359; Bernd Moeller, 'Die Rezeption Luthers in der frühen Reformation', in *Reformations-Theorien*, eds. Hamm, Moeller, Wendebourg, pp. 22–7.
10   For the difference of opinions see Bernd Moeller, 'Die Rezeption Luthers in der frühen Reformation', in *Reformations-Theorien*, ed. Hamm, Moeller, Wendebourg, pp. 22–7; Bernd Moeller, 'Luthers Erfolg', in *Luther in seiner Zeit*, ed. Greschat and Lottes, pp. 89–105; Hans-Jürgen Goertz, 'Eine "bewegte" Epoche. Zur Heterogenität reformatorischer Bewegungen', in *Reformiertes Erbe*, ed. Heiko Oberman et al., (Zurich, 1993), pp. 103–25; Susan C. Karant-Nunn, 'What was Preached in the German Cities in the Early Years of the Reformation?' *Wildwuchs* versus Lutheran Unity', in *The Process of Change in Early Modern Europe*, ed. Phillip N. Bebb and Sherrin Marshall (Athens, Ohio, 1988), pp. 81–96; Miriam Usher Chrisman, *Conflicting Visions of Reform. German Lay Propaganda Pamphlets, 1519–1530* (New Jersey, 1996).

harmony overwhelm us. All of the leaders of the early Reformation were ultimately inspired by Luther's dialogue with the Catholic church, and the vast majority of participants recognized that there were essential theological principles at stake in the debate. There may have been contrasts in stress placed on certain aspects of the Word, differences of accent and understanding amidst the flux of opinions, and different visions of reform derived from the same biblical maxims, but at the root of it all was a common stock of basic religious ideas. These ideas, as Moeller illustrates, were at the heart of the preaching and publishing revolution as it was experienced in the German cities.

There was in fact more than just a group of related ideas held in common by the early reformers. One idea in particular inspired the whole event. For all of the major Protestant thinkers of the sixteenth century, from Luther to Zwingli, Osiander to Calvin, the central theme of evangelical theology was the doctrine of justification. Luther thought that the doctrine of justification 'is the lord and prince of all forms of doctrine and rules all conscience and the whole Church. Without it the whole world is stale and naught but darkness; no error but will steal in and rule, be it absent.' Justification was not just a defining tenet of the Lutheran church, but the centre of the Christian faith. 'Take away the justification article and you do away with the Church,' wrote Luther in 1531, 'for it can then withstand no error. Except within this article the Holy Ghost neither will nor can be with us.'[11] Other Protestant reformers thought in similar terms, though they may not have identified so strongly with Luther's own ideas on justification. But for all of them, this 'lord and prince of all forms of doctrine' was the theological insight that distinguished the Protestant faith from the theology of the Catholic church.

What was the Reformation doctrine of justification? This is the question that animates the contribution by Berndt Hamm (chapter 3). It too is a difficult theme, for Hamm is not limiting his study to the thought of one major reformer, but rather extending the range of his analysis to all of the main thinkers (Luther, Melanchthon, Zwingli, Calvin) in an effort to identify the *essential* Reformation doctrine of justification. Essential, in this context, is defined by Hamm as that body of thought 'which cannot be described as just one possible position within the medieval theological system'. In other words, the Reformation doctrine of justification, in order for it to distinguish itself from the Catholic inheritance, had to be 'mould-breaking'; it had to project an entirely new understanding of the relationship between sinful man and a righteous God.

11   Ernst Walter Zeeden, *The Legacy of Luther*, tr. Ruth Mary Bethell (London, 1954), p. 6.

Hamm identifies this breach by way of a contextual, historical approach. In the medieval church, like the later Reformation church, justification was related to the idea of being made righteous. In the medieval church, however, the believer was an active subject before God; he could participate in his salvation. It was a complicated theory, but in essence the church claimed that justification was expressed when man was made righteous and his soul was transformed through the quality of God's grace. Schools of theological thought fought bitterly over the extent to which the individual could contribute to his own salvation, but it was generally held that medieval man could acquire grace by doing works of appropriate merit or worthiness.[12] 'God's forgiveness of sins and justification of man,' as Hamm observes, 'is made possible by the granting of grace to man and by his subsequent good works and freedom from acts of mortal sin; these aspects of his nature then also become the condition of his sanctification after death.' Thus the process whereby man becomes righteous, justified before God, was subject to reasons and preconditions. The Reformation doctrine of justification, in contrast, was unconditional. The sinner had an outright promise of unconditional salvation. There was nothing that could be done, no reasons given or preconditions that had to be met. Christ had already made us righteous in the sight of God with his saving death. Salvation was no longer dependent on merit (for nothing could be done to alleviate man's sinful nature), but rather guaranteed by the righteousness of Christ. 'The new relationship in which grace justifies us,' Hamm observes, 'means that God sees man in the light of Christ's righteousness, and allows it to stand for the righteousness of sinners.' This was the essential or 'mould-breaking' idea in Reformation theology, and it was shared by all of the major reformers. Righteousness was not a state that could be acquired, as Catholicism taught, but a condition which exists beyond ourselves in Christ (*extra nos* in the words of the theologians). And that is why Luther's famous insight speaks of justification through faith alone. 'For faith is the means whereby man is led from his moral subjective existence,' explains Hamm, 'into the final validity of the righteousness of Christ, in which he is preserved for salvation – outside himself, where God looks graciously on him.' With this new understanding, centuries of Catholic belief were cast off.

The Reformation doctrine of justification represented a radical conceptual break with the medieval theological tradition, but also it reflected, in part, a common intellectual and social trend. The Catholic

---

12   Euan Cameron, *The European Reformation* (Oxford, 1991), pp. 79–93; Alister E. McGrath, *Iustitia Dei. A History of the Christian Doctrine of Justification* (2 vols, Cambridge, 1986), vol 1, pp. 155–79.

church on the eve of the Reformation was in search of a centre. In both its doctrine and its forms of worship, there was a need and a desire to reduce the complexity, to make the relationship between man and the divine more direct, more immediate. For the late-medieval spiritual elite, this meant the right execution of a Christian life, and it meant living each day, as the author Thomas à Kempis advised, in imitation of Christ. The ordinary parishioner, however, who could not hope to find this union in the cloistered life, contemplation, or prayer, had to trust in the ministrations of the Catholic church. The need for a direct or a centred relationship with God was just as strong, but there was no route to salvation other than the one offered by the church. The believer had to participate in the complex and perpetual cycle of salvation preserved by Catholic dogma. The union with God was thus far from simple and direct, and any perceived focal point or centre to medieval religion was kept at a distance by the demands of the penitential cycle. The Reformation doctrine of justification, however, broke with the relative complexity of the medieval church and offered the faithful a focus or a centre to their faith. Hamm has termed this a 'normative centering', for it represented a turn away from the medieval cycle of religion (along with its mental, psychological, and economic burdens) towards a new relationship between the believer and God. Christ was now the centre of the faith; there was a move away from the systems of late-medieval religiosity to a more direct Christ-centred religion of the Word.[13] Salvation was in Christ and his Word. That is why the Reformation doctrine of justification posed such a powerful threat to the medieval Catholic church. 'The whole typical late medieval yearning for security and the certainty of grace and salvation,' as Hamm observes in his contribution, 'finds an outlet and a solution here.' Few words in European history have led to such fundamental change.

II

In the German lands, as in France, the Swiss cantons, the Netherlands, and in other parts of central and eastern Europe, the Reformation first took hold in the cities and surrounding towns. Historians have long recognized this, and today the importance of civic culture for the Protestant movement is widely accepted. To claim that the Reformation was first experienced as an 'urban event' is now a commonplace of modern

---

13   Berndt Hamm, 'Reformation als normative Zentrierung von Religion und Gesellschaft', *Jahrbuch für Biblische Theologie*, 7 (1992), pp. 241–79; Hamm, 'Einheit und Vielfalt der Reformation – oder: was die Reformation zur Reformation machte', in *Reformations-Theorien*, ed. Hamm, Moeller, Wendebourg, pp. 57–127.

historiography. There is no great mystery in this. The urban setting was the natural location for the reception and dissemination of Reformation ideas, for that is where the reformers first held their sermons, the evangelical authors first published their pamphlets, and the message was first diffused. Public life in the sixteenth century was civic life, and in so far as there was a common cultural tradition in this period, it was urban based. With a view to the place of origin, the Reformation was necessarily an event which first took root in the urban setting.[14] This was especially true for the Reformation in Germany and Switzerland, where civic culture had reached a high stage of development. As Luther himself appreciated, the earliest supporters of the evangelical movement were found behind the city walls, and it was this union between urban culture and the new faith which made it possible for the Reformation to take shape initially and then to survive. Moreover, this union also made it possible for a movement rooted in the realm of religious ideas to translate into social reality. The evangelical movement had spread to the cities and towns, the people were acting on the message they were hearing, and the Word was transformed into collective action. Urban culture had turned a debate between churchmen into a social revolution. That is why the story of the Reformation's legacy to the western world begins in the Swiss and German cities.

In his *Address to the Christian Nobility of the German Nation* Luther first drew widespread public attention to the need for reform. At certain points in the tract, Luther addressed the territorial princes and the urban magistrates as equals, as authorities with similar powers of rule, and in general this reflected a fact about political culture in the German lands. Although the city councils ruled over smaller territories, the character of rule was similar to that enjoyed by a prince. In the most privileged examples – and usually this meant the free Imperial cities (*Reichsstädte*) rather than the territorial cities (*Landstädte*) – the urban councils had the right to tax their subjects, to regulate economic affairs, to create and enforce laws, to govern over the local church, to enter into federations or alliances, to assemble armed forces, and to wage defensive wars. In all but name, city councils in the free Imperial cities ruled as lords. Unlike the princely states, however, powers of rule did not reside in a single sovereign or hereditary institution. In the cities, in contrast to the territories, power was situated in four contending figurations of rule – city councils, urban guilds, urban communes, and the traditional laws and customs of the city. Claims to power might therefore overlap, but common to all forms of civic governance was the concept and praxis

14 See the discussion and the literature cited in Cameron, *The European Reformation*, pp. 210–63; 475–87; Heinz Schilling, *Die Stadt in der frühen Neuzeit* (Munich, 1993), pp. 94–112.

of community. The basic inner structure of urban rule was communal or corporate in nature. Citizens (and for the most part this meant male householders) were bound together through oath in a politico-legal association based upon notions of freedom, peace, common law, and independent government. In theory, this meant that rule was derived from, and functioned for, the civic commune. The commune or the common good (*Gemeinnutz*) was the highest political value. Civic government was instituted to ensure that the values and relations which bound the community together as a free association were preserved. It was a form of political culture with a powerful ethical component at its core; and even if few city councils really practised a communal form of rule, the idea that sovereignty was derived from the commune in order to serve the commune hung over the cities' past 'like a ghost'.[15]

The urban culture of communality proved especially receptive to the early Reformation message, and this was the deep affinity that bound the reform movement to the cities. All social relations in this age needed religious legitimatization, and there could be no better endorsement of urban values than the message of the evangelical movement. Reformers spoke of brotherly love and the need to live in harmony as good Christians, and these were words that a culture tied to the values of the common good could readily appreciate. More than this, many believed that Luther's movement, and the preaching of the Word in particular, would at last complete the sacral corporation, the *corpus christianum* so longed for in the medieval world.[16] For any religion which transformed the relationship between the individual and God would transform the relationship between the community and God, necessarily so in an age when religion was imagined and experienced at both an individual and a collective level. As a consequence, cities did not look to the Reformation just to legitimize urban culture, but to sacralize it.[17]

This deep affinity between the early reform movement and the cities is the subject of the contribution by Thomas A. Brady, Jr. (chapter 4). Values of communalism or corporatism, long at the heart of urban culture, in concert with the powerful political standing of Imperial cities such as Nuremberg, Strasbourg, and Augsburg, tied the progress of the early Reformation to the fate of the cities. In Nuremberg, for instance,

15   Gerhard Dilcher and Thomas A. Brady, Jr., in *Resistance, Representation, and Community*, ed. Peter Blickle (Oxford, 1997), pp. 249; 217–55; Bob Scribner, 'Communities and the Nature of Power', in *Germany. A New Social and Economic History*, ed. Bob Scribner (London, 1996), pp. 291–326.
16   Bernd Moeller, *Imperial Cities and the Reformation*, trs. H. C. Erik Midelfort and Mark U. Edwards, Jr. (Durham, 1982), p. 49.
17   Berndt Hamm, *Bürgertum und Glaube. Konturen der städtischen Reformation* (Göttingen, 1996), pp. 51–102.

the evangelical movement soon attracted a strong following, not just among the educated elite, but also among the 'common man' inside and outside the city walls. As Brady suggests in his contribution, the evangelical movement offered all Nuremberg inhabitants 'a common vehicle for liberation from an oppression that they, for the moment, sensed to be a common one'. Granted, notions of liberation clearly differed, but they were all rooted in the idea of community, and they all had profound consequences once translated into social action. To the city councillors, the Reformation meant liberation from external ecclesiastical authorities, while at the same time it legitimized and strengthened the system of rule put in place in order to protect the 'common good' and the sacral corporation. To the common man, in contrast, the Word of God and its stress on equality, community, and brotherly love spoke of new forms of social relations and governance. Both visions had a chance to develop in the Imperial city, but without doubt the convictions of the common man threatened to bring about the most sweeping change. On the eve of the Peasants' War of 1525 Nuremberg's artisans and labourers were demanding the removal of the Catholic clergymen and the appointment of evangelical preachers in their stead. They insisted that the Word of God should lead to a reform of the church, and that its message of brotherly love should serve as the moral norm for social relations. In more practical political terms, they refused to render tithes, they called for a reduction in the fees and dues paid to the city, and they petitioned for the right to participate in government. Religious demands had thus been shaped by the political environment, a process the Nuremberg city council acknowledged with some unease in June of 1524 when it called attention to the 'malicious letters and notes (which do nothing more than lead to unrest and contempt for authority) that have been posted in the churches and the squares here in the city'.[18]

As the Imperial diets met in Nuremberg from 1522 to 1524, the governing council could only stand by and watch as the Reformation took hold in the cities. Emperor Charles V had already issued the Edict of Worms in 1521 in an effort to outlaw and suppress Lutheran teachings, claiming that Luther's ideas led 'to nothing else but unrest, division, war, murder, robbery and pillaging and in general the destruction of the Christian commonwealth', but despite constant Imperial insistence, the city authorities were unable to enforce the edict.[19] By this stage, as Brady makes clear, support for the reform movement had become too

18   Günter Vogler, 'Erwartung – Enttäuschung – Befriedigung. Reformatorischer Umbruch in der Reichsstadt Nürnberg', in *Die frühe Reformation in Deutschland als Umbruch*, eds. Stephen E. Buckwalter and Bernd Moeller (Gütersloh, 1998), p. 390.
19   Heinrich Richard Schmidt, *Reichsstädte, Reich und Reformation* (Stuttgart, 1986), p. 42.

powerful and widespread among the commoners. When the regency council ordered the suppression of the movement and the suspension of the changes in worship introduced in the city churches, the Nuremberg authorities, recognizing the depth of support for the 'Luther Affair', simply claimed 'that is not within the power of the honourable council at the present time'.[20] Luther's religious protest had created a new political dynamic in the German lands. Domestically, urban councils had begun to implement changes and adapt the reform movement to their systems of rule; externally, city politics, tolerant if not fully supportive of the evangelical movement, now ran counter to the politics of Charles V, a man who still thought in terms of Catholic empire. The religious issue was now at the centre of the agenda; it had created clear divisions. Urban culture, bound to the religious principles and the social energy of the Reformation, turned its back on the vision of empire. It was a fateful moment for urban politics, indeed a fateful moment for the course of European history. Rather than look to the Catholic Emperor, the cities sought to defend a common religion in confessional unions and military alliances. For the first time in German history, cities joined together with territorial princes in defence of a common cause. The Reformation had transformed European politics. Ultimately, however, as the cities were never perceived as equal partners, the change of policy brought about by the Reformation led to the weakening of the urban front. Germany remained a land of territorial princes, while the cities, having alienated the Emperor, became their prey. But few would have predicted this result in the early 1520s, when it seemed that the fusion of urban culture and the evangelical message would bring about the rule of the common man.[21]

The relationship between the evangelical movement and the early-modern political culture of communalism is also the subject of the contribution by Peter Blickle (chapter 5). Blickle extends the notion, both with reference to the role played by the community in the thought and actions of the initial reformers and the geographical reach of the early Reformation. No less than urban culture, Blickle argues, the culture of the countryside proved receptive to the cause of reform. The cities may have been the heartland of the early Reformation, and urban society may have set the pace, but the spread of the movement to the rural hinterlands was not an inevitability or an accident. On the contrary, Blickle sees an essential affinity between the evangelical faith and the type of political culture familiar to the parishioners of central and southern

20   Schmidt, p. 163.
21   Thomas A. Brady, Jr., *Turning Swiss. Cities and Empire, 1450–1550* (Cambridge, 1985), pp. 215; 125–225; Thomas A. Brady, Jr., *Protestant Politics: Jacob Sturm (1489–1553) and the German Reformation* (New Jersey, 1995), pp. 149–88.

Germany. In short, we cannot understand the success of the reform movement of the sixteenth century until we take full account of the culture and praxis of communalism. This affinity, a fusion of evangelical theology with the communal spirit, was what in fact characterized the early Reformation movement, both in its first manifestation as a church built around the community *and* as a theology conditioned by its age. 'To my mind,' Blickle writes in his contribution, 'the *communal spirit* that developed in Europe in the late Middle Ages provides the best explanation of the theology of the reformers (and hence of their ethics and politics), in so far – and this is an important proviso – as it can be deduced at all from concrete historical circumstances.'

In essence, communal spirit is a reference to the nature of political culture at the local level. Throughout the late-medieval period, local communes, local political communities, were evolving at the expense of traditional monarchical forms of governance.[22] Communal assemblies developed sophisticated systems of rule based upon the principles of common good, peace, and extended political participation. On the eve of the Reformation, as a result, the German lands were home to two notions or traditions of rule: a vertical notion of sovereignty, the lord and his subjects, and a horizontal notion of communalism, a political unit bound by an oath. In the Rhaetian Freestate, for instance, a confederation of autonomous political communes in the southern Empire, both communalism and monarchism provided the context for rule. The Rhaetian communes comprising the federation used traditional notions of feudalism to justify their right to rule over their subjects (or fellow members), but they rejected all notions and claims of sovereignty that threatened their culture of communalism. 'The bishop is the lord, but the peasants are master', was the measured formula of the Protestant minister of Chur.[23] But clearly it was the peasants – the commune – that carried the most weight.

This communal spirit played a role in both the urban and the rural reform movements, to such an extent that Blickle believes the most appropriate way to understand the Reformation up to the outbreak of the Peasants' War in 1525 is to think of it as a Communal Reformation. Like the cities, though more susceptible to the flux of feudal relations, rural communities had developed fairly sophisticated systems of rule at

22   Blickle has presented the full sweep of communalism in two edited volumes: Peter Blickle, ed. *Landgemeinde und Stadtgemeinde in Mitteleuropa: ein struktureller Vergleich* (Munich, 1991); Peter Blickle, ed. *Theorien kommunaler Ordnung in Europa* (Munich, 1996).
23   Randolph C. Head, *Early Modern Democracy in the Grisons. Social Order and Political Language in a Swiss Mountain Canton, 1470–1620* (Cambridge, 1995), p. 120; *passim*.

the local level. This process was most marked in Switzerland and Germany (the setting for the early Reformation), where, as one scholar has summarized it, 'the basic form of association in both town and country was the commune (*Gemeinde*), which possessed, or sought to possess, autochthonous rights to regulate its own affairs. This included the administration of justice, maintenance of peace within the community, economic functions such as distribution of common land or grazing, administration of church finances and church fabric, and in some places communal appointment of pastors.'[24] Again like the cities, rural society looked to the ideal of the common good (*Gemeinnutz*) to legitimate the method of rule. This tradition of political practice and ideal community not only predisposed the parishioners to find the Gospel's message of 'brotherly love' appealing: in so far as evangelical theology was tied to practical experience, the culture of communalism actually gave shape to the early Reformation message. According to Blickle, 'the original, undistorted, unadulterated character of the reformation is its manifestation as a communal reformation'.[25] In both Memmingen and Wendelstein, to cite the examples Blickle gives, the early Reformation was experienced as a Communal Reformation. The parishioners demanded the preaching of the Word, they insisted on greater control over the local church and its finances, and they called for the right to have power over the parish clergyman, including his appointment and dismissal. Similar demands were made, though in much more threatening terms, throughout Germany and Switzerland during the period of peasant unrest. Even the leading reformers, men such as Martin Luther, Huldrych Zwingli, and Martin Bucer, conceived of church reform in terms of the commune and collective worship. Unless we understand the relationship between this political culture and the early reform movement, Blickle insists, we will never grasp the essential importance of the Reformation as a historical event. Nor will we ever recover its true legacy for the people of Europe.

III

In 1727 the chapter of Salzburg elected a new archbishop, Leopold Anton, Freiherr von Firmian. Educated as a Jesuit, Firmian had little tolerance for other Christian denominations, and he soon decided to root

---

24   Robert W. Scribner, 'Communalism: Universal Category or Ideological Construct? A Debate in the Historiography of Early Modern Germany and Switzerland', *The Historical Journal*, 37 (1994), p. 199.
25   Peter Blickle, *Communal Reformation. The Quest for Salvation in Sixteenth-Century Germany*, tr. Thomas Dunlap (London, 1992), p. xiv.

out the Protestant homesteads scattered throughout the alpine districts of his archdiocese. Faced with this threat, the Protestants, most of whom were rather modest cattle farmers, submitted a petition to the *corpus evangelicorum* (which represented Protestant interests at the Imperial diets) and detailed how Catholic bullying had become a part of their daily lives. Undaunted, Firmian stepped up his efforts, and on 11 November 1731 the archdiocese issued a emigration edict designed to 'extirpate and uproot these unruly, seditious, and rebellious folk wholly and henceforth'.[26] This edict set in motion one of the most famous events in the confessional history of Europe, the expulsion of the Salzburg Protestants (1731–2). Thousands of alpine residents had to pack up their belongings and leave their land of generations on account of their religion. The emigrants were not long without a home, however, for the Protestant Elector of Brandenburg, Frederick William, had heard of their plight and offered a formal patent of invitation to the Salzburg Protestants to settle in Prussian Lithuania. Frederick William, as his supporters described it, saviour of the Protestant faith, had rescued his fellow believers from the hold of the Catholic foe. So the emigration began, and a history or legend grew up around the event. In his poem *Die Alpen* (1728), for instance, Albrecht von Haller had already described the Salzburg Protestants as a people characterized by integrity, independence, and moral probity. They were a people of the book, living together in pious households built on thrift, hard work, loyalty, and faith. The expulsion of such people, later authors opined, could only be the work of a godless ruler in a godless land. Protestants did not miss the chance to make parallels with the exodus of the Israelites. And if their predicament had been brought about by the tyranny of a bishop, slave to a false religion, the legends and histories left Europe in no doubt that it was their distinctly Protestant virtues that enabled them to survive. The entire event, in fact, was imagined in religious terms.

The Salzburg emigration took place two hundred years after the Reformation, but it was brought about by the confessional developments of the sixteenth century. It occurred in an age when the context of personal and political relations was deeply influenced by religion, and the personal faith of every European was bound to the public profile of the state. The Reformation had created an international society which defined itself in terms of religious belief. A sense of identity was communicated through education, first with the catechisms after the church service, then at the schools staffed with servants of the church, and finally at the universities or the higher educational establishments

---

26 Mack Walker, *The Salzburg Transaction. Expulsion and Redemption in Eighteenth-Century Germany* (London, 1992), p. 62; *passim*.

(such as the Jesuit schools). Detailed and explicit confessions (or state-ments) of the faith spelled out the difference between true and false reli-gion, and each member of the church was expected to honour the public confession in its entirety. Right belief was not a matter for the individ-ual to decide. The faithful belonged to a distinct religious confession, and that confession was legitimized by the state. Moreover, it was the God-given obligation of the state to ensure that unity and purity of faith were observed. As a consequence, and with increasing inflexibility, the subject population was reined in by the powers of discipline; they were not only told what to believe, but how they should act on those beliefs. It became the goal of every European leader to create the perfect con-fessional state, a union of ruler and ruled bound by a single faith. That is why the Salzburg archbishop felt it necessary to expel the alpine Protestants from his lands, and that is why the Protestant Elector of Brandenburg moved to receive them.

The relationship between the rise of the confessional state and the Reformation is analysed in the contribution by Wolfgang Reinhard (chapter 6). Historians have long recognized that the sixteenth century was marked by the formation of powerful new confessions. Far from weakening the status of the church, religious divisions led to the further consolidation of Christian culture. Europe was no longer joined in the Catholic fold, but never before had the church had so much power in society, and never before had the faithful shared such a strong sense of religious identity. But it was a process that went beyond the church; all of European culture and society was touched by it. Recognizing this, Wolfgang Reinhard, along with his fellow German historian Heinz Schilling, has tried to make sense of this historical process by developing the paradigm of confessionalization. Rather than limiting itself to a study of the traditional aspects of religious development (syntheses of the faith, educational initiatives, liturgical innovations), confessionalization looks at the role played by religion in the restructuring, the strengthening, and indeed the modernization of society. 'Thus confessionalization,' in the words of one scholar, 'does not mean the process which led to the for-mation of confessions or the development of the major church struc-tures, but rather the process which enabled the spirit of confessional Christianity to penetrate, transform and then reform the state, culture, the legal and intellectual realm, and indeed society *tout court*.'[27]

In his contribution, Reinhard suggests that confessionalization is best thought of as 'an early phase of modern state formation' which affected

---

27   Johannes Wallmann, 'Lutherische Konfessionalisierung – ein Überblick', in *Die lutherische Konfessionalisierung in Deutschland*, ed. Hans-Christoph Rublack (Güter-sloh, 1992), p. 35.

all of Europe, not just the states of a certain confession. 'The undisputed theological oppositions,' he writes, 'were by no means expressed in practical life in the form of consistent structural divergencies.' In other words, confessionalization was a 'universal phenomenon' with certain essential characteristics. It was not particular to Catholicism or Protestantism; it was a structural development which occurred in the same way, at the same time, throughout most of Europe. Given the sheer number of different territorial powers in the Holy Roman Empire, it should come as no surprise that the process of confessionalization was at its most intense in the German lands. But it was not just a German phenomenon. The Catholic confessionalization of the French province of Avignon, for instance, relied on the same methods, and could hope for the same results, as the confessionalization of any Protestant state in the Empire. Only the religious expectations behind the process differed.[28]

Confessionalization was thus marked by certain common features, and these cut across the boundaries of religious conviction. To start with, each of the major Christian churches of the post-Reformation era had developed fairly detailed and fairly inflexible statements of their respective religions. Lutherans could learn what to believe in the *Augsburg Confession* (1530) and the *Formula of Concord* (1580), Catholics in *The Roman Catechism* (1566), while the members of the Reformed church, which had a number of confessional statements to choose from, could turn to *The Heidelberg Catechism* (1563). These theological summaries then formed the basis of the total reform of culture and society set in motion after the Reformation. Or, to cite the words of Heinz Schilling, 'religious change, conceived as social change, thus serves as a heuristic indicator for the secularizing forces within the entire process'.[29] This process occurred in most of the major states in Europe, from the Protestant territories in Germany to the traditional Catholic lands of Italy and Spain. As Reinhard points out in his contribution, this was experienced at the social and political level in a number of ways. Education, inspired and directed by the confessional programmes, was standardized, so that all of the students were exposed to the same notions of religious orthodoxy and the same set of social ideals. In essence, it was a campaign of indoctrination. At the more general level,

---

28   Compare *Die Territorien des Reichs im Zeitalter der Reformation und Konfessionalisierung*, ed. Anton Schindling and Walter Ziegler (5 vols, Münster, 1989–1992); Marc Venard, *Réforme protestante, Réforme catholique dans la province d'Avignon au XVIe Siècle* (Paris, 1993), pp. 389–902.
29   Heinz Schilling, 'Confessional Europe', in *Handbook of European History, 1400–1600: Late Middle Ages, Renaissance and Reformation*, ed. Thomas A. Brady, Jr., Heiko A. Oberman, and James D. Tracy (Leiden, 1995), vol. 2, p. 643.

in the books people read or the public culture they shared, the confessional state drew upon the church confessions to develop and project the public sense of religious identity. And in all of this, as Reinhard makes clear, the state had become the main beneficiary. Never before had the secular rulers been invested with such powers of rule, for as heads of the state church, placed into office by God, they now had the obligation to care for both the secular *and* the spiritual welfare of the subject population. Little wonder historians often see an intensification of social disciplining in this age. All of this, Reinhard argues, from the evolution of common identities to the consolidation and modernization of the state, has its roots in the process of confessionalization. There might have been some subtle differences between the Catholic and the Protestant approach, but in its essential outlines, confessionalization was a universal phenomenon, and most of the European states were shaped by it to some degree.[30] It was a legacy of the Reformation, even if it was unforeseen.

Concepts like confessionalization can help us appreciate the meaning of the Reformation, for it is easier to assess the importance of a historical process if we can visualize it (in terms of the state, the family, the individual conscience) than if we try to make sense of it in the abstract terms common to theology or intellectual history. There is a risk involved, however, and it resides in the confusion of cause and effect. Once we start associating the Reformation so closely with the characteristics of modern European society, and once we start thinking of it as a turning point in history, as a rupture or a break with the medieval period, then it becomes difficult to understand the event on its own terms. We tend to abstract from the present to arrive at an understanding of the past, to the point where many of the things we hold to be modern we trace back to important events like the Reformation, events which are assumed to mark a turning point in the development of European history. And the problem is compounded when history is invoked to explain national development, rather than just general development. In German scholarship, as one scholar has observed, the Reformation has long been considered 'the crucial and (in a quite literal sense of the term) epoch-making event by

---

30   For some insights that have come to light since the appearance of Reinhard's article, see Heinz Schilling, 'Die Konfessionalisierung von Kirche, Staat und Gesellschaft – Profil, Leistung, Defizite und Perspektiven eines geschichtswissenschaftlichen Paradigmas', in *Die katholische Konfessionalisierung*, ed. Wolfgang Reinhard and Heinz Schilling (Gütersloh, 1995), pp. 1–49; Wolfgang Reinhard, 'Was ist katholische Konfessionalisierung?' in *Die katholische Konfessionalisierung*, eds. Reinhard and Schilling, pp. 419–52; Hans-Christoph Rublack, 'Zur Problemlage der Forschung zur lutherischen Orthodoxie in Deutschland', in *Die lutherische Konfessionalisierung in Deutschland*, ed. Rublack, pp. 13–32.

which the nature of an entire national community and of its history has been defined'.[31] For many scholars working within this tradition it is difficult to imagine the Reformation without thinking of its imputed effects on the evolution of German society. And as a consequence it is difficult to speak of the essence of the Reformation in Germany without appeals to the modern age.

The relationship between the Reformation and the modern age is the theme of the contribution by Richard van Dülmen (chapter 7). Modernity, he observes in the introduction to his analysis, is impossible to imagine without calling to mind the Reformation movement, even if it is difficult to give a full account of the developments and associations involved. For modernity was not just a functional consequence of the religious divisions of the sixteenth century. Many of the values and virtues of modern society, and many of the qualities that are assumed to distinguish the present age from past periods, find their source in the Reformation. We value the Reformation because we live in an age which has been shaped by it, and we think of the Reformation as the turn towards modernity because that is where we find the first signs of ourselves. Thus the issue at the heart of van Dülmen's study is not only how the evangelical movement ultimately set in motion a series of historical developments which led to the modernization of Europe. A theme of equal importance is this close affinity between the modern age and its *perception* of the Reformation. For it has not always been understood in these terms. To the first few generations of reformers, for example, Luther was perceived as the instrument of God, and the reform movement was understood as the Holy Spirit at work in the world. A century or so later, however, it was less the power of prophecy or sacred history which held the story together so much as theological orthodoxy. But this approach started to unravel in later centuries, and thinkers began to look beyond confessions of the faith and sacred histories and started to rely more on secular or rational explanations. The Reformation thus fell prey to another myth of unity, this one grouping everything together under the banners of progress and profit, the advancement of the general welfare, rationality and freedom of conscience.[32] It was the German sociologist Max Weber, perhaps, who did the most to turn this association into a habit of mind. For it was his theories, and in particular his work *The Protestant Ethic and the Spirit of Capitalism* (1904), that

---

31   Jaroslav Pelikan, 'Leopold von Ranke as Historian of the Reformation: What Ranke did for the Reformation – What the Reformation did for Ranke', in *Leopold von Ranke and the Shaping of the Historical Discipline*, ed. Georg G. Iggers and James M. Powell (Syracuse, 1990), p. 90.
32   Dickens and Tonkin, *The Reformation in Historical Thought*, pp. 7–282; Wohlfeil, *Einführung in die Geschichte der deutschen Reformation*, pp. 45–57.

gave intellectual substance to the alleged association between the modern qualities of rationality, duty, individuality and the essence of Protestantism. The purpose of Weber's research was to 'chart Protestant asceticism as the foundation of modern vocational civilization', and his work has since influenced generations of scholars. Religious conviction was seen as the reason why European society developed the way it did – and with this insight, the Reformation enters the modern age.

More than just theories or habits of mind bear out this association. There is good reason to speak of a relationship between the Reformation and the modern age. Granted, few scholars today would think of the rise of Protestantism as an inevitable turn towards modernity, and fewer still would make explicit reference to theories (such as those associated with Max Weber) that afford the Reformation such a causal role in the emergence of modern industrial Europe.[33] And yet, there is no doubt that many of the qualities and certainties of the modern age originated with the Reformation. The proof, as van Dülmen illustrates, is in the details. In the first instance, the confessional divisions of the sixteenth century created a new awareness. Europe was now home to religious pluralism. At one level this led to the rationalization and standardization of a common confessional identity (the process of confessionalization discussed above by Wolfgang Reinhard); at another level its effects were more subtle and personal, giving rise to modern notions of religious tolerance and a more private experience of faith. In Protestantism, the believer stood before God without sacramental intermediary, and the personal demands were greater. Modern notions of individuality, as van Dülmen has suggested elsewhere, owe many of their roots to the religious developments of the sixteenth century.[34] In a broader context, the Reformation acted as a spur to the modernization of the state. Clear divisions were established between church and state, with each 'kingdom' of rule given its own set of responsibilities. We think of this separation of the secular and the spiritual as a rational or a modern development.

Also counted among the Reformation's contributions to the modernizing process are the improvements made in education, the secularization of marriage (along with the resultant moral reform of the household), and the revaluation of secular activity brought about by Protestantism's positive endorsement of work. This brings us back to Max Weber and his view that the Reformation gave rise to new forms of thought and conduct. Protestantism is a religion based on the Word, he

33   Hartmut Lehmann, *Max Webers 'Protestantische Ethik'* (Göttingen, 1996), pp. 42–9.
34   Richard van Dülmen, *Die Entdeckung des Individuums. 1500–1800* (Frankfurt, 1997), pp. 19–25.

argued; it requires a command of the text, along with the courage to interpret the text. By its very nature it demands greater vocation and application from the believer, and a greater sense of agency and destiny takes hold of the individual as a result. Seen in this light, as van Dülmen points out, it is difficult to imagine modern Europe without first calling to mind the Reformation, and it is difficult to take stock of the qualities and values common to the modern age without making some sort of association with the rise of Protestantism. Indeed, even Max Weber's wife, Marianne, found it necessary to open the 1929 biography of her husband with an account of how Weber himself was the stock of a long line of industrious and pious people who had been expelled from Salzburg in 1731 'on account of their Protestant faith'.[35] Perhaps the father of the theory was in need of some sort of legitimization as well, or perhaps it was just habit of mind.

IV

'I declare,' wrote Martin Luther in 1528, 'I have made a reformation which will make the popes' ears ring and hearts burst.' Revolutions have been launched in gentler tones than this, but Luther's words are typical of the sense of destiny and expectation at the heart of the evangelical movement in the 1520s. Most of the early supporters of the Reformation were confident that the Word of God would effect a total reform of the church and its people. Most were also convinced that there would be a return (a revolution) to a state of secular and spiritual relations grounded in biblical norms. The world would be turned upside down. With this in mind, perhaps it *is* best to think of the early Reformation as a type of revolution.

In essence Luther had already launched a revolution against the church when he attacked the clergy, the monasteries, and the Pope, whom he termed the 'destroyer of Christianity' and the Antichrist. Other reformers followed suit, drawing on the revolutionary spirit of anticlericalism animating the people of northern and central Europe, from the nobles to the peasants, the burgers to the knights.[36] At the same time, evangelical pamphleteers such as Heinrich von Kettenbach elevated the Reformation principle of *sola scriptura* (scripture alone) to a war cry against the 'human fables, papal bulls, spiritless laws, and Imperial mandates' of traditional Catholic Europe. The moment had come, Kettenbach and others concluded, for the Catholic clergy, the

35   Walker, *The Salzburg Transaction*, p. 189.
36   Hans-Jürgen Goertz, *Antiklerikalismus und Reformation* (Göttingen, 1995), pp. 26–9; *passim*.

'plunderers of the bodies, souls, honour, and goods', to make way for Christ's church. And leading the charge, at least in the eyes of the early reformers, was the laity, for the laity had become heirs to the Word of God. In part this was a logical consequence of Luther's notion of the Priesthood of All Believers, a theological principle which necessarily put the common man on equal terms with the clerical estate. But the belief that the laity would be the first to inherit the fruits of the Reformation was also a projection of the revolutionary expectations of the early reformers. In the literature of the evangelical movement, the laity emerge as wise, competent, and capable of understanding God's word. They would build the new church. This was the real revolution, this belief that the common layman now had the competence to decide the fate of the church. Luther believed it, and that is why he boasted to the Elector of Saxony that he lived in an age which was witness to 'young children praying more devoutly, believing more firmly, and discoursing more eloquently on God and Christ than, in the old days, all the learned monks and doctors'. Even Johannes Cochlaeus, the great Catholic polemicist, acknowledged it. That is why he complained about the spread of Luther's Bible and how the 'cobblers and women and all of the laity, who have at best an incomplete understanding of German letters, read it without pause, as if it were the font of all truth'. They carry the text around with them, he continued, and learn it by heart, and once they feel they have learned enough, they begin to debate over religious matters 'not only with other Catholic laypeople, but with priests and monks, indeed even with masters and doctors of theology'.[37] To judge by these early commentators, the fate of the Reformation was in the hands of the laity.

How far removed seem the words and spirit of the commentators in the centuries that followed. In place of praise for a pious church-going lay population, the Lutheran pastors of Germany on the eve of Eng-lightenment have nothing but disappointment to relate. The parishioners now resent the Word of God, for they feel that it leads to the preaching of the Law. Evangelical pastors were no longer respected for their ability to interpret the Gospel from the pulpit. Instead, they were denounced as 'lords and bishops' who wished to rule over the village. The parishioners sinned as they had sinned in the medieval age. Despite the optimism of the early Reformation, there had been no moral reform of the parishes; and when the parishioners were called to account for it, they would simply claim: 'One cannot always live up to heaven'. Even in their beliefs, they seemed to have been untouched by the Reformation.

37   Steven Ozment, *Protestants. The Birth of a Revolution* (London, 1993), pp. 47; 48; 38–90; Fuchs, 'Martin Luther', pp. 85–6.

Church attendance remained poor; and when they did attend, whether it was a sermon or communion or a baptism, it was done out of social obligation. They came away without knowing 'what it all means'. 'Alas' wrote a Protestant pastor in the seventeenth century, in a lament he put to verse, In these last days,

> The state of the common man is such
> That he does not believe in God's work
> And he behaves as though blind and deaf.
> Arrogantly he says
> Is all this still true?
> But when God afflicts people
> Greatly and punishes them . . .
> Then faith is conveniently at hand.

The layman was no longer interested in the Word of God. And he no longer aspired to read the Bible or to understand Scripture on his own. 'The common folk lie buried in great ignorance and stupidity; they need to be taught the first letters of the Word of God', was how the pastors viewed the state of affairs. 'While working who can think of God? That is impossible', was how the parishioners answered their critics. 'If one wants to read and pray, one has to sit down or walk, and get a book, and we do not always have the time for that.'[38] The age of chasing after Catholic doctors with Scripture in hand, as Cochlaeus described it, had passed. No doubt the Protestant commentators exaggerated to make the situation look worse than it was, but if there is truth in this, even in small part, it would seem that the Reformation had failed to accomplish many of its central objectives.

The relationship between the expressed objectives of the early Protestant reformers and their impact on Reformation Germany is the theme of the contribution by Gerald Strauss (chapter 8). Strauss couches his analysis in terms of 'success and failure,' and he does this because he believes there are clear criteria with which to judge the Reformation achievement. Luther and his supporters hoped that the Word would effect a reform of Christian conscience. The Reformation, in the first instance, was a matter of personal faith. Once the inner man was touched (through the Word) by the Holy Spirit, the reform of society in its head and members would naturally and necessarily follow. Thus the early reformers put great stress on education; they were convinced that

---

38   Hans-Christoph Rublack, 'Success and Failure of the Reformation: Popular "Apologies" from the Seventeenth and Eighteenth Centuries', in *Germania Illustrata*, eds. Andrew C. Fix and Susan C. Karant-Nunn (Kirksville, 1992), pp. 147; 149; 150–1; 153; 154; 141–65.

proper religious instruction would implant the faith in young minds. The Reformation, in the words of Strauss, 'embarked on a conscious and, for the first time, remarkably systematic endeavour to develop in the young new and better impulses, to implant inclinations in consonance with the reformers' religious and civic ideals, to fashion dispositions in which Christian ideas of right thought and action could take root, and to shape personalities capable of turning the young into new men – into the human elements of a Christian society that would live by evangelical principles.'[39] It seemed an endeavour that could not fail, for the pedagogical principles of the day insisted on repetition and memorization as the keys to educational success, and there had never been a better aid to rote learning than the Protestant catechisms of the sixteenth century. Moreover it was a campaign which had the backing of the state. As in most things, as Strauss remarks in his contribution, 'political ends came inevitably to be fused with religious objectives'.

Nevertheless, despite the support of the state, and despite the strong sense of purpose and destiny behind the endeavour, the educational experiment appears to have been a failure. Strauss reaches this conclusion through a study of the visitation returns, the annual reports on the state of religious affairs in the parishes. According to the visitation records housed in the German archives, the subject population of the major Lutheran territories had not been reformed by the Word of God. Indeed, using these records as a guide, there is little to suggest that a Reformation of religion had taken hold at all. Neither parish morality, nor the quality of parish religion, had been markedly affected by the reform campaign. In Luther's land of Electoral Saxony, Strauss observes, 'no change had taken place,' and the situation was no better in the territories of Brandenburg, Wolfenbüttel, Grubenhagen, Kalenberg, Lauenberg, Oldenburg, or the Imperial cities of Ulm, Nuremberg, and Strasbourg. Granted, in the larger Latin schools there was evidence of improvement, but 'very little of this transferred itself to the general adult population on whose everyday lives and thoughts the formal religion, Catholic or Protestant, seems to have made little impact'. In light of these results, Strauss can come to no other conclusion: 'A century of Protestantism had brought about little or no change in the common religious conscience and the ways in which ordinary men and women conducted their lives.'[40] In short, judged by its own standards, the Reformation had failed. No doubt many of the Lutheran pastors of the seventeenth and the eighteenth centuries cited above would have agreed.

39   Gerald Strauss, *Luther's House of Learning. Indoctrination of the Young in the German Reformation* (London, 1978), p. 2.
40   Strauss, *Luther's House of Learning*, p. 299.

Since the publication of Strauss's findings a number of works have appeared which challenge and even reject his conclusions. Research has been done on the visitation process in select Imperial cities, for instance, and it would seem that the pedagogical experiment in the urban setting was more successful than its rural equivalent. Some scholars have suggested that a study limited to the German lands should not be applied to the Reformation as a whole, while others have questioned the suitability of the sources that were used. Visitation records are, by design, testimony to failure.[41] But the real issue is not what the sources have to tell us about the relative success or failure of local reform initiatives. The real issue is the *sense* of failure shared by the generations that tried to realize the dream of reform. The evidence is there, as Strauss makes clear, to suggest that the Reformation did not achieve what Luther and his supporters hoped it would. But still more powerful was the perception of failure, the widespread belief that the reform movement had fallen short of its original objectives. This realization coloured the thoughts of later Protestant pastors, and it should colour ours. For the Reformation was not experienced as a faultless unfolding of theological ideas put into practice. Nor was it merely the logic behind the structural developments which mark the modern age, such as secularization, confessionalization, or the growth of social disciplining. The Reformation was an encounter between the will of the state and the individual in the parish, and it is best understood in terms of mediation and accommodation, rather than acculturation or domination. The reformers accomplished some of their aims, but fell short of others, and their ultimate legacy was far removed from their original intentions.[42] This is what the work of Strauss suggests to us, that we might try to understand the Reformation as a narrative of consequences never intended, and a narrative of failure as well.

For the vast majority of people in medieval Europe, religion was not experienced in terms of abstract doctrine, but rather in the practical realities of ritual and custom. Like all Christian devotion in this age, parish religion was determined by the law of the Catholic church – public rites and ceremonies had to be approved, worship was focused on the liturgical office, and each member of the church had to partake in the sacraments. The sacraments, in return, sanctified the believers, and made them part of the Christian community. But medieval Christians had a very active style of piety, and whenever it was possible to manipulate or personalize Catholic forms of worship they were quick to set

41   For the most recent survey see Geoffrey Parker, 'Success and Failure during the First Century of the Reformation', *Past and Present*, 136 (1992), pp. 43–82.
42   C. Scott Dixon, *The Reformation and Rural Society. The Parishes of Brandenburg-Ansbach-Kulmbach, 1528–1603* (Cambridge, 1996), pp. 102–207.

their stamp. Witness the spread and popularity of the *Corpus Christi* processions in the late medieval period, the localization of the Virgin Mary as a figure of devotion, or the cult of the saints.[43] Where they were able, the people of medieval Europe took the Catholic church to their hearts and shaped it in their image. And this was one of the main problems facing the reformers of the sixteenth century. For as difficult as it was to make people remember the lines of a Protestant catechism, it was an even greater task to make people forget their religion of centuries.

The effect of the Reformation on the mental world of the sixteenth-century parishioner is the theme of the contribution by Robert W. Scribner (chapter 9). If medieval religion was steeped in ritual and imagery, Protestantism was a religion of the book. Luther and the other reformers stressed the efficacy of God's Word and the saving power of faith. Beyond belief, there was nothing that could be done, no ritual or observance, to secure salvation. In place of the 'superstitious' practices of the Catholic church, the reformers set out to create a Christian community bound by understanding and faith. There was no room for trust in false religious practices or doubt in the power of belief. 'The Reformation removed this ambiguity,' as Scribner observes in his study, 'by taking the "magical" elements out of Christian religion, eliminating the ideas that religious ritual had any automatic efficacy, that material objects could be endowed with any sort of sacred power, and that human actions could have a supernatural effect.' The most powerful magical elements in use, however, were those lodged deepest in the heart of popular religion – the sacraments and sacramentals of the Catholic church.

Sacraments guard the central rites of the Christian church; they are signs of God's promise, and in the view of the Catholic church (or its Thomist tradition) they contain grace. Moreover, the benefit derived from a sacrament is automatic; it does not depend on the moral quality of the administrant. Sacramentals, in contrast, are not held to be necessary to human salvation. A sacramental is associated with piety and veneration, and it can be almost anything that has been blessed and exorcised by the priest. The most familiar would be blessed water and salt, but a sacramental could also be a sign, a rite, a blessing or a prayer, or it could be an object appropriate to certain feast days, such as palms, ashes, candles, or herbs. Unlike the sacraments, the sacramentals were not automatically efficacious, but rather reliant on the disposition of those handling them. In the popular mind, however, their powers were guaranteed.[44] Sacramentals were no less effective than sacraments, and no

43   Francis Rapp, *L'église et la vie religieuse en Occident à la fin du Moyen Age* (Paris, 1971), pp. 143–62.
44   R. W. Scribner, *Popular Culture and Popular Movements in Reformation Germany* (London, 1987), pp. 1–47.

less charged with sacral power. They could work magic. Indeed, as Scribner remarks, the sacramentals enjoyed a status where 'any firm lines between religion and magic could become blurred', and that is why he begins his analysis with a look at the role of sacramentals in both Catholic and Protestant religious culture. It is a revealing approach. For in the age of Reformation, sacramentals were not only testimonials to the diversity of Catholic worship; they were testimonials to a type of religious belief. Catholic parishioners believed that the sacramentals contained the power of the divine and could bring benefit (due to their sacral power) if they were used in the appropriate way. To Protestants, however, this was anathema. Christ had blessed the earth with his saving death, and nothing could be done to tempt or harness his favour. 'This viewpoint,' Scribner observes, 'destroyed the basis for sacraments and sacramentals, indeed for any kind of ritual by means of which this-worldly symbolic action could have any transcendental efficacy.' The reform of sacramentals was thus not just a clash between two different religious cultures, but two different world views.

Protestantism's campaign against the sacramentals and the magical aspects of popular religion made some inroads, as Scribner points out, but it did not rid the parishes of popular beliefs, and it did not lead to the desacralization or disenchantment of the world. This was only to be expected, for a strong sense of the supernatural and a deep fear of the diabolical remained common even to men such as Luther and Calvin. They did not think to rid the universe of its charms. But they did object to the idea that the faithful could do anything with powers of their own to win God's favour or secure the benefits of the divine, and that is why they hoped to do away with the belief in the sacramentals. Popular religion had a deep hold, however, and it proved difficult to reform the traditional forms of parish religion. In the German principality of Brandenburg-Ansbach-Kulmbach, for instance, the Lutheran authorities set out to purge the parishes of the widespread trust in the supernatural efficacy of the Catholic sacramentals, but aside from those objects of devotion or veneration that had been physically removed from places of worship, sacramentals were as popular as before.[45] Using the sacramentals as a window on the dialogue between the Reformation and popular belief it seems clear, as Scribner observes, that the reforming campaign 'did not remove the popular desire for some kind of instrumental application of sacred power to deal with the exigencies of daily life'.

This does not mean that popular mentalities were unaffected by the Reformation. Sacramentals, along with many of the other traditional

45   Dixon, *The Reformation and Rural Society*, pp. 162–76.

protective remedies of the Catholic church, had been reduced in number, if not availability. Protestant pastors, in addition, constantly denounced the efficacy of sacramentals as tools of worship, and went so far as to condemn their use as superstitious and irreligious. As a consequence, the Protestant faithful became much more aware of their helplessness before God, as well as man's vulnerability in the sacred order. Scribner sees this as giving rise to 'complex mental and cultural modifications', and he views it as a shift from a world infused with localized forms of sacrality to a universe charged with the belief that all human action could provoke supernatural intervention. The Protestant faithful were much more likely to see a relationship between moral disorder and the processes of the natural world than their Catholic ancestors.[46] Protestants also became much more aware that certain forms of popular religious practice were viewed as supersitious or magical by the Reformation church, and this too caused subtle mental and cultural modifications. In the absence of the Catholic sacramentals, the parishioners looked to harness the powers of their own church, and for the Protestants this necessarily led back to the Word. Forms of Protestant magic evolved: blessings and prayers based on Gospel verse, the words of Saint John on a piece of paper. Bibles, hymnals, and catechisms became holy things, a type of sacramental object. 'We can certainly speak of a distinctive Protestant form of sacramentalism,' Scribner concludes, 'albeit one far weaker than its Catholic counterpart.' But it was sacramentalism nonetheless, and it warns us against thinking of the Reformation in terms of simple narratives or stark contrasts. The Reformation did not desacralize or disenchant the world, even the world of popular religious practice. Instead, there was a subtle shift of ideas, a transfer of meaning from one group of symbols and gestures to another. This originated in the sixteenth century during the process of Reformation, and it has continued ever since. Some scholars have even suggested that the transfer of meaning might now almost be complete, with the sacral world of the parish dwarfed by the symbolic might of the state.[47]

46   Bob Scribner, 'Reformation and Desacralisation: from Sacramental World to Moralised Universe', in *Problems in the Historical Anthropology of Early Modern Europe*, eds. R. Po-Chia Hsia and R. W. Scribner (Wiesbaden, 1997), pp. 75–92.
47   See the discussion in Friedrich Wilhelm Graf, ' "Dechristianisierung." Zur Problemgeschichte eines kulturpolitischen Topos', in *Säkularisierung, Dechristianisierung, Rechristianisierung im neuzeitlichen Europa*, ed. Hartmut Lehmann (Göttingen, 1997), pp. 32–66.

V

Taken together, the contributions in this volume offer the reader an idea of the scale and variety of recent work on the German Reformation. They do not, however, provide a unified or consistent narrative history of the event. There is no single vision of the movement or its long-term consequences. The contributors have asked different questions of the Reformation, and as a result both the approach and the focus of their analyses are fundamentally different. For those who have written on the early phase of the evangelical movement, for instance, its essence is best associated with the religious ideas which first moved the reformers to challenge the teachings of the Catholic church. Certain theological insights, in particular the evangelical doctrine of justification, are held to mark such a profound break with the past that we might trace the origins of the Reformation back to a moment of spiritual insight. Others have followed the filiation of religious ideas through to their union with the social and political forces of the day. Reformation, from this secular perspective, made its greatest impact on the German world once it was cast in the speech and culture of daily experience. That is why historians speak of an urban Reformation, for the Reformation in the cities was a distinct historical event, bound and shaped by the forces unique to the civic environment. The same reasoning lies behind the notion of a Communal Reformation, an idea which holds that religious culture, and indeed the religious imagination, was conditioned by the social and political realities of communal life. The Reformation, in this view, was a fusion of text and context, and it nearly transformed the political constitution of early modern Germany.

But the legacy of the Reformation, as other thinkers in this volume have suggested, is with us in the present as much as it might be discovered in the past. Our own age, the modern age, owes a profound debt to the confessional history of the sixteenth century. For religion has played a fundamental role in many of the developments that distinguish the modern age – from the evolution of collective identities, to the growth of the nation-state, to the dynamics of international politics, Even some of the values we hold as individuals, or the qualities we might look for in other people (honesty, industry, intelligence, moral probity), trace a direct line back to the Reformation. It seems an unlikely chain of influence, from the changes wrought by the evangelical doctrine of justification to the human condition of modern times, but religion has always had a broad range of influence. And that makes it all the more surprising to discover, as the final contributions attest, that the very changes the evangelicals hoped to effect through the Reformation were the most reluctant to take hold. Religious culture at the parish level was slow to conform to the Protestant vision of faith, while the deeper habits of thought, the magical or sacramental mentality of popular religion, would survive for centuries. Indeed, if we were to judge by the criteria of the reformers themselves, we might wonder whether the change of religion has had any permanent affect. Judging by the criteria of past and present centuries, however, it is clear that the Reformation has had a profound and lasting influence on the course of European history. But then our own understanding of the movement must be imagined in terms that would have been foreign to men such as Martin Luther, Huldrych Zwingli, or any other of the early reformers, for we stand at a distance from the event, we have a broader perspective, and we are now more aware that the most important events of the past have causes and consequences which only come to light after years of study. This is what any essential reading of the German Reformation would hope to demonstrate.

2

What was Preached in German Towns in the Early Reformation?

Bernd Moeller

Originally appeared as Bernd Moeller, 'Was wurde in der Frühzeit der Reformation in den deutschen Städten gepredigt?' *Archiv für Reformationsgeschichte*, 75 (1984), pp. 176–93.

Editor's Introduction

Historians of the German Reformation generally agree that the sermon was fundamentally important for the diffusion and ultimate institutionalization of the reform movement. In an age when the majority of people could not read, ideas were often spread by word of mouth rather than the printed page, and most parishioners would have heard evangelical teachings for the first time from a reformer preaching from a church pulpit. Of course, there were other ways in which the message might be spread by word of mouth – in private households, in alehouse sittings, in open-air readings, in university lecture halls. But the sermon remained the most effective and most popular way to broadcast the message.

Despite the central importance of the sermon to the Reformation, however, very little is known about what was actually preached in the early years of the movement. The most famous and impressive of reformers, men such as Martin Luther and Andreas Osiander, had their sermons gathered and published, but most evangelical clergymen left no trace behind of what they preached. As a consequence, our knowledge of the intellectual content of the early Reformation has always been lacking. In the following contribution by Bernd Moeller, however, this issue is dealt with in a systematic way for the first time. Moeller bases his study on the analysis of thirty-two sermon summaries, short published statements or confessions of personal faith written by the pastors of select German cities. All of the summaries were published between 1522 and 1529, before the evangelical movement had become formalized in confessions of the faith, and all of the summaries claim to represent (or simply replicate) a sermon once held in a town church. Thus the authors, all of whom were educated clergymen who spoke out in defence of the reform movement in the 1520s, were directing their sermons at an urban audience. This point, as Moeller makes clear, is significant, for it speaks of the close relationship between the Reformation and the German city. Without the sermon Luther's message would not have reached the parishioners as quickly and as effectively as it did; and without the urban setting, the reformers would have lacked both the popular backing and the institutional framework that transformed their words into a social and intellectual movement.

What then was preached in the urban sermons? What were the central theological subjects or themes of the early Reformation sermon? On the basis of his analysis, Moeller concludes that there was an essential unity to the evangelical movement of the 1520s. He speaks of a fundamental theological consensus, characterized in its essentials by a sense of 'Lutheran conformity'. All of the reform preachers were in fundamental agreement with the central insights of Luther's early theology. The main themes of the sermons touched on justification, the church, the Christian way of life, and the Last Things (the sense of final judgement); and while they approached these topics in different ways, all of the authors grounded their sermons in the essential theological principles of the Reformation. Occasionally the church was described in terms which emphasized Luther's notion of the Priesthood of All Believers, but for all of the early reformers the essential focus of the church was Christ and the Reformation principle of salvation through his grace alone (*sola gratia*). Two other central principles of the Reformation were also common in the sermon summaries: the idea of scripture alone (*sola scriptura*) as the only source of Christian truth, and Luther's theological insight of justification through faith alone (*sola fide*). Repeatedly the clergymen made reference to the Bible as the sole source of religious authority. Scripture alone was the standard of religious truth; all other earthly conceits must answer to the Word of God. Indeed, for many of the early evangelicals (as for Luther himself) the Reformation was nothing more than the Word of God released from its long captivity. Equally, the doctrine of justification through faith alone was also central to the sermons preached in the cities. Granted, the sermons conveyed the idea in different ways; some preachers spoke of the importance of faith for salvation, and thus tried to relate Luther's insight directly, while others spoke of the relationship between faith, sin, and brotherly love. But the central idea of justification through faith alone remained consistent.

In making the case for a theological consensus among the evangelical preachers of the 1520s Moeller is offering a novel interpretation of the early Reformation. Historians have long described the first decade or so of the reform movement as a time which lacked unity and coherence. Clergymen spoke in general terms of the reform of the church or the need to preach the Word of God, but there was no intellectual consistency to their message. Instead, historians have used terms such as 'wild growth' to characterize the unrestrained flux of ideas during the early Reformation. Events seem to lend weight to this interpretation, for this was the decade that witnessed both the rise of Anabaptism and the outbreak of the Peasants' War of 1525. Any sense of unity, historians have therefore concluded, will not be found in the ideas themselves, but rather in the parishioners' collective response. Moeller's study of the sermon summaries, in contrast, argues against the notion of a 'wild growth' of religious ideas and speaks of a consistent and unified vision of reform. The early Reformation, as Moeller sees it, was marked by a fundamental theological consensus. The early evangelical preachers understood Luther's main theological insights and tried to relate these insights to their urban congregations. Moeller thus finds a core of evangelical conviction in a world charged by religious ideas.

What was Preached in German Towns in the Early Reformation?

Bernd Moeller

I

The question that constitutes the title of this chapter[1] is a crucial issue in the current state of Reformation studies. The study of sermons preached in towns in the early Reformation period is more than simply an arbitrary section of Reformation history. Rather, the question relates to the whole of the historical process we call the Reformation. If it can be answered, we may expect to gain important insights into the emergence and development of that historical process.

In research today, so far as I can see, it is agreed that the key words 'town' and 'sermon' denote two major factors that help us to understand the communication and distribution of Luther's ideas, and the way in which collective convictions were formed in the context of the Reformation. No one seriously disputes that in its origins and its dynamic, the early Reformation was essentially an urban phenomenon,[2] or that preaching was the main way in which it operated.[3] However, it is not so certain whether my title question can be answered; in fact it may be said at once that in the present state of research we do not know just what *was* being preached in German towns in the early Reformation.

Individual accounts of striking sermons, of course, are not absent from chronicles and letters. Now and then the text of a sermon is reported, or even more than the text in the case of some outstanding urban preachers such as Huldrych Zwingli in Zurich and Andreas Osiander in Nuremberg, to say nothing as yet of Martin Luther. However, there are serious deficiencies in our representative, broad-

1   It derives from a lecture given in all at seven places between 1980 and 1983. The last occasion (on 16 August 1983) was at a seminar during the sixth Luther-forschungskongress in Erfurt. The version printed would never have been possible without the many stimulating ideas put to me in the discussions following my lectures.
2   There is a textbook formula to the effect that: 'Urban feeling in favour of the Reformation in towns, and consequently the Evangelical towns themselves, were vital factors for the success of the Reformation in Germany and its influence internationally.' R. Wohlfeil, *Einführung in die Geschichte der deutschen Reformation* (Munich, 1982), p. 118.
3   '... the Reformation itself was predominantly a preaching revival'. R. W. Scribner, *For the Sake of Simple Folk* (Cambridge, 1982), p. 2.

based knowledge of the kind of material regarded as general and 'usual': the very aspect of these sermons that gave them their historical importance. For unlike other means of communication – the books, leaflets and pictures that fostered agitation[4] – sermons helped the new doctrine to cross the social divide between the literate and the illiterate and reach the entire urban population. Where the citizenry as a whole was more or less in favour of the introduction of Reformation ideas, the spreading of the unadorned gospel message and the abolition of the mass (as we know was indeed the case in many towns), then as a rule sermons containing the ideas of the Reformation, had preceded the formation of such opinions. The normal urban course of events was for a preacher – a priest, a member of a preaching order, a monk or occasionally a layman, usually someone who had himself been influenced by reading Luther – to expound Reformation doctrines from the pulpit and create a stir with his preaching. His hearers were swept away with him, and there were practical consequences as a result.

The absence of more detailed knowledge has led to much speculation in studies of the subject, not just on what is assumed to have been the content of the sermons but also on the resultant pro-Reformation convictions entertained by the citizens and the motivations behind urban Reformation policy. More particularly, there is widespread scepticism concerning these convictions and motivations – for instance, the definition coined by Franz Lau, the 'wild growth of Reformation ideas',[5] is currently applied to this early period. Much doubt has also been cast on the idea that Luther's doctrines and aims made their way into individual towns and the minds of individual citizens, and on the consistency of the early Reformation – was it guided by uniform ideas, by theological ideas, indeed by any ideas at all, or was it perhaps governed by some quite different historical dynamic?

II

I have already referred elsewhere[6] to sources that have previously been overlooked, in the form of the 'sermon summaries' in Reformation pam-

---

4   On this point cf. Scribner's book cited in note 3, and my review of it in *Historische Zeitschrift* 237, 1983, pp. 707–10.

5   F. Lau and E. Bizer, *Reformatonsgeschichte Deutschlands* (Göttingen, 1964), ch. 17ff. This point is taken up, approvingly, by H. J. Goertz, 'Aufstand gegen den Priester. Antiklerikalismus und reformatorische Bewegungen', in Peter Blickle (ed.), *Bauer, Reich und Reformation, Festschrift für G. Franz* (Stuttgart, 1982), pp. 182–209, *passim.*

6   B. Moeller, 'Stadt und Buch. Bemerkungen zur Struktur der reformatorsichen Bewegung in Deutschland', in W. J. Mommsen (ed.), *Stadtbürgertum und Adel in der*

phlets. This genre seems to offer a firmer footing in the issue that concerns us here. The present article refers back to my earlier studies and seeks to take them further.

These 'sermon summaries', as I have called them, are found in pamphlets and books in which a preacher who is an adherent of Luther addresses the people of a town where he used to be active. In most cases these preachers had been forced to leave because their sermons advocated Reformation, and in several cases they are written by men who had worked in the town concerned in the pre-Reformation period. The writer's intention is always to impart to the citizens of a town the essential and indispensable elements of the evangelical faith, i.e. the true Christian faith, and to do so concisely in the form of a summary. It is normally claimed that the book contains the sum of all the sermons preached by the author in that town. Sometimes the contents are not so coherently structured. On several occasions they print model sermons claiming to contain the sum of the author's ideas; sometimes they even contain commentaries on an entire book of the Bible.[7] There are also cases where earlier sermons are retracted in the light of new understanding.

Many of these writings are in the style of a conversation between the author and those he is addressing. All the expositions clearly aim to be approachable and authentic. The passionately felt experiences and eventful lives that lie behind most of these books are sometimes described at length – the radical confrontations of the time find vivid expression, depicting the struggle for truth at the risk of life itself. What all these writings have in common is the 'summary' element: they claim to be offering something definitive; it might be called the 'iron rations' of faith. They also share a common situation: the author used to be

Reformation (Stuttgart, 1979), pp. 25–39; ibid., 'Einige Bemerkungen zum Thema: Predigten in reformatorischen Flugschriften', in H. J. Köhler (ed.), *Flugschriften als Massenmedium der Reformationszeit* (Stuttgart, 1981), pp. 261–88. K. Stackmann and I are still planning to publish our studies of these writings as a monograph, but many other claims on our time have unfortunately led to its completion being repeatedly postponed. However, since the book will eventually appear [Bernd Moeller and Karl Stackmann, *Städtische Predigt in der Frühzeit der Reformation. Eine Untersuchung deutscher Flugschriften der Jahre 1522 bis 1529*, Göttingen, 1996], I will confine myself in the present chapter basically to giving references to the quotations.
7   Caspar Hedio, 'In die erst epi // stel S. Joannis des Euange= // listen . . .', 1524 (Hedio's preface to an edition of Oecolampadius's commentary on the First Epistle of John, in E. Weller, *Repertorium typographicum*, Nördlingen, 1864, reprinted 1961, no. 3075, copy in the Landesbibliothek Stuttgart); Jakob Otter, 'Die Epistel San= // cti Pauli an Titū / gepredigt . . .', 1524, in Weller, no. 3092, copy in the Universitätsbibliothek Heidelberg); ibid., 'Das erst Buch Mosi / // geprediget . . .', 1528, in J. Benzing, *Bibliographie Haguenovienne*, Baden-Baden, 1973, p. 112, copy in the Stadtbibliothek Augsburg).

familiar to those he is addressing and now they are separated. An exiled preacher often informs the reader that he is writing in response to requests that have reached him from the town itself, whose citizens have requested such a summary as a replacement, in the form of his book, for the living preacher now lost to them. As one of the preachers explains his intentions, in the book 'I return not in body but in spirit'.[8]

Taken as a whole, the material is of considerable extent and variety. In all, thirty-two writings of this kind have so far been found, in a total of fifty-six editions. There are twenty-six authors, addressing themselves to twenty-seven towns. The entire extent of the summaries amounts to some 1500 original printed pages; some 50,000 such books may have been available.

Without exception, they date from the period between 1522[9] and 1529,[10] and most of them are from 1523 and 1524. The year 1523, with fourteen titles, accounts for almost half the material. Geographically, the texts come from a wide areas, but there are some striking and revealing groupings: nine of the twenty-seven towns are in central Germany, from Mühlhausen[11] in the west to Cottbus[12] in the east, and from Magdeburg[13] in the north to Arnstadt[14] in the south. To some extent Elbogen near Eger in Bohemia,[15] Iglau in Moravia[16] and Bamberg in Franconia[17] form another geographical unit. Thirteen of the towns

8 Johann Eberlin, 'Ain kurtzer gschrifftlicher bericht . . .', 1523, in L. Enders (ed.), *Johann Eberlin von Günzburg, Sämtliche Schriften* (Halle, 1896–1902), 4 vols, vol. 2, p. 173.

9 The earliest of these writings seems to be by Jakob Strauss, 'Ain trostliche versten // dige leer . . .', in A. Kuczynski, *Thesaurus libellorum historiam Reformationis illustrantium* (Leipzig, 1890), reprinted 1969, no. 3608, copy in the SuUB Göttingen.

10 Johannes Langer, 'Vrsach der lere . . .', in Kuczynski, no. 1244; copy in the UB Heidelberg.

11 Johann Rothmeler, 'Eyn sendebryff / an dye / betrub // ten / Cristen . . .', 1525, in H. Claus, *Der deutsche Bauernkrieg im Druckschaffen der Jahre 1524–1526* (Gotha, 1975), no. 86; copy in the Hofbibl. Aschaffenburg).

12 Johannes Briessmann, 'Vnterricht vnd ermanung . . .', 1523, in P. Hohenemser, *Flugschriftensammlung Gustav Freytag* (Frankfurt, 1925), reprinted 1966, no. 2963, copy in the SuUB Göttingen.

13 Johann Fritzhans, 'Johan: Fritzschans // an ein Erbarn: Er= / / samen / weyssen radt . . .', 1523, in *Geschichtliche Blaetter für Stadt und Land Magdeburg* 15,1880, p. 227; copy in the Duke August-Bibl. Wolfenbüttel.

14 Caspar Güttel, 'Schuczrede . . .', 1522, in G. W. Panzer, *Annalen der ältern deutschen Literatur 2*, Hildesheim, 1961, no. 1476, copy in the SuUB Göttingen.

15 Wolfgang Rappolt, 'Eyn kurtze Epistel . . .', 1525, in Kuczynski, no. 2204, copy in the Staatsbibl. Munich.

16 Paul Speratus, 'Wie man trotzen sol // auffs Creutz . . .', 1524, in Kuczynski, no. 3601, copy in the SuUB Göttingen.

17 Johann Schwanhauser, 'Ain Trostbrief . . .', 1525, in Kuczynski, no. 2426, copy in the SuUB Göttingen.

are in south-west Germany, in an area bordered by Weißenburg[18] and Strasbourg in Alsace,[19] and including Mainz,[20] Miltenberg,[21] Bopfingen,[22] Ulm,[23] Riedlingen an der Donau,[24] Rheinfelden[25] and Neuenburg[26] above and below Basle on the Rhine. Farther-flung towns are Altötting in Bavaria[27] and Hall in the Tyrol.[28] This was a large area then, but the areas that are not covered are no less characteristic than those that are given mention. I believe it is mere chance that German-speaking Switzerland, so dynamically involved in the early Reformation, is only marginally represented by the frontier town of Rheinfelden[29] and by a single author, the former Franciscan Dr Sebastian Meyer of Berne, who in fact addresses himself to the imperial city of Strasbourg.[30] The absence of representation in the Hanseatic cities on the North Sea and the Baltic, with their early pro-Reformation tendencies, could also be put down to chance. However, it must be significant that the entire west of the Empire north of Mainz goes unrepresented, and no such records are preserved either from the north-west and north of Germany above Magdeburg or from the north-east and east down to Bohemia. A picture

18   Martin Bucer, 'Martin Butzers // an ein christlichen Rath vñ // Gemeyn der statt Weissen- // burg Summary . . .', 1523, in R. Stupperich (ed.), *Martin Bucers Deutsche Schriften* 1 (Gütersloh, 1960), pp. 79–149.
19   Sebastian Meyer, 'Doctor Sebastian // Mayers / etwañ Predicant . . .', 1524 in Kuczynski, no. 1868, copy in the Staatl. Bibl. Regensburg).
20   Hedio, 'In die erst epistel'.
21   Johann Drach, 'Epistel an die Gemeyne zu // Miltenberg . . .', 1523, in Weller, no. 2832, copy in the SuUB Göttingen; ibid., Epistel an die // Gemeine tzu // Milten= // berg . . .', 1523, in Weller, no 2831, copy in the Zentralbibl. Zurich; ibid., 'Eyn Christenlich= // er Sendebrieff . . .', 1524, in Weller, no. 2833; copy in the Duke August-Bibl. Wolfenbüttel.
22   Wolfgang Vogel, 'Ayn trostlicher sendbrieff . . .', 1526, in Kuczynski, no. 2712, copy in the Staatsbibl. Munich.
23   Johann Eberlin, *Ain kurtzer gschrifftlicher bericht*, in Enders, *Johann Eberlin von Günzburg*, vol. 2, pp. 173–92; ibid., 'Die ander getrew // vermanung . . .', 1523, in Enders, *Johann Eberlin von Günzburg*, vol. 3, 1902, pp. 1–40; Heinrich von Kettenbach, 'Ein Sermon . . .', 1523, in O. Clemen (ed.), *Flugschriften aus den ersten Jahren der Reformation* (Leipzig, 1907–11), 4 vols, reprinted 1967, vol. 2, pp. 104–25.
24   Johannes Zwick, 'Geschrifft . . .', 1526, in Weller, no. 4042, copy in the UB Heidelberg.
25   Johann Eberlin, 'Ein schoner spiegel . . .', 1523, in Enders, *Johann Eberlin von Günzburg*, vol. 3, pp. 97–109.
26   Otho Binder, 'Eyn nütze Christenliche // ermanung . . .', 1525, in Weller, no. 3325, copy in the Hofbibl. Aschaffenburg.
27   Wolfgang Russ, 'Ayn Sermon . . .', 1523, in Kuczynski, no. 2300, copy in the SuUB Göttingen; ibid., 'Ayn entschuldigung . . .', 1523, in Kuczynski, no. 2299, copy in the Staatsbibl. Munich.
28   Strauss, 'Ain trostliche versten'.
29   Eberlin, 'Ein schoner spiegel'.
30   Meyer, 'Doctor Sebastian // Mayers / etwañ Predicant'.

clearly emerges of what are generally accepted as the focal points of the early Reformation – the two main areas of Saxony and Thuringia on the one hand, the south-west of Germany on the other. These are, respectively, the region in which Luther lived and worked and the region influenced by Zwingli. Moreover, the distribution illustrates the predominance of urban environments and the generally slow progress made by the Reformation in penetrating the Low German linguistic area.

The diversity of these urban areas is also extremely interesting; they include large cities such as Strasbourg[31] and Magdeburg[32] and typical imperial cities like Weil[33] and Mühlhausen,[34] as well as towns such as Zwickau[35] and Miltenberg[36] situated in principalities, early princely residences such as Weimar,[37] a small knightly town (Neckarsteinach)[38] and other small places including Kenzingen im Breisgau,[39] Riedlingen an der Donau[40] and Stolberg am Harz,[41] rural enough for their citizens to cultivate the land. Then there were episcopal towns like Naumburg,[42] Bamberg[43] and Mainz,[44] and mining towns such as Annaberg[45] and Hall in the Tyrol[46] – in fact every type of urban area is represented, and so is every kind of economic, social and political situation. Only villages do not feature on the list: so far as we know, no Reformation preacher collected the content of his sermons in a pamphlet addressed to villagers, and there is no reason why he should have done so. In general the peasants could not read; they had to be read to by people from towns. The fact that our material shows the early Reformation concentrating on urban areas thus appears both impressive and characteristic.

31 Meyer, 'Doctor Sebastian // Mayers / etwañ Predicant'.
32 Fritzhans, 'Johan: Fritzschans an ein Erbarn'.
33 Theobald Billicanus, 'An die Christe= // lich kirch . . .', 1522, in Kuczynski, no. 258, copy in the Landesbibl. Stuttgart.
34 Rothmeler, 'Eyn sendebryff'.
35 Caspar Güttel, 'Eyn Christlich= // er /ym wort Gottes ge= // gründter ausszug . . .', 1523, in Panzer, no. 1895, copy in the SuUB Göttingen.
36 Drach, 'Epistel an die Gemeyne'.
37 Johann Voit, 'Eyn Sermonn // vō Newen Jare . . .', 1523, in Weller, no. 2729, copy in the Bodleian Libr. Oxford.
38 Otter, 'Das erst Buch'.
39 Otter, 'Die Epistel'.
40 Zwick, 'Geschrifft'.
41 Simon Hoffmann, 'Ain sermonn // geschen am Ostertag . . .', 1523, in Panzer, no. 1906, copy in the Bischöfl. Bibl. Paderborn.
42 Langer, 'Vrsach der lere'.
43 Schwanhauser, 'Ain Trostbrief'.
44 Hedio, 'In die erst epistel'.
45 Friedrich Mykonius, 'Eyn Freüntlich // Ermanung vnd trostung . . .', 1524, in Weller, no. 3059, copy in the Staatl. Bibl. Regensburg.
46 Strauss, 'Ain trostliche versten'.

Further study of the places where these writings originated also shows a geographical concentration. After the authors had fled the places where they were formerly active, most of them settled in one of only three cities: Wittenberg,[47] Nuremberg[48] and Strasbourg.[49] The last-named imperial city in particular, judging from our material, proves to have been a centre of the propagation of early Reformation tenets for its entire region.

As for the writers themselves, they were all clerics, as might be expected, and had almost all been active in the pre-Reformation church – only Schweblin's pamphlet addressed to the people of Pforzheim[50] has at least a preface by a lawyer, Nikolaus Gerbel of Strasbourg, well known for his friendship with Luther. More interesting, and one might also say more characteristic of the early Reformation, is the fact that the remaining twenty-five clerical authors divide roughly into two sections: twelve had previously been priests in the secular community, while thirteen had been monks, probably all from mendicant orders with a strong preponderance of Franciscans (at least seven).

In addition, it can be shown that almost all the authors had pursued academic studies; no less than eight were doctors, and six of these were doctors of theology. The educational standards of these men were thus well above the normal educational standard of a cleric in the late Middle Ages, and this fact too fits the general image of the early Reformation preachers, who must have been something of an elite among the clergy. Another striking fact is that four universities clearly predominate among the places where they studied – Wittenberg, Erfurt, Heidelberg and Basle – and apart from Wittenberg, which was a special case, the other three are those very universities which we know, from other sources, occupied a special position within the academic world, being centres for the formation of circles of friends and action groups of young graduates who followed or at least sympathized with Luther – although as a whole the universities regarded the new movement with many reservations or rejected it outright.

As for the authors' age, the majority were relatively young men, or at least younger than Luther, who was forty in 1523, so that most of them were in their thirties. Many of them were also well known as the writers of other Reformation pamphlets, for instance Johann Eberlin von Günzburg;[51] most interestingly of all, however, many rose to promi-

---

47   Briessmann, Drach, Eberlin, Fritzhans, Speratus, Strauss.
48   Schwanhauser, Vogel.
49   Binder, Bucer, Hedio, Otter, Schweblin/Gerbel.
50   Hans Schweblin, 'Ein Sermon // auf Misericordia domini . . .', 1524, in Kuczynski, no. 2435; copy in the Stand- & Univ. Bibl. Frankfurt am Main.
51   Eberlin, *Ain kurtzer gschrifftlicher bericht.*

nence later. They included the later reformers Bucer[52] and Hedio[53] of Strasbourg; Briessmann[54] and Speratus[55] of the duchy of Prussia; Wolfgang Vogel,[56] executed in Nuremberg in 1527 as an Anabaptist; and Billican,[57] who later returned to the Catholic church. However, the authors also included some preachers who are quite unknown to us except through these writings.

III

So much for the external circumstances in which this group of pamphlets came to be written; by now the historical importance I would claim for them is perhaps perceptible in outline. As I see it, these thirty-two summaries of urban sermons deserve to be regarded and evaluated as representative texts: that is to say, they seem to present a typical picture of urban preaching in the early Reformation. They should to some extent provide a comprehensive and relatively reliable answer to the question: 'What was the normal or average content of sermons preached in towns?' At least, they should do so with more precision than has been possible with previous material and methods.

Our discussion therefore leads to the question: 'What is in these texts? What theological subjects of urban preaching do they illustrate?' In some ways it is easier to answer the question than might really be expected in view of the widely dispersed origins of the material. The theological content is homogeneous to a surprising, indeed an astonishing extent. There are no essential or obvious differences of content relating to either geographical locations or types of towns, to either the origins of the preachers or their different destinies and achievements at a later date. Of course there are differences of length, and some display a certain degree of linguistic sophistication and literary skill, while others are more rough-hewn, using simple, inelegant and vague language. They express differences in their authors' levels of theological education, and they make varying intellectual demands on their readers. Leaving such considerations aside, however, the texts agree in their main theological statements, their basic lines of argument and the most important points they make. That is to say, they convey the impression that from Cottbus to Rheinfelden and Berne, from Hall in the Tyrol to

---

52 Bucer, 'Martin Butzers an ein christlichen Rath'.
53 Hedio, 'In die erst epistel'.
54 Briessmann, 'Vnterricht vnd ermanung'.
55 Speratus, 'Wie man trotzen sol'.
56 Vogel, 'Ayn trostlicher sendbrieff'.
57 Billicanus, 'An die Christelich kirch'.

Magdeburg, more or less the same thing was being preached everywhere in the early period of the Reformation.

So what exactly was it? First of all, fundamentally these sermons were all exclusively concerned with the doctrine of salvation. That is to say, at heart the summaries concentrate solely on the theological tenets of the third article of the creed. The material can in essence be reduced to four subjects: the preachers spoke of justification, the church, the Christian way of life and the Last Things.

The last of these four subjects in some respects suggests the framework and orientation of the sermons as a whole. All the texts are imbued with great inner tension; they reflect awareness of a radical, indeed almost total rejection of the existing state of affairs. They are battle cries. However, the battlefield is generally conceived as an *eschatological situation* – the Last Judgement and the Kingdom of God seem close at hand and opposition in the form of the Catholic church is depicted as anti-Christian (to a great extent they use the German terms *endchristisch* and *antichristisch* interchangeably). Heiko Oberman's theory[58] that Luther's eschatological orientation sets him apart from the rest of the Reformation finds no support in our texts, and so cannot be confirmed for this early period.

'I have brought you not my word, but the gospel and God's word'[59] – this lapidary statement, expressing an idea in common to all these writings, also defines the authors' own positions as eschatological. They speak of a time full of grace, a 'golden and joyous' time,[60] already experienced or being experienced by the people they are addressing; although 'the whole world . . . has denied Christ'[61] God himself is now at work, and the future lies ahead – 'Make haste, brother, make haste, or you will be left behind.'[62]

The central theological argument upon which these preachers base their consciousness of superiority and their forceful claim to possess the truth is reference back to the Bible. They are convinced that 'now the truth is awakened by God's spirit, and Holy Scripture has risen strong from the grave', as Johannes Briessmann cogently puts it.[63] The

---

58   H. A. Oberman, 'Martin Luther Vorläufer der Reformation', in Eberhard Jüngel (ed.), *Verifikationen, Festschrift für Gerhard Ebeling zum 70. Geburtstag* (Tübingen, 1982), pp. 91–119.
59   Briessmann, 'Vnterricht vnd ermanung', A 4 a.
60   Vogel, 'Ayn trostlicher sendbrieff', C 2 a.
61   Hoffmann, 'Ain sermonn', A 4 b.
62   Russ, 'Ayn entschuldigung', B 3 a.
63   Briessmann, 'Vnterricht vnd ermanung', A 3 b. The image was probably not Briessmann's own but derived from Luther it also occurs in the iconographic polemics of the time. Cf. the examples in the exhibition catalogue *Martin Luther und die Reformation in Deutschland* (Frankfurt, 1983), no. 279, p. 291.

original gospel, the 'evangelical Christian truth'[64] that 'was once the comfort . . . of every Christian heart',[65] can now be heard again.

An interesting stylistic device frequently found in these pamphlets illustrates the historical and theological convictions of their authors: in many cases they write their letters to the urban congregations from which they are parted in more or less exact imitation of the epistles of the Apostle Paul, also addressed to urban communities, thus seeking to emphasize their claim that the momentous situation of early Christianity had recurred.[66] In line with this belief, they constantly turn their opponents' accusation that they are introducing innovations upside down: they argue that instead it is the teaching of their opponents, 'at odds with the teaching of Christ', that is new, while evangelical doctrines, through which they themselves have been freed from the 'anti-Christian darkness' prevailing in past centuries, represent the 'true old teaching', 'the teaching of faith according to the word of God'.[67]

The word of God, the Bible, has now been reawakened, and thus the book that is so different in scope from any other book in the world acquires new validity. The Bible does not require one to 'believe a history that was and that happened' but to 'place all faith, help and trust in this Christ'.[68] In this sense, the *preaching* of the gospel always assumes central importance for the writers – the idea is that as we hear the gospel Christ 'falls' into our hearts,[69] and Christ is 'born' of the word of God 'heard and believed',[70] while the Holy Ghost 'brings it about'[71] that we

---

64   Russ, 'Ayn entschuldigung', A 4 b.

65   Binder, 'Eyn nütze Christenliche ermanung', A 2 a.

66   Cf. Schwanhauser, 'Ain Trostbrief', A 2 a. He writes 'after the manner of the holy apostles who sent their epistles to the places where they had preached and where they could not now come.' Our authors probably imitated this stylistic approach from Luther, who also uses it relatively frequently in the early years of the Reformation, first in his 'Epistel oder Unterricht von den Heiligen, an die Kirche (die Christen) zu Erfurt', dated 10 July 1522 (*Luthers Werke*, Weimar edition 10/2, pp. 164–8). Billikan reprinted this 'epistle' of Luther's in the appendix to his pamphlet to the town of Weil (Billicanus, 'An die Christelich kirch'), which in its turn is the first in our series of sermon summaries to imitate the style of a Pauline epistle. He is followed most obviously by Bucer, Drach (all three pamphlets), Mykonius, Hedio, Schwanhauser and Rothmeler. We may assume that there was literary influence. However, the same stylistic device was popular elsewhere at this time. Zwingli uses it, for instance, in his epistle to the brothers in Augsburg of December 1524 (*Zwinglis Werke* 3 [corpus ref. 90], pp. 500–2).

67   Meyer, 'Doctor Sebastian Mayers etwañ Predicant', A B; Schwanhauser, 'Ain Trostbrief', D 2 a.

68   Fritzhans, 'Johan: Fritzschans an ein Erbarn', C 4 a.

69   Drach, 'Epistel an die Gemeine . . .', A 3 b.

70   Eberlin, 'Die ander getrew vermahnung', 14.

71   Speratus, 'Wie man trotzen sol', E 3 bf.

recognize the word we have heard as God's word. 'All that was said by Christ is not for the apostles or the saints alone, but is given to me and said to me', ran a saying of the Miltenberg preacher Johann Drach,[72] and this basic concept recurs explicitly in more than half our texts.

Consequently the elements of the Reformation *doctrine of justification* are to be found literally in all the sermon summaries. The fundamental theological convictions that dominate this entire body of writing are the generality and totality of human sin, unconditional acceptance into salvation exclusively on the grounds of faith in Christ and the rejection of any idea that a man's own works and achievements can help him on the way to salvation.

A prominent theme which takes up a good deal of space in this context is the effort made by the authors to show their readers the meaning of *faith*. There is clearly both a theological and an emotional centre to the sermons in this point, evident not least in the fact that here they are far from employing uniform patterns of language and of ideas. Among other elements, it is noticeable that they quite often call on the terminology and concepts of mysticism: in faith, Christ lives in us, 'moves and works and has his being',[73] and we are in him, indeed 'we are Christ', says Bucer of Strasbourg,[74] we become one body with him and accompany him 'to heaven as member of him' (in the words of Fritzhans of Magdeburg).[75] The authors expatiate on renunciation of the world and self-denial, the possibility of judgement and consciousness of freedom in belief: 'If you believe . . . then it is not possible that your heart should not laugh for joy in God and be free, confident and courageous', is Jakob Otter's way of summing up the idea.[76] His countryman Otho Binder coins an even more lapidary phrase: 'A Christian must always be a daredevil'.[77] Only once is any failure of faith mentioned, by the former Franciscan Friedrich Mykonius writing to Annaberg in Saxony, and mentioning that in the tribulations of his monastic imprisonment he was 'assailed so unexpectedly . . . that I did not know how I might cling to God and his word', and who could hardly remind himself 'how to seize upon Christ so that he would not fall away from me'.[78]

These authors regularly and vehemently reject their opponents' accusation that their doctrine of salvation, entirely focused on grace

72   Drach, 'Sendebrieff', C a.
73   Briessmann, 'Vnterricht vnd ermanung', B b.
74   Bucer, 'Martin Butzers an ein christlichen Rath', p. 96.
75   Fritzhans, 'Johan: Fritzschans an ein Erbarn', C 3 b.
76   Otter, 'Die Epistel', N 4 b.
77   Binder, 'Eyn nütze Christenliche ermanung', C 3 b.
78   Mykonius, 'Eyn Freüntlich Ermanung', C b.

and faith, leads to moral laxity. In fact they claim that the opposite is the case, although they do indeed utterly reject the medieval theory and practice of good works. Skilfully and at length, they argue against the whole idea of monastic life, the religious cult of images, devotion to the saints and pilgrimages, and secular and monastic piety in works, tackling the subject comprehensively and full on. The medieval teaching of the church is described as a human doctrine, a doctrine of works, a false doctrine, but their theological point is that it appears to be self-seeking, conceived for the 'use of man alone': 'a teaching for human comfort, and for securing themselves'.[79]

To sum up briefly the opposing stance of the Reformation, it was, as each of these pamphlets repeats, that 'where there is faith, there too is Love'.[80] Logically, there can be no question of a Christian's doing good for his own pleasure; rather, he does good solely for the sake of his neighbour and thus serves 'Christ himself in his neighbour',[81] in the footsteps of Christ himself – an idea put with theological cogency by Caspar Hedio in saying that 'you should devote yourself entirely to your neighbour, as Christ did for you'.[82] Faith and love are very closely connected – the two commandments of the gospel and Jesus' parable of the tree and the fruits are probably the most-quoted scriptural passages in these pamphlets. Faith is 'the foundation and grounds of firm, true love',[83] because it teaches us to look away from ourselves and love proceeds from it 'without compulsion'.[84] Faith 'inclines' towards love,[85] 'may not fail',[86] 'never tires',[87] 'does not stand still'[88] – in Briessmann's simple and straightforward phrasing, it is 'impossible'[89] that faith should remain without love.

'Priests and the cloister are against God';[90] 'If we look at the Pope with his followers, why, there lies the true origin of all godlessness in this world';[91] 'The devil has long upheld the kingdom of anti-Christ and the church of the godless, maintaining them under the name of the Chris-

---

79 Güttel, 'Schutzrede', B b.
80 Binder, 'Eyn nütze Christenliche ermanung', C 4 b.
81 Bucer, 'Martin Butzers an ein christlichen Rath', p. 88.
82 Hedio, 'In die erst epistel', aa 5 b.
83 Billicanus, 'An die Christelich kirch', A 2 a.
84 Drach, 'Epistel an die Gemeyne . . .', B b.
85 Billicanus, 'An die Christelich kirch', A 2 a; Eberlin, 'Ein schoner spiegel', p. 103.
86 Güttel, 'Eyn Christlicher . . . auszug', B 3 a.
87 Binder, 'Eyn nütze Christenliche ermanung', C 4 b; Otter, 'Die Epistel', E 2 b.
88 Kettenbach, 'Ein Sermon', p. 108.
89 Briessmann, 'Vnterricht vnd ermanung', B 2 a.
90 Eberlin, 'Ein schoner spiegel', p. 101.
91 Speratus, 'Wie man trotzen sol', G 2 a.

tian church'[92] – it must have been obvious that such comments, found in abundance in these pamphlets and expressing basic *criticism of the church*, indeed total rejection of it, derive in every case from quite precise theological arguments, and are substantially founded on criticism of the existing Catholic church's doctrine of salvation and practices related to it. This is confirmed by condemnations of the Pope's exercise of power, the worldliness of the bishops, the avarice of priests and the immorality of monks – to crown everything in this dismal picture, so to speak, the existing church of sacraments and benefices represents a distortion of true sacred ministry even in its personnel.

Consequently statements about the *church* are also central to the sermon summaries – according to Eberlin, the Article on the church is the 'angle of the door through which all other difficult points enter in and are understood',[93] an observation showing remarkable and still relevant theological insight into the structures of ecclesiastical controversy. The true church is defined in a variety of phrasings as a community of the faithful, or with even more theological concentration as 'the place where God's word is kept'.[94] The Reformation doctrine that priesthood is an attribute of all the faithful is widely elaborated, in contrast to the view that clerics are set apart: Jesus was a layman, the apostles were craftsmen and peasants.[95] Consequently the gospel does not belong to priests alone: 'it is ours as well as theirs, but really it is more ours than theirs'.[96] Everyone can learn and understand it, and laymen are equal or actually superior to priests in their understanding of faith.[97] which is even ascribed to women.[98] As a result, the appointment of *pastors* is the business of the community, and there are arguments against their exemption from tolls, taxes and communal service, besides the rule of celibacy. Their office is to convey the word of God and their obligations include preaching as well as the administration of the three remaining sacraments of baptism, communion and confession – although on the whole these receive only marginal mention in passing.

The most important aspect of the service of love incumbent upon Christians, as it is represented in the sermon summaries, is *to care for the poor*. There are frequent exhortations for funds previously spent on

92   Binder, 'Eyn nütze Christenliche ermanung', D 5 a.
93   Eberlin, 'Bericht', p. 174.
94   Fritzhans, 'Johan: Fritzschans an ein Erbarn', B 3 b.
95   Bucer, 'Martin Butzers an ein christlichen Rath', p. 85; Russ, 'Ayn Sermon', A 4 a.
96   Speratus, 'Wie man trotzen sol', F 3 b.
97   Bucer, 'Martin Butzers an ein christlichen Rath', p. 82; Eberlin, 'Ein schoner spiegel', p. 103; Drach, 'Epistel an die Gemeyne . . .', C 3 a; Schwanhauser., 'Ain Trostbrief', B b and *passim*.
98   Otter, 'Epistel an die Gemeyne,' H b and passim.

religious foundations to be diverted to the poor, and the preachers frequently refer to charitable institutions that already exist or that they recommend should be founded in the towns to which they are writing. In general the new order of the Christian life and the Christian church was expected to work relatively straightforwardly with the authorities, including town councils, described by Eberlin, for instance, as 'showing the Christian way in community offices'.[99] Sometimes an idealistic picture is painted in the colours of Reformation theology, showing a new kind of urban society finding what it really needs – peace and communal existence – through obedience to the word of God and the faith of true Christians, active in love. Adherents of the medieval church with its egotistic view of salvation, on the other hand, are dismissed as ' disloyal . . . to the common people'[100] and are described as spreading 'disharmony, much to the detriment of the land and the people'.[101]

These comments are particularly worth noting where the authors are writing about situations very unfavourable to Reformation doctrines, for instance where a minority of evangelically-minded people is confronted by a town council supporting the old beliefs in a strongly Catholic principality. In such circumstances our authors regularly on the one hand distance themselves critically from encroachment on the spiritual area by the authorities, while on the other hand they recommend those to whom they are writing not to oppose even such authorities as may be called 'tyrants and hotheads',[102] or 'successors to Herod and Pilate',[103] except at the most by passive means. The writers recommend that one should 'plead with them, beg them and show them all friendship', to persuade them to allow free preaching of the gospel.[104] *Resistance and violence*, however, are not presented as options.

Instead, what the preachers have to say to their congregations (most of them subject to trials and tribulations) usually ends in the instruction to *suffer*. One series of pamphlets, in fact, expounds a whole theology of suffering in relation to Christ's cross. Suffering is a necessary part of Christian life: this is a theme that recurs frequently, and Johann Drach prints the key words with initial capitals: 'The Cross must be borne; where there is no Cross, there is no Christ'.[105] However, suffering is not to be sought for its own sake, as in the monastic practice of asceticism,

---

99 Eberlin, 'Die ander getrew vermanung', p. 3
100 Eberlin, 'Die ander getrew vermanung', p. 19; cf. the entire account in ibid., 9ff.
101 Voit, 'Eyn Sermonn', C 4 a.
102 Schwanhauser, 'Ain Trostbrief', B 2 b.
103 Strauss, 'Ain trostliche versten', A 2 a.
104 Binder, 'Eyn nütze Christenliche ermanung', D 2 a.
105 Drach, 'Epistel an die Gemeine', A 4 a.

but is to be accepted at God's hands even unto a willingness to die. Some of the preachers feel obliged to defend themselves against the charge of avoiding martyrdom in their own past flight from a town. Again, there are themes reminiscent of the mystical interpretation of suffering in several of the pamphlets, but it is noticeable that the writers always try to base these ideas on christology. Suffering is our lot in emulation of Christ; the gospel without the cross would be no gospel at all. Thus the cross not only reminds Christians of Christ's suffering, it also reminds them that justification is by faith alone – 'the bridegroom, Christ, embraces his bride, the community, only with the cross'.[106]

Willingness to bear the *cross*, then according to Sebastian Meyer, is the Christian state of perfection,[107] and according to Drach the cross brings righteousness and salvation.[108] Calling on the theological theme that had helped them to make their profound and moving new discovery, these preachers also employ the theology of the cross to overcome the worst threat that new discovery entailed.

IV

The resumé above surveys the theological content of the sermon summaries. I will conclude by bringing together the results of my study and trying to interpret them with the help of four observations.

1   The thirty-two urban sermon summaries show – thus providing a considerable corrective to current scholarly opinion on the subject – that in the early years of the Reformation there was no indeterminate and primitive 'wild growth' of theological ideas in the urban pulpits of Germany where its adherents preached. Instead, their theological doctrine was uniform and relatively consistent in outline and in its main statements, resting on a fundamental theological consensus. Even the less skilled of the authors, some of whom wrote in a rather clumsy style, obviously seek to express such a fundamental consensus. They saw themselves as a unified community of 'evangelicals', citing their great masters – Luther in particular is frequently mentioned – and aiming to agree with them.

2   The opinion, prevalent in wide areas of Reformation studies, that the point of departure and overriding theme in the early Reformation was *criticism of the church*, or anticlericalism, is not confirmed in that

106   Drach, 'Epistel an die Gemeine', A b; almost the same wording may be found in Mykonius. 'Eyn Freüntlich Ermanung', C a.
107   Meyer, 'Doctor Sebastian Mayers etwañ Predicant', E 4 a.
108   Drach, 'Epistel an die Gemeine', A 2 b.

precise form by these texts. Indeed, so far as the texts go they contradict it. The sermons provide no evidence to support the idea that the popularity of Luther's cause and its success in urban areas were to some extent based on the reiteration of late medieval criticisms of the church, and that the Reformation associated itself and agreed with such criticisms.[109] Instead, it seems to have been largely the specifically new element of Reformation thought, whereby criticism of the church was based on the doctrine of justification, that found approval and carried conviction – to the preachers who accepted and then propounded these ideas with particular forcefulness, and probably then to their urban communities brought up in the medieval religious tradition of justification by works. The new quality in criticism of the church during the Reformation seems to have been the factor that gave it its compelling power. Moreover, the generally high theological demands made by these pamphlets constitute their most surprising characteristic, although as with such great reformers as Luther and Zwingli, the theology is in fact very practical and closely connected with real life. In so far as elements of social criticism do occur in the texts, it is noticeable that they hardly ever refer to secular systems. I may summarize this point by saying that their social criticism was confined to criticism of the clergy.

3   If we try to survey the theology viewpoints put forward in these writings without putting too much theological strain on the texts – that is, if we do not underestimate their mainly popular and practical purpose – then what they say can be reduced to a common denominator. The basic theological consensus they provide consists to a remarkable extent in agreement with the fundamental theological statements of Luther. It should be noted that almost all these sermon summaries date from a phase of the Reformation when the later schisms between Lutheranism, Zwinglianism and south German theology, or between the Reformation proponents of ecclesiastical reform and such sects as Anabaptists and spiritualists, had not yet come into being. Some of the authors, as mentioned above, later joined groups which moved away from Luther or which he condemned. In terms of ecclesiastical history, however, the impression given by the pamphlets studied here is that very few features of these later schisms could yet be detected or foreseen – to my mind, the only clear distinction is in the fact that discussion of the issue of images is confined almost exclusively to south German authors, while a

109   R. van Dülmen, *Reformation als Revolution*, Frankfurt, 1977, p. 23f.: 'The effective part of Luther's preaching was first to articulate and draw to the notice of the congregation the generally deplorable current state of religious and social affairs, and only then to preach his gospel with its new interpretation of the relation between God and man'. Cf. also the article by H. J. Goertz mentioned above in note 5, 'Aufstand'.

certain liking for mystical phraseology is more common among the central German preachers. Later theological differences within Protestantism are foreshadowed in, for instance, discussion of the sacraments and communion or of the doctrine of justification. They do not contradict or oppose the views put forward in these writings, but they are perceptible in rudimentary form. However, even at certain theologically delicate points these texts adopt a mainly uniform view: they all describe love as the result and not the form of faith, they all apply Luther's double meaning[110] to the concept of Christian freedom and they all accept that the law has been superseded as a means of salvation. The idea that justification enables man to obey the law is foreign to them.

4   Ultimately, then, the opinion often propounded to the effect that Luther did not really make his mark in the early Reformation, and his success was based instead on misconceptions, derives no support from these sermon summaries. I have in mind an essentially different interpretation of the development: there was no general 'wild growth' of ideas, and instead the early Reformation, up to around 1525 and the year of the Peasants' War, is marked by a *Lutheran conformity*, at least in urban areas: by a doctrine that was remarkably consistent, by uniform teachings and maxims, uniform condemnations and recommendations – in fact by a party spirit. After 1525, of course, the picture changes, but we may conclude that Lutheran conformity was surely what made the early Reformation a great historical force and the theologian Martin Luther a figure of international historical importance.

110   H. A. Oberman does not agree, in 'Headwaters of the Reformation' (*Luther and the Dawn of the Modern Era*, ed. ibid., Leiden, 1974, pp. 40–88): 'It is on [the] threshold between the first and second proposition of *De libertate* that we may find one of the characteristic lines of demarcation between the *initia Lutheri* and the *initia reformationis*.'

3

What was the Reformation Doctrine of Justification?

Berndt Hamm

Originally appeared as Berndt Hamm, 'Was ist reformatorische Rechtfertigungslehre?' in *Zeitschrift für Theologie und Kirche*, 83 (1986), pp. 1–38.

Editor's Introduction

Throughout the sixteenth century the theme of justification (that is, how sinful man could stand in a right relationship with God) remained at the heart of the confessional dialogue. Indeed, the entire Reformation movement, in a sense, was born in response to Luther's question: 'How may I find a gracious God?' Of course, the Christian church itself was a shepherd to this concern, so naturally this was not the first time the question had been raised. The medieval church had its own corpus of ideas on the subject, and by Luther's day there was a wide variety of related theory on the notion of justification. Most of the theory had become extremely complex, and few ordinary parishioners would have been familiar with Catholic teaching on salvation or redemption. Theological debate was left to the schools or ways (*viae*) of scholastic thought, such as the ancient way (*via antiqua*), an intellectual tradition associated with Thomas Aquinas and Duns Scotus, and the modern way (*via moderna*), whose inspirational figures included William of Ockham and Gregory of Rimini. The reformers would necessarily engage in a dialogue with these traditions of thought. In fact many of them, Luther included, were deeply influenced by the methods and the ideas of the scholastic schools. But for the average medieval parishioner, the concern with justification was not expressed in terms of abstract theological doctrine. The system of worship in the Catholic church was in place to answer this need.

In the medieval church, the believer participated in a process or a cycle of salvation. Mankind fell prey to sin, the sinner then went to confession, the priest granted absolution, fixed a penance, and with the penance the sins were forgiven and the penitent returned to a state of grace. Moreover, through penance the sinner would be transformed by God's grace, infused into the soul to facilitate redemption, and this would in turn promote acts of love and good works, which would then earn the sinner merit or worthiness before God. All of the schools would have accepted this general description of the pastoral process. They would not have agreed, however, over how much mankind could actually contribute to the process, or indeed whether the sinner could accomplish anything at all without divine grace. For some theologians within the *via moderna* school, for instance, the cycle of salvation was imagined in terms of a covenant between God and man. God had established the conditions necessary for salvation. Of his own will, rather than any eternal necessity, God had bound his activity within the rules of the covenant, and he would respond reliably to the conditions he had set. If the believer fulfilled certain demands (or, as the theologians summarized it, committed to 'doing what lies within you') he or she would acquire semi-merit (*meritum de congruo*). Through the covenant, the sinner was then rewarded with 'uncreated grace' which in turn produced good works. The combination of God's grace and the believer's own good works (though good works, as mentioned, aided by the grace of God) resulted in the sinner's acceptance. None of this could be accomplished without the assistance of God. In this view, human works had no inherent value; on their own they did not merit salvation, but God had promised to accept them as worthy of salvation. Even greater emphasis was placed on the role of God by thinkers such as Gregory of Rimini, who thought that mankind could do nothing but sin, and salvation was entirely dependent on an act of free grace from God. But all schools, even the strict Augustinians, thought in terms of the cycle of salvation and the central importance of the Church and the sacraments to the process. Ultimately, grace was acquired through penitential exercises, through good works.

The Reformation (or evangelical) doctrine of justification, as Berndt Hamm demonstrates, represented a radical break with the medieval inheritance, for it spoke of an outright promise of unconditional salvation. Indeed, Hamm defines the Reformation doctrine of justification as precisely that which 'broke the mould of the medieval theological system'. There were no reasons or conditions that had to be met; there was no system of worship, no cycle of redemption by means of which God's grace was acquired. Justification, in Luther's famous words, was through faith alone. As he wrote in his tract *The Freedom of a Christian* (1520): 'This is that Christian liberty, our faith, which does not induce us to live in idleness or wickedness but makes the law and works unnecessary for any man's righteousness and salvation.' As Hamm illustrates, this notion of justification was based upon a complex of interrelated theological insights. But the essential and most marked difference was that salvation was not achieved through penitential exercises or good works. The believer could do nothing to contribute to his or her salvation. Justification was through faith alone, trust in Jesus Christ, a theological insight often expressed by its Latin tag *sola fide*–faith alone. The soul was not purified of sin, as in the medieval cycle of worship, but rather covered by the 'cloak' of divine forgiveness won for us by Christ. There was no longer a process of renewal or an infusion of God's grace. Righteousness was perceived as a state beyond ourselves (*extra nos*) won by the intervention of Christ. God sees mankind in the light of Christ's righteousness, which alters the status of the sinner in the sight of God (*coram Deo*). All of this was derived from Luther's reading of Paul, in particular Romans 1 : 17 ('For therein is the righteousness of God revealed from faith to faith: as it is written, The just shall live by faith'). And this, in turn, was the fruit of another principle which divided the reformers and the defenders of the Catholic church – the total evangelical reliance on Scripture alone (*sola scriptura*). Only the Word of God could provide a foundation for the church. And only the Gospel of Christ, the promise of free grace, could ensure salvation. 'This, then,' wrote Luther in *The Freedom of a Christian*, 'is how through faith alone without works the soul is justified by the Word of God, sanctified, made true, peaceful, and free, filled with every blessing and truly made a child of God, as John 1 : 12 says: "But to all who . . . believed in his name, he gave power to become children of God."'

As Hamm demonstrates, the doctrine of unconditional salvation was the 'mould-breaking' aspect of evangelical theology. This doctrine divided the reformers and the Catholic authorities, and it remained the theological essence of the Reformation movement. In discussions of its origins, it is usually attributed to Luther, but it was an understanding of Christian salvation shared by all of the major reformers of the sixteenth century, from Huldrych Zwingli to Philip Melanchthon to John Calvin. It led to a complete break with the church of medieval Catholicism. A culture of worship based on the notion of good works was no longer viable, for there was no active 'work' that the sinner could do to earn or merit salvation. The idea of the church as the sole repository of God's grace was abandoned. The believer no longer had to rely on the church or its ministers to stand in a right relationship with God. As a consequence, religious life was simplified. The reformers turned against the penitential cycle, the cult of the saints, the use of images and sacramentals, and the monastic orders. Centuries of Catholic inheritance was rejected outright, because there was no place for traditional worship in a church built upon the Reformation doctrine of justification through faith alone.

What was the Reformation Doctrine of Justification?

Berndt Hamm

The question I hope to answer in this chapter contains a problematical dimension of breadth – and not just on account of the *genius loci* of Erlangen. I am not asking: 'What is the *Lutheran* doctrine of justification?' but 'What is the *Reformation* doctrine of justification?' That is to say, what links the Wittenberg Reformation of Luther and Melanchthon, the Reformation of Zwingli in Zurich and Calvin's Geneva-based Reformation in their opposition to medieval Catholic doctrine and the reforming Catholicism of the sixteenth century? The limits I have set to my subject will be obvious, in that I do not intend to discuss Reformation theology in general but only the Reformation doctrine of justification; however, that is a merely apparent limitation, since to those four historically influential leading figures of the Reformation the central point, indeed the whole meaning, of their theology lay in the doctrine of justification.[1]

Is there merely *one* Reformation doctrine of justification, however, in contrast to the wide variety of medieval Roman Catholic doctrinal systems? Let us briefly survey this wider range of issues. Reformation historians in recent decades have encouraged an awareness of the diversity of currents in the Reformation to such an extent that it is becoming increasingly difficult to retain a grasp on those features that are common to the Reformation as a whole, and to define their content precisely. This is particularly true of the doctrine of justification. The various Reformation positions are seen as drifting so far apart on this point that either they appear to have no common ground any more,[2] or

This essay is an extended version of my inaugural lecture at the University of Erlangen on 26 June 1985.

1   Cf. E. Wolf, 'Die Rechtfertigungslehre als Mitte und Grenze reformatorischer Theologie', 1949/50, in Wolf, *Peregrinatio II* (Munich, 1965), pp. 11–21, particularly the comment: 'The doctrine of justification, consequently, is not to be understood as the natural property of the Evangelical church, always available, but as ground that must always be reconquered. It should not be regarded as a "dogma' in terms of theological history, or a theologumenon to be revised more or less intensively at a certain opportune or appropriate time; it means an ever-indispensable consciousness that theological self-examination is central to the life of the church' (p. 11).

2   Cf., for instance, U. Gäbler, *Huldrych Zwingli. Eine Einführung in sein Leben und sein Werk* (Munich, 1983), p. 47: 'In view of the diversity of theological positions among

what they do have in common is formulated in such vague and amorphous terms, such as the principle of grace, that it no longer seems possible to trace any clear dividing line between it and the Catholic concept of grace.[3] It is at this point, and with a certain sense of resignation, that historians come up against enthusiastic ecumenicists who in any case believe that the doctrine of justification does not divide the churches,[4] and this opinion can then be linked to a historical line of argument claiming that the reformers, in particular Luther, were not really attacking a truly 'catholic' doctrine of justification. Instead, their attacks are claimed to have been provoked by the degenerate, Ockham-infected doctrine of the late Middle Ages and then forced into certain prejudices which turn out to have no real basis when compared with a 'fully catholic' theology of grace such as Thomism with some Augustinian influence.[5] And thus the contours become blurred. If we also note how far the question of what is really evangelical has been drawn into the search of today's Evangelical churches for the self-confidence of a con-

sixteenth-century Protestants, it is impossible to trace a historically distinct outline of the term "evangelical". Although it generally used to be identified with the theology of the reformer of Wittenberg – and in confessional Lutheran studies it still is – the precise content of the term is less and less frequently discussed in written studies. It may still be in use, but one must indicate that it has come to be detached from the traditional church and its doctrine.'

[Throughout the text, the German term *reformatorisch* has been translated into 'evangelical'. This seemed an appropriate solution, as it is now common for scholars to term the early Reformation the 'evangelical movement', while the English equivalent of the German term ('reformational') is not in use. 'Evangelical' also captures the essential religious convictions at the heart of the early Reformation movement, including its emphasis on the Gospel and the atoning death of Christ. S. D.]

3   Cf., for instance, H. Scheible, 'Reform, Reformation, Revolution. Grundsätze zur Beurteilung der Flugschriften', in *Archiv für Reformationsgeschichte*, 65 (1974), pp. 108–34, 117.

4   On the Catholic side the names of H. Küng, S. Pfürtner, O. H. Pesch and V. Pfnür spring to mind. On the Lutheran side, P. Brunner in particular tends this way in his essay 'Reform – Reformation, Einst – Heute', 1967, in Brunner, *Bemühungen um die einigende Wahrheit. Aufsätze* (Göttingen, 1977), pp. 9–33, esp. pp. 28–31. It is significant that in this article Brunner expressly quotes Melanchthon's doctrine that degrees of heavenly reward would be assessed by the merit of a man's works (*Apologie* §366, quoted from the German translation by Justus Jonas § 368f; *Die Bekenntnisschriften der evangelisch-lutherischen Kirche*, Göttingen, 1930 229, 21–27 and 229.59–230.7), for exactly this kind of doctrine lies outside the bounds of any Reformation doctrine of justification. Cf. also the work of Brunner's pupil H. G. Pöhlmann, *Rechtfertigung. Die gegenwärtige kontroverstheologische Problematik der Rechtfertigungslehre zwischen der evangelisch-lutherischen und der römisch-katholischen Kirche* (Tübingen, 1971).

5   Cf., for instance, E. Iserloh, *Luther und Reformation. Beiträge zu einem ökumenischen Lutherverständnis* (Der Christ in der Welt, XI/4), Aschaffenberg, 1974, esp. p. 24f; cf. also earlier works by J. Lortz, L. Bouyer and W. H. van de Pol.

fessional identity, then we can understand how difficult it is for the ecclesiastical historian to separate this historical issue from the embrace of dogmatism, for the less clear our historical definition of the evangelical is, the more forceful and unchecked the dogmatic premises applied to the study of this complex subject become. A glance at the discussion of Luther's turning towards ideas of Reformation and what it really entailed will amply demonstrate my point.[6] Against the impressive background of all the currents of the Reformation[7] and the tensions and contrasts between many genuine reform initiatives, it seems to me all the more important to ask again what was so particular to the Reformation in its central doctrine of justification, and to answer the historical question by applying historical criteria.

I shall do so in the following stages: having established the criteria (I), I shall then discuss the general medieval Catholic doctrine of justification (II), and then, in contrast, what was both common to the individual reformers' understanding of justification and what features of it were particular to the Reformation (III). Finally, I shall show where this significantly evangelical factor can first be clearly perceived in historical terms (IV), where it can become reinforced and intensified in certain doctrinal developments, and where, on the other hand, its distinct features are lost or even abandoned (V).

I   Criteria for Defining the Reformation Doctrine of Justification

By comparison with many other *reformationes*, the specific feature of the sixteenth-century Reformation was that it was a movement of radical change from the ecclesiastical and theological system of the Middle Ages in its return to study of the scriptures. Historically, therefore, it is only logical to say that whatever broke the mould of the medieval theological system in returning to the word of God in the Bible, and whatever can no longer be explained as an extreme position within the range of medieval theological variation, is of the Reformation. However, there is certainly wide scope for discretion in determining what it was about the Reformation doctrine of justification that actually did break the mould

6   Cf. the studies by O. H. Pesch: 'Zur Frage nach Luthers reformatorischer Wende', in *Catholica* 20, 1966, pp. 216–43, 264–80; in B. Lohse (ed.), *Der Durchbruch der reformatorischen Erkenntnis bei Luther* (Wege der Forschung, 123) (Darmstadt, 1968), pp. 445–505; and 'Neuere Beiträge zur Frage nach Luthers "reformatorischer Wende"', in *Catholica* 37 (1983), pp. 259–87; 38 (1984), pp. 66–133.

7   Cf. H. A. Oberman, 'Headwaters of the Reformation. Initia Lutheri – Initia Reformationis', in Oberman (ed.), *Luther and the Dawn of the Modern Era*. Papers for the Fourth International Congress for Luther Research (1974), pp. 40–88.

of the system. Consequently two further and more precise criteria may be added in our search for the features essential to an understanding of the Reformation doctrine of justification.

1   Historically, there is little point in understanding the essential features of the Reformation in such a narrow sense – perhaps on the basis of certain interpretations of remarks made by Luther[8] – that our criterion would prove Zwingli or even Calvin to be the proponents of non-Reformation theology. Or to put it in more positive terms: the nature of Reformation theology must always be defined by comparison. The objective common ground between the reformers when they move away from medieval systems must find a place in our definition of its features. Consequently, the question of what is characteristic of the Reformation is also the question of what is common ground shared by all the reformers, and is not just specifically Lutheran.[9]

2   Another criterion to be taken into account in defining the mould-breaking element of the Reformation doctrine of justification is to determine what the theological exponents of Catholicism in the sixteenth century thought of the doctrine. What features of the doctrine were perceived as 'mould-breaking' and what features (in their eyes) could be integrated? By those exponents I mean representatives of all scholastic orientations, not only Ockhamism and Scotism but also a Thomism and

8   For instance, E. Bizer and his followers who support a late date for Luther's turning to ideas of Reformation, particularly O. Bayer, 'Die reformatorische Wende in Luthers Theologie', in *Zeitschrift für Theologie und Kirche* 66 (1969), pp. 115–50; ibid., *Promissio. Geschichte der reformatorischen Wende in Luthers Theologie* (Forschungen zur Kirchen- und Dogmengeschichte, 24) (Göttingen, 1971).

9   We can thus ascertain what the evangelical doctrine of justification actually was by comparing Luther, Melanchthon, Zwingli and Calvin. I believe that the differences between these four most important of the reformers in their views of the doctrine of justification are wide and representative enough to keep our definition of its strictly evangelical character from becoming too narrow. At the same time, the crucial common ground between them in their opposition to the doctrinal systems of the Roman Catholic church appears quite clearly, as it certainly would not if Osiander and the anti-authoritarian reformers, represented by some very diverse figures, were to be included in a study of the Reformation doctrine of justification. That 'left wing' did indeed subscribe entirely to what we call the Reformation and to Reformation theology, but not every evangelical position in the sixteenth century necessarily contains a genuine Reformation doctrine of justification, that is, one clearly distinct from the Catholic understanding of grace and morality. Where a doctrine of justification no longer contains the fundamental features of opposition to Catholicism, to be studied below from comparison between Luther, Melanchthon, Zwingli and Calvin, its evangelical character is in doubt – not for dogmatic but for purely historical reasons, since application of the historical description 'evangelical' is appropriate only where there has been an obvious break with the ecclesiastical and doctrinal system of the Middle Ages.

Augustinianism that were extremely sensitive to questions of the theology of grace. It is by comparison with men who grappled with the Reformation doctrine of *solus Christus* and *sola gratia* as openly as Johannes von Staupitz,[10] Johannes Gropper,[11] Gasparo Contarini[12] and Girolamo Seripando[13] that a clear outline of what was evangelical will emerge and must be checked.[14] In this context, the religious negotiations between Protestants and Roman Catholic controversialist theologians aiming for unity on the one hand,[15] and the debates and doctrinal statements of the Council of Trent[16] tending towards distinction and separation on the other, will be of great significance for our study of the issue.

10 Cf. H. A. Oberman, *Werden und Wertung der Reformation. Vom Wegestreit zum Glaubenskampf* (Tübingen, 1977), pp. 97–118; B. Hamm, *Frömmigkeitstheologie am Anfang des 16. Jahrhunderts* (Beiträge zur historischen Theologie, 65) (Tübingen, 1982), pp. 234–43 (bibl.).
11 Cf. R. Braunisch, *Die Theologie der Rechtfertigung im "Enchiridion" (1538) des Johannes Gropper. Sein Kritischer Dialog mit Philipp Melanchthon* (Reformationsgeschichtliche Studien und Texte, 109), Aschendorff, 1974.
12 Cf. H. Rückert, *Die theologische Entwicklung Gasparo Contarinis* (Arbeiten zur Kirchengeschichte, 6), Bonn, 1926.
13 Ibid., *Die Rechtfertigungslehre auf dem Tridentinischen Konzil* (Arbeiten zur Kirchengeschichte, 3), Bonn, 1925, pp. 230–8; A. Forster, *Gesetz und Evangelium bei Seripando* (Paderborn, 1963).
14 Of course we must always consider how far such theologians were already influenced by the Reformation doctrine of justification. There can thus be common ground between reforming Catholic theologians and the leaders of the Reformation, and even though it *is* common ground it may contain features that are specifically and genuinely of the Reformation.
15 Cf. B. Lohse in *HDGThG* II, ed. C. Andresen, 1980, pp. 102–8 (bibl.).
16 Cf. W. Dantine, ibid., pp. 453–64 (bibl., esp. the works by Rückert, Oberman and Joest). In comparing the decrees and canons of Trent with the doctrine of the reformers, one must always remember that the Council of Trent narrowed orthodoxy down considerably by comparison with the doctrinal diversity and broad spectrum of Catholic theology in the Middle Ages. What the Council rejected and condemned as non-Catholic was far from being non-Catholic as that term would have been understood in the Middle Ages and the first half of the sixteenth century. Anyone contrasting 'Catholic theology' with 'Reformation theology' should thus be aware of what medieval Catholic theology permitted. In particular, the 'Augustinian' school of the Augustinian Eremites order must not be overlooked, nor above all should the combination of radical Augustinianism and nominalism in the theology of grace propounded by Gregory of Rimini and his pupils. In speaking of nominalism a great many Catholic and Evangelical scholars still automatically think of Ockhamism, although with its specific doctrine of grace Ockhamism – in its own turn by no means always unambiguous – is only one aspect of nominalism. On the symbiosis of Augustinianism and nominalism cf. recently M. Schulze, ' "Via Gregorii" in Forschung und Quellen', in H. A. Oberman (ed.), *Gregor von Rimini. Werk und Wirkung bis zur Reformation* (Berlin, 1981), pp. 1–126; A. Zumkeller, *Erbsünde, Gnade, Rechtfertigung und Verdienst nach der Lehre der Erfurter Augustinertheologen des Spätmittelalters* (Cass, 35), Würzburg, 1984, esp. 2–9.

If we set out from the criterion defined above, that Reformation features are mould-breaking and cannot be described as just *one* possible position within the medieval theological system, then one thing should be clear: access to a definition of the Reformation doctrine of justification can be acquired only by studying the characteristics of medieval Catholic doctrines of grace and salvation, and what they have in common. I shall now turn to that question.

II   Medieval Catholic Doctrine[17]

Let us imagine a late medieval man with a strong consciousness of his sinfulness, living in fear of the divine judge and the punishments of hell

17   It is not only sensible but necessary for us to take our bearings in the following account from those medieval doctrines of salvation that, comparatively speaking, come closest to the Reformation doctrine. I am thinking of a doctrine of grace strongly influenced by Augustine's Anti-Pelagianism, for instance in the late works of Thomas Aquinas (*Summa theologiae*), in the Augustinian Eremite Aegidius Romanus, and in Gregory of Rimini. These theologians laid particular emphasis on the distance between natural morality and the justifying operation of grace. The differences separating this Augustinian theology of grace from the theology of the reformers also apply (indeed, they apply in particular) to the Scotist and Ockhamist doctrine of grace. To that extent we can detect a common basic feature of medieval theology. On *one* point, however, we must make a reservation. The Scotists and Ockhamists agree with the nominalist tendencies of the Augustinian Gregory of Rimini in stressing the fact that the infused 'habit of grace' of *caritas* and the works proceeding from it do *not* lead with absolute inevitability to the divine *acceptatio ad vitam aeternam*. In his sovereign power (*de potentia dei absoluta*) God could still withhold eternal bliss from the man to whom grace has been given. The causal and conditional connection between human morality – that is, its fulfilment of divine law and the attainment of salvation – is thus not directly derived from the nature of man in possession of justifying grace. Only God's freely given promise lies at the root of this causal relationship and thus the connection between merit and reward. In the context of this order of salvation, ordained by God thus and not otherwise, and therefore immutable (*de potentia dei ordinata*), the quality of the habit of grace and the morality of good works can indeed develop fully: a characteristic feature of the Catholic understanding of salvation. The scope of the *potentia dei absoluta* thus makes no difference to the immanent stringency of the concept of salvation in the model of justification described below. The nominalists too see salvation *de facto* as depending on the essential quality and actual morality of man. However, wide differences then arise between those theologians who, like William of Ockham, will even allow natural man the possibility of selfless love of God, and those like Gregory of Rimini who consider a morally good action possible only on condition of the granting of grace and the actual support of God (the *auxilium speciale dei*). Even Gregory of Rimini, however, insists on the morality of human acts as a condition of fitness for salvation. On the tradition of the freely given promise of God in the Middle Ages, cf. B. Hamm, *Promissio, Pactum, Ordinatio. Freiheit und Selbstbindung Gottes in der scholastischen Gnadenlehre* (Beiträge zur historischen Theologie, 54), Tübingen, 1977.

and purgatory. Let us further imagine that this man acts as he is expected to do by the scholastic theologians. He will be constantly repenting of his sins, confessing to the priest and receiving the sacrament of absolution. He will hope devoutly that God has forgiven him his sins for Christ's sake and is inclined to show him grace. But he knows at the same time that this is not enough to get him into Paradise. He sees the way of probation lying ahead of him, the way of obedience to the law, the way of good works that must be done out of unselfish love for God and for his neighbour. Through such works he will on the one hand make amends (*satisfactio*) for the temporal punishment of sin he bears, and on the other he will acquire merit (*merita*).[18] He will earn continuation in the divine grace, an increase of grace, entrance into eternal life, and finally an increase in the sanctification of eternal life. All this is the object of his works, made possible by active love. Of course, supposing for instance that this man has heard Johannes von Staupitz preach in Nuremberg,[19] he knows that he can never do such good works of his own sinful nature, but only through the supernatural quality of grace infused in him by God and transforming him. Furthermore, he will have a sense of the inadequacy of his works of love:[20] he will feel that even they can never fully atone for his temporal sin and earn a heavenly reward, but the power of the Passion of Christ must always compensate for his inadequacy,[21] and thus that in the end, when his works are accepted by God and he is granted eternal life, God is rewarding only his own gifts to mankind,[22] and always through the interceding power of

18   The actual content of the concept of merit and the basis on which its possibility is founded are very variable in scholastic theology; cf. Hamm, ibid., pp. 437–62.
19   Nuremberg sermons of 1517 (Lazarus Spengler's copy). *Johann von Staupitzens sämmtliche Werke I: Deutsche Schriften*, ed. J. K. F. Knaake (Potsdam, 1867), pp. 15–42.
20   Cf. A. Zumkeller, 'Das Ungenügen der menschlichen Werke bei den deutschen Predigern des Spätmittelalters', in *Zeitschrift für katholische Theologie* 81 (1959), pp. 265–305.
21   Staupitz applies the idea of inadequacy with particular force to the affect of repentance; cf. theologishen L. Graf zu Dohna and R. Wetzel, 'Die Reue Christi. Zum theologischen Ort der Busse bei Johann von Staupitz', in *SMGB* 94 (1983), pp. 457–82; Hamm, *Frömmigkeitstheologie*, pp. 240–2. The christological idea of compensation as held in the late Middle Ages, mainly by the Augustinian Eremites, is taken up in pre-Tridentine reforming theology, particularly by supporters of the doctrine of double *iustitia* (Gropper, Pigge, Contarini, Seripando); cf. Braunisch, *Die Theologie der Rechtfertigung*, pp. 419–37.
22   According to Augustine's influential formulation, for instance in *De gratia et lib. arb.* 6, 15 (PL 44, 891); 'Si ergo dei dona sunt bona merita tua, non deus coronat merita tua tamquam merita tua, sed tamquam dona sua.' *Tract. in Ioan.* 3, 10 (*CChr. SL* 36, 25, 25f): 'Coronat autem in nobis deus dona misericordiae suae.'

Christ.[23] Even all this, however, will not lead our medieval man to feel a confident certainty of grace and salvation. He will still feel sure (if he sees himself in the light of scholastic doctrines) that he can attain salvation only through works of love, and he will still be convinced that these works must derive from the nature of the human being himself, that is, from a quality of selfless divine love constantly present in him and expelling the affect and the act of hostility to God, that is to say, original sin and mortal sin. However, he will also feel sure that he can never know with complete certainty if he really possesses that love and is thus in a state of grace that will justify him.[24] In pious self-analysis, his conscience will remain anxiously intent on his own condition, however often he is told and assured that everything happens through grace and for the sake of Christ, for the reality of Christ must become the reality in him of a new state of being and acting. At the end of his life, after all, the same Christ who died for him and works in him through grace will call him to reckoning, a stern judge, and will then decide whether he has kept the law of love.

Now let us try to perceive the scholastic understanding of justification as set out in this model of late medieval experience. Here, and indeed here above all, where the primacy and the transforming power of grace are emphasized in line with Augustine's anti-Pelagianism, justification is identified with the idea of being made righteous. The nature of justification, its *forma*, is the new quality of grace shown in love, a quality that is acquired by man, and here indeed the giving and working of God[25] has become so much his own that they are the wellspring of his own free movement and a self-realization resulting from his actions, with the aim of achieving eternal life. The person of the man

23 The scholastic concept saw merit and satisfaction on mankind's part as possible only in so far as man's finite actions and sufferings are founded in the infinite value of the merit and satisfaction of Jesus Christ. Johannes von Paltz, referring to Johannes Duns Scotus, consequently says of *satisfactio*: 'Verum est, quod deo per nos satisfacere non possumus, sed tamen in virtute passionis Christi possumus satisfacere; quia illa passio in tantum acceptatur a deo trino, ut virtute eius acceptetur satisfactio illa, quae secundum se accepta non posset esse satisfactio.' Johannes von Paltz, *Supplementum Coelifodinae*, 1504, ed. B. Hamm (Spätmittelalter und Reformation, 3), Berlin, 1983, p. 290, 11–14.
24 On the uncertainty of grace and election, cf. Hamm, 'Frömmigkeitstheologie', pp. 222–6 (distinguishing between subjective and objective levels of certainty).
25 The freedom of the *liberum arbitrium*, to medieval followers of Augustine, means simply the participation of the man to whom grace has been shown; the operation of God is transformed into the spontaneous operation of man, and man as an entity guided by God also operates of himself, as an active subject (as distinct from acting under compulsion, *coactio*). Cf. Thomas Aquinas, *S.th.* I–III q. 113 art. 3.

assumes the aspect of an active subject[26] before God, and only in this way can he win eternal life. The working of God as the autonomous first cause opens up to man the possibility of cooperation (*cooperatio*) in his own salvation through the outpouring of grace and perhaps in addition through the actual aid of God's grace.[27]

Here we come to the understanding of the nature of existence characteristic of the medieval doctrine of salvation,[28] an ontology of righteousness determining man's righteous conduct and relation to salvation from the viewpoint of his moral quality, and teleologically relating that morality in action to man's final acceptance into sanctification. A crucial point is the dominant idea here of causality or contingency: the justification of the sinner, his pardon and acceptance as a child of God, are expressed when he is made righteous and his soul transformed through the quality of grace. Only if sin is really set aside is it conceivable that a man's sins can be forgiven and not held against him. Here, in the transformation wrought by the infused habit of grace, lies the real factor making acceptance of the sinner possible[29] – its 'sole formal cause' (*unica formalis causa*), as the Council of Trent puts it.[30] However,

26 Johannes von Staupitz formulates this idea in accordance with the theological tradition whereby the good works of the justified, although they are the works of God, are *formaliter* present in man; *Libellus de exsecutione aeternae praedestinationis*, 1517, § 40, ed. L. Graf zu Dohna and R. Wetzel (Spätmittelalter und Reformation, 14), Berlin, 1979, p. 124. The *formaliter* here, according to the editor's comment, means 'subjective', that is, it describes the *esse* of the works as in a subjective relation to the substance of the human person.

27 The necessity of the actual aid of God's grace of God for every morally good act is emphasized by Gregory of Rimini and his pupils; cf. C. P. Burger, 'Der Augustinschüler gegen die modernen Pelagianer: Das *auxilium speciale dei* in der Gnadenlehre Gregors von Rimini', in Oberman (ed.), *Gregor von Rimini*, pp. 195–240.

28 Theologians influenced by nominalism also understand the nature of being in a similar way, although they are more interested than the representatives of the *Via antiqua* in unusual than in habitual actions. They too are concerned about the moral nature of man in the doctrine of justification, whether in regard to the 'habit' of love or to the separate acts of love of the justified, and they too see morality as a human factor that is a condition of acceptance into salvation.

29 Cf., for instance, the answer given by Thomas Aquinas to the question 'Utrum ad remissionem culpae, quae est iustificatio impii, requiratur gratiae infusio', and in particular his concern with the argument that the forgiveness of sin consists in the *reputatio divina*, and thus requires no *infusio gratiae*: *S.th.* I–III q. 113 art. 2 arg. 2 and ad 2. Cf. also ibid., art. 8 ad 1: from God's point of view (*ex parte dei iustificantis*) the infusion of grace precedes the forgiveness of sins, not temporally but in an objectively logical sense (*ordine naturae*), for the infused habit of grace is *causa remissionis culpae*.

30 *Decretum de iustificatione*, c. 7 (D/S No. 1529). Cf. ibid. can. 11 (No. 1561): 'Si quis dixerit homines iustificari vel sola imputatione iustitiae Christi vel sola peccatorum remissione, exclusa gratia et caritate, quae in cordibus eorum per spiritum sanctum diffundatur atque illis inhaereat, aut etiam gratiam, qua iustificamur, esse tantum favorem dei: anathema sit.'

this means that the process whereby the sinner is made righteous, a process expressed in moral virtues and good works, is the reason, the necessary prerequisite and condition for the final absolution of man at the Last Judgement. For where the grounds of the reality of justification are seen as residing in the nature and actions of man, the justification of the sinner in this life is always provisional and incomplete, and will come to a final conclusion only in the judgement that will absolve man and find him righteous *because of* his righteous nature and actions. In scholastic thought, then, the two great significant aspects of the Christian life are separate: first the acceptance of man into grace (the *acceptatio ad gratiam*) occurring when he is made righteous in the process of justification, then his acceptance into salvation at the end of his life (the *acceptatio ad vitam aeternam*).[31] Final absolution is *on the grounds* of righteous actions and obedience to the law, although also, and always, for the sake of Christ. Here a causal and contingent relationship prevails, and it is also articulated in the concepts of satisfaction and merit.[32] The fact that the works of love are described as satisfactory and meritorious shows that they are the necessary prerequisite or at least the *causa sine qua non* for making man's sanctification possible. The Council of Trent consequently condemns the doctrine that the Gospel constitutes a 'naked and absolute' (i.e. unconditional) 'promise of eternal life', that is to say, sanctification given 'without condition of the fulfilment of the commandments' (*sine condicione observationis mandatorum*).[33]

III The Reformation Doctrine of Justification

1 The unconditionally given acceptance of mankind

This doctrine, condemned by the Council of Trent as un-Catholic and stating that the sinner is given an outright promise of unconditional salvation, was at the centre of the Reformation doctrine of justification as we encounter it in Luther, Melanchthon, Zwingli and Calvin.[34] In the

31 Cf., for instance, Johannes von Paltz, *Supplementum Coelifodinae*, p. 227, 5–7: 'Respondetur, quod est duplex acceptatio: una quantum ad praesentem iustitiam, altera quantum ad finalem remunerationem.'

32 On the medieval connection between the concept of merit and ideas of causality cf. Hamm, *Promissio*, pp. 443f. and 485–9.

33 *Decretum de iustificatione*, can. 20 (D/S No. 1570): 'Si quis hominem iustificatum et quantumlibet perfectum dixerit non teneri ad observantiam mandatorum dei et ecclesiae, sed tantum ad credendum, quasi vero evangelium sit nuda et absoluta promissio vitae aeternae sine condicione observationis mandatorum: anathema sit.'

34 Cf. Luther, *Resolutiones*, thesis 38 (*Weimarer Ausgabe*, 596, pp. 7–9): 'Cave ergo, ne quando in tuam contritionem ullo modo confidas, sed in nudissimum verbum

Confessio Augustana Variata, Melanchthon says that the promise of forgiveness of sins and of eternal life is certain, since it does not depend on
the condition of our worthiness (*ex condicione nostrae dignitatis*) but is
given for Christ's sake. Melanchthon sees the whole consolation of the
terrified conscience in this unconditionality, the fact that forgiveness is
linked neither to preceding nor to subsequent works.[35] Calvin puts it
similarly when he sees the characteristic feature of the promises of the
law in its structure of conditionality, the *condicio*: only on condition that
the commandment of the law to love is kept does its promise of life come
into effect.[36] It is not so with the gospel: its promises of justice do not
depend on the *condicio operum,* but are unconditional, resting solely on
the mercy of God and the righteousness of Christ interceding for us.[37]
This unconditional promise, the unconditional acceptance of the sinner
into righteousness and sanctification, is what Calvin calls justification
(*iustificatio*).[38]

It is not a matter of terminology. The term *iustificatio* plays a very sub-
sidiary part in the writings of Zwingli compared with those of the other
three reformers, and Luther by no means confines it to the precise sense

optimi et fidelissimi tui salvatoris Jesu Christi; cor tuum fallet te, ille te non fallet vel
habitus vel desideratus.'

35 'Quamquam igitur evangelium requirit poenitentiam, tamen, ut remissio peccatorum certa sit, docet eam gratis donari, hoc est non pendere ex condicione dignitatis nostrae nec dari propter ulla praecedentia opera aut dignitatem sequentium
. . . ideo Paulus dicit: "gratis salvati estis" [Eph. 2, 5]. Item: "ideo ex fide gratis, ut sit
firma promissio" [Rom. 4, 16], hoc est: ita erit certa remissio, cum sciemus eam non
pendere ex condicione nostrae dignitatis, sed donari propter Christum. Haec est
firma et necessaria consolatio piis et perterrefactis mentibus.' CAvar (1540), art.
4 (*Melanchthons Werke in Auswahl,* ed. R. Stupperich, VI, Gütersloh, 1955, p. 15,
11–16, 24–30).

36 Cf., for instance, *Inst.,* 1559, III, 17, 6 (OS IV, 258, 27–32): 'Legales promissiones appello, non quae ubique sparsae sunt in libris Mosaicis (quando in illis
quoque evangelicae multae occurrunt), sed quae proprie ad legis ministerium per-
tinent. Eiusmodi promissiones, quocunque nomine vocare libeat, sub condicione "Si
feceris quod tibi praecipitur" paratam esse remunerationem denuntiant'. Cf. ibid. III,
11, 17 (IV, 200, 34–201, 7); III, 17, 2 (IV, 254, 30 f.); III, 13, 3 (IV, 218, 8).

37 Ibid. III, 11, 17 (IV, 200, 33–201, 15), and finally: 'Certe et lex ipsa suas habet
promissiones. Quare in promissionibus evangelicis distinctum aliquid ac diversum
esse oportet, nisi velimus fateri ineptam esse collationem. Quale autem istud erit,
nisi quod gratuitae sunt ac sola dei misericordia suffultae, cum legis promissiones
ab operum condicione pendeant.' Cf. ibid. III, 2, 29 (IV, 39, 6–11) for the distinction
between *promissio gratuita* and *promissio condicionalis.*

38 Cf., for instance, ibid. III, 11, 2 (IV, 183, 4–10): 'Contra iustificabitur ille fide,
qui operum iustitia exclusus Christi iustitiam per fidem apprehendit, qua vestitus in
dei conspectu non ut peccator, sed tamquam iustus apparet. Ita nos iustificationem
simpliciter interpretamur acceptionem, qua nos deus in gratiam receptos pro iustis
habet. Eamque in peccatorum remissione ac iustitiae Christi imputatione positam
esse dicimus.'

of God's absolution received in faith, as do the late Melanchthon and Calvin; he also relates divine justification to the living process of justification in human existence.[39] As for the term *condicio*, one might search both Luther and Zwingli in vain for an explicit account of the unconditionality of grace and salvation. The Reformation was concerned not with the term but with the essence of unconditionality: the unconditionality of the process whereby the godless sinner is justified before God and accepted by God into salvation. How can I become just before God and be saved, in view of the total commitment of will and of achievement that God's law demands of me? How can I, as one who breaks that law, be accepted into the family and inheritance of God? This is the essence of the idea of justification at the heart of every fully developed theological system in the Reformation.[40] The connection between justification and unconditionality, as the reformers saw it, requires an explanation that will correctly locate its essential difference from medieval theology.

To be precise, we are concerned with the nature of the relationship between divine acceptance of the sinner and the sinner's actual change of life. The close connection between justification and absolution is not a matter of controversy. All the great reformers emphatically taught that justification, the absolution and acceptance of godless man, is fundamentally connected with man's sanctification and renewal in love and the works of love. The difference from Catholicism does not lie here, as if there could be a new divine beginning without renewal in man, and the act of judgement were an abstract and involuntary act of God concerned with himself, not a creative calling of man to life. After Luther, Calvin in particular shows how deeply the connection of justification and sanctification can be founded in the Reformation; to Calvin, the indissoluble link arises from the community of the faithful in Christ.[41] For 'Christ justifies no one whom he does not at the same time (*simul*) sanctify', Calvin writes in the *Institutio*.[42] Those who would separate the two would tear Christ apart. 'Would you therefore achieve justice in Christ?' Calvin continues. 'Then you must first possess Christ. However, you cannot possess Christ at all without at the same time

---

39 Cf. P. Althaus, *Die Theologie Martin Luthers* (Gütersloh, 1980), p. 197.

40 This question, characteristic of the Reformation as a whole, is still central where the answer blurs the dividing line between Reformation and medieval Catholic doctrines, for instance in Andreas Osiander the elder.

41 Cf. W. Kolfhaus, *Christusgemeinschaft bei Johannes Calvin* (Beiträge zur Geschichte und Lehre der Reformierten Kirche, 3), Neukirchen, 1939.

42 'Nullum ergo Christus iustificat, quem non simul sanctificet. Sunt enim perpetuo et individuo nexu coniuncta haec beneficia, ut quos sapientia sua illuminat, eos redimat, quos redimit, iustificet, quos iustificat, sanctificet.' *Inst.* (1559), III, 16, 1 (OS IV, 249, 8–11).

participating in his sanctification . . . the Lord gives us both at once (justification and sanctification), never the one without the other.'[43] The reason is in the inseparable community of Christ with the Holy Spirit, so that our community with Christ is always at the same time community with his renewing spirit.[44] In a treatise of 1547 against the decrees of the Council of Trent Calvin explicitly says that the question is not whether Christ also sanctifies those whom he justifies. The entire argument, rather, turns around the cause of justification: 'Sed tota nostra disceptatio est de causa iustificationis.'[45] The question is where the acceptance of man, the totality of his justification and his salvation before God, have their foundation.

We have seen how in medieval Catholic theology neither the acceptance of the sinner into the process of justification nor his acceptance for eternal salvation is seen as causeless, that is, without foundation in sanctification and the renewal of human morality. Absolution and acceptance by God never occur without such cause. God's forgiveness of sins and justification of man is made possible by the granting of grace to man and by his subsequent good works and freedom from acts of mortal sin; these aspects of his nature then also become the condition of his sanctification after death. These ideas of the possible and necessary grounds of righteousness and sanctification are what the reformers dispute. It is here that the Reformation doctrine of justification

---

43   'Vis ergo iustitiam in Christo adipisci? Christum ante possideas oportet; possidere autem non potes, quin fias sanctificationis eius particeps; quia in frusta discerpi non potest. Cum ergo haec beneficia [i.e. *iustitia* and *sanctificatio*] nonnisi se ipsum erogando fruenda nobis dominus concedat, utrunque simul largitur: alterum nunquam sine altero.' Ibid., III, 16, 1 (IV, 249, 14–19). On the idea that to separate justification from sanctification would be to tear Christ apart, cf. also note 46.

44   Cf. the account and texts in T. Stadtland, *Rechtfertigung und Heiligung bei Calvin* (Beiträge zur Geschichte und Lehre der Reformierten Kirche, 32), Neukirchen, 1972, p. 129f.

45   A distinction may be drawn between justification and sanctification, but they cannot be divided: '. . . perpetuo coniunctae sint ac cohaereant duae istae res: sanctificatio et iustificatio. Sed perperam inde infertur unam ac eandem esse. Exempli gratia: Solis lumen, etsi nunquam separatur a calore, non tamen calor existimandus est; nemoque tam rudis invenitur, qui non unum ab altero distinguat. Fatemur ergo, simul atque iustificatur quispiam, necessario innovationem quoque sequi. Neque vero de eo ambigitur, an sanctificet Christus nec ne, quoscunque iustificat. Hoc enim esset lacerare evangelium adeoque Christum ipsum discerpere, si quis iustitiam, quam fide consequimur, separare velit a poenitentia. Sed tota nostra disceptatio est de causa iustificationis. Hanc Tridentini patres duplicem esse fingunt: ac si partim remissione peccatorum, partim spirituali regneratione iusti essemus; vel, ut aliis verbis exprimam quod sentiunt: ac si partim imputatione, partim qualitate iustitia nostra constaret. Ego autem unicam et simplicem esse assero, quae tota continetur gratuita dei acceptione. Eam praeterea extra nos constituo, quia in solo Christo iusti sumus.' *Acta Synodi Tridentini cum antidoto* (CR 35, 448).

breaks the mould. There can be no valid cause for man to be justified before God; not even God himself stands in such a causal relation to man and his actions. The acceptance of God, his bestowal of grace on his creature, is not subject to reasons or conditions, although justification always has consequences in the shape of sanctification in the renewing power of love and the works of love.

2 Radical sin

The way taken by the reformers in reaching this view of unconditionality is through insight into man's pitiable nature and sinful frailty before God. To the scholastic understanding, the life of man is always marked in one way or another by sin. However, sin dividing man from God, original and mortal sin that of its nature excludes the love of God, is a human fault that can be remedied. The infusion of the habit of grace compensates for this lack in man by making him a creature that loves God,[46] and thus goes to meet God through obedience to the law. The reformers, however, particularly Luther, thought and taught that the original sin of rebellion against God was not a human fault that could be cancelled out, but was the perverse and basic tendency of the whole person until death. Throughout his life, the Christian remains an unrealized being, incapable of love for God and his neighbour, trapped in a self-centred way of life, lacking even the roots of humanity.

3 Grace preceding perfect righteousness

This understanding of radical sin has its precise counterpart in the understanding of grace. Just as sin is not an aspect of man, but is the whole man, justifying grace is not an appendage of man, a quality inherent in him, something that man as subject possesses. Grace, in direct contrast to the scholastic doctrine, is nothing but God himself in his mercy, the grace of God, God giving himself in community with the sinner. Grace is not something made in man, but his new standing in the sight of God. Since man is guilty before God, and owes total righteousness and selfless love throughout his life, the reality and possibility of God's grace can have no foundation based in man. Furthermore, even if man could obey God's law and owe nothing to God's favour, as a

46 Here we may disregard the scholastic doctrines that allow the possibility of acts of divine love even in the natural state, before the reception of *caritas* – in line with our basic proposition (see note 18 above) to take medieval theology seriously where it most strongly emphasizes the gulf between nature and grace.

created being he would not be worthy or deserving of the boundless grace and splendour of God;[47] to quote Luther: 'God has laid it down that man is to be saved not by the law but by Christ.'[48] To the godless, then, grace becomes real in the form of groundless acceptance into the family of God, the beginning of a new relationship. A conceptual approach in terms of the relationship replaces the traditional qualititive and moral attitude. Sin remains real in ourselves, but outside ourselves (*extra nos*), in the relationship, that is to say, we are justified in the way in which we are seen by God (*coram deo*).

A little further interpretation of what Luther and the other reformers understood by this relationship of grace should be added. The propitiatory righteousness of Jesus Christ acting vicariously for us is of fundamental importance. It alone is the cause of justification, it alone provides satisfaction and wins merit. The new relationship in which grace justifies us means that God sees man in the light of Christ's righteousness, and allows it to stand for the righteousness of sinners. That in turn means that through Christ man acquires a total righteousness that he could never qualitatively possess as a frail sinner and a created being with such a being's limitations.

Luther, and Melanchthon and Calvin with him, express this understanding of justification in terms of the relation by speaking of the imputation to us of righteousness (*reputatio, imputatio*), and by describing the righteousness of Christ imputed to the sinner as a righteousness that is external and alien to mankind (*iustitia aliena, externa*). It is indeed truly given to us, but it never exists *in* us, only in the manner of its acceptance and of divine absolution. 'Righteousness' is the acknowledgement of the sinner before the judgement seat of God in the face of accusations against him from all sides, including his own heart. This extremely forensic terminology articulates the change from the scholastic understanding of the nature of man in particularly concentrated form;[49]

47   Cf. Zwingli, 'Eine kurze christliche Einleitung', in *Huldreich Zwinglis sämtliche Werke* (abbreviation Z) II, 637, 3–6 and 24–26: 'And even if we were always devout and without frailty, and served God all our days according to his will, yet man's life is unworthy of long, immeasurable eternity.'

48   'Est autem quaestio non, utrum lex vel opera rationis iustificent, sed an lex facta in spiritu iustificet. Respondemus autem, quod non, et quod homo, qui per omnia legem virtute spiritus sancti impleret, tamen debeat implorare misericordiam dei, qui constituit non per legem, sed per Christum salvare.' *Weimarer Ausgabe*, TR 1, 32, 9–13, no. 85.

49   Cf. O. H. Pesch, *Theologie der Rechtfertigung bei Martin Luther und Thomas von Aquin* (Walberg, Ger. Albertus-Magnus-Academie. Walberger Studien, 7, T 4), Mainz, 1967, repr. 1985, p. 182: 'Secondly, the requisite distinction from scholastic doctrine can best be perceived through forensic understanding. We may indeed wonder, with some justice, whether Elert is right in suggesting that scholasticism bases its certainty of justification not on faith but on "empirical facts". However, it

however, the example of Zwingli clearly shows how the basic attitude of the Reformation to the doctrine of justification can still be the same where this specific kind of terminology is not to the fore. Once again, the crucial point is not the forensic terminology but the nature of what it implies. Zwingli never equates the righteousness we derive from Christ with the righteousness of renewal expressed by good works and wrought in us by the Holy Spirit. He too sees the righteousness of Christ as the pre-given totality of our acceptance for salvation in the forgiveness of our sins, while the renewal itself is the partial element in an existence shattered by sin. Our righteousness and innocence, preserving us before the judgement of God, as Zwingli constantly emphasizes, are nothing but the righteousness of the son of God interceding for us.[50] 'Everyone who is in Christ,' he says, 'is saved in the perfection of the law and by it. To be "in Christ" means to have faith in him and to continue firm in our belief.'[51]

Although Zwingli seamlessly links righteousness received in faith with the sanctification of life under the dominant perspective of the workings of the divine spirit, and although he therefore identifies belief and love in his concept of faith,[52] his own theology displays the characteristic profile of the Reformation doctrine of justification: indissoluble as the link between justification and sanctification appears to the reformers,[53] they all, even Zwingli, clearly point out that, in contrast to

is true that on the issue of justification, the scholastics enquire not about empirically verifiable processes but about *internal* processes, about *man*, while Luther, on the other hand, is concerned with the new attitude of *God* to man. In fact a forensic understanding thus does express the most important difference between the Reformation and scholasticism.'

50 Cf., for instance, Zwingli, *Auslegen und Gründe der Schlussreden* (Zurich, Froschower, 1523); Art. 5 (Z II, 40, 26–28); B. Hamm, *Zwinglis Reformation der Freiheit* (Neukirchen-Vluyn, 1988). As yet there is no complete study, free of polemics and apologetics, of Zwingli's understanding of righteousness and justification. The monograph by H. Schmid, *Zwinglis Lehre von der göttlichen und menschlichen Gerechtigkeit'* (Studien zur Dogmengeschichte und systematischen Theologie, 12), Zurich, 1959, does not give a precise account of the specifically evangelical features of Zwingli's doctrine of justification.

51 In 'Epist. ad Rom.', on Rom. 10, 4 (M. Schuler and J. Schulthess, *Huldrici Zwinglii Opera* VI/2, 1838, 112): 'Omnis, qui est in Christo, est in perfectione legis et per hoc salvus. In Christo esse est ei fidere et firma fide haerere.'

52 Cf., for instance, *Commentarius de vera et falsa religione*, 'De merito' (Z III, 848, 29, and 849, 33).

53 This is particularly true, to an even greater degree, of those reformers who saw justification and sanctification less *a parte hominis* than from the perspective of the works of God. Since in Zwingli the main viewpoint is always the omnipotence of the spirit of God, justification and sanctification, faith and love, the fruits of love and its social consequences, seen from that angle, all cohere to form a spiritual unity, with faith in God alone at its centre, wrought by the spirit. This theocentric perspective

scholastic theology, justification is not the same thing as to be made righteous. Justification as the totality of obedience to the law and of righteousness, given to the sinner in advance through Christ and protecting him, that perfect righteousness in the sight of God, can never be congruent with partial renewal through the spirit of love. This tenet also means that the sinner's acceptance into the grace and salvation justifying him can never derive the basis of its existence from the change to a Christian way of life. Justification through the righteousness of Christ which is outside us, and the process whereby we become just within ourselves in a sanctified life, are always separate, like cause and effect, like the immeasurable fullness of God and the emptiness of created beings, the purity of the innocent and the guilt of outcast, ever-sinful man. To this extent there is agreement between the reformers, if not terminologically then on a common 'evangelical conviction of the unconditional predominance of "alien righteousness (*iustitia aliena*)"' (Dantine).[54] And Elert is right to locate the crucial difference from scholasticism in this 'alien righteousness'.[55]

4   Simul iustus et peccator

In the thinking of the Reformation, the approach to this distinction and to the irreversibility of cause and effect is directly connected with the approach to the idea of what is *simul*, existing 'at the same time'. *Simul*, in the Reformation[56] means simultaneity, the inseparable and yet distinct existence side by side of four carefully distinguished aspects of the Christian's life;[57] and in fact the emphasis on simultaneity derives only from this distinction. Simultaneous realities are (1) sin lasting all our lives, and received by the Christian in the form of penance; (2) the right-

of unity, however, must not be misunderstood. As soon as the question of the cause of salvation is raised, and attention is directed to the created being, Zwingli distinguishes clearly between the righteousness of the son of God passively received in devout faith, and the activity of the loving human being; the latter can never be a cause of salvation but always shows the workings of the abundance of righteousness and salvation that has been received.

54   Dantine, in *HDGThG* II, p. 459.

55   W. Elert, *Morphologie des Luthertums* I (Munich, 1931), repr. 1965, pp. 68–70. However, Elert confines his definition of this opposition to Luther.

56   On the 'evangelical' character of the idea inherent in the Lutheran formula *simul iustus et peccator*, cf. W. Link, *Das Ringen Luthers um die Freiheit der Theologie von der Philosophie* (Forschungen zur Geschichte und Lehre des Protestantismus, IX/3), 1940, repr. 1979, pp. 77f.

57   The classic text in which these four realities of sin and justice are first ranged side by side in Reformation theology is in Luther's course of lectures on the Epistle to the Romans, Rom 4, 7f (*Weimarer Ausgabe* 56, 269. 21–273, 2).

eousness in the sight of God won for us by Christ (*extra nos*), and received in the form of faith; (3) the righteousness of renewal in sanctification that wrestles with sin, active in the form of love; and (4) liberation from our sinful natures and complete renewal after death, already present in the form of hope. This fourfold reality is expressed in Luther's famous phrase *simul iustus et peccator*, 'a just man and at the same time a sinner'.[58] Yet again, however, the Reformation doctrine of justification does not depend upon such formulaic expressions. So far as I am aware Zwingli, who was a great deal more independent of Luther than Melanchthon and Calvin, did not employ this formula, but the simultaneity of the fourfold reality of sin and righteousness is at the very heart of the content of his theology.[59] He too makes it clear that because man always stands before God as a created being and a sinner, the totality of his simultaneous righteousness must always be outside himself, in Christ, must antedate all the good works of his new life, and must always be considered the sole grounds for the reality and possibility of salvation.

5 The eschatological final validity of justification

Having located the new element in the Reformation understanding of sin and grace, we must now go a step further. Since in Reformation thinking justification is the *unconditional* acceptance of the sinner, for Christ's sake and not because of any previous, present or future quality in his life and morals, and is always founded outside us in God himself – since that is the case, justification acquires an eschatological meaning in the Reformation that is foreign to it in Catholic theology.[60] In scholastic thinking, as we have seen, man's acceptance into grace and righteousness in justification, and his acceptance into sanctification at the Last Judgement, are two separate things, divided by the way of life inherent in obedience to the law and the principles of satisfaction and merit. Man's morality is the prerequisite of his final acceptance. Reformation unconditionality brought the two aspects together: the sinner

58   Cf. the pioneering work of R. Hermann, *Luthers These 'Gerecht und Sünder zugleich'* (Göttingen, 1930), repr. 1960. The Lutheran *simul* is not Pauline but does signify a further creative development of St Paul's interpretation, and thus represents a genuine assimilation of Pauline thinking at a period much concerned with the refinement of the scholastic theology of sin and grace; cf. W. Joest, 'Paulus und das Luthersche Simul Iustus et Peccator', in *Kerygma und Dogma* 1 (1955), pp. 269–320.
59   Cf. G. W. Locher, *Huldrych Zwingli in neuer Sicht. Zehn Beiträge zur Theologie der Zürcher Reformation* (Zurich, 1969), p. 230 (quoting texts).
60   Cf. U. Asendorf, *Eschatologie bei Luther* (Göttingen, 1967), pp. 36–48.

has already been accepted for salvation through his justification and in advance of his new life and good works, despite the enduring power of sin. This is the eschatological final validity of justification. Through the acceptance of the sinner, his entering into the righteousness of Christ, something final has taken place; it cannot be superseded even by the Last Judgement, but will then be brought out of concealment into the revelation of bliss. Why does his acceptance for sanctification become so conclusively a present event in the justification of godless man? Because in giving grace to man God is giving not a thing but himself, in his whole and undivided love, and God himself cannot be superseded.[61]

At the same time, this conclusive finality in Reformation theology derives from Christ. The justice of Jesus Christ interceding for human guilt thus makes the here and now of justification the *eschaton*, the final event in the divine plan, since Jesus Christ 'is the same yesterday, and today, and forever' (Heb. 13.8) and consequently his protective righteousness is eternal too.[62] The godless are therefore safe in his righteousness for all eternity.[63] In the last resort the dogma of Christ's divinity is at the heart of this line of argument: through his divine nature, and through his human suffering and death in man's stead, he is part of the divine eternity. This is the sole reason why the 'existence in Christ' of the justified already denotes existence in everlasting bliss.

Luther and the other reformers with him express this final acceptance of mankind in Christ by saying that in the act of justification the sinner becomes 'righteous *and* saved', *iustus et salvus*,[64] that is, not righteous now and saved at some future date, but already the recipient of righteousness and salvation in faith. Luther, for instance, comments in his Little Catechism on the sacrament of communion: 'We are shown it in this saying: given for you and shed in forgiveness of sins, that is to say,

61 Cf. H. Rückert, *Vorträge und Aufsätze zur historischen Theologie* (1972), p. 306f.
62 Cf. A. Sperl, *Melanchthon zwischen Humanismus und Reformation* (Forschungen zur Geschichte und Lehre des Protestantismus, X/15), Munich, 1959, pp. 48–61 (on Luther).
63 Cf. Calvin, *Inst.* (1599) III, 24, 6 (OS IV, 416, 38–417, 14).
64 Cf. for instance Luther's famous preface to the first volume of the complete edition of his Latin writings, Wittenberg, 5 March 1545 (*Weimarer Ausgabe* 54, 183, 27–9): '... deinde primitias cognitionis et fidei Christi hauseram, scilicet non operibus, sed fide Christi nos iustos et salvos fieri.' In retrospect, Luther writes that he came to this conclusion after the most careful public and private reading of holy scripture and after teaching it for a period of seven years ('sacras litteras diligentissime privatim et publice legeram et docueram per septem annos'). Since we know that Luther gave his first public course of biblical lectures after attaining the degree of Baccalaureus biblicus on 9 March 1509, we can date his conclusion to 1515 (assuming he used the manner of counting customary at the time, including both the first and last years involved) and thus, at the latest, to his lectures on the Epistle to the Romans.

in the sacrament such words offer forgiveness of sins, life and salvation. For where there is forgiveness of sins [to Luther, this was what justification entailed] there is also life and salvation.'[65] Calvin puts it thus: 'Through faith in Christ we achieve not only the ability to win righteousness and become sanctified, but they are both [*iustitia* and *salus*] given to us [through faith].'[66] The faithful, as he says, are those who 'have achieved sanctification' already through their community with Christ.[67]

In this context we repeatedly encounter the Pauline image of the 'heir of God' (Rom. 8.17; Gal. 4.7). By adoption or birth through his justification, the sinner becomes the child and heir of God and his glory: 'He has not earned his position as heir to that fortune through his work, nor does he work and act so that he may become heir to it, but when he was born he was already heir to those patrimonial estates on the grounds of birth, not as a result of his own merit. Even if he persists steadfastly in his work he asks no reward, for he knows that all is his already.' The justified man, then, as God's heir, is already in possession of salvation; he is an heir before he performs any works, and is not paid for them later; he is a child and not a servant.[68]

6 The certainty of salvation

Salvation means the unconditional and thus final acceptance of the godless, an acceptance that cannot be reversed. The epoch-making break with medieval theology in this tenet becomes even clearer when we see that the unconditional nature of salvation propounded by the reformers makes it possible for the sinner to equate certainty of *salvation* with certainty of *belief*. The historical point at which the opposition between the Reformation and Catholicism first emerged on this question was Luther's interrogation by Cardinal Cajetan in Augsburg in October 1518.[69] When the Thomist Cajetan read Luther's resolutions on

65 *Die Bekenntnisschriften der evangelisch-lutherischen Kirche* (Göttingen, 1930), 520, 24–30.

66 'Non enim aut comparandae iustitiae aut salutis tantum acquirendae facultatem fide Christi obtingere significant, sed utrunque nobis donari.' *Inst.* (1559) III, 15, 6 (OS IV, 245, 17–19).

67 Ibid. (IV, 245, 12–16).

68 Quotation from Zwingli, *Expositio fidei*, in Schuler & Schulthess, *Huldrici Zwinglii Opera* IV, 1841, p. 63; quoted from the German translation in: *Zwingli Hauptschriften* II, 1948, 344. Cf., for instance, Luther, *Rhapsodia seu concepta in librum De loco iustificationis* (*Weimarer Ausgabe* 30/II, 670, 21–32).

69 Cf. G. Hennig, *Cajetan und Luther. Ein historischer Beitrag zur Begegnung von Thomismus und Reformation* (Arbeiten zur Theologie, 7), Stuttgart, 1966; Hamm, *Frömmigkeitstheologie*, p. 225f.

indulgences he recognized this point, with admirable acuity, as the greatest threat to the papal church: subjective certainty of salvation on the part of the believer could replace obedience to the church. In line with tradition, Cajetan would allow only the idea of objective certainty of belief, which to him meant the sacrament of penance: the Christian, obedient to the faith of the church, must be convinced that generally speaking the priest's absolution freed men from the guilt of sin, and that those who receive the sacrament in a fit state of mind, truly repenting of their sins, will acquire grace that justifies them. According to Cajetan, on the other hand, a subjective certainty of faith is not permitted to the Christian; that is, he can never have undoubted certainty on the question of whether he himself is in a state of grace, for no one can know if he truly repents of his sins and has received the sacrament worthily. Cajetan accuses Luther of mingling the objective and subjective aspects of the certainty of faith, and the new Reformation approach to the question of the certainty of belief does indeed reside in this combination of the objective and subjective. Luther and the other reformers after him make a connection between the objective validity of the actions of Christ, of the New Testament and its promise, and the advent of his promise in the shape of subjective certainty of faith in the man who receives it. This connection is possible only in the light of unconditionality. Only because the question of whether the person receiving grace is worthy or unworthy becomes irrelevant, only because the sinner's gaze no longer remains fixed on himself with his imperfect repentance and his inability to love, only because this subjective uncertainty is no longer necessary and the sinner's attention is diverted away from his own potential for works and towards Jesus Christ as the sole grounds of salvation, does the subjective certainty of salvation become possible: man is unconditionally accepted by God for salvation although he is a sinner, indeed *as* a sinner. Unconditional certainty, to the reformers, is thus the outcome of unconditional grace.[70]

In their view, moreover, this certainty of being safe in Christ is the source of all that they call the peace, calm, joy and consolation of a Christian life. The whole typical late medieval yearning for security and the certainty of grace and salvation[71] finds an outlet and a solution here.

70　In neither Melanchthon and Zwingli nor in Calvin, however, are unconditional grace and certainty bound to the effective power of external consent, as we encounter it in Luther after 1518, particularly in his dispute with Cajetan.

71　Cf. Hamm, *Frömmigkeitstheologie*, pp. 216ff (chapter 5: 'Im Umkreis der Suche nach Gnaden- und Heilsgarantien'.)

7   Freedom and the absence of freedom

The central concept of Christian freedom must also be mentioned at this point. Every Reformation doctrine of justification is essentially a doctrine of freedom. Above all it means freedom from the law, even in Zwingli and Calvin, and not just freedom from human statutes but even from the divine law of love that still holds good. Christ frees the sinner's conscience from the accusation and condemnatory curse of disobedience to the law, and from the pressure of his obligation to obey that law as a condition of salvation, so that now – backed by the total obedience to the law shown by Jesus Christ – he can obey the law 'freely and cheerfully'.[72] Again, everything depends on the idea of salvation unconditionally given, free of insistence on the law.

This Christian freedom, according to the Reformation understanding of it, is protected by a radical doctrine of our lack of freedom. For only where the sinner's freedom to decide is taken from him by God, where God's gift of grace and man's own remaining in that grace do not in the last resort depend upon man's free will, do the reformers see the doctrine of *solus Christus* and unconditional grace maintained. In this, like the anti-Pelagian Augustine and his medieval followers, they take up the fight against the moralism of all periods which rests on the basic axiom that man has moral autonomy in his freedom to decide. This insistence on the sinner's lack of freedom is not specifically of the Reformation and did not of itself break the mould of the scholastic systems. However, for all the major reformers, including the young Melanchthon of the *Loci communes*,[73] a strict doctrine of predestination forms the foundation of their Reformation doctrine of justification. And the understanding of justification that is specifically evangelical, the unconditional gift of salvation, is essentially and indeed indissolubly bound up with the doctrine of election and the absence of freedom.

The new element in Reformation ideas of predestination, as opposed to those of the scholastics, is perceptible where it becomes clear that not a speculative but a highly soteriological and christological interest in the believer's certainty of salvation is controlling the line of doctrinal argument. Where the idea of conditionality has collapsed, the believer knows his salvation is assured by God's immutable decision alone: no power,

---

72   A favourite phrase of Zwingli's: e.g. in Z II, 649, 32.
73   For Melanchthon's radical doctrine of determination see the *Loci communes* of 1521, the section 'De hominis viribus et de libero arbitrio', *Melanchthons Werke in Auswahl*, ed. R. Stupperich, II/1 (1952), pp. 8–17.

not even his own sin, can part him from God's unconditional will for his salvation.[74]

8 By faith alone

Is it not possible, however, that with faith playing so important a part in salvation, with the typically evangelical principle of *sola fide*, a subtle element of conditionality creeps into the doctrine of justification by the back door? We here encounter an area of problems concerning faith and the word within which the various Reformation positions are relatively far apart. Even behind this diversity of views, of course, common evangelical ground in contrast to medieval Catholic doctrine as a whole is clearly perceptible, and so we should now look at the Reformation principle of 'by faith alone'. The Reformation concept of faith, unlike the cognitive aspect of scholasticism usually identified with the affective concept of faith, derives its nature from rejecting reliance on good works and from its close connection with the word of the Gospel. In this context the Reformation principle of *sola fide*, which may look like the last bastion of conditionality, on the contrary becomes a principle of *un*conditionality. But I must explain this proposition further.

What exactly does it mean to say that man is justified by faith *alone*, not by the works of the law? To the reformers, it meant that the sole grounds and cause of justification reside in God's mercy in Jesus Christ, not any morality inherent in man and manifesting itself in works.[75] Faith, in their eyes, is not located on man's active plane as a spiritual quality, a virtue or a work. Instead, it is a purely receptive mode – and not just because faith is a gift of the Holy Spirit (to the scholastics, after all, grace was also a divine gift), but because of its very nature it means

74 Cf. Luther, *De servo arbitrio* (*Weimarer Ausgabe* 18, 783, 28–33): 'At nunc, cum deus salutem meam extra meum arbitrium tollens in suum receperit et non meo opere aut cursu, sed sua gratia et misericordia promiserit me servare, securus et certus sum, quod ille fidelis sit et mihi non mentietur, tum potens et magnus, ut nulli daemones, nullae adversitates eum frangere aut me illi rapere poterunt.' We may also compare the manner in which Calvin, in the *Inst.* (1559), presents the doctrine of predestination as a doctrine of consolation, e.g. III, 15, 8 (OS IV, 247, 22–248, 7).

75 Cf. Melanchthon, *Loci theologici* (CR 21, 750): 'Quare cum dicitur "fide iustificamur", non aliud dicitur, quam quod propter filium dei accipiamus remissionem peccatorum et reputemur iusti. Et quia oportet apprehendi hoc beneficium, dicitur "fide", id est fiducia misericordiae promissae propter Christum. Intelligatur ergo propositio correlative: "fide sumus iusti", id est per misericordiam propter filium dei sumus iusti seu accepti.' On the (exclusively) christological central point of justification by faith in Luther, cf. esp. H. J. Iwand, *Rechtfertigungslehre und Christusglaube* (Leipzig, 1930), repr. 1966.

that the sinner's attention is directed away from himself,[76] away from any condition on which his own salvation depends,[77] and shelters in the righteousness of Christ. This is the confidence of the believer: he is sure that in faith he is taken outside himself, away from the necessity of proving himself to God in works, and instead is taken into the righteousness of Christ. Luther put it thus: 'Entering into Christ is the faith that gathers us together in the wealth of divine righteousness.'[78] Zwingli states that faith is 'peace and security in the merit of Christ'.[79]

The eschatological final validity of justification that I have mentioned corresponds exactly to the supremacy of this faith, divorced from all virtues and morality. In scholasticism the primacy of faith represents only a beginning; it has only a 'temporal root' as a necessary interim stage in the process of justification.[80] Not faith, but the quality of grace through love determines the specific order of being of the justified; the quality of that grace 'forms' faith. That is to say, only such a quality authenticates faith and its validity in justification, and only active love makes possible the dynamic and teleology of good works in the form of satisfaction and merits rendering mankind acceptable into salvation. The Council of Trent therefore tried to 'hold the necessity and the impossibility of "faith" in equilibrium'.[81] Reformation theology insists that all is given to faith and faith alone. It is a justifying, saving faith: *fides iustificans et salvifica*. For faith is the means whereby man is led from his moral subjective existence into the final validity of the righteousness of Christ, in which he is preserved for salvation – outside himself, where God looks graciously on him. Faith therefore derives its justifying form not from internal love but through the external righteousness of Christ, to which it is bound in trust. The medieval *fides caritate formata* is replaced by the Reformation *fides Christo formata*, the 'faith that lives in

---

76   Cf. Calvin, *Inst.* (1559) III, 19, 2 (OS IV, 283, 16f.): 'averso a nobis aspectu unum Christum intueri'.

77   Cf. Calvin, Comm. On Hab. 2. 4 (CR 71, 529): 'Ergo [homo] nihil affert proprium, quia fides quasi precario mutuatur, quod non est penes hominem.'

78   'Ingressus in Christum est fides, quae nos colligit in divitias iustitiae dei.' *Operationes in Psalmos* (*Weimarer Ausgabe* 5, 408, 4f.).

79   *Auslegen und Gründe der Schlussreden*, 1523, Art. 20 (Z II, 182, 4–9): 'Faith is nothing other than a secure certainty whereby man relies on the merit of Christ, and it is not a work . . . but it is peace and security in the merit of Christ, which security and faith comes not from man but from God.' Cf. Calvin, Comm. On Rom. 3. 21 (CR 49, 58): 'Ideo fide iustificamur, quia in solam dei misericordiam et gratuitas eius promissiones nos recumbere necesse est.' *Inst.* (1559) III, 11, 18 (OS IV, 202, 8f.): 'fides sine operum adminiculo tota in dei misericordiam recumbit'.

80   W. Joest, 'Die tridentinische Rechtfertigungslehre', in *Kerygma und Dogma* 9 (1963), pp. 41–69, here 65.

81   Dantine, in *HDGThG* II, p. 464.

Christ'.[82] In such fulfilment, faith is of course internal too and before the exposition of any system of ethics it denotes rebirth and the transformational vitality of the inner man.[83] This creative advent of the righteousness of Christ into the very centre of man's existence, into his conscience, heart and mind, is part of justification.

The reformers see the fact that faith is also extremely active, operating through love and its works, in a different context. That activity is not a matter of doing good works in order to acquire justification and salvation; it derives from salvation that has already been received. When St Paul (Gal. 5.6) says that faith 'worketh through love', Luther explains that he is speaking, 'not of becoming just, but of the life of the just. *Fieri et agere* is one thing, *esse et facere* another, as boys learn *verbum passivum* and *verbum activum* at school.'[84] The sphere in which faith is active in love does not, as in scholasticism, constitute its justifying nature; faith is justified only passively,[85] in that the sinner is accepted into salvation in advance of any good works he may perform. Every Reformation doctrine of justification in fact (though not necessarily in terminology) distinguishes in this way between the passive and active nature of faith, between its *soteriology* and its *ethics*.[86]

9   The bond between faith and the biblical word

As I pointed out above, passive faith meant taking of man out of himself. As a believer, he stood outside himself and in Christ. To the reformers

82   Cf. H. A. Oberman, ' "Iustitia Christi" und "Iustitia dei". Luther und die scholastischen Lehren von der Rechtfertigung', in Lohse (ed.), *Durchbruch*, pp. 413–44, here 436 and note 45; T. Mannermaa, 'Das Verhältnis von Glaube und Liebe in der Theologie Luthers', in M. Ruokanen (ed.), *Luther in Finnland*, SLAG, A22 (Helsinki, 1984), pp. 99–110, 102f; B. Hägglund, 'Was ist mit Luthers "Rechtfertigungs"-lehre gemeint?', in *Zugänge zu Luther*, Publication of the Luther-Akademie Ratzeburg 6 (1984), pp. 110–20, here 117.
83   Cf. the quotations from Luther in Hägglund, ibid., pp. 114–17.
84   *Weimarer Ausgabe* B 9, 407, 40–2 (No. 3614, 10 or 11 May 1541); cf. K.-H. zur Mühlen, 'Die Einigung über den Rechtfertigungsartikel auf dem Regensburger Religionsgespräch von 1541 – eine verpasste Chance?', in *Zeitschrift für Theologie und Kirche* 76, 1979, pp. 331–59, here 352f. Cf. also Calvin's interpretation of Gal. 5. 6 in *Inst.* (1559) III, 11, 20 (OS IV, 204, 18–22): 'Fatemur quidem cum Paulo non aliam fidem iustificare quam illam caritate efficacem; sed ab illa caritatis efficacia iustificandi vim non sumit. Imo non alia ratione iustificat, nisi quia in communicationem iustitiae Christi nos inducit.'
85   Cf. Calvin, ibid. III, 13, 5 (IV, 220, 24–26): 'Nam quoad iustificationem res est mere passiva fides, nihil afferens nostrum ad conciliandam dei gratiam, sed a Christo recipiens, quod nobis deest.'
86   Cf. Hägglund, 'Luthers "Rechtfertigungs"-lehre', p. 118.

this meant that faith was located in the biblical word of God, the gospel of Jesus Christ, and only there – outside man himself – did it have a firm foothold. This point brings us to the Reformation principle of scripture and the word. At the heart of the activities of all the reformers we find the bond between man and God's word: his conscience was bound to that word alone and was thus free from all the words of men. The faith of man was bound to the word of holy scripture addressed to him and to the preaching that continued this biblical message. Zwingli, unlike Luther, did not think this meant that in the workings of his spirit *God* had also bound himself to his *verbum externum*.[87] However, Zwingli too stresses that *man* and his faith are bound to the biblical word.[88] Man must not base his trust on what he himself says, for he is a sinful creature, called to answer for himself yet not responsible for himself; in his faith he should cling only to the revelations of God's liberating word. This view of faith shows the direct connection between the scriptural principle of the Reformation and the principle of grace that brings justification: man's false reliance on his own word reflects a distortion in himself, a belief in what he himself has achieved in works as well as words. Conversely, the reformers saw belief in God's word alone and reliance on holy scripture as faith solely in the grace of God, who forgives sins, gives absolution and accepts us into salvation.

Through grace and the scriptures, that is, the promise of the Gospel, man is led out of himself, out of his self-accusation and self-justification and any kind of 'pious' ministering to himself. We have seen how 'grace' in the thinking of the Reformation is determined not through the internal dimension of human qualities, but in relation to the external dimension of the righteousness of Christ, in which God unconditionally gives himself in grace. Grace is a reality that always flows in afresh from ouside, not from any inner experience of reality; it justifies man and brings absolution from the accusations of sin. This attitude precisely reflects the importance of the word in the Reformation and the bond between faith and the biblical word. For the word is a relational process: the sinner is taken out of himself, away from anything he himself could say, and is liberated from the realities of virtue and morality. Through the word that brings absolution, forgiveness and a promise, the totality and final validity of his acceptance become present to the sinner and precede any partial achievement of righteousness.

---

87 Cf. Locher, *Huldrych Zwingli*, p. 222f.
88 Cf. on the following B. Hamm, 'Freiheit zur Freude – der Weg des Schweizer Reformators Huldrych Zwingli', in *Evangelisch-reformatorisches Kirchenblatt für Bayern* (1984), no. 3, pp. 5–11, here 8.

10   Breaking the mould: the contrast with medieval theology

Let us return to our initial question: what was specifically evangelical in the Reformation doctrine of justification? Historically, as I have pointed out, the evangelical element lies in the mould-breaking contrasts between the theology of the various reformers and the medieval Catholic systems. We have explored the frontiers of the medieval understanding of grace, which are also the frontiers of sixteenth-century Catholic controversialist theology, while on the other hand we have defined what is common ground in the evangelical antitheses to Catholicism, or at least what was common ground to the four reformers who most influenced the structure of Protestantism in the sixteenth century in their theological doctrine of justification. A considerable body of mould-breaking contrasts has emerged in the process. They are found in the understanding of sin and grace, and the way in which sin and righteousness can be regarded as simultaneous in Reformation thinking; they are found in the eschatological determination of justification, in the doctrine of the certainty of salvation and the understanding of freedom from the law; finally, they are found in the role of faith and the bond between the scriptural principle and the principle of grace. If we ask what binds these various aspects of Reformation thinking together, we shall see that the unconditional nature of salvation is the overriding theme: an abundance of righteousness and salvation is given to the godless man in his justification. His total, unconditional acceptance by God for Christ's sake precedes any partial renewal of the still sinful man himself: such rudiments of the regenerating sanctification of man can never become a condition in which his value before God is founded, but are merely the consequence and creative advent of the abundance and totality of grace bestowed upon him. The reformers express this immutable consequential relationship in describing 'good works' – by which they mean all the reality of man renewed – as the fruits and signs of faith and of justification received in faith.[89] This is the doctrine that the church fathers condemned at the Council of Trent: 'If a man says . . . that good works are only the fruits and signs of justification already achieved, not the cause of an increase in justification, then let him be anathema!'[90]

89   Cf. Luther, *Rhapsodia* (*Weimarer Ausgabe* 30/II, 663, 5f.): 'Et opera fidei signa sunt et fructus iustitiae. Sic opera incredulitatis signa et fructus iniustitiae sunt.'
90   'Si quis dixerit iustitiam acceptam non conservari atque etiam non augeri coram deo per bona opera, sed opera ipsa fructus solummodo et signa esse iustificationis adeptae, non etiam ipsius augendae causam: anathema sit.' Concilium Tridentinum, *Decretum de iustificatione*, can. 24 (D/S No. 1574).

II   The evangelical understanding of the person

Behind this epoch-making change in the understanding of justification and salvation, as Wilfried Joest has shown, lies a new view of the person.[91] To a great extent Joest's account of it in Luther can also be applied to Melanchthon, Zwingli and Calvin. The Reformation no longer defines the human person before God in the manner of medieval philosophy and theology, that is, as the substance of the natural or spiritual man, distinguished by reasonable and voluntary possession of himself, a subject with qualities deriving from his essence and a morality made manifest in works. To the reformers the presence of the human personality before God entails a break with the subjectivity of the sinner: he is taken out of himself, and outside himself he is in Christ. The person accepted by God is thus not man in the mode of ethical realization, but man solely *coram deo*, as he is seen by God,[92] in what has become the basis of his salvation through Christ.[93]

IV   Luther's Lectures on the Epistle to the Romans as Evidence of the Reformation Doctrine of Justification

This understanding of the person as wholly man who is yet wholly absolved by God and accepted into salvation has manifested itself to us under various aspects of unconditionality. If we ask where this break with the medieval Catholic doctrine of justification first becomes historically perceptible in the Reformation, we must look at the early stages of Luther's evangelical theology. Having begun by determining historical criteria for the use of the term 'evangelical' and thus the content of the Reformation element in the doctrine of justification, let us conclude

91   W. Joest, *Ontologie der Person bei Luther*, 1967; ibid. 'Martin Luther', in *Gestalten der Kirchengeschichte*, ed. M. Greschat, V (Stuttgart, 1981), pp. 129–85, here 156–9 (on man as person).
92   Cf. G. Ebeling, *Luther. Einführung in sein Denken* (1964), pp. 219–38 (the person in Christ and in the world), esp. pp. 220–30 (the fundamental meaning of the *coram* relation in Luther).
93   Seen in this way, 'self-realization' does not enter into Reformation Christianity: the realization of man, yes, but not *self*-realization. For the person accepted by God is never man in the mode of ethical realization. He has *been* realized, in that an abundance of righteousness and salvation and thus total and unconditional acceptance have become his through Christ; man is therefore free from the compulsion to realize himself and be concerned for himself, and can give himself up to loving care for his neighbours (which is where the realization of his new nature begins, in the reality of sanctification). On the other hand, man is truly realized only in death and resurrection, when he passes into eternal freedom.

by looking at the interesting question of the content and timing of Luther's turn towards evangelical thinking. The features of the general understanding of justification in the Reformation, as set out in my comparative analysis above, bring us to Luther's lectures on the Epistle to the Romans of 1515/16. If we move forward historically from the scholastic systems to study the Reformation as a whole, without setting out from too narrowly defined a postulate in the systematic and theological essence of what is truly evangelical, then we shall find that the break with the medieval system came in this work *at the latest*. The structural antithesis of Reformation theology is not yet fully worked out in the lectures on Romans. It was not until 1518 that Luther developed the relationship between faith and the word in the process of justification into the assessment of the external word as the pledge which, in his view, makes the certainty of salvation possible. However, we should not think that the mould-breaking element was not present in Luther's theology until the Reformation doctrine of justification was mature and complete, with all its features in place. Although the lectures on the Epistle to the Romans occupy a central place in the development of Luther's Reformation theology, they already clearly illustrate the break with the Middle Ages.

The way in which various different aspects come together in this work makes it particularly impressive. I will mention only some of the most important:

- a radical approach to the understanding of sin, typical of the Reformation;[94]
- also characteristic of the Reformation is the definition of grace as proceeding exclusively from the favour of God shown in absolution; Luther intensifies his understanding of grace in the new concept of *iustitia dei*, a righteousness conveyed by God, who draws the nature of the sinner into his own righteous nature by justifying him;[95]
- the evangelical understanding of the righteousness of the sinner, in that the righteousness of Jesus Christ is credited to him (*iustus ex reputatione*),[96] and in this connection the forensic emphasis on the *extra nos*;[97]

94   Cf., for instance, *Weimarer Ausgabe* 56, 271, 1–272, 2.
95   Cf. *Weimarer Ausgabe* 56, 172, 3–5.
96   Cf., for instance, *Weimarer Ausgabe* 56, 272, 18.
97   Cf., for instance, *Weimarer Ausgabe* 56, 268, 26–269, 19; cf. also K.-H. zur Mühlen, *Nos extra nos. Luthers Theologie zwischen Mystik und Scholastik'* (Beiträge zur historischen Theologie, 46), Tübingen, 1972, on the Epistle to the Romans, pp. 93–176.

- hence the Reformation development of the doctrine *simul iustus et peccator*,[98] and the first emergence of the theme of christological exchange and interchange, which is particularly forceful in Luther's Reformation doctrine of justification: 'This (Christ) has made his righteousness mine and has made my sin his.';[99]
- freedom from the law, seen in the Reformation as freedom from a conditional understanding of the law (obedience to the law as a condition of acceptance into salvation);[100]
- the Reformation identification of the justification of the godless with his acceptance into salvation, eschatological final validity, and the total righteousness credited to him in advance of any partial renewal of his life;
- the basic view, evident in all these aspects, that salvation is unconditional and has no grounds *a parte hominis*: forgiveness of sins, righteousness and sanctification are bestowed only for Christ's sake and never because of any partial involvement of human virtues and morals, satisfaction or merit;
- and finally the basically new understanding in the Reformation of the person: the righteousness of the person *coram deo* is by its nature outside itself, in Christ and in the eyes of God.[101]

None of this can still be accommodated in the scope for variation found in medieval theologies, even if we take their most extreme stances on the theological doctrine of grace. Against the background of the reformers' common ground in the doctrine of justification, even thinkers like Gregory of Rimini and Johannes von Staupitz appear the exponents of a very Catholic theology, and in fact comparison with them shows how far away Luther had moved from this Augustinian scholasticism and the devotional theology of the late Middle Ages as early as his course of lectures on the Epistle to the Romans.[102] Comparison with Catholic

98   Cf. notes 58, 59 above.
99   'Hic suam iustitiam meam fecit et meum peccatum suum fecit.' *Weimarer Ausgabe* 56, 204, 18f. On this text and its context cf. H. J. Iwand, 'Glaubensgerechtigkeit', in *Gesammelte Aufsätze* II, ed. G. Sauter, TB 64, 1980, pp. 118–20; B. Hamm, 'Martin Luthers Entdeckung der evangelischen Freiheit', in *Zeitschrift für Theologie und Kirche* 80 (1983), pp. 50–68, here 59f.
100   Cf., for instance, *Weimarer Ausgabe* 56, 274, 11–275, 16.
101   Cf., for instance, *Weimarer Ausgabe* 56, 158, 10–159, 14.
102   Cf. D. C. Steinmetz, *Luther and Staupitz. An Essay in the Intellectual Origins of the Protestant Reformation* (Duke Monographs in Medieval and Renaissance Studies, 4), Durham, NC, 1980 (this work pays special attention to Luther's lectures on the Epistle to the Romans). There is no similar comparative study on Gregory of Rimini and Luther; for Gregory's doctrine of grace, see most recently Burger, 'Der Augustinschüler gegen die modernen Pelagianer'; cf. also note 18.

controversialist theologians of the sixteenth century such as Gropper, Contarini and Seripando leads to the same conclusion. Even at the time of his lectures on Romans, Luther was aware of the fundamental antithesis of his ideas to scholasticism, as is clear from his general polemic against the *theologi scholastici* ('O *stulti*, O pig-theologians!')[103] and their amalgamation of theology with Aristotelian philosophy.[104] The direct confrontation with Catholic thinking is new by comparison with Luther's earlier lectures on the Psalms, in which he can still cite the doctrine of the sinner's duty *facere quod in se est* and add an approving *recte dicunt doctores*.[105] Another new feature is the fact that in putting forward his opposition to scholasticism in his lectures on Romans, Luther also depicts his own theological past as one of wrestling while he was held captive in error.[106]

In this confrontation between scholasticism and the elucidation of his own position, Luther sees the crucial contrast as the conflict between two entirely different ways of thinking and speaking. It is, as he likes to put it, the contrast between the *modus loquendi theologicus* or *modus loquendi Apostoli (Pauli)*, that is, the biblical approach to theology, and the *modus loquendi philosophicus* or *metaphysicus seu moralis*, an approach to theology that is guided by philosophy, and is non-biblical, metaphysical and moral.[107] The metaphysical and moral approach, as Luther understands it, is characteristic of the entire scholastic and medieval understanding of theology. He sees the interest of scholastic theology as being bent on human morality, man's moral quality before God, and his natural quality in accordance with his creation, its diminution through sin and its restoration and improvement through the metaphysical quality of grace. Luther sees the Pauline approach to theology, on the other hand, as leaving aside the entire field of virtue and morality, physics and metaphysics, and man's ability to act for better or worse. He is not concerned with man's human ability but with his new creation by God, and a new relationship between merciful God and sinful man in which man is outside himself in Christ. Consequently Luther can formulate the whole mould-breaking antithesis to the Catholic doctrine of the Middle Ages, the contrast between the two approaches, cogently as follows: Paul says that man is removed but sin remains.

103   *Weimarer Ausgabe* 56, 273, 4; 274, 14.
104   Cf., for instance, *Weimarer Ausgabe* 56, 273, 3–274, 2.
105   *Weimarer Ausgabe* 4, 262, 4–7.
106   Cf. *Weimarer Ausgabe* 56, 274, 2–11 (in connection with his understanding of *remissio peccatorum*).
107   Cf. L. Grane, *Modus loquendi theologicus. Luthers Kampf um die Erneuerung der Theologie (1515–1518)* (Acta Theologica Danica, 12), Leiden, 1975, esp. pp. 94–96 (on *Weimarer Ausgabe* 56, 334, 2ff).

The moral approach, however, says that sin is removed and man remains.[108]

This and other formulations of antitheses in the lectures on Romans mark the epoch-making turning point between scholasticism and the Reformation. The question of how far Luther's *Dictata super Psalterium* (1513–15) already subscribe to the Reformation doctrine of justification may be left open; the clarity and the sharp distinctions drawn in the lectures on Romans are absent from that work. Here Luther's early theology of humility still seems bound to the conditional structure of the medieval theology of grace and judgement,[109] although the break with scholasticism is already perceptible, particularly in the field of hermeneutics,[110] in Luther's understanding of sin[111] and in his relational view of personal righteousness *coram deo*.[112] The first lecture on the psalms is obviously a transitional work between two periods neither clearly of the Reformation nor – if we are looking for the roots of Luther's Reformation theology – unambiguously not of the Reformation.

V Further Prospects: the Intensification and the Boundaries of the Reformation Doctrine of Justification

Our object has been to trace the characteristic evangelical element in the doctrine of justification, and a study of the common ground between the reformers was a determining factor. In relation at least to further prospects, however, I must not omit to say that this characteristic element, the essence of Reformation thinking, can at certain points undergo reinforcement and intensification in many reformers, while in others it is diluted so far as to be unrecognizable.

I would speak of the reinforcement or intensification of the Reformation doctrine of justification when, in marked contrast to medieval or contemporary Catholic theology, the subject of unconditionality

---

108 'Modus loquendi Apostoli et modus metaphysicus seu moralis sunt contrarii. Quia Apostolus loquitur, ut significet, sonet hominem potius auferri peccato remanente velut relicto et hominem expurgari a peccato potius quam econtra. Humanus autem sensus econtra peccatum auferri homine manente et hominem potius purgari loquitur. Sed Apostoli sensus optime proprius et perfecte divinus est.' *Weimarer Ausgabe* 56, 334, 14–19.

109 Cf. Hamm, 'Martin Luthers Entdeckung', p. 56.

110 Cf. G. Ebeling, 'Die Anfänge von Luthers Hermeneutik', 1951, in ibid., *Lutherstudien* I (1971), pp. 1–68.

111 All his life man is a sinner in the sight of God: for instance, *Weimarer Ausgabe* 3, 289, 6f.

112 Cf., for instance, *Weimarer Ausgabe* 3, 287, 20–293, 21.

emerges even more strongly than was already obvious in our study of the common ground between Luther, Melanchthon, Zwingli and Calvin. I will cite a few examples: by comparison with the consensus of the reformers, there is certainly some intensification in Luther's new understanding of the righteousness of God, for here he works out God's unconditional communication with sinful man to the point where God in his righteousness abandons his own self to participate with man.[113] He thus fundamentally does away with the traditional understanding of satisfaction, whereby Christ provides satisfaction before God's avenging righteousness;[114] this comes out particularly clearly in the theme of the fortunate interchange, the direct exchange between the righteousness of God and the sin of man. Another intensification of Reformation thinking is Luther's new understanding of the word, breaking with the western and Augustinian tradition of the hermeneutics of signification.[115] The fact that God's word not only conveys meaning and points the way, but is an active word creating faith and effectively conveying forgiveness and salvation, liberates faith even more from considerations of virtue and qualities, and makes man fully at home outside himself and in the word. In his understanding of faith Zwingli also finds a way – admittedly a different way – of stressing the unconditionality of salvation. Strictly speaking, he says, human faith is not the cause of salvation and does not bring our salvation about; it is done solely through God's free election.[116] Faith is merely the consequence and the sign of election; election is not a consequence of faith.[117] God, then, can save even unbelievers.[118] Here assurances against the misunderstanding of faith as a condition and cause of salvation are built into the theology of justification. We find similar assurances expressed by Calvin, although in a considerably diluted manner,[119] when he emphasizes the fact that

113   Cf. *Weimarer Ausgabe* 56, 172, 3–5; cf. also Iwand, 'Glaubensgerechtigkeit', pp. 107–11: 'God's own righteousness includes us in it rather than excluding us.'
114   The understanding of *iustitia dei* in the other reformers (apart from Andreas Osiander and Johannes Brenz), on the other hand, moves exclusively in the traditional context of righteousness that judges and recompenses.
115   Cf. Bayer, *Promissio*, pp. 161ff (Part II).
116   Cf. *Freundliche Verglimpfung über die Predigt Luthers wider die Schwärmer* (Z V, 781, 21–7).
117   Cf. *Fidei ratio* (Z VI, 2, 799, 15–18); *De providentia dei* (Z VI, 3, 169–192: *De fide*, esp. 181, 11 f.; 183, 11–184, 3).
118   Zwingli is thinking of dead infants (including unbaptized infants) and certain elect heathens of antiquity. On infants, cf. the text from *Fidei ratio* quoted in note 118; on the heathens the text, also quoted in note 118, from *De providentia dei* (182, 15–183, 6); cf. also R. Pfister, *Die Seligkeit erwählter Heiden bei Zwingli. Eine Untersuchung zu seiner Theologie* (1952).
119   Calvin can still call faith the *causa formalis vel instrumentalis* of salvation; *Inst.* (1559) III, 14, 17 (OS IV, 235, 27f.). To Zwingli, on the other hand, faith is merely

faith does not justify through itself or through any intrinsic power (*virtus intrinseca*). In the real sense, God himself alone justifies us, and Christ justifies us because he was given us for the sake of righteousness; faith itself is only a receptive, empty vessel.[120]

Intensifications of Reformation thought all attempt to make conceptual distinctions illustrating the fact that the regenerative sanctification of man does not stand in any fundamental or causal relation to the acceptance of the sinner into grace and salvation. For instance, distinctions are drawn between faith and love (Luther, Melanchthon, Calvin), justification with sanctification and renewal (Melanchthon and Calvin) or regeneration and renewal (developed in particular by Matthias Flacius Illyricus).[121] In this area, orthodoxy concentrated on the famous maxim *Qui bene distinguit, bene docet*. Such differences are logical abstractions intended to clarify the issue of cause and effect through precise conceptual distinctions, and to illustrate the fact that justification is unconditional and separate from any alteration of the sinner's life on his own part. A logical and causal distinction, however, is of its nature not identical with the distinction between a temporal 'before' and 'after'.[122] To take the example of Calvin, he does not see the distinctions mentioned above as impairing the unity of the connection between faith and love or between justification and renewal;[123] faith is always love at the same time, and justification is always renewal as well.

The boundaries of the Reformation doctrine of justification, the place where it begins to lose its clear contours, is also the nerve-centre where the causality and unconditionality of justification and sanctification are located. The boundary is crossed when the quality and morality of natural or spiritual man are again seen to some extent as the real or potential reason for the sinner's justification and the outcome when he faces judgement. Setting out from this point, one may question, in

---

in the nature of a sign and has no causal function; cf. Locher, *Huldrych Zwingli*, p. 219.

120   Ibid. III, 11, 7 (IV, 188, 24–189, 9); cf. III, 18, 8 (IV, 279, 1–3. 7–10); III, 18, 10 (IV, 281, 9–13).

121   On Flacius, cf. B. Hägglund, 'Rechtfertigung – Wiedergeburt – Erneuerung in der nachreformatorischen Theologie', in *Kerygma und Dogma* 5 (1959), pp. 318–37, here 326f. Regeneration, to Flacius, is the imputed relational process of man's adoption as a child of God. While Flacius is not content with forensic categories but equates the crediting of Christ's merit to man (forensic justification) with *regeneratio* (as distinct from *renovatio*), he makes it clear that justification is not merely an external verdict but indicates a profound change of the inner man (in faith) preceding any gradual renewal of the heart.

122   Cf. the very instructive quotation from Hesshusen's *Examen theologicum*, 1587, in Hägglund, 'Rechtfertigung', p. 336.

123   Cf. notes 42–6 above.

particular, Osiander's effectively judicial understanding of justifica-tion,[124] and the later Melanchthon's doctrine of freedom. In principle we must accept that some reformers and writers of evangelical theology promoted the scriptural Reformation principle of the word in opposition to the Roman Catholic church and its authorities, but without develop-ing any doctrine of justification that was really of the Reformation and that broke away from dogmatic Catholic systems.[125] Historically, then, it is inappropriate to limit our ideas of the essence of the Reformation to the doctrine of justification and the criticisms of the church that arose directly from it. That does not, of course, alter the fact that the stimulating *centre* of the Reformation was its theology, and the struc-tural centre of that theology was the doctrine of justification as I have tried to outline it here.

124 It was from this that the whole difficulty of agreement on the article on justification arose at the Regensburg Conversation on Religion of 1541. For instance, when the formula agreed says that those who have done greater or more works attain a higher degree of sanctification on account of the increase of their faith and their love (*propter augmentum fidei et caritatis*), we have the classic formu-lation of a non-Reformation doctrine in line with Catholic thinking. The agreed formula, however, also contains Reformation elements of Melanchthonian theology. Text in ARCEG VI (1974), 52, 33–54, 37.
125 This corresponds to the observations on the Reformation pamphlets in Scheible, 'Reform, Reformation, Revolution'.

4

The Reformation of the Common Man, 1521–1524

Thomas A. Brady, Jr.

Originally appeared as Thomas A. Brady, Jr., *Turning Swiss. Cities and Empire, 1450–1550* (Cambridge: Cambridge University Press, 1985), pp. 151–83.

Editor's Introduction

Urban culture was where the Reformation movement found its first supporters and its first institutional context. Without the cities, Luther's protest would not have spread throughout the German lands as quickly as it did. In the larger cities, the 'Luther Affair' first came to the attention of the educated elite. The Humanist sodalities, in particular, were quick to support Luther in his cause against (as they saw it) the twin evils of an outmoded scholastic theology and a Catholic church resistant to reform. In Nuremberg, for instance, members of the Humanist society – which included such local dignitaries as the poet Willibald Pirckheimer, the lawyer Christoph Scheurl, the city councillor Caspar Nützel (who translated Luther's ninety-five theses into German), the painter Albrecht Dürer, and the city secretary Lazarus Spengler – were the first to follow events. Spengler is also representative of another group of urban citizens that quickly expressed interest in the movement – the urban oligarchy. By the early 1520s many of the major cities in the German lands were ruled by councils with Lutheran sympathizers in positions of power. Spengler, for example, published a tract in support of Luther as early as 1519. The larger Imperial cities, powerful municipalities such as Nuremberg, Augsburg, or Strasbourg, could weather the differences of religious opinion among the ruling elite without compromising traditions of rule. But a problem arose once the city governments were faced with a subject populace demanding the introduction of the Reformation. This is exactly what happened in the early 1520s, as the evangelical movement gathered supporters among the artisans and labourers, as well as the peasant farmers beyond the city walls.

Thomas A. Brady, Jr. illustrates how these popular demands for the introduction of reform forced the city councils to take control of the movement. Preaching mandates were published, public gatherings were prohibited, the selling of Lutheran books or anticlerical pictures in the public squares was suppressed, the authorities kept a close watch out for quarrels over religion, and public preaching was subject to increased supervision – or outlawed altogether. This happened at various stages throughout the Empire, though some city governments reacted with greater hesitation than others. In Nuremberg, the intensity of popular support forced councillors to introduce religious changes. The Catholic Mass was suspended, evangelical preachers were put in office, the monasteries were closed and placed under the control of the council, a public disputation gave the Reformation it public legitimacy, and the appropriate religious reforms were introduced. Strasbourg followed a similar course (though in a Zwinglian rather than a Lutheran vein) as did most of the other cities surveyed by Brady (Augsburg, Frankfurt, Ulm, Constance, Esslingen, Nördlingen). By the mid-1520s, these German cities had introduced the Reformation, and it was now the task of the urban governments to negotiate the delicate political situation brought about by the change of religion.

Luther's hearing before the Emperor Charles V and the other imperial authorities took place in April of 1521. On 18 April 1521 Luther gave his defence before the imperial diet, wherein he claimed that he was captive to the Word of God, and he refused to recant what he had written. Unless Scripture could prove it otherwise, he was bound by what he believed. In response, Charles V placed him under the ban of Empire, and on 26 May 1521 the Edict of Worms was published, thus making Luther an outlaw in the realm. With the Edict of Worms and the papal bull of excommunication, it now became both a secular and a spiritual crime to offer Luther safe harbour or to support any of his teachings. This gave rise to political divisions between the estates (Stände) of the Empire, for while a number of princely territories and Imperial cities refused to act against the reform movement (even in its association with Luther), the Emperor Charles V regarded the movement as heretical and vowed to root it out. The debate took place at the level of the Imperial diet (Reichstag), a meeting of the estates usually called by the Emperor and arranged into three colleges: The college of electors (the seven rulers who elected the Emperor), the college of princes, and the college staffed by the representatives of the Imperial cities (Reichsstädte) which sat in two blocs (Rheinish and Swabian). There were lesser forums as well – the cities met in separate diets, for instance, as did the estates of an individual territory – but the Imperial diet was the grand stage, and it was at the series of diets held in Nuremberg (1522 to 1524) that the religious question first brought serious division to Imperial politics.

By looking at the development of the evangelical movement within the cities, as well as the effect of the urban Reformation on the course of Imperial politics, Brady illustrates how religious ideas came to transform the context of social and political relations in the Empire. By 1524, the system of governance was essentially in a state of stalemate. The Emperor had been unable to enforce the Edict of Worms through the diets; the governing council, recently moved to Esslingen, remained ineffectual; and the Swabian League, the Empire's peace-keeping force, did not act. At the same time the Reformation took hold in the cities. Support for the evangelical movement continued to grow among the common man. The same religious ideas that had brought deadlock to Imperial politics inspired the religious and political thinking of the parishioners. To an extent, the Peasants' War of 1525, an event Friedrich Engels termed 'the grandest revolutionary effort of the German people', would cast a shadow over these developments and return the Empire to its former political state. But as Brady makes clear, the Reformation had brought about a fundamental change in German culture and German politics. The brief alliance between the Reformation and the common man may have ended with the decline of the urban front and the rout of the peasants in the war of 1525, but the memory would long have its role in German history.

The Reformation of the Common Man, 1521–1524

Thomas A. Brady, Jr.

In 1871, the founding year of the Prussian-German empire that arose on the ruins of the Holy Roman Empire, a Bavarian jurist described the free cities' liberating role in the German Reformation: 'The Reformation was not simply prepared in the cities, there it was also first put into practice. There, where civil freedom was greatest, in the free cities, came the earliest reforms. Then, from the cities the spirit of the Reformation and the Reformation itself spread out in ever widening circles.'[1] A century of research has placed beyond doubt the cities' role as the nurseries of the Reformation movement, where the Evangelical cause was transformed from a provincial issue into a mighty German movement. After it came the 'Princes' Reformation', which gave German Protestantism its historic shape,[2] but which also drew institutions, personnel, values, and symbols from the 'urban Reformation'.[3]

When Charles V set a new, hard policy on the religious question in 1524, he put tremendous pressure on the urban governments, within whose communes Luther's followers were stirring vigorous social movements: groups of committed persons united in collective actions with a common consciousness, who wanted or attempted rapid and immediate changes to the existing religious order, sometimes through noninstitu-

1   Quoted by Rublack, 'Forschungsbericht', 10 n. 7, who notes that Maurer wrote one hundred years before A. G. Dickens's celebrated comment that 'the German Reformation was an urban event.' Dickens, *German Nation*, 182, The massive literature on the urban Reformation is surveyed by Rublack, 'Forschungsbericht'; G. Müller, *Reformation und Stadt*; and Greyerz, 'Stadt und Reformation' (my thanks to Kaspar von Greyerz for letting me read this in typescript). For a briefer overview, see Brady, 'Social History', 167–72.
2   Dickens, *German Nation*, 221. Whereas Dickens laments the subsequent domination of the Lutheran princes, which he believes fostered 'legalism rather than . . . religious and political liberty', Oberman contends that, despite 'the acute disadvantages' of the princes' reform, intellectual freedom was better served by the Lutheran reformation than the urban one. *Werden and Wertung*, 346, 361–7 (English: *Masters*, 272, 284–8). Heinz Schilling's very important conclusions (*Konfessionskonflikt*, 387–91) to some degree parallel Oberman's, though he makes far less of theology. All three scholars agree on the role of the cities as the nurseries of German Protestantism.
3   See Press, 'Stadt und territoriale Konfessionsbildung', 251–96; Schilling, *Konfessionskonflikt*, 168–76.

tional means.[4] Calling themselves 'Evangelical', they wanted to free Christianity from centuries of 'human additions' to the Bible. By 1524, the size and militancy of such movements made it impossible for their governments, whatever the oligarchs' personal views, to enforce strictly the Imperial ban on Luther's works and ideas.[5]

In this massive and unprecedented intervention, the Common Man made history. Already by 1524, before the great insurrection on the land was fairly underway, popular action had inspired or frightened urban governments into defying the emperor and the law, thereby damaging severely and irreparably the old partnership between Crown and cities. By the deep winter of 1524–5, when the valleys and uplands of the South seethed with incipient revolution, the latest form of the Habsburg system's urban wing, the urban front, was already a wreck.

The Common Man in the Urban Reformation

> Das evangeli frone
> auss gotts gnad fürher bracht
> Martinus Luther schone,
> das vor lang was veracht,
> mit füssen was vertreten
> und lag ganz in dem staub;
> das hat er sauber gjeten,
> wie wol in nit hat beten
> der romanisten raub.[6]

When the Edict of Worms was issued on 8 May, 1521, the southern urban governments hardly rushed to publish it locally, nor did they hurry to censor the printers.[7] The tide of books, pamphlets, and broadsides quickly became a flood, as printers, illustrators, and authors rushed to promote Luther as a holy man and his cause as a holy cause, drawing upon symbols and language that were 'deeply embedded in the

---

4 See Moeller, *Reichsstadt*, 19–34 (English: *Imperial Cities*, 54–69); Dickens, *German Nation*, 102–34; Scribner, 'Social Movement', 54, 77–8, on whose definition I depend here. On the movement's phases, see Blickle, 'Social Protest', 5–7.
5 Wohlfeil, 'Wormser Reichstag', 148–51.
6 'It has come from God's own grace that the wondrous Martin Luther has restored the Gospels' splendor; for long years it was despised, trod under the feet of men, and left lying in the dust. He did this with great skill, despite the strong objections of the robbing Roman horde.' Liliencron, *Volkslieder*, 3:510, no. 393, stanza 3.
7 Brecht, 'Wormser Edikt', 476.

culture and belief of those brought up in the old faith'.[8] The cities, centers of all communication – oral, visual and written, learned and lay – became the breeding ground for a mighty movement, though for a few years 'the Luther affair' seemed to disappear from the stage of Imperial politics.[9] The rulers of the towns, however, knew quite well what was going on within their walls, and it troubled them.

From the very beginning, the Evangelical movement had to be a matter for public attention, because 'the concern for the sustaining of the civic commonweal gave even the forms of piety a pubic relevance, which from the first necessarily made the issues of the veneration of saints and of images especially pressing'.[10] One may go further and say that clerical involvement also made the movements public, for clergy were public persons, and the movement began as an attack of one group of clergy on another. The Evangelical leaders were well-educated clergymen from urban backgrounds, sons of patricians, merchants, and artisans.[11] They gained hearings largely because they offered answers to long-posed questions, and they sowed seed on long-prepared soil. Even where such answers and such seed were not, from the preachers' perspective, central to their gospel, they hoped that by addressing such questions – usury, tithes, clerical immunities, clerical indiscipline – they would win a hearing for pure doctrine. Luther showed the way by trying to touch every sensitive nerve of his day, at the price of sowing unclarity about his message, though not about his person. Some of his partisans came to see the world through his central message; others did not. But in these years their cause was a common one.[12] The urban preachers sensed this and tried skillfully to adapt Luther's message to the hegemonic corporate-communal values of their fellow citizens.[13] The building of followings, however, no matter how militant, was but

8   Scribner, *Simple Folk*, 245. For very different approaches to printing and the Reformation, see Moeller, 'Stadt und Buch', 25–39 (and Scribner's critical 'How Many Could Read?'); Chrisman, *Lay Culture*, ch. 7. The current state of research on pamphlets is accessible in Köhler, *Flugschriften.*
9   Noted by Brecht, 'Wormser Edikt', 479.
10   Oberman, *Werden und Wertung*, 238 (English: *Masters*, 188).
11   Scribner, 'Practice and Principle', 99–106.
12   Oberman believes that, at this point in the history of the movement, Luther was more significant as symbol than as teacher. Oberman, 'Gospel of Social Unrest', 43. I agree.
13   This conclusion of Moeller, *Reichsstadt*, esp. 34–55 (English: *Imperial Cities*, 69–90), has been heartily seconded by Schilling, *Konfessionskonflikt*, 45, 142–3. Both Moeller ('Stadt und Buch', 38–9) and Schilling (*Konfessionskonflikt*, 376 n. 17a) have criticized my view of the sacral commune as both a leading idea, in the Marxian sense, and a shared value, which at times could be defended by the commons against their rulers, as happened as Strasbourg in 1548 (Brady, *Ruling Class*, chap. 8) and Lemgo in 1609 (Schilling, *Konfessionskonflikt*, 241–71).

the first step in a process that had to end with the support and protection, willing or grudging, of the urban oligarchies, who alone could shield the movement from its enemies.

The Evangelical preachers' freedom to act grew out of the pre-Reformation clergy's freedom from reform, which had flowed from the many checks on a bishop's power to discipline his clergy.[14] This clerical freedom, rooted in the pre-Reformation deadlock over control of the Church, often threatened good order and civic peace, a fact may oligarchs, engaged or not, Lutheran or Catholic, recognized. At Strasbourg, for example, Augustin Drenss (d. 1552), a big man in the Gardeners' guild, complained that the wooing of his sister by the young preacher Caspar Hedio (1494–1552) was merely one more case of a lustful priest violating the sanctity of an upright Christian home. It mattered little to Drenss that Hedio called himself an 'Evangelical'.[15] At Nuremberg, Christoph Kress, a Lutheran, complained that 'nothing bothers me more than to see the escaped monks and priests running about. If I had my way, they could go to the Devil'.[16] And at Augsburg, Ulrich Arzt, a Catholic, wrote amid the upheaval of 1525 that 'we townsmen are to blame, and I fear it will bring down the honorable cities. Had we got rid of these preachers and allowed their own superiors to punish them, as is just, these things would now be settled and overcome'.[17]

If such opinions were common among the oligarchs, one may fairly ask, how did the Evangelical movement ever succeed in the cities? The social character of the urban Reformation has, indeed, long been a hotly debated subject. According to a thesis formulated for northern Germany and subsequently extended to the southern cities, 'the Reformation was never the work of a town council', and there was 'a general antipathy to the Reformation especially among the patricians'.[18] That is much too categorical, for the early Reformation movement

> embraced various forces and interests. They included oligarchs and humanists, artisans and journeymen, clergymen and artists, peasants and plebians, who differed from one another in their views on both the theoretical and practical aspects of the Reformation, and who reacted differently to different situations.[19]

14   This is superbly documented by Rapp, *Réformes.*
15   Brady, *Ruling Class*, 231–2, 307 (May 1524).
16   Kress to Gerwig Blarer, Nuremberg, 7 Nov., 1523, in Blarer, *Briefe und Akten,* 1:26, no. 44, lines 21–4.
17   Vogt, 'Correspondenz, I', 367, no. 123.
18   Lau, 'Der Bauernkrieg', 119; Moeller, *Reichsstadt,* 25, 27 (English: *Imperial Cities,* 60–1, 63).
19   Vogler, *Nürnberg,* 323.

These groups briefly saw in the Evangelical movement a common vehicle for liberation from an oppression that they, for the moment, sensed to be a common one, though later the movement began to break into different, sometimes opposed, streams. At the beginning, however, from all classes were recruited 'Evangelicals', that is, men and women who believed that, for the sake either of individual salvation or the integrity of Christian life in this world, or both, the rightly understood Bible required the abolition of certain religious traditions and the curbing of ecclesiastical power.

Townsmen of good family had, to be sure, special reasons for opposing such a movement, ranging from career advantages in the old Church to familial attachments to religious orders to native oligarchical conservatism.[20] Wealthy and politically powerful men nonetheless emerged as early patrons of and participants in the Evangelical movement, before it moved from the monasteries and private homes to the pulpits, shops, guildhalls, and taverns. In a few southern cities, true, such as Rottweil and Schwäbisch Gmünd, ruling patricians closed ranks against the Evangelicals, especially when they also took up the cause of political reform.[21] In most other cities, however, the upper classes did little to defend Catholicism in an organized way after about 1526.

There was much in the reformers' messages to attract the urban oligarchs. The pure gospel 'could be understood by burghers and peasants as the common good translated into theological terms',[22] which justified liberating the urban churches from external authority and bringing whole sectors of clerical activity under welcome governmental control: poor relief, schools, marriage law, clerical citizenship and guild membership, parish organization and the administration of parish and monastic properties. Through cooperation with the popular movements and the preachers, the town councils expanded and intensified their sovereignty over churches and citizens, and this domestication of urban religion converted the ecclesiastical order from a disruptive into an integrative element in civic life.[23]

As it moved out into the churches, shops, and taverns, however, the movement developed clearly dangerous forms of action, such as iconoclastic riots, and it pressed the governments to clearly illegal measures, such as the dissolution of religious houses. The preachers had a nose for exploiting existing grievances, such as demands for greater political participation, and the urban commons gradually became the motor of the movement, as large numbers – we need not assume undocumented

---

20   See Brady, *Ruling Class*, 215–30; Christensen, *Art*, 71–2.
21   Brecht, 'Rottweil'; Naujoks, *Obrigkeitsgedanke*, 60–4, 96–102.
22   Blickle, *Reformation im Reich*, 131.
23   Scribner, 'Sozialkontrolle'; Wettges, *Reformation*, 66–8.

majorities – of ordinary folk supported through their guilds the program of religious change.[24] Where the guilds embraced very large shares of the adult-male population – about thirty-five hundred at Strasbourg, a city of some twenty thousand, and almost twenty-three hundred in slightly smaller Ulm[25] – the governments had to deal with the movements through negotiation rather than coercion. The movements had nonetheless to be mastered in the name of the historic civic norms of peace, justice and unity.

The true danger from the Evangelical movement for the oligarchies lay in the fact that, even where the clergy could be controlled, the principle of biblicism stayed to haunt the governments. The identification of the Bible, understood as the *lex Christi*, with the common good admitted of different interpretations, according to whether the Bible was used to legitimate or to criticize existing social structures and practices. Just this ambiguity turned Christoph Fürer (1481–1537) of Nuremberg against the Evangelicals, who 'are making the common people so godless that they will lack all good discipline and human morals'.[26] The realism of his fear is suggested by the remarks of Ott, an Augsburg ropemaker, who was overheard in 1524 to damn the 'dishonorable priests and the rich . . . , who pile up goods and money and keep the truth from us'. 'We have always been Evangelicals', Ott blurted out, 'and we still are today. But, truly, we have been fed many lies. If we truly followed the gospel, we would all have to be like brothers.'[27] Why should the Bible slice through the lordship of bishop and priest but stop at that of artisan master, landlord, and town councillor? Should Christians not also treat their fellow citizens as 'brothers' in Ott's sense? Had the movement for 'godly law', 'Christian commonweal', and fraternal cooperation won out, revolution would have come to the village, the town hall, the guild-hall and the shop. Whether one calls this program 'the gospel of social unrest' or 'biblicism vs. feudalism',[28] it could be tolerated by no one who believed that peace, justice, and unity could be established and preserved only from above.

The common challenge the Evangelical movement posed to the urban governments is symbolized by the common measure they first used to gain control of it, the preaching edicts of 1523 and 1524. These laws commanded the clergy to preach 'nothing but the gospel' and leave off

---

24 Wettges, *Reformation*, 117. For the example of Basel, see Füglister, *Handwerksregiment*.
25 Rott, 'Artisanat', 158; Nebinger, 'Abstimmungslisten', 26.
26 Quoted by Reicke, *Geschichte*, 839.
27 StA Augsburg, Urgichten 1524, Produkt 3, at 27 Sept., 1524 (my thanks to Hans-Christoph Rublack for this text).
28 The first phrase is Oberman's, the second Blickle's.

'all provocative and insulting comments, including everything which tends to rouse the Common Man to anger or confusion or to a rebellion against his rulers, lay or ecclesiastical . . .'.[29] Between 29 January, 1523, and 5 April, 1524, such laws were issued at Zurich, Worms, Basel, Bern, Mulhouse, Augsburg, Strasbourg, Constance, Frankfurt am Main, and Sankt Gallen.[30] Their family resemblance derived both from consultation and from a common descent from the Imperial Diet's decree of 9 February, 1523, by which preachers were to be ordered 'to shun everything that might stir up the Common Man against the rulers or confuse the ordinary Christian; but they should preach and teach only the holy gospel as interpreted by the writings that the holy Christian Church has approved and accepted'.[31] Such laws were proof not of an official partisanship for Evangelical religion but of the urban governments' determination to bring the internal divisions under control through the exercise of their *jus pacificandi*.[32]

This cause, bringing the Evangelical movement under control, became the duty of every oligarch pledged to preserve peace, justice and unity, though growing dispute about God's honor and the common good made the duty's discharge ever more difficult. Gradually, however, the town councils went beyond the biblicist minimum of the preaching edicts and began to claim divine authority for their actions. Memmingen's council wrote in 1527, for example, that 'because we wish to defend God's honor, and because we have received our authority from God Himself, we are inclined and determined to issue a law forbidding concubinage and prostitution to all our citizens, both clerical and lay'.[33] Specific changes ought to be seen less as inevitable products of individual politicians' conversions[34] than as actions of urban governments, which, pushed from below by their commons and harangued by the preachers, came to see that the new gospel offered welcome solutions to nagging old problems. The revolutionary events of 1524 and 1525, as Christoph Kress once admitted, pushed the governments farther than

29   Moeller, 'L'édit strasbourgeois', 58. On the origin of the crucial phrase, see Augustijn, ' "Allein das heilig Evangelium" ', 150–65.
30   Moeller, 'L'édit strasbourgeois', 51–61; Vögeli, *Schriften*, 1:154–5; Rublack, *Einführung*, 244 n. 21; H. Lutz, *Peutinger*, 227; Jahns, *Frankfurt*, 35; Oberman, *Werden und Wertung*, 250–1 (*English: Masters*, 196–7).
31   *RTA*, *jR*, 3:747–8, no. 117. The Governing Council's enforcing edict of 6 March, 1523, is in ibid., 447–52, no. 84.
32   Oberman, *Werden und Wertung*, 241–50; the following quote is at 249 (English: *Masters*, 196).
33   Burgomaster and Senate of Memmingen to Ambrosius Blarer, Nov. 27, 1527, in Schiess, *Briefwechsel*, 1:143, and also in Dobel, *Memmingen*, 2:50–1.
34   Brecht, 'Politik'.

they had ever intended to go.[35] Few urban politicians dreamed, however, that with the preaching edicts they had embarked on a course that would make them arbiters of Christian doctrine and sole enforcers of Christian morals, a role for which little in their traditions, education, or experience had prepared them.[36]

Urban Oligarchies and Reformation Movement, 1524

> Nun wirt das bletlein umbgekart
> und fürgewänt ain ander art.
> Ich main si all, die sölicher gestalt
> erheben sich gaistlicher gwalt
> in reichtumb, bracht und übermūt,
> zern von des armen schwaiss und blūt,
> den si mit unrecht oft und vil
> thūn zwingen zū irem būbanspil
> zū geben alls was er vermag.
> . . . .
> Wo man vom evangeli sagt,
> So hat man in gar bald verjagt.[37]

By the early months of 1524, the fabric of established authority in many a free city was creaking under the strain of maintaining law and order. Though some have written of a 'victory' or 'breakthrough' of the Reformation in 1524, the movement's destructive or purgative phase culminated only with the abolition of the central act of Catholic worship, the Mass, which happened at Zurich in 1527, at Memmingen, Strasbourg and Basel in 1529, at Ulm in 1531, and at Augsburg, Ravensburg and Biberach an der Riss never.[38] During the first months of 1524, by

35 Leonhard von Eck to Duke William of Bavaria, Feb. 27, 1525, in Vogt, *Die bayrische Politik*, 399.
36 See Brady, *Ruling Class*, 192–3; Broadhead, 'Politics and Expediency', 55–70.
37 'Now the page is turning to show another side. I mean to show up them all, who make themselves priests, who live in wealth, luxury, and arrogance and feed on the poor man's sweat and blood. They do so much harm themselves and force others as well to give them all they have. . . . Wherever the Gospel has its say, they've been driven all away.' Liliencron, *Volkslieder*, 3:366, no. 352, lines 25–33, 43–4.
38 On the victory thesis, which I discussed in *Ruling Class*, 204–5, much new light is shed by Rublack, *Nördlingen*, especially 263; and Abray, *The People's Reformation*, who shows that none of the fundamental issues was settled at Strasbourg during the 1520s and 1530s. See Oberman, *Werden und Wertung*, 348 (English: *Masters*, 273), on the Reformation's geographical limitations and 'loss of substance', comments he repeats in 'Stadtreformation', 88. Bolder is Ozment, *Age of Reform*, 437–8, though his gloomy conclusion rests on theological rather than historical criteria.

contrast, the movement was in most southern cities just exhibiting its muscle in public for the first time.

Rarely did solid oligarchic opposition keep the Evangelicals from sweeping rapidly to victory, though at a few places – Regensburg was one – the government did indeed plod after the popular movement.[39] In most of the larger cities, however, rich and powerful individuals and families lent protection and aid to the Evangelical movement from the first. Nowhere was this aid more decisive than at Nuremberg, where, even before a truly Lutheran presence emerged, the cream of local society had gathered around Johann von Staupitz (d. 1524), the reform-minded General Vicar of the Augustinians. Anton Tucher was there, and Hieronymus Ebner, along with Caspar Nützel, Hieronymus Holzschuher, Endres and Martin Tucher, and Sigmund and Christoph Fürer, representatives of a 'typical South German Christian humanism, shaped by Erasmian biblicism, which is repeatedly and justifiably regarded as an important point of contact for the Reformation in the cities'.[40] The senate of Nuremberg, though it did temporize, also called the first Lutheran preachers to the city in 1522 and protected them from the bishop of Bamberg. By early 1523, Hans von der Planitz was reporting to Elector Frederick that a serious official move against the preachers would provoke an insurrection; soon Nuremberg was gaining a reputation for heresy.[41] The presence of the Governing Council and the High Court,[42] plus the staging of three Imperial Diets at Nuremberg between 1522 and 1524, may well have heightened the senate's caution, and the growth of radical stirrings in the countryside, where many Nuremberg patricians had substantial seigneurial holdings, prompted careful reflection about following words with deeds.[43] The

39   Wettges, *Reformation*, 53.
40   Seebass, 'Reformation in Nürnberg', 254. This account is based on ibid., 252–69 (English: 'Reformation in Nürnberg', 17–40); idem, 'Stadt und Kirche in Nürnberg', 66–86; Vogler, *Nürnberg*, 33–134; Strauss, *Nuremberg*, 154–74; and Wettges, *Reformation*, 23–7, 33–8, 62–5, 97–102. Engelhardt, *Reformation in Nürnberg*, is useful for details but narrowly confessional in perspective.
41   Planitz is cited by H. von Schubert, *Lazarus Spengler*, 379–83. See Vogler, *Nürnberg*, especially 95–118. On Nuremberg's reputation, see Abbot Georg Truchsess of Wernitz-Anhausen to Gerwig Blarer, Jan. 9, 1524, in Blarer, *Briefe und Akten*, 1:28, no. 45; Strauss, *Nuremberg*, 174.
42   The attitude of the Governing Council toward the Evangelical movement is not clear. See Engelhardt, *Reformation*, 1:129; H. von Schubert, *Lazarus Spengler*, chap. 8; Richter, *Reichstag zu Nürnberg* 1524, 12. Archduke Ferdinand wrote to Charles V, Innsbruck, May 12, 1523, about 'aulcuns, et en especial de cellui qu'est au lieu du duc de Saxe, nommé Plains [Planitz], lequel avec plusjeurs ses adherans sans aucune craincte de dieu ne vergoigne du monde s'emploient tres detestablement . . .' W. Bauer and Lacroix, *Korrespondenz*, 1:59, no. 36, para. 10.
43   Vogler, *Nürnberg*, 27–8, 83–134.

government therefore both protected Lutheran preachers against the bishop and Catholic ceremonies against the Evangelicals, though there can be no doubt about the deep penetration of Evangelical ideas into the best homes. Many of the officeholders, for example, who marched in procession on Corpus Christi and Saint Sebald's Day, 1524 – the last ever held at Nuremberg in this era – probably did so from respect for tradition rather than conviction.[44] The senate also tolerated as its public spokesman the notoriously Lutheran city secretary, Lazarus Spengler (1479–1534), whose efforts Luther compared with the labors of the prophets of old.[45] The situation at Nuremberg during the Imperial Diet of 1524 thus suggests that the transitional phase of discussion and tolerance of parties would come to an end, once Nuremberg escaped the limelight of Imperial government.

Events at Augsburg ran a similar course at a slower pace.[46] Some very big men early joined the typically clerical circles of initial Evangelicals, including three of the four burgomasters – Georg Vetter (d. 1536), Ulrich Rehlinger (d. 1547) and Hieronymus Imhof (1468–1539) – plus such other leading politicians as Conrad Herwart, Lucas Welser and the younger Martin Weiss. Against them stood an 'old guard' headed by the fierce Ulrich Arzt, and between the parties Conrad Peutinger pursued his 'middle way', tending and mending Augsburg's lines to the Imperial court.[47] A report of 1522, that half the Augsburgers supported the Evangelicals, surely exaggerated; but two years later Clemens Sender, a Benedictine chronicler, noted that 'in the year of Our Lord 1524 Lutheranism grew very rapidly at Augsburg, and heresy got the upper hand'.[48] This was close enough to the truth that the papal legate, Cardinal Lorenzo Campeggio (1474–1539), was advised in March 1524 that he should enter Augsburg at noontime, when the craftsmen were indoors eating lunch.[49] Despite the growing number of Evangelicals in the government, however, the intense external pressures on Augsburg – from the Habsburg courts, the Bavarian dukes, and the bishop of Augsburg – made its magistrates more cautious and reluctant to act

44   Soden, *Beiträge*, 159–60.
45   *WA TR*, no. 5426. H. von Schubert's unfinished biography is by no means superseded by Grimm, *Lazarus Spengler*, but Berndt Hamm's forthcoming work will put the subject on a new basis.
46   To the fundamental work by F. Roth, *Reformationsgeschichte*, should be added Broadhead, 'Internal Politics' (of which there is a useful extract in his 'Popular Pressure'), and Wettges, *Reformation*, 27–31, 38–49, 102–7.
47   F. Roth, *Reformationsgeschichte*, 1:53–73, 87–94, 136; H. Lutz, *Peutinger*, 222–8.
48   Sender, 'Chronik', 154.
49   Rem, 'Cronica newer geschichte', 144, translating 'handwercksvolck' as 'craftsmen' rather than 'laborers' (as 'Broadhead, 'Popular Pressure', 80).

than their Nuremberg counterparts. This inertia was to lead to the movement's getting out of hand during 1524.

Outside the Confederacy, no other large city of South Germany moved so swiftly to accommodate the Evangelicals as Strasbourg did.[50] By the end of 1523, the movement had gained powerful patrons and adherents, such as the Ammeisters Claus Kniebis (1479–1552), Martin Herlin (d. 1547), and Daniel Mieg (c.1484–1541), the future Ammeister Mathis Pfarrer (1489–1568) – who was also Sebastian Brant's son-in-law – the rich merchant Conrad Joham (d. 1551), and Egenolf Röder von Diersburg (1475–1550), a prominent nobleman with important connections in Middle Baden.[51] Hot words over religion flew in the senate chamber during 1523, and the memorial Mass for Ammeister Heinrich Ingold just before Christmas was the last such Mass ever sung in Strasbourg's cathedral.[52] When the new senators took office in January 1524, the Evangelicals – militants and moderates together – held a majority, and on 25 January they liquidated the clergy's ancient immunity and began to attack the monasteries. There were nonetheless very cautious men among the oligarchs, such as Jacob Sturm, whose judgment on the religious parties was that 'both sides are Christians, may God have mercy!'[53] External pressures and influences were much weaker here than at Augsburg or Ulm. The one Imperial councillor in the government, for example, was Friedrich Prechter (d. 1528), the Fugger agent in Alsace, but he played a very minor role in public affairs.[54] All in all, Strasbourg appeared in early 1524 to be the major free city sailing most nearly in Zurich's wake.

Though somewhat smaller in size, Ulm resembled Strasbourg in social structure and politics.[55] Religious change came slowly to this capital of the Swabian League, though the Evangelicals did win over prominent laymen, among them Bernhard Besserer, who was as conservative and cautious as Strasbourg's Sturm. During 1523, the government's attitude began to soften, and by December it was reported that the new religion 'has so rooted and grown in the people, that even with force it would be very hard to put down'.[56] Ulm had no out-

50   This is based on Chrisman, *Strasbourg*; Lienhard, 'La Réforme à Strasbourg, I–II.'
51   Brady, *Ruling Class*, 209–10.
52   Ibid., 205, 229.
53   Brady, ' "Sind also zu beiden theilen Christen",' 76.
54   F.-J. Fuchs, 'Les foires et le rayonnement économique', 307–13; Feyler, *Beziehungen*, 178.
55   On Ulm, see Geiger, *Reichsstadt Ulm*; Naujoks, *Obrigkeitsgedanke*; Brecht, 'Ulm'; Walther, 'Bernhard Besserer'.
56   Quoted by Naujoks, *Obrigkeitsgedanke*, 53.

standing clerical figure to lead popular pressure against the government, which moved no faster than events forced it to do.

The story of a fifth large city, Frankfurt am Main, contrasts neatly with that of Strasbourg.[57] The patricians, who had surrendered only one-third (versus Strasbourg's two-thirds) of the offices to the guilds, still dominated the town's economy through the chartered fairs, which drew merchants from far and wide. The three collegial churches also enjoyed Imperial protection. The archbishop of Mainz maintained a much greater authority at Frankfurt than did the bishops – Bamberg, Augsburg, Strasbourg and Constance – whose jurisdictions covered Nuremberg, Augsburg, Strasbourg and Ulm. The external pressures on Frankfurt's government were thus relatively strong. Lutheran ideas first spread here, as elsewhere, among humanist clergymen, and the movement was greatly aided by the patronage of two leading patrician politicians, Philipp Fürstenberger (1479–1540) and Hamann von Holzhausen (1467–1536). Later than in other cities, the movement spilled out of patrician homes and monasteries into the churches and shops, but by early 1524 it had mounted little or no direct action.

This survey of five larger towns may be supplemented by views of three middling ones, Constance, Esslingen and Nördlingen. Constance, squeezed between bishop and Austria, had lost the rich Thurgau in 1499 and its chance to turn Swiss in 1510, and, having no stable past to which to cling, proved very open to change.[58] One sign of this openness was the early and strong movement of leading patricians into the Evangelical party, such as Burgomaster Bartholomäus Blarer (d. 1524) and Hans Schulthaiss (d. 1538), the richest man in Constance.[59] The special intimacy, indeed, that developed here between preachers and politicians rested on the fact that the two leading preachers, Ambrosius Blarer (d. 1564) and Johann Zwick (d. 1542), were natives who had brothers in the government. Very early, these circles split from the Erasmians at the episcopal court and provoked some of the earliest episcopal countermeasures in all of South Germany. When Archduke Ferdinand demanded action against Lutheran literature in early 1524, the council expelled his local agent, whom the Evangelicals regarded as 'an enemy of human salvation'.[60] Constance's situation meant that every Evangelical action drew strength from the nearness of Zurich, whereas every counteraction must be tarred with episcopal or Austrian

57   This is based on Jahns, *Frankfurt*, 16–36.
58   This is based on Rublack, *Einführung*, 20–6, 34–7; idem, 'Aussenpolitik'; idem, 'Politische Situation'; Moeller, *Johannes Zwick*; Bender, *Reformationsbündnisse*, chap. 2.
59   Rublack, *Einführung*, 16–17, 62–6; Buck, *Anfänge*, 60–9, 519–22.
60   Rublack, *Einführung*, 36–7.

brushes, so that by early 1524 Constance had become, after Strasbourg, the most nearly Evangelical urban government.

The movement came to Esslingen later than to Constance, though its leading politician, Hans Holdermann, wondered already at Worms, 'as to what will become of the monk's affair, I believe that no one really knows, for I think that it contains a wholly new understanding of things, which not everyone can yet see'.[61] The movement developed slowly at Esslingen, though the government kept a careful watch on its growth in other towns. The town council protected Catholic clergy and services without suppressing the Evangelicals, and, with one eye on the Habsburg regime at Stuttgart and the other on the Swabian League, remained master in its own house all through the 1520s. The transfer of the Governing Council and High Court, which freed the movement from some constraints in Nuremberg, retarded its growth in Esslingen and allowed the council to pursue a temporizing policy 'more for the security of public order and civic unity than for loyalty to the Church'.[62] Pressure from below nonetheless emerged in mid-January 1524, when some citizens asked for Michael Stifel's restoration to his pulpit and for regular Sunday preaching in the convents. As late as the end of April 1524, Esslingen's government boasted that the town had no 'Lutheran disturbance', though a few days later began the first expulsions for anti-clerical agitation.[63]

Nördlingen, a final example, was a Franconian cloth town of middling size (about seven thousand).[64] The Evangelical movement surfaced here in 1522 with anticlerical agitation, tithe resistance, and breaches of the fast. Although the government expelled a local Carmelite, Kaspar Kantz, when he married a butcher's daughter in 1523, it took no other action until the anticlerical demonstrations of 1524. As in Esslingen, in Nördlingen the presence of Evangelical sympathizers in the town council did not lead to official action, beyond bare toleration, until after the first popular demonstrations.

This survey of eight cities to early 1524 confirms a recent judgment that the situation from 1521 to the end of 1523 'has the marks of a transition or advent', which was characterized by 'the expectation, that something must and would change', though nothing was yet decided.[65] The Evangelical movement had developed out of its original milieu – monasteries, patrician parlors and printshops – into public places; it had

---

61 This is based on Naujoks, *Obrigkeitsgedanke*; Borst, *Geschichte*, 218–19, 224–6; Rublack, 'Reformatorische Bewegung', from which the quote is taken, p. 196.
62 Rublack, 'Reformatorische Bewegung', 203.
63 Krabbe and Rublack, *Akten*, 18–20, nos. 2–4.
64 This is based on Rublack, *Nördlingen*, 94–100.
65 H. Schmidt, 'Reichsstädte', 290; and see excellent summary on 123–61.

taken shape under clerical leadership and petitioned for protection of Evangelical clergymen, but it had not yet moved to disturbances of the civic peace. The degree of official cooperation with popular demands for change seems to have related directly to the strength and intensities of external pressures on the oligarchies: from the bishops and neighbouring princes; from the two Habsburg courts; from the privileged status of vital economic operations, such as trading firms and fairs; and from the presence of organs of Imperial government – the Diet, the Governing Council, and the High Court. Such forces kept the oligarchies from acting, no matter how deeply the new ideas penetrated powerful families, until in 1524 there arose a kind of political scissors, of which one blade was the urban commons' direct pressure for religious change, and the other was Charles V's new determination to scotch the Lutheran heresy. The convergence of these two blades made it impossible for most urban governments to continue the policy of benign inaction. The pressure from the commons developed more or less dangerously, depending on whether the social distance between oligarchy and commons was relatively great (Nuremberg, Augsburg and Frankfurt) or small (Strasbourg, Ulm and Constance), and on whether there were politically significant guilds (Strasbourg, Ulm, Constance and Esslingen), relatively weak ones (Augsburg, Frankfurt), or none at all (Nuremberg). In the absence of guilds, even in the presence of great social differences, the craftsmen and tradesmen had no established institutions through which to press their grievances and demands on their governments. Where the social gap was wide and the guilds prominent, as at Augsburg, the oligarchy was the least mobile and the Evangelicals most likely to take their message into socially sensitive areas. Each of these factors – external forces, social structure and constitution – contributed to the urban governments' variegatedly common situation.

Though some of the town council's early acts on religion could be justified by its mandate to keep the peace and interpreted as well within the local traditions of church – state relations, by the early weeks of 1524, when the Third Imperial Diet of Nuremberg convened, the limits of tradition were being overstepped, or soon would be, at Strasbourg, Constance and perhaps Nuremberg. Each new challenge by or to episcopal authority brought closer the day when the Edict of Worms would be enforced. The edict was no dead letter. The Governing Council's supplementary enforcing edict of 20 February, 1522,[66] had been published

---

66   *RTA, jR*, 3:21–4. See Brecht, 'Wormser Edikt', 476, against Borth, *Luthersache*, 132, who calls it 'mild'. On its enforcement in South Germany, see Brecht, 'Wormser Edikt', 477–8; Oberman, *Werden und Wertung*, 305–8 (English: *Masters*, 241–2) on 'the onset of the Counter-Reformation'.

by Duke George the Bearded in his parts of Saxony and by the bishop of Freising, and Stuttgart's own edict was to be followed by others in Western Austria. The Swabian League had nonetheless not yet been stirred to become the guardian of orthodoxy in South Germany, though it very soon would be,[67] and the free cities' governments felt as yet a palpable threat neither from above nor from below. This situation was about to change.

The 'Luther Affair' Surfaces, Nuremberg, 1524

In steten sind aufgstanden
vil predicanten frum,
hand dwarheit gnommen zhanden
und forchten in nit drum,
erboten zdisputieren
menglichem in der welt;
ob iemants könd probieren,
dass sie das volk verfüren,
solt helfen sie kein gelt.[68]

An odd calm about the Luther affair had prevailed in Imperial politics since the Diet of Worms in 1521. The Second Diet of Nuremberg in 1522-3 had reformulated the German powers' grievances against the papacy, bishops and clergy and had listened to Pope Adrian's somber confession of the clergy's contribution to the current disorders and laxity.[69] Nor, to judge from the extant acts, did the religious question disturb the Urban Diet's deliberations during four sessions between July 1522 and the following June.[70] The subject did surface, however, at the Urban Diet of Speyer in November 1523, when the government of Wissembourg asked for advice about the excommunication of two of its clergymen by the bishop of Speyer. The cities decided not to aid Wissembourg, for the bishop's action was justified by the Governing Council's mandate of 6 March, 1523, against divisive preaching, and an opinion to this effect was signed by envoys from Strasbourg, Frankfurt, Nuremberg and Ulm in the name of all the free cities, who 'still

---

67 Rublack, *Nördlingen*, 139–45.
68 'In the cities has arisen many a pious man to preach God's own true Gospel without the slightest fear. They've offered to debate it with anyone at all. If any can now prove that they lead the folk astray, they'll get nothing as their pay.' Liliencron, *Volkslieder*, 3:510, no. 393, stanza 5.
69 G. Müller, *Kurie*, 14; Oberman, *Werden und Wertung*, 305–6 (English: *Masters*, 241); H. Schmidt, 'Reichsstädte', 191–230.
70 H. Schmidt, 'Reichsstädte', 182–3.

stood on the ground of the Church'.[71] For the urban oligarchies, as for the German ruling classes as a whole, down to the end of 1523 the religious question had not disturbed the traditional patterns of politics.

When the Imperial Diet opened ceremoniously at Nuremberg on 14 January, 1524, no sign showed that this calm would not prevail. The Diet's agenda, drafted for Archduke Ferdinand by the Governing Council, gave highest priority to the reorganization and financing of the Governing Council and High Court.[72] What no one at Nuremberg knew, and especially not Ferdinand, was that Jean Hannart had come from Spain with a secret instruction, which raised the Luther affair once more to prominence and demanded that the monk's doctrine 'must be suppressed and not allowed to spread'.[73] Apparently – the initiative is still unclear – Charles had decided to bring the religious question to a head and solve it through the Diet's reaffirmation of the Edict of Worms. Perhaps he was responding to the complaint, voiced by Pope Clement VII's German legate, Lorenzo Campeggio, that 'the Edict of Worms is not obeyed by many lay and ecclesiastical princes. How that could happen in the Empire, he [Campeggio] doesn't understand'.[74] Whatever the background, Charles's action was certainly spectacular, if not quite 'revolutionary',[75] for he demanded 'that every ruler make sure that his subjects live according to His Majesty's edicts'.[76] The Diet eventually declared itself willing to enforce the edict, but only to the extent that 'the Common Man' was thereby given no cause for 'rebellion, disobedience, murder, or slaughter'[77] – a qualification that effectively took back with one hand what it gave with the other – and asked for a 'national' council of the Church in the Empire to meet at Speyer in September.[78] The Diet acted thus less out of sympathy for Luther than from instinctive resistance to the emperor when he operated, as Charles now did,

---

71   Ibid., 231–40, with new documents; the quote is from 240.
72   *RTA, jR*, 4:273, no. 32. See Rublack, *Nördlingen*, 133; and H. Schmidt, 'Reichsstädte', 291–335, whose account is fullest and clearest.
73   *RTA, jR*, 4:295, para. 3. Headley, *Emperor*, 129, sheds new light on Hannart's instruction.
74   *RTA, jR*, 4:487, no. 106. See Mogge, 'Studien', 88–9. There are new perspectives on Charles's religious policy during the 1520s in Reinhard, 'Vorstellungen', and Rabe, 'Befunde', especially 101, who notes that the religious question did not play a large role in the emperor's correspondence.
75   Borth, *Luthersache*, 147, based on *RTA, jR*, 4:500. See Brecht, 'Politik', 189.
76   *RTA, jR*, 4:295, no. 34. See H. Schmidt, 'Reichsstädte', 292–3.
77   *RTA, jR*, 4:507, no. 113. This echoed the urban governments' argument that they couldn't enforce the law for fear of the Common Man.
78   Ibid., 301, no. 36. See Mogge, 'Studien', 91; H. Schmidt, 'Reichsstädte', 299–305.

hand in glove with the pope, and from a fine sense for the mounting unrest among their subjects.

The Cities' House displayed a remarkable solidarity in the discussions of the religious question, which began only after the arrival of Cardinal Campeggio in mid-March and continued until 19 April.[79] Although they heartily approved the idea of a 'national' council, the cities protested en bloc against the reinstatement of the Edict of Worms, and their representatives refused to sign the Diet's recess. In their memorial to the rest of the Diet, the cities raised above all the spectre of revolt,

> because now the Common Man everywhere thirsts after God's Word and the Gospel, which . . . have recently spread much more widely than before . . . If we accept, approve, or allow to be enforced even the slightest barrier to the Gospel's spread, the honorable free and Imperial cities . . . could not only not enforce such a law, but they would doubtless provoke widespread disturbances, rebellion, murder, bloodshed, yes, total ruin and every sort of evil . . . The honorable free and Imperial cities, whom these developments would cause the greatest harm, damage and ruin, must prevent them and protect themselves and their people from such injury and ruin.[80]

This document set the keynote for all subsequent efforts to keep the urban front together despite the division over religion: Without taking formal sides with either Evangelical religion or Catholicism, the cities stressed the futility of all outside attempts to suppress the former, in view of the Common Man's support for the Evangelical cause and his propensity for rebellion. The cities thus took de facto a pro-Evangelical position without taking sides on doctrinal grounds.[81] The policy was formulated by a committee with a pro-Evangelical majority from Nuremberg, Strasbourg and Ulm, but it was weakened by removal of positively pro-Evangelical elements to accommodate Cologne and other Catholic governments.[82]

The actions of the Cities' House of the Diet at Nuremberg provide the first evidence that pro-Evangelical governments and politicians were beginning to set the tone in the urban front. Only nine cities took much active role in the deliberations, and Nuremberg and Strasbourg seem to have taken the leading parts. On the question of the council, the cities decided to follow Strasbourg's Hans Bock rather than Nuremberg's

79 H. Schmidt, 'Reichsstädte', 305–33; G. Schmidt, Städtetag, 479–83.
80 RTA, jR, 4:506–8, no. 113, here at 507, lines 27–37, and 508, lines 1–6. The call for a council is at p. 508, lines 20–2.
81 G. Schmidt, Städtetag, 481; Scribner, 'Cologne'.
82 G. Schmidt, Städtetag, 482–3, who found the document at Frankfurt.

Spengler. Spengler counseled delay, believing that 'the longer it goes on, the more, praise be to God, the Word of God will spread to and take root in all parts of the land, so that nothing can be undertaken against it'.[83] The current dilemma was a test for the city folk, 'whether or not they are Christians', and if they stood fast, Christ would defend his own, 'for I am certain that Christ is Lord also over his enemies and thus is mighty enough to sustain this cause . . . against many foes'.[84] 'However mighty, awesome, or powerful they might be', he declared, the opposition 'cannot hitch the stirrup one notch higher than where God long ago ordained and decreed it to be'.[85] The danger of a council, he warned, was that it might rule against the Evangelicals.

Strasbourg's government, by contrast, wanted the religious question referred to a council. This policy, first broached by the Imperial Diet at Nuremberg in January 1523,[86] had been taken up at Strasbourg no later than the following December, before the Evangelicals had a clear majority.[87] Bock's instruction for Nuremberg had lamented the misunderstandings and disputes over religion, which only a free, public hearing of the preachers could dispel; 'whatever a free council or Christian assembly [gemein] would then decide, the government and commune of Strasbourg, which have ever been and still are an obedient, Christian member of the Holy Roman Empire, would support and accept'.[88] The urban envoys at Nuremberg endorsed this policy and rejected the reinstatement of the Edict of Worms as unenforceable. This formula, which united Evangelical and Catholic envoys and thus preserved urban solidarity, 'was neither a theological demonstration nor a beacon, but a decision based on considerations of political utility'.[89]

---

83   *RTA, jR*, 4:491, no. 107.
84   Ibid., 238–9, no. 28, and see 50 n. 1.
85   Ibid., 490, lines 14–15, 27–36, and see 492–3 for his rejection of a council. The document is summarized by Brecht, 'Politik', 188, who exaggerates Spengler's role.
86   *RTA, jR*, 3:424, lines 23–5, no. 79. See Bernhard Wurmser von Vendenheim and Daniel Mieg to the Stettmeister and Senate of Strasbourg, Nuremberg, 4 Feb. 1523, in ibid., 924, lines 7–8, no. 250.
87   The instruction for the Urban Diet at Speyer in Dec. 1523 is in *Annales de Sébastien Brant*, no. 4484. Moeller, 'Zwinglis Disputationen, II': 222, is properly cautious about drawing conclusions from it about religious policy, but Brecht, 'Politik', 188–9, is not. On the context, see my *Ruling Class*, 205–8.
88   *PCSS*, 1:87–8, no. 162; there is a better text in Bucer, *Deutsche Schriften*, 1:345–7. Brecht, 'Politik', 189 n. 33, believes that the idea may have come from Bucer, but this cannot be proved. For discussions at Strasbourg, see *Annales de Sébastien Brant*, no. 4495; *PCSS*, 1: no. 166.
89   G. Schmidt, *Städtetag*, 482, who criticizes Brecht, 'Politik', 190–1.

During the spring and summer of 1524, the popular movement in the free cities 'reached its first peak'.[90] At Strasbourg five parishes, those of the 'little people' – fishermen, gardeners, and craftsmen – moved to select their own preachers; and by summer's end the government ordered the purge of all religious images from the churches.[91] At Augsburg, the government's immobility brought the city to the brink of an uprising over the dismissal of Johann Schilling, who preached that 'if the government will not act, the commune must'.[92] After nearly eighteen hundred Augsburgers gathered before the city hall on 6 August, shouting for their favorite, on the ninth the senators appeared in full armor and cowed the crowd outside, and they sealed their courage by sending two old weavers 'with bloody hands from life into death'.[93] Jacob Fugger closed his office, buried his cash, and fled to Biberach an der Riss. At Ulm, the government called in June the first official Evangelical preacher, Konrad Sam (1483–1533), after a citizens' petition on 22 May had demanded that Catholic preaching be prohibited.[94] At Constance, where matters were more advanced, the preachers and their Catholic opponents were already squaring off for a disputation à la Zurich.[95] There were riots and demonstrations against the Catholic clergy in many towns, not least in Frankfurt am Main.[96]

No other city seethed more tumultuously during the summer than did Nuremberg, whose population, now relieved of the Imperial government's presence, took up the Evangelical cause in all seriousness. Lutheran preaching had already become an everyday matter, and it was said during Easter Week 1524 that 'the preachers here preach more sharply than ever before against the pope, cardinals, and bishops'.[97] Important changes were made in Catholic ceremonies during these weeks, and Andreas Osiander (1498–1552) turned his rhetorical guns on both clerical and lay authorities. 'He is now also attacking the lay authority', one report ran, 'to the degree that the subjects might well rise up against it.'[98] In truth, peasants around nearby Forchheim had

90   H. Schmidt, 'Reichsstädte', 464, who surveys the subject on 444–64.
91   Chrisman, *Strasbourg*, 114–16, 138–40, 144; Brady, *Ruling Class*, 166–8; Bornert, *La réforme protestante*, 133–4.
92   H. Lutz, *Peutinger*, 235; F. Roth, *Reformationsgeschichte*, 1:155–70; Wettges, *Reformation*, 104–6; Broadhead, 'Internal Politics', 114–63. To the sources listed by H. Lutz, *Peutinger*, 392 n. 1, should be added Hans Ungelter's report of Aug. 13, 1524, in Klüpfel, *Urkunden*, 2:279–80.
93   H. Lutz, *Peutinger*, 235.
94   Keim, *Reichsstadt Ulm*, 64–6, 86–8; Naujoks, *Obrigkeitsgedanke*, 57–8; Brecht, 'Ulm', 98.
95   Rublack, *Einführung*, 40–1.
96   Jahns, *Frankfurt*, 35–6.
97   Quoted by Vogler, *Nürnberg*, 58; see 58–63.
98   Quoted in ibid., 59.

recently rebelled, and Nuremberg artisans were joining them.[99] The movement's first peak also created painful stresses within Nuremberg's oligarchy, dividing families and friends. Susanna Stromer, a nun of very good family, poured out her distress to Katharina, widow of Caspar Kress:

> Ursula Topler has no good reason for leaving her convent, only that she was treated too laxly and that her monk and friends sent her Lutheran books. I've not had such a bad life in the convent, and I've never wanted to take a husband.
>
> . . . Dearest Auntie, I trust that you will stick to the old ways and won't forget entirely the poor nuns here. God searches out his own in all classes of society, finds good and bad everywhere; and the good shouldn't be wiped out because of the bad. This is God's punishment on the clergy, and I hope that His divine goodness will yet turn things around and make them turn out for the best.[100]

Yet the movement could not be held back at Nuremberg, and soon Huldrych Zwingli was saluting the Nurembergers as comrades in arms.[101]

The rumblings in their own commons did not disrupt the urban front – not yet. The cities came together again in an Urban Diet at Speyer in mid-July 1524. Although the agenda contained six separate points, yet, as Nuremberg pointed out, it 'is true that among other articles this matter, which has been called the new, misleading doctrine, is not the least, in fact, we would call it the most important, the principal matter'.[102] It had, in other words, replaced the customs duty, monopolies, and the Spanish embassy as the most pressing subject. The leadership of Strasbourg and Nuremberg, established at the recent Imperial Diet,[103] still held, though the two governments could not agree on a policy. Nuremberg wanted the cities to frame another appeal to Charles V – their favorite tactic – to ask for a more moderate law, and they insisted that each city should prepare its own case for the national council at Speyer in the fall. The Strasbourgeois, however, were instructed to urge the cities to form a stronger unity and to put their

99   Pfeiffer, 'Einführung', 112–33; Seebass, 'Stadt und Kirche in Nürnberg', 73. On the rural disorders, see Vogler, 'Vorspiel'.
100   Pfeiffer, Quellen, 306–7 (after 4 Dec., 1524).
101   Zwingli to Willibald Pirckheimer, Zurich, 24 Oct., 1524: 'Futurum arbitror, ut Norimberga et Tigurum aliquando in eodem iungantur foedere . . . ' Ibid., 293, from Z, 8: no. 349.
102   Quoted by H. Schmidt, 'Reichsstädte', 465.
103   Simon Reibeisen to the bishop of Strasbourg, 17 April, 1524, in RTA, jR, 4:173, lines 27–32, no. 25. The published sources for the Urban Diet of Speyer, 13–18 July, 1524, are collected by Brecht, 'Politik.'

houses in order through stricter censorship and firmer controls on preaching, so 'that nothing should be presented and preached but the holy divine scriptures, to the enhancement of God's honor and love of neighbor, and brotherly concord should be preserved. And all other doctrines, which contradict the holy scriptures and lead to rebellion and discord, should be abolished.'[104] The cities must also face the national council as one body, and they 'should prepare a common memorial to justify the chief points: that the priests are taking wives; that the Eucharist is received by laymen under both species; and that no one is bound by church law to confess sins, to fast, and other such things'. As to the Edict of Worms, the emperor must be told that enforcement 'is not possible', and that 'where it is enforced, it would lead to great rebellion and conflict between commune and government, and between clergy and laity'.

Probably the Strasbourgeois tried to make the urban front more decidedly Evangelical than was possible, especially as concerned the preparations for the national council.[105] The Urban Diet could nevertheless agree that the Edict of Worms, restated and given teeth by a mandate from the Governing Council, was simply unenforceable in the cities, and Strasbourg, Nuremberg, Frankfurt, and Ulm agreed to represent this refusal of full obedience to the Governing Council.[106] Some other cities were not willing to go this far, and none was willing to join Strasbourg and Ulm in planning an urban military league to defend the cities in religious matters.[107] The time was unripe for an *Evangelical* urban front. The Urban Diet's letter of grievance to Charles V, however, spoke of a fear every urban officeholder could share:

> In the past the honorable free and Imperial cities . . . have always shown every possible form of obedience to the Roman emperors and kings . . . yet this edict is so framed that many of them cannot enforce all of its articles without provoking serious uprisings, the destruction of law and order, and dissension between commons and regimes and between clergy and laity. This will all lead to murder and bloodshed, and the honorable free and Imperial cities will thereby be alienated from His Imperial Majesty, and the Holy Roman Empire will be pushed toward certain ruin.[108]

104   *PCSS*, 1:92, no. 171, and there too, the following quotes.
105   H. Schmidt, 'Reichsstädte', 467.
106   The recess is in StA Ulm, A 527.
107   G. Schmidt, *Städtetag*, 485–6.
108   Förstemann, *Neues Urkundenbuch*, 1:211, no. 855, dated to July or early Aug. but almost certainly drafted about 18 July, 1524. For the Ulmers' position, see Naujoks, *Obrigkeitsgedanke*, 57; the Nurembergers' policy is noted by Brecht, 'Politik', 196, from Pfeiffer, *Quellen*, 158–63.

As these lines were written, armed peasants were already patrolling the valleys in the southern Black Forest, harbingers of the coming revolution.

These summer months were the urban front's Indian summer. To be sure, the advance of the Evangelical movements in some prominent cities gradually shifted the tone in the Urban Diet in a pro-Evangelical direction, but not so strongly that the cities had been split by the religious question. The urban commons were nevertheless pushing their governments farther and farther into illegality and open heterodoxy. The appeal to a national council, which had been framed by the entire Imperial Diet, preserved, for the moment, the urban governments' freedom of action to meet the pressure from below with concessions. This could continue, probably, so long as the other blade of the scissors did not begin to close.

The Fall of the Urban Front

> Also ists vast aufgangen
> in allem deutschen land,
> zu Wittemberg angfangen,
> den Entchrist bracht in shand.[109]

While in Germany the Luther affair was developing from the disobedience of a provincial professor into a movement of tremendous power, at Charles V's court in Spain it could not even be discussed. Or so wrote Margrave Hans of Brandenburg in mid-1525 to his brother, Casimir, confessing that he knew little about the new doctrine, about which no one at court would enlighten him, for fear of angering Charles.[110] Charles himself did not have to rely on ecclesiastical channels for his knowledge of heresy's progress, for Archduke Ferdinand's letters expressed mounting concern about it.

One of the most important things Ferdinand had learned since his arrival in 1522 was that the Habsburg power in Germany was truly in danger. He entered an Austria aboil with unrest and rebellion. His agents in Tyrol met armed resistance from country folk, who demanded to be put directly under the emperor, while radicals convened their own assemblies in the Lower Austrian duchies and called for death to the

---

109 'The movement come from Wittenberg has spread on every breeze through the whole German land and brought Antichrist to his knees.' Liliencron, *Volkslieder*, 3:510, no. 393, stanza 4.
110 Friedensburg, *Vorgeschichte*, 104 n. 2.

nobles.[111] Some of his subjects warned him, he reported, that they had to have a natural prince or else they'd turn Swiss.[112] The shade of Maximilian van Bergen, who had not lived to see Ferdinand's Austrian progress, must have smiled. Ferdinand also seems to have comprehended that the unrest racing through his and his brother's lands represented the common desire to extend to entire lands the principles of communal-federal life as learned in the village, district, mining and urban communes and in the territorial diets. It was with good reason, therefore, that he congratulated Charles on the smashing of the Castilian *comuneros*, whose ultimate demand might very well have suited his own Austrian subjects: 'The notions of the nobles and heathens belong to the past; the entire kingdom should live as one commune in peace and justice under one king and one law.'[113] As a prince of strong dynastic consciousness, but also as a younger brother who very much wanted authority independent from an elder one, Ferdinand strove to convince Charles that conditions in Germany required Ferdinand's election as King of the Romans and successor to Charles, if the decline of Habsburg prestige there were to be arrested.[114]

In reporting to Charles the progress of the German heresy, Ferdinand added to his other motives a desire to protect the religion of his ancestors. 'Sire', he wrote to Charles from Nuremberg at the end of 1523, 'the Lutheran sect reigns so thoroughly in this land of Germany that the good Christians hardly think they can declare themselves and be known as such.'[115] At Constance, heresy was being openly preached, 'and such is no less preached here in Nuremberg and in all the other Imperial cities. Also, the people refuse to pay tithes, eat meat on Friday, take the sacrament without first confessing, and do other things of that sort.'[116] Charles reacted to these and other reports with his 'great displeasure,

---

111   V. von Kraus, *Zur Geschichte Oesterreichs*; Lhotsky, *Zeitalter*, 81–92, 98–104; Fichtner, *Ferdinand I of Austria*, 22–5.
112   Archduke Ferdinand's instruction, Nuremberg, Nov. 1522: 'Ains disent vouloir avoir seigneur naturel out aultrement ilz se rendront Suysses . . .' W. Bauer and Lacroix, *Korrespondenz*, 1:23, no. 21. Somewhat later, it was said in the Governing Council, 'Dass auch etzlich reichsstett sich zu den schweiczern schlahen [könnten].' Quoted by Grabner, *Reichsregiment*, 101.
113   Quoted by Brandi, *Kaiser Karl V*, 1:121–2 (English: *Emperor Charles V*, 148), the saying comes from the Valencian Germanía. Ferdinand's congratulation is in W. Bauer and Lacroix, *Korrespondenz*, 1:31, no. 23, para. 2. See Haliczer, *Comuneros*, 131, 176–9, for the *comuneros*' ideals.
114   Laubach, 'Nachfolge', 6–10.
115   W. Bauer and Lacroix, *Korrespondenz*, 1:89–90, no. 50, para. 26.
116   Ibid. See Rublack, *Einführung*, 213, no. 50. Fichtner, *Ferdinand I of Austria*, 6–7, 110–17, 141–2, 148–9, 209–17, 228–31, sheds new light on Ferdinand's religious opinions.

that the Lutheran sect dominates in all Germany'.[117] The Third Diet of Nuremberg was just about to end, and Ferdinand fanned the flame by adding – and here the truth gave blessed support to his own ambition – that 'in the Lutheran matter . . . [there is] the greatest moment and danger'.[118] He then clinched the argument through a messenger he sent to Charles in June 1524, suggesting that the Germans might force 'the electors to elect a new [i.e., a Lutheran] king'.[119] Charles, who had paid dearly for the Imperial candidacy of Elector Frederick the Wise of Saxony in 1519, knew what that meant.

Charles, meanwhile, in the spirit of his current policy and convinced, apparently, that the leading southern free cities were indeed fonts of the heresy, wrote to Nuremberg to express his displeasure 'that you and the other estates support Luther so much'. He charged the government with allowing Lutheran books to be printed and sold, thereby encouraging others to similar acts of disobedience. Nuremberg should abandon Lutheranism, 'since most of the others in the Holy Empire will follow your example', and because otherwise the city would lose its liberties.[120] The wisdom of this harder approach was confirmed by Ferdinand in August, when he reported that the free cities, assembled at Speyer (in July), had decided to defend the cause of Luther, 'with whose doctrine they are so thoroughly infected that you cannot imagine it'.[121] Lest Ferdinand be accused of merely trying to increase the pressure on Charles to give him more independence, Jean Hannart, who was no friend to Ferdinand, reported from Germany in the same vein.[122] From Charles's perspective, therefore, the southern free cities, which in the late summer of 1523 had emerged as the best potential supporters of stronger Habsburg rule in the Empire, a year later had become the nurseries of a

---

117   W. Bauer and Lacroix, *Korrespondenz*, 1:108, no. 62, para. 14 (Burgos, 15 April, 1524).
118   Archduke Ferdinand to Charles V, Nuremberg, April 27, 1524, in ibid., 115, no. 65, para. 7.
119   Archduke Ferdinand's instruction for Karel de Bredam, Stuttgart, 13 June, 1524, in ibid., 158, no. 76, para. 16.
120   E. Franz, *Nürnberg*, 87–8. A similar letter from the Governing Council, dated 18 April, 1524, went to Strasbourg. *PCSS*, 1:92 n. 1.
121   Archduke Ferdinand to Charles V, Vienna, 14 Aug., 1524, in W. Bauer and Lacroix, *Korrespondenz*, 1:210–11, no. 85, para. 3.
122   Jean Hannart wrote on 26 April, 1524: 'Item il fault grandement peser le fait de ladite secte luterane, pour ce quelle est desia fort esparse en toute la lemaignes ingendrant beaucoup de maulx et desobeissance du peuple, tant contre les gens deglise comme vers les superieurs et justices. Et fait sur ce paz a noter, que toutes les villes imperiales ont proteste contre lexecution dudit mandat de Worms, et a ceste occasion non voulu seeller ledit departement et recez.' Lanz, *Korrespondenz*, 1:127, no. 55.

movement that, if successful, would undermine the church whose symbols and authority lent legitimacy to the Habsburg sense of dynastic calling.

It remained to find an instrument to bring the cities in line. The Imperial Diet was unsuitable, because it had called for a national council. The Governing Council lay then in the throes of its transfer to Esslingen, a move that would increase princely suspicion of it.[123] Of the Swabian League, on the other hand, some expected much as a bulwark against the Lutheran onslaught,[124] but the League's council contained a strong voice from the cities, the objects of repression, and it had princely enemies as well. It was never to be an entirely reliable instrument for the defense of Catholicism in South Germany.

The idea of a new military league, the first of those confessional leagues that would dominate German political life until 1648, probably came from Lorenzo Campeggio, the papal legate, and Duke William of Bavaria.[125] It was called the 'Regensburg Pact', because of its creation by Archduke Ferdinand, Dukes William and Louis of Bavaria, and twelve South German bishops at Regensburg between 27 June and 7 July, 1524. Its aims were enforcement of the Edict of Worms and a church reform to take the wind from Lutheran sails. Though this league fell victim to the anti-Habsburg turn of Bavarian policy in 1525, it had some lasting success in splitting some of the smaller Upper Swabian free cities – Ueberlingen, Ravensburg, Leutkirch, Wangen and Pfullendorf – away from the increasingly Evangelical Urban Diet.[126] The Regensburg Pact also threw Duke William, rather than Archduke Ferdinand, into the spotlight as the political leader of a nascent Catholic party in the South. William had come early to the conclusion that the bishops alone

---

123   Baumgarten, *Geschichte*, 2:330–2. See Jean Hannart to Charles V, Nuremberg, 6 March, 1524, in Lanz, *Korrespondenz*, 1:105, no. 52. On the Governing Council's religious complexion at this time, see Archduke Ferdinand to Charles V, 12 May, 1523, in W. Bauer and Lacroix, *Korrespondenz*, 1:59, no. 36, para. 10. Ferdinand wrote to Charles from Nuremberg, 18 Dec., 1523, that 'd'autrepart led. regiment et la ligue de Zwave [Schwaben] ne s'accordent point bien ne est possibles, car ilz sont totalement contraires . . .' Ibid., 84, no. 50, para. 9.

124   Gerwig Blarer to Dr. Johann Fabri, May 18, 1524, in Blarer, *Briefe und Akten*, 1:31, lines 3–4, no. 50. See G. Müller, *Kurie*, 286; Rublack, *Nördlingen*, 139–42. There was also a princely opposition to the League, for which see Salomies, *Pläne*, 36–7.

125   H. Lutz, 'Das konfessionelle Zeitalter, I', 314. On the Regensburg Pact, see Friedensburg, 'Regensburger Convent', and Borth, *Luthersache*, 161–8. Many sources for it are in *ARC*, 1:294ff.

126   H. Schmidt, 'Reichsstädte', 473–6.

could not halt the Lutheran advance,[127] and his role as a leader of the Catholic party happily united the defence of the faith with a weakening of Habsburg influence.

The dreamy calm of Indian summer broke in late September 1524, when Charles's decision on the Diet's request arrived from Spain. There would be no national council at Speyer on Saint Martin's Day; and the Edict of Worms would be enforced to the letter.[128] With this Edict of Burgos fell the death blow, not to the Urban Diet or the tradition of urban cooperation, but to the urban front – that is, to the promise of making urban solidarity effective through a new kind of partnership with the monarch.[129] When Charles's reply to the Diet became known, the Edict of Worms stood alone as valid Imperial law on the Lutheran question. The emperor's decision fell as a hammer blow on the urban front, not so much because the Speyer assembly might have achieved a solution to the religious question – there was little hope of that – but for two other reasons. First, it came at a time when the Evangelical movement was making perceptible progress, week by week, in the cities, pushing the governments further and further toward partisanship for the new religion. Secondly, it found the South on the brink of the greatest social upheaval in German history, the great Revolution of 1525, called 'the German Peasants' War'.[130]

The movement of the leading urban governments toward public defence of the Evangelical cause was no figment of Archduke Ferdinand's imagination. Two Nurembergers, Hieronymus Ebner and Caspar Nützel, described the recent Urban Diet to Elector Frederick the Wise: 'The free cities have appeared in great numbers, and others have sent proxies, to a meeting at Speyer [in mid-July], where they decided unanimously to hold to the Word of God, come what may.'[131] Count Palatine Frederick, too, noted a new sense of unity in this Urban Diet and thought it meant future trouble for the

---

127   Duke William of Bavaria to Duke Ernest of Bavaria, 2 Jan., 1524, in ARC, 1:162–3, quoted by H. Lutz, 'Das konfessionelle Zeitalter, I', 313 n. 2. The text has a phrase that is usually taken as proof of Evangelical sentiments, 'die gottliche ehre und unser heiliger glauben'.

128   The edict is in Förstemann, Neues Urkundenbuch, 1:204–5. Brecht, 'Politik', 197–202, describes these events, though he elsewhere (193) seems to confuse an edict of 18 April, 1524, drafted in Charles's name by the Governing Council, with the edict sent from Spain. Borth, Luthersache, 158 n. 233, lists the three edicts.

129   G. Schmidt, Städtetag, 478, rightly criticizes me (in 'Jacob Sturm and the Lutherans', 202) for construing the effects too drastically.

130   Oberman, 'Gospel of Social Unrest', explains why the term is inappropriate.

131   Förstemann, Neues Urkundenbuch, 1:213, no. 87.

princes.[132] The surviving documents drafted in free cities for the national council at Speyer reveal an impressive new commitment to Evangelical principles and language, though not necessarily to specifically Lutheran ones, and breathe the strong biblicism native to the urban Reformation.[133]

The news from Spain reinforced the slide toward an urban front committed to the Evangelical cause. This is visible in the Urban Diet that met at Ulm on Saint Nicholas's Day (6 December), 1524. Some small Upper Swabian Catholic towns boycotted the assembly, but most of the big folk were represented: Strasbourg by two Evangelicals, Egenolf Röder von Diersburg and Martin Herlin; Nuremberg by two burgomasters, Christoph Tetzel and Clemens Volckamer; Augsburg by Antoni Bimel, who already stood under Zwingli's influence; Constance by Jakob Zeller, a strongly Evangelical guildsman; and Esslingen by Hans Holdermann, who kept his distance from the Evangelicals without opposing them.[134] The Edict of Burgos frightened away the Frankfurters, who wrote that 'we must obey this edict [of Worms] insofar as we are able, so that we cannot send anyone to this meeting without incurring considerable risk'.[135] Called at Nuremberg's request, this Urban Diet dealt officially with 'Luther's doctrine' for the first time.[136]

It is not true, as has been alleged, that the Urban Diet of Ulm on 6 through 13 December, 1524, displayed 'the primacy of the Reformation religious principle in the cities' common policy in 1524'.[137] Despite the deliberate absence of a large number of cities, the Diet did not adopt the views of Lazarus Spengler, who criticized his own masters, and those of the other cities, for their timidity.

132   Count Palatine Frederick to Counts Palatine Ottheinrich and Philip, 5 Aug., 1524, in Friedensburg, *Reichstag zu Speier*, 10. Under his presidency, the Governing Council began to move against cities for failure to enforce the Edict of Worms. Naujoks, *Obrigkeitsgedanke*, 58.
133   H. Schmidt, 'Reichsstädte', 476–85, who cogently criticizes Brecht, 'Politik', 219–20, for making the document too specifically Lutheran.
134   Brady, *Ruling Class*, 317–18, 342–3. Nuremberg's envoys are listed in the recess, in StA Ulm, A 529, fol. 24^v. See also F. Roth, *Reformationsgeschichte*, 1:88, 102 n. 7; Rublack, *Einführung*, 107–8; idem, 'Bewegung', 197; Krabbe and Rublack, *Akten*, nos. 162–5.
135   Jahns, *Frankfurt*, 36. Frankfurt did send a proxy to Ulm. StA Ulm, A 529, fol. 25^r.
136   The meeting was called at Nuremberg's request (StA Ulm, A 529, fol. 3^r) to consider Luther's doctrine (ibid., fol. 2^r). Thirty envoys attended (ibid., fols. 3^r–4^r). The recess is in ibid., fols. 2^r–25^v.
137   Brecht, 'Politik', 202. See G. Schmidt, 'Haltung', 197–8.

They should not be so timid in this matter, which concerns not only this government but all the Empire's subjects, and which is not the cause of any one person, but God's cause. They shouldn't start at every carnival mask, such as are used daily to frighten them; but, as Christian people, they should trust God, His word and righteousness, because they seek nothing else than His honor, their subjects' welfare, and the good of all Christendom – not their own interests. If you trust God more than men, He will become your helper in His own good time, and He will never abandon those who trust in Him. Viewed in the light of God's grace, this matter is not so dangerous that the council should abandon those whose hearts are in the right place or do anything that is improper or disadvantageous before God and the world, for the government would otherwise give a public example for abandoning the gospel.[138]

The entire Evangelical movement, Spengler trumpeted, is 'a great . . . courageous . . . assembly, which will permit no power to wrest it from the gospel and the Word of God', and the best way to defend it is through an embassy to inform Charles V about the conditions in the Empire. The Constancers wanted to go even farther and send 'learned and pious men' to Spain to instruct the emperor in the new doctrine and its religious and social benefits.[139]

The Urban Diet at Ulm heard the Edict of Burgos read and then resolved

not to sit by and do nothing, but to act diligently . . . and, with God's grace, to seek suitable ways, means and assistance in nullifying the severity of said penal edict, or in counteracting it effectively. For if this is not done, the efforts of the free and Imperial cities' grim and hateful foes – especially the fish whose water is removed by the holy, indestructible Word of God [i.e., the bishops] – will produce evil worse than any pen can describe . . .[140]

The best remedy would be a 'Christian letter' [*ein Christenlich schrifft*] to warn the emperor that 'it is not humanly possible for the free and Imperial cities to enforce this edict on the Common Man or other subjects or to force them to give up the Word and call of God, without uprisings, ruin, destruction, and bloodshed within our communes'. This was the same argument the cities had employed at the Third Diet of Nuremberg and again at the Urban Diet at Speyer in July 1524. This time, however,

138   Pfeiffer, *Quellen*, 176; the following quote is at 172.
139   Spengler's memorial is in ibid., 168–77; and the Constance document is printed by Vögeli, *Schriften*, 2, 1:656. See Brecht, 'Politik', 199–202; H. Schmidt, 'Reichsstädte', 485–502; G. Schmidt, *Städtetag*, 487–90.
140   StA Ulm, A 529, fol. 4ᵛ; the following quote is at fol. 5ʳ.

a new spirit, intensely religious and direct, animated their pleas. 'For we confess by our consciences', they wrote to Charles,

> and on our souls' salvation, that in this we seek nothing else and ask for nothing more earnestly from God, than that His divine honor, praise and honor of His holy name, and also brotherly love, to be advanced. Also, [we desire] that His authentic Word be preached to all men throughout the whole world for salvation and solace, and that the prosperity, welfare, and prestige of the Holy Roman Empire and of Your Imperial Majesty be increased.[141]

The envoys were careful, to be sure, to distance themselves from Luther and his doctrine.

> It has not been, and is not now, our intention, desire, or opinion to defend in any way or to support Luther's person or his doctrine, particularly where the latter is supposed to be against the Word of God and the holy gospel. For we consider Luther to be a man, who can err as other men do. We were not baptized in the said Luther's name or that of any other man. He did not suffer for us, and he did not bear and pay for our sins. But we believe in God the Almighty as our Creator and head of His Christian churches, Who saved us through the death of His only beloved Son, Jesus Christ, and Whose Word and gospel we will support, so long as He gives us grace.[142]

There is nonetheless an unmistakably Evangelical ring to their denunciation of all laws and edicts issued 'to forbid us in any way the Word of God, from which alone we have life, through which we must be preserved and be saved, and which alone we want to protect against all human doctrines, teachings, and opinions'. Nothing like this, surely, had ever before been submitted to Charles V. The Urban Diet of Ulm also worked out a plan of collective security to aid those cities that were being prosecuted for violations of the Edict of Worms, such as those by the bishop of Speyer against Wissembourg and Landau and that of the bishop of Augsburg against Kaufbeuren. It was not the much-discussed urban league, but it was a step in that direction.[143]

While the Urban Diet deliberated and framed conclusions, South Germany rolled on toward revolution. The social landscape sprouted volcanoes, as peasants rose in arms in the bishopric of Bamberg,

---

141   Pfeiffer, *Quellen*, 310, who prints the full text (308–11) from StA Ulm, A 529, fols, 5ᵛ–10ᵛ. See Brecht, 'Politik', 200–1.

142   Pfeiffer, *Quellen*, 308–9, and there, too, the following quote.

143   StA Ulm, A 529, fols, 11ʳ, 11ᵛ–12ʳ, 12ʳ–17ʳ, 19ʳ⁻ᵛ, 21ʳ–22. Well over 90 per cent of the text deals with this issue.

the southern Black Forest and Switzerland. At Wendelstein near Schwabach in Franconia, they drove out their pastor and claimed the right to install a new one, and at Thayngen near Schaffhausen they did the same.[144] From its starting point in the Black Forest, the revolt had spread since early summer into the Klettgau and the Hegau, the politically spongy boundary zone between Swabia and the Confederacy.[145] Nowhere did the urban Evangelical movements and the rural uprisings, both nourished by communalism, converge more successfully than along the higher reaches of the Upper Rhine, where Balthasar Hubmaier (1481–1528), a Swabian radical with a strong anti-Jewish record, drew together around Waldshut all the complaints of the Common Man – against the priests, the Jews, the merchants, and the Austrian government.[146]

The fundamental theme of these movements was expressed by the upland subjects of the great abbey of Sankt Blasien in the southern Black Forest, who declared that they simply wanted to be free, like other 'peoples' [*Landschaften*] and pay no more dues.[147] The Evangelicals' desire for religious self-rule converged with and mightily strengthened the much broader and older movement for self-rule in general, which had sprung from the erosion and defeat of feudal lordship. Had it not been for the preachers and printers of the early 1520s, who spread common symbols and slogans of encouragement and resistance, possibly the *Bundschuh* actions of 1502 and 1513–17 would now appear as mere aftershocks of the Swabian War of 1499, not as preliminary tremors to the Revolution of 1525.

And so, while the urban governments, pressed from below by their own commons, came to the brink of declaring all-out partisanship for the Evangelical cause, and while their sovereign, who was convinced that the cities were nursing heresy, the mother of rebellion, tightened the pressure on them from above, all around the public peace and the self-confidence of lords were melting away before the fires of revolt. This conflagration would reveal both the fundamental weaknesses of the Habsburg power in South Germany and how impotent the free cities were without effective royal leadership.

144   G. Franz, *Der deutsche Bauernkrieg*, 100–1. See, in general, ibid., 99–112; Blickle, *Revolution von 1525*, 24, 28, 38, 160, 206, 214, 220, 223, 249–50, 277.

145   G. Franz, *Der deutsche Bauernkrieg*, 104–18; idem, *Bauernkrieg. Aktenband*, 241, no. 83.

146   G. Franz, *Der deutsche Bauernkrieg*, 110–13; Scott, 'Reformation and Peasants' War'.

147   G. Franz, *Der deutsche Bauernkrieg*, 107. On the rural movement's phases, see Blickle, 'Social Protest', 7–9.

References

Manuscript sources

Augsburg, Stadtarchiv. Litteralien-Sammlung
    Oct. 8, 1519
    Aug. 24, 1523
    Aug. 20, 1525
    Oct. 28, 1525
    April 2, 1526
    Dec. 9, 1528

Basel, Staatsarchiv
    Deutschland B 2 I
    Kirchen-Akten A 8
    Politisches L 2,I; M 8,3

Chicago. The Newberry Library
    Ms. 63, Oraciones varies

Esslingen, Stadtarchiv
    Bürgerbuch II 79

Göttingen, Niedersächsische Staats- und Universitätsbibliothek
    Ms. Hist. 154, Chronik der Stadt Strassburg

Marburg, Hessisches Staatsarchiv
    Politisches Archiv des Landgrafen Philipp 389

Strasbourg, Archives Municipales
    AA 309   IV 33/7   IV 68/122   RP1540
    AA 313   IV 33/9   IV 68/128
    AA 319   IV 33/14
    AA 374b

Stuttgart, Hauptstaatsarchiv
    A 2, Bd. 396

Ulm, Stadtarchiv
    A 521
    A 529

Printed sources

This list contains all books and articles, published and unpublished, cited in the notes to this chapter. Because of the method of citation by short title, sources have not been separated from secondary literature. The entries are alphabetized by author, editor, translator, or title.

Abray, Lorna Jane. *The People's Reformation: Magistrates, Clergy, and Commons in Strasbourg, 1520–1598*. Ithaca, NY, and London, 1985.

Augustijn, Cornelis. ' "Allein das heilig Evangelium.' Het mandaat van het Reichsregiment 6 maart 1523.' *Nederlands Archief voor Kerkgeschiedenis*, new series 48 (1967–8): 150–65.

Bauer, Wilhelm, and Robert Lacroix, eds. *Die Korrespondenz Ferdinands I.* 3 vols. Veröffentlichungen der Kommission für neuere Geschichte Oesterreichs, nos. 29–31. Vienna, 1912–38.

Bender, Wilhelm. *Zwinglis Reformationsbündnisse. Untersuchungen zur Rechts-und Sozialgeschichte der Burgrechtsverträge eidgenössischer und oberdeutscher Städte zur Ausbreitung und Sicherung der Reformation Huldrych Zwinglis*. Ph.D. dissertation, University of Berlin. Zurich and Stuttgart, 1970.

Blarer, Gerwig. *Briefe und Akten*, ed. Heinrich Günter. 2 vols. Württembergische Geschichtsquellen, nos 16–17. Stuttgart, 1914–21.

Blickle, Peter. *Die Reformation im Reich*. Uni-Taschenbücher, no. 1181. Stuttgart, 1982.

———. *Die Revolution von 1525*. Rev. edn. Munich, 1981.

———. 'Social Protest and Reformation Theology.' In *Religion, Politics, and Social Protest: Three Studies on Early Modern Germany*, ed. Kaspar von Greyerz, pp. 1–23. Publications of the German Historical Institute London. London, 1984.

Bornert, René. *La réforme protestante du culte à Strasbourg au XVIe siècle (1523–1598). Approche sociologique et interprétation théologique*. Studies in Medieval and Reformation Thought, no. 28. Leiden, 1981.

Borst, Otto. *Geschichte der Stadt Esslingen am Neckar*. 3rd edn. Esslingen, 1978.

Borth, Wilhelm. *Die Luthersache (causa Lutheri) 1517–1524. Die Anfänge der Reformation als Frage von Politik und Recht*. Historische Studien, no. 414. Lübeck and Hamburg, 1970.

Brady, Thomas A., Jr. *Ruling Class, Regime and Reformation at Strasbourg, 1520–1555*. Studies in Medieval and Reformation Thought, no. 23. Leiden, 1978.

———. ' "Sind also zu beiden theilen Christen des Gott erbarm." Le mémoire de Jacques Sturm sur le culte public à Strasbourg (août 1525).' In *Horizons européens de la Réforme en Alsace. Mélanges offerts à Jean Rott pour son 65e anniversaire*, ed. Marijn de Kroon and Marc Lienhard, pp. 69–79. Publications de la Société Savante d'Alsace et des Régions de l'Est, no. 17. Strasbourg, 1980.

———. 'Social History.' In *Reformation Europe: A Guide to Research*, ed. Steven Ozment, pp. 161–81. St. Louis, 1982.

Brandi, Karl. *The Emperor Charles V: The Growth and Destiny of a Man and of a World-Empire*. Trans. C. V. Wedgwood. 1939. Reprint. London, 1965.

———. *Kaiser Karl V. Werden und Schicksal einer Persönlichkeit und eines Weltreiches*. Vol. 1. 6th edn. Munich, 1961. Vol. 2. 2nd edn. Darmstadt, 1967.

Brecht, Martin. 'Die gemeinsame Politik der Reichsstädte und die Reformation.' *Zeitschrift der Savigny-Stiftung für Rechtsgeschichte, Kanonistische Abteilung* 49 (1977): 180–263.

——. 'Die gescheiterte Reformation in Rottweil.' *Blätter für württembergische Kirchengeschichte* 75 (1975): 5–22.

——. 'Ulm und die deutsche Reformation.' *Ulm und Oberschwaben* 42/43 (1978): 96–119.

——. 'Das Wormser Edikt in Süddeutschland.' In *Der Reichstag zu Worms von 1521*, ed. Fritz Reuter, pp. 475–89. Worms, 1971.

Broadhead, Philip. 'Internal Politics and Civic Society in Augsburg during the Era of the Early Reformation, 1518–37.' Ph.D. dissertation, University of Kent, 1981.

——. 'Politics and Expediency in the Augsburg Reformation.' In *Reformation Principle and Practice. Essays in Honour of Arthur Geoffrey Dickens*, ed. Peter N. Brooks, pp. 55–70. London, 1980.

——. 'Popular Pressure for Reform in Augsburg, 1524–1534.' In *The Urban Classes, the Nobility and the Reformation. Studies on the Social History of the Reformation in England and Germany*, ed. Wolfgang J. Mommsen, R. Alter, and R. W. Scribner, pp. 80–7. Publications of the German Historical Institute London, no. 5. Stuttgart, 1979.

Buck, Hermann. *Die Anfänge der Konstanzer Reformationsprozesse. Oesterreich, Eidgenossenschaft und Schmalkaldischer Bund 1510/22–1531*. Schriften zur Kirchen- und Rechtgeschichte, nos. 29–31. Tübingen, 1964.

Chrisman, Miriam Usher. *Lay Culture, Learned Culture: Books and Social Change in Strasbourg, 1480–1599*. New Haven and London, 1982.

——. *Strasbourg and the Reform: A Study in the Process of Change*. New Haven and London, 1967.

Christensen, Carl C. *Art and the Reformation in Germany*. Studies in the Reformation, no. 2. Athens, Ohio, and Detroit, 1979.

Dickens, Arthur Geoffrey. *The German Nation and Martin Luther*. London and New York, 1974.

Dobel, Friedrich. *Memmingen im Reformationszeitalter*. 5 vols. Augsburg, 1877–8.

Engelhardt, Adolf. *Die Reformation in Nürnberg*. 3 vols. Nürnberg, 1936–9.

Feyler, Anna. *Die Beziehungen des Hauses Württemberg zur schweizerischen Eidgenossenschaft in der ersten Hälfte des 16. Jahrhunderts*. Ph.D. dissertation, University of Zurich. Zurich, 1905.

Fichtner, Paula Sutter. *Ferdinand I of Austria: The Politics of Dynasticism in the Age of the Reformation*. East European Monographs, 100. Boulder, Colo., 1982.

Förstemann, Carl Eduard, ed. *Neues Urkundenbuch zur Geschichte der evangelischen Kirchen-Reformation*. Hamburg, 1842.

Franz, Eugen. *Nürnberg, Kaiser und Reich. Studien zur reichsstädtischen Aussenpolitik*. Munich, 1930.

Franz, Günther. *Der deutsche Bauernkrieg*. 7th edn. Bad Homburg v. d. H., 1965.

——. *Der deutsche Bauernkrieg. Aktenband*. 3rd edn. Darmstadt, 1972.

Friedensburg, Walter. 'Der Regensburger Convent von 1524.' In *Historische Aufsätze dem Andenken an Georg Waitz gewidmet*, pp. 502–39. Hannover, 1886.

——. *Zur Vorgeschichte des Gotha-Torgauischen Bündnisses der Evangelischen 1525–1526*. Marburg, 1884.

Fuchs, François-Joseph. 'Les foires et le rayonnement économique de la ville en Europe (XVIe siècle).' In *Histoire de Strasbourg des origines à nos jours*, ed. Georges Livet and Francis Rapp, vol. 2: *Strasbourg des grandes invasions au XVIe siècle*, pp. 259–361. Strasbourg, 1981.

Füglister, Hans. *Handwerksregiment. Untersuchungen und Materialien zur sozialen und politischen Struktur der Stadt Basel in der ersten hälfte des 16. Jahrhunderts.* Basler Beiträge zur Geschichtswissenschaft, no. 143. Basel, 1981.

Geiger, Gottfried. *Die Reichsstadt Ulm vor der Reformation. Städtisches und kirchliches Leben am Ausgang des Mittelalters.* Forschungen zur Geschichte der Stadt Ulm, no. 11. Ulm, 1971.

Grabner, Adolf. *Zur Geschichte des zweiten Nürnberger Reichsregimentes 1521–1528.* Historische Studien, no. 41. Berlin, 1903.

Greyerz, Kaspar von. 'Stadt und Reformation. Stand und Aufgaben der Forschung.' *Archiv für Reformationsgeschichte* 76 (1985).

Grimm, Harold J. *Lazarus Spengler, a Lay Leader of the Reformation.* Columbus, 1978.

Haliczer, Stephen. *The Comuneros of Castile: The Forging of a Revolution, 1475–1521.* Madison, Wis., 1981.

Headley, John M. *The Emperor and His Chancellor: A Study of the Imperial Chancellery under Gattinara.* Cambridge, 1983.

Jahns, Sigrid. *Frankfurt, Reformation und Schmalkaldischer Bund. Die Reformations-, Reichs- und Bündnispolitik der Reichsstadt Frankfurt am Main 1525–1536.* Studien zur Frankfurter Geschichte, no. 9. Frankfurt a. M., 1976.

Keim, Karl Theodor. *Die Reformation in der Reichsstadt Ulm.* Stuttgart, 1851.

Klüpfel, Karl, ed. *Urkunden zur Geschichte des Schwäbischen Bundes (1488–1533).* 2 vols. Bibliothek des Litterarischen Vereins in Stuttgart, nos. 14, 31. Tübingen, 1846–53.

Köhler, Hans-Joachim, ed. *Flugschriften als Massenmedium der Reformationszeit. Beiträge zum Tübinger Symposion 1980.* Spätmittelalter und Frühe Neuzeit. Tübinger Beiträge zur Geschichtsforschung, no. 13. Stuttgart, 1981.

Krabbe, Helmut and Hans-Christoph Rublack, eds. *Akten zur Esslinger Reformationsgeschichte.* Esslinger Studien, Schriftenreihe, no. 5. Esslingen, 1981.

Kraus, Viktor von., ed. 'Itinerarium Maximiliani I. 1508–1518, mit einleitenden Bemerkungen über das Kanzeleiwesen Maximilians I.' *Archiv für österreichische Geschichte* 87 (1899): 229–318.

——. *Zur Geschichte Oesterreichs unter Ferdinand I. Ein Bild ständischer Parteikämpfe.* Vienna, 1873.

Lanz, Karl, ed. *Korrespondenz des Kaisers Karl V.* 3 vols. Leipzig, 1844–6. Reprint. Frankfurt a. M., 1966.

Lau, Franz. 'Der Bauernkrieg und das angebliche Ende der lutherischen Reformation als spontaner Volksbewegung.' *Luther-Jahrbuch* 26 (1959): 109–34.

Lhotsky, Alphons. *Das Zeitalter des Hauses Oesterreich. Die ersten Jahre der Regierung Ferdinands I. in Oesterreich (1520–1527).* Veröffentlichungen der Kommission für die Geschichte Oesterreichs, no. 4. Vienna, 1971.

Lienhard, Marc. 'La Réforme à Strasbourg', parts 1, 2. In *Histoire de Strasbourg des origines à nos jours*, ed. Georges Livet and Francis Rapp, vol. 2: *Strasbourg des grandes invasions au XVIe siècle*, pp. 363–432, 433–540. Strasbourg, 1981.

Liliencron, Rochus Freiherr von, ed. *Die historischen Volkslieder der Deutschen*. 5 vols. Leipzig, 1865–96.

Lutz, Heinrich. *Conrad Peutinger. Beiträge zu einer politischen Biographie*. Abhandlungen zur Geschichte der Stadt Augsburg, no. 9. Augsburg, 1958.

――. 'Das konfessionelle Zeitalter', part 1. In *Handbuch der bayerischen Geschichte*, ed. Max Spindler, vol. 2: *Das alte Bayern*, pp. 297–350. Munich, 1966.

Moeller, Bernd. 'L'édit strasbourgeois sur la prédication du 1.12.1523 dans son contexte historique.' In *Strasbourg au coeur religieux du XVIe siècle*, ed. Georges Livet, Francis Rapp, and Jean Rott, pp. 51–61. Publications de la Société Savante d'Alsace et des Régions de l'Est, series 'Grandes Publications', no. 12. Strasbourg, 1977.

――. *Johannes Zwick und die Reformation in Konstanz*. Quellen und Forschungen zur Reformationschichte, no. 28. Gütersloh, 1961.

――. *Reichsstadt und Reformation*. Schriften des Vereins für Reformationsgeschichte, no. 180. Gütersloh, 1962.

――. 'Stadt und Buch. Bemerkungen zur Struktur der reformatorischen Bewegung in Deutschland.' In *The Urban Classes, the Nobility and the Reformation. Studies on the Social History of the Reformation in England and Germany*, ed. Wolfgang J. Mommsen, R. Alter, and R. W. Scribner, pp. 25–39. Publications of the German Historical Institute, London, no. 5. Stuttgart, 1979.

――. 'Zwinglis Disputationen. Studien zu den Anfängen der Kirchenbildung und des Synodalwesens im Protestantismus.' *Zeitschrift der Savigny-Stiftung für Rechtsgeschichte, Kanonistische Abteilung* 56 (1970): 275–334; 60 (1974): 213–364.

Mogge, Birgitta. 'Studien zum Nürnberger Reichstag von 1524' *Mitteilungen des Vereins für Geschichte der Stadt Nürnberg* 62 (1975): 84–101.

Müller, Gerhard. *Die römische Kurie und die Reformation 1523–1534. Kirche und Politik während des Pontifikates Clemens' VII*. Quellen und Forschungen zur Reformationsgeschichte, no. 38. Gütersloh, 1969.

Naujoks, Eberhard. *Obrigkeitsgedanke, Zunftverfassung und Reformation. Studien zur Verfassungsgeschichte von Ulm, Esslingen und Schwäb. Gmünd*. Veröffentlichungen der Kommission für geschichtliche Landeskunde in Baden-Württemberg, series B, no. 3. Stuttgart, 1958.

Nebinger, Gerhart. 'Die Abstimmunglisten von 1530 über die Reformation der Reichsstadt Ulm.' *Blätter des Bayerischen Landesvereins für Familienkunde* 14, no. 2 (1980): 1–36.

Oberman, Heiko A. 'The Gospel of Social Unrest: 450 Years after the so-called "German Peasants" War' of 1525.' *Harvard Theological Review* 69 (1976): 103–29.

――. *Werden und Wertung der Reformation. Vom Wegestreit zum Glaubenskampf*. Vol. 2 of *Spätscholastik und Reformation*. 2d ed. Tübingen, 1979.

Ozment, Steven. *The Age of Reform, 1250–1550: An Intellectual and Religious History of Late Medieval and Reformation Europe*. New Haven and London, 1980.

Pfeiffer, Gerhard. 'Die Einführung der Reformation in Nürnberg als kirchen-rechtliches und bekenntniskundliches Problem.' *Blätter für deutsche Landes-geschichte* 89 (1952): 112–33.
——. Ed. *Quellen zur Nürnberger Reformationsgeschichte. Von der Duldung liturgis-cher Aenderungen bis zur Ausübung des Kirchenregiments durch den Rat (Juni 1524–Juni 1525).* Einzelarbeiten aus der Kirchengeschichte Bayerns, no. 55. Nuremberg, 1968.
Press, Volker. 'Stadt und territoriale Konfessionsbildung.' In *Kirche und gesellschaftlicher Wandel in deutschen und niederländischen Städten der werdenden Neuzeit,* ed. Franz Petri, pp. 251–96. Städteforschung, series A, no. 10. Cologne and Vienna, 1980.
Rabe, Horst. 'Befunde und Ueberlegungen zur Religionspolitik Karls V. am Vorabend des Augsburger Reichstags 1530.' In *Confessio Augustana und Confutatio. Der Augsburger Reichstag 1530 und die Einheit der Kirche. Interna-tionales Symposion der Gesellschaft zur Herausgabe des Corpus Catholicorum in Augsburg vom 3.–7. September 1979,* ed. Erwin Iserloh, pp. 101–20. Refor-mationsgeschichtliche Studien und Texte, no. 118. Münster (Westphalia), 1980.
Rapp, Francis. 'Jean Geiler de Kaysersberg (1445–1510), le prédicateur de la Cathédrale de Strasbourg.' In *Grandes figures de l'humanisme alsacien. Courants, milieux, destins,* ed. Francis Rapp and Georges Livet, pp. 25–39. Publications de la Société Savante d'Alsace et des Régions de l'Est, series 'Grandes Publi-cations', no. 14. Strasbourg, 1978.
——. *Réformes et réformation à Strasbourg. Eglise et société dans le diocèse de Stras-bourg (1450–1525).* Paris, 1974.
Reicke, Emil *Geschichte der Reichsstadt Nürnberg.* Nuremberg, 1896.
——. 'Willibald Pirckheimer und die Reichsstadt Nürnberg. im Schwabenkrieg.' *Jahrbuch für schweizerische Geschichte* 45 (1920): 133–89.
Reinhard, Wolfgang. 'Die kirchenpolitischen Vorstellungen Kaiser Karls V ihre Grundlagen und ihr Wandel.' In *Confessio Augustana und Confutation Der Augs-burger Reichstag 1530 und die Einheit der Kirche. Internationale. Symposion der Gesellschaft zur Herausgabe des Corpus Catholicorum in Augsburg vom 3.–7. Sep-tember 1979,* ed. Erwin Iserloh, pp. 62–100. Reformations-geschichtliche Studien und Texte, no. 118. Münster (Westphalia), 1980.
Rem, Wilhelm. 'Cronica newer geschichte, 1512–1527.' In *Chroniken der deutschen Städte,* vol. 25, pp. 1–265. Leipzig, 1896. Reprint. Göttingen, 1966.
Richter, Ernst Arwed. *Der Reichstag zu Nürnberg 1524.* Ph.D. dissertation, Leipzig, 1880.
Roth, Friedrich. *Augsburgs Reformationsgeschichte.* 4 vols. Munich, 1901–11.
——. *Die Einführung der Reformation in Nürnberg 1517–1528.* Würzburg, 1885.
Rott, Jean. 'Artisanat et mouvements sociaux à Strasbourg autour de 1525.' In *Artisans et ouvriers d'Alsace,* pp. 137–70. Publications de la Société Savante d'Alsace et des Regions de l'Est, no. 9. Strasbourg, 1965.
Rublack, Hans-Christoph. 'Die Aussenpolitik der Reichsstadt Konstanz während der Reformationszeit.' In *Der Konstanzer Reformator Ambrosius Blarer 1492–1564. Gedenkschrift zu seinem 400. Todestag,* ed. Bernd Moeller, pp. 56–80. Constance and Stuttgart, 1964.

———. *Eine Bürgerliche Reformation. Nördlingen.* Quellen und Forschungen zur Reformationsgeschichte, no. 51. Gütersloh, 1982.

———. *Die Einführung der Reformation in Konstanz von den Anfängen bis zum Abschluss 1531.* Quellen und Forschungen zur Reformationsgeschichte, no. 40. Gütersloh, 1971.

———. 'Forschungsbericht Stadt und Reformation.' In *Stadt und Kirche im 16. Jahrhundert,* ed. Bernd Moeller, pp. 9–26. Schriften des Vereins für Reformationsgeschichte, no. 190. Gütersloh, 1978.

———. 'Politische Situation und reformatorische Politik in der Frühphase der Reformation in Konstanz.' In *Kontinuität und Umbruch. Theologie und Frömmigkeit in Flugschriften und Kleinliteratur an der Wende vom 15. zum 16. Jahrhundert,* ed. Josef Nolte, Helga Tompert, and Christoph Windhorst. pp. 316–34. Spätmittelalter und Frühe Neuzeit. Tübinger Beiträge zur Geschichtsforschung, no. 2. Stuttgart, 1980.

———. 'Reformatorische Bewegung und städtische Kirchenpolitik in Esslingen.' In *Städtische Gesellschaft und Reformation,* ed. Ingrid Bátori, pp. 191–220. Spätmittelalter und Frühe Neuzeit. Tübinger Beiträge zur Geschichtsforschung, no. 12. Stuttgart, 1980.

Salomies, Marti. *Die Pläne Kaiser Karls V. für eine Reichsreform mit Hilfe eines allgemeinen Bundes.* Annales Academiae Scientiarum Fennicae, series B, vol. 83, part 1. Helsinki, 1953.

Schiess, Traugott, ed. *Briefwechsel der Brüder Ambrosius und Thomas Blarer.* 3 vols. Freiburg im Breisgau, 1908–12.

Schilling, Heinz. *Konfessionskonflikt und Staatsbildung. Eine Fallstudie über das Verhältnis von religiösem und sozialem Wandel in der Frühneuzeit am Beispiel der Grafschaft Lippe.* Quellen und Forschungen zur Reformationsgeschichte, no. 48. Gütersloh, 1981.

Schmidt, Georg. 'Die Haltung des Städtecorpus zur Reformation und die Nürnberger Bündnispolitik.' *Archiv für Reformationsgeschichte* 74 (1984): 194–233.

———. 'Reichsstadt und Territorialstaat. Esslingen, Württemberg und das Städtecorpus um die Mitte des 16. Jahrhunderts.' *Esslinger Studien* 21 (1982): 71–104.

———. *Der Städtetag in der Reichsverfassung. Eine Studie zur korporativen Politik der Freien und Reichsstädte in der ersten Hälfte des 16. Jahrhunderts.* Veröffentlichungen des Instituts für Europäische Geschichte Mainz, 112. Wiesbaden, 1984.

Schmidt, Heinrich R. 'Reichsstädte, Reich, Reformation. Korporative Religionspolitik 1521–1529/30.' Ph.D. dissertation, Saarbrücken, 1983.

Schubert, Hans von. *Lazarus Spengler und die Reformation in Nürnberg.* Ed. Hajo Holborn. Quellen und Forschungen zur Reformationsgeschichte, no. 17. Leipzig, 1934. Reprinted. New York, 1971.

Scribner, Robert W. *For the Sake of Simple Folk: Popular Propaganda for German Reformation.* Cambridge Studies in Oral and Literate Culture, no. 2. Cambridge, 1981.

———. 'Practice and Principle in the German Towns: Preachers and People.' In

Reformation Principle and Practice. Essays presented to A. G. Dickens, ed. P. N. Brooks, pp. 97–117. London, 1980.

——. 'The Reformation as a Social Movement.' In *The Urban Classes, the Nobility and the Reformation. Studies on the Social History of the Reformation in England and Germany*, ed. Wolfgang J. Mommsen, R. Alter, and R. W. Scribner, pp. 49–79. Publications of German Historical Institute London, no. 5. Stuttgart, 1979.

——. 'Sozialkontrolle und die Möglichkeit einer städtischen Reformation.' In *Stadt und Kirche im 16. Jahrhundert*, ed. Bernd Moeller, pp. 57–65. Schriften des Vereins für Reformationsgeschichte no. 190. Gütersloh, 1978.

Seebass, Gottfried. 'Die Reformation in Nürnberg.' *Mitteilungen des Vereins für Geschichte der Stadt Nürnberg* 55 (1966/67): 252–69.

——. 'The Reformation in Nürnberg.' In *The Social History of the Reformation*, ed. Lawrence P. Buck and Jonathan W. Zophy, pp. 17–40. Columbus, 1972.

——. 'Stadt und Kirche in Nürnberg im Zeitalter der Reformation.' In *Stadt und Kirche im 16. Jahrhundert*, ed. Bernd Moeller, pp. 66–86. Schriften des Vereins für Reformationsgeschichte, no. 190. Gütersloh, 1978.

Sender, Clemens. 'Die Chronik von Clemens Sender von den ältesten Zeiten der Stadt bis zum Jahre 1536.' In *Chroniken der deutschen Städte*, vol. 23, pp. 1–404. Leipzig, 1894. Reprinted. Göttingen, 1966.

Soden, Franz von. *Beiträge zur Geschichte der Reformation und der Sitten jener Zeit mit besonderem Hinblick auf Christoph Scheurl II.* Nürnberg, 1855.

Strauss, Gerald, ed. and trans. *Manifestations of Discontent in Germany on the Eve of the Reformation.* Bloomington, Ind., 1971.

——. *Nuremberg in the Sixteenth Century.* New York, 1966.

Vögeli, Jörg. *Schriften zur Reformation in Konstanz 1519–1538.* Ed. Alfred Vögeli. 2 vols. in 3. Schriften zur Kirchen- und Rechtsgeschichte, nos. 39–40. Tübingen and Basel, 1972–3.

Vogler, Günter. *Nürnberg 1524/25. Studien zur Geschichte der reformatorischen Bewegung in der Reichsstadt.* Berlin, 1982.

——. 'Ein Vorspiel des deutschen Bauernkriegs im Nürnberger Landgebiet 1524.' In *Der Bauer im Klassenkampf*, ed. Gerhard Heitz et al., pp. 49–81. Berlin, 1975.

Vogt, Wilhelm. *Die bayrische Politik im Bauernkrieg und der Kanzler Dr. Leonhard von Eck, das Haupt des Schwäbischen Bundes.* Nördlingen, 1883.

——. Ed. 'Die Correspondenz des schwäbischen Bundeshauptmannes Ulrich Arzt von Augsburg aus den Jahren 1524–1527. Ein Beitrag zur Geschichte des Schwäbischen Bundes und des Bauernkrieges.' *Zeitschrift des Historischen Vereins für Schwaben und Neuburg* 6 (1878): 281–404; 7 (1879): 233–380; 9 (1892): 1–62; 10 (1883): 1–298.

Walther, Heinrich G. 'Bernhard Besserer und die Politik der Reichsstadt Ulm während der Reformationszeit.' *Ulm und Oberschwaben* 27 (1930): 1–69.

Wettges, Wolfram. *Reformation und Progaganda. Studien zur Kommunikation des Aufruhrs in süddeutschen Reichsstädten.* Geschichte und Gesellschaft. Bochumer Historische Studien, no. 17. Stuttgart, 1978.

Wohlfeil, Rainer. 'Der Speyerer Reichstag von 1526.' *Blätter für pfälzische Kirchengeschichte und religiöse Volkskunde* 43 (1976): 5–20.

——. 'Der Wormser Reichstag von 1521 (Gesamtdarstellung).' In *Der Reichstag zu Worms von 1521,* ed. Fritz Reuter, pp. 59–154. Worms, 1971.

5

Reformation and Communal Spirit: The Reply of the Theologians to Constitutional Change in the Late Middle Ages

Peter Blickle

Originally appeared as Peter Blickle, *Reformation und kommunaler Geist. Die Antwort der Theologen auf den Verfassungswandel im Spätmittelalter* (Schriften des Historischen Kollegs, 44) (Munich, 1996).

Editor's Introduction

The sixteenth century marked an important stage in the development of political culture in the Holy Roman Empire. Princely sovereignty remained the dominant form of rule, but an alternative tradition of governance had taken hold in the towns and villages of the German lands. Throughout the medieval period settlements and communities had sprung up all over central Europe. Some communities had foundation charters with extensive political privileges, and many of these later developed into important urban centres. Others, the smaller villages and hamlets, simply evolved out of praxis and circumstance: peasants gathered together to create a clearing, to herd their livestock in common fields, or to band together in a common defensive union. As the communities grew in size and complexity, and as economic conditions demanded even more co-operation and co-ordination, local systems of government developed alongside traditional feudal relations. The unit of rule that emerged in both town and country was the commune (*Gemeinde*), a sworn association of residents (usually male householders) who were bound together to protect the local peace and ensure order at the local level. Over time, the culture of communalism began to dominate political life, and fairly sophisticated organs of government emerged as a result. In the countryside, for instance, village assemblies elected their own officials and placed them in offices specifically devised to serve local interests. Once in office, the elected officials were bound to enforce the village ordinances and bring transgressors before the village court. All of this, from the creation of offices to the enforcement of order, was done in the name of the common good (*Gemeinnutz*). The central concern was the preservation of peace and order in the town and villages. Communalism was thus a tradition of rule which grew out of the historical conditions of the age. It was often best understood in relation to its perceived opposites, rule for personal gain (*Eigennutz*) or the rule of the lord (*Herrennutz*).

According to Peter Blickle, this political culture was so pervasive that even the Reformation is best understood within the context of communalism. All three of the major reformers (Martin Luther, Huldrych Zwingli, and John Calvin) thought of the Reformation church in terms of the commune. Luther's early writings encouraged the local communities to introduce reform measures without waiting on the approval of the bishop. Indeed, in 1523, in his open letter to the community of Leisnig, Luther outlined for the first time his understanding of the evangelical church. The sure mark of the church, Luther noted, was the preaching of the Word, the pure gospel, and 'it undeniably follows,' he wrote, 'that bishops, religious foundations, monasteries, and all who are associated with them have long ceased to be Christians or Christian congregations'. Tradition is not a sure sign of the church, and as a consequence Catholicism forfeits its right to claim precedence. In its place, Luther imagines a church built on the basis of the commune. The Christian congregation, not the popes or the bishops or indeed any of the Catholic clergy, has the right to judge Christian teaching, for 'we must act according to Scripture and call and institute from among ourselves those who are found to be qualified and whom God has enlightened with reason and endowed with gifts to do so.' For Luther, the right to elect the pastor was in the hands of the congregation; even if the bishops wanted to install an evangelical preacher, 'they still could not and should not do so without the will, the election, and the call of the congregation'. Luther would later draw back from these statements and look to the prince to guide the church, but his original vision was coloured by the ideals of communalism. Calvin and Zwingli, as Blickle makes clear, thought along the same lines.

Understanding the early reform movement as a Communal Reformation sheds light on the Reformation as a historical process. For it was not until the theological ideas of the reformers had been received by the parishioners and then put into practice that the full weight of the Reformation was actually felt. This occurred in the early 1520s, as the parishioners began to think of the evangelical movement in terms of the commune. One of the best examples of this (and one which Blickle uses to illustrate his thesis) was the early reform movement in the Franconian village of Wendelstein. In 1524, as the parishioners welcomed a new clergyman to their parish church, they broadcast (and later published) a list of demands, and a notion of the Reformation, which historians have termed the *Wendelstein Church Ordinance*. In this ordinance, the villagers claim that the congregation has the power to appoint and dismiss the pastor, and they have the God-given right to judge his teaching. The pastor, they add, is 'nothing more than an attendant and servant of the commune' called into office by the community in order to preach the Word of God. In this document, the main elements of the Communal Reformation were in evidence: the villagers demanded the preaching of the Word, the right to elect and dismiss the local pastor, the right to judge the clergy's teaching, the right to manage local church affairs (including the maintenance of the tithe payments), and the right to subject the clergy to secular jurisdiction. Demands such as these, though more violent in tone, would be voiced throughout Germany the following year with the Peasants' War of 1525.

The vision of reform projected by the Wendelstein villagers was shared by many parishioners in the German lands. The faithful, inspired by the evangelical preachers, turned to the gospel for guidance and inspiration. The result was an understanding of the Christian church shaped by their own cultural and political experiences, and that is why Blickle speaks of a Communal Reformation. Moreover, it was not just the parishioners who thought in these terms. To a considerable extent, these same experiences had given shape to the early Reformation as it was projected by Martin Luther, Huldrych Zwingli, and John Calvin. Even in the realm of religious ideas, the culture of communalism left its mark.

Reformation and Communal Spirit: The Reply of the Theologians to Constitutional Change in the Late Middle Ages

Peter Blickle

The Reformation lies like an erratic block in the landscape of German history. Whenever it seemed difficult to understand the present, the Reformation was cited to explain it, with reference not so much to the abstract idea of the Reformation itself as to its personification in the figure of the reformer Martin Luther.

When the old Holy Roman Empire of the German Nation was dissolved and Germany had to find new political systems, Georg Friedrich Wilhelm Hegel formulated the dictum that, 'In Luther the subject finds the role intended for it in the history of the spirit: to be the organ of truth.'[1] Hegel saw the history of the spirit as the history of its freedom, and Luther occupies such a prominent place in it that the philosopher is said to have celebrated every 31 October, the anniversary of Luther's nailing his theses to the church door in 1517, with a particularly good bottle.[2] On the occasion of Thomas Mann's seventieth birthday in 1945, when he was trying to explain German history to an American public in view of the collapse of the Third Reich,[3] he was obviously unable to

1   Walter Mostert, article 'Luther III', in *Theologische Realenzyklopädie*, vol. 21 (Berlin and New York, 1991), p. 574. Hegel sees Luther standing at a turning-point in world history. 'In the Lutheran church, the subjectivity and assurance of the individual is as necessary as the objectivity of truth. To Lutherans, truth is not a painted object, but the subject itself is to become a true subject in exchanging its particular substance for the substance of truth, and making this truth its own. The subjective spirit thus becomes free in the truth, negating its particularity and realizing itself in the truth, so that Christian freedom is genuinely achieved.' Quoted from Mostert (after Hegel's lectures on the philosophy of history).

2   For the anecdotal nature of this story, see Joachim Ritter, 'Hegel und die Reformation', in Ritter, *Metaphysik und Politik. Studien zu Aristoteles und Hegel* (Frankfurt am Main, 1969), pp. 310–17, esp. p. 311.

3   Thomas Mann, *Reden und Aufsätze*, vol. 3 (*Gesammelte Werke*, vol. 11), Frankfurt am Main, 1960, pp. 1126–48, these quotations p. 1133ff. Mann strongly emphasizes the dialectical nature of Luther's concept of freedom (Luther was a 'hero of freedom' but a hero of freedom 'in the German style, since he did not understand freedom at all', all ideas of political freedom being repugnant to him). Here Mann is taking up a line of argument already supported by Marx (see the following note).

do so without reference to Luther who, as Mann says, 'gave tremendous impetus to the freedom of scholarship, of criticism and of philosophical speculation', and 'advanced the cause of European democracy' by 'establishing the idea of man's immediate relationship with his God'. Mann did concede that 'the unadulterated German, separatist, anti-Catholic and anti-European approach' which he saw embodied in Luther also alienated and indeed alarmed him. When Germany was divided into two states, Luther was cited (although only in the east) as one of the founders of the modern age. The German Democratic Republic saw itself as the legitimate heir and indeed the ultimate fulfilment of the *early bourgeois revolution*, determined in the first instance entirely by the person of Martin Luther. This idea derived from Karl Marx, who considered that while the Germans were outstandingly good at revolutionary theory – he was not referring only to himself but expressly mentioned Martin Luther – they were not so good at revolutionary practice.[4] Seen in this light, the practice of the theory produced East German socialism.

When the German tragedy of the Third Reich impinged upon the consciousness of the western world, however, it paused in alarm, and shrank from continuing the usual line traced from Luther to Bismarck on into the present.[5] The importance of reference to Luther decreased as the intellectual and social sciences in Germany, using historical methods, began to see the modern age as founded in the Enlightenment. This was a friendly gesture to France and England, and with the political integration of the Federal Republic of Germany into the west, it suggested that the way to a morally improved Germany should be sought in wider historical contexts than merely the German tradition. The Reformation thus lost some of its former importance. Significantly, on the 1983 quincentenary of Luther's birth, as far as I know the most lavishly celebrated historical event in Germany of the last forty years, there was no suggestion that he was responsible for the present order of things.

4   Marx works out these ideas in his critique of Hegel's legal philosophy. See Karl Marx, *Werke, Artikel, Entwürfe März 1843 bis August 1844* (Karl Marx – Friedrich Engels, *Gesamtausgabe* [MEGA], vols 1–2), Berlin, p. 177: 'For Germany's *revolutionary* past is theoretical; it is the *Reformation*. It is in the *philosopher's* brain today, as it was in the *monk's* brain then, that the revolution begins.' His famous comment on Luther's dialectic of liberation follows: '*Luther*, however, replaced servitude out of *piety* by servitude out of *conviction* [. . .].' Cf. the brilliant (from the Marxist viewpoint) essay by the young Günter Vogler, 'Marx, Engels und die Konzeption einer frühbürgerlichen Revolution in Deutschland', in *Zeitschrift für Geschichtswissenschaft* 17 (1969), pp. 704–17.
5   Cf. Hartmut Lehmann, 'Martin Luther als deutscher Nationalheld im 19. Jahrhundert', in *Luther* 55 (1984), pp. 53–65, esp. p. 57.

Niklas Luhmann finds himself unable to continue connecting the Reformation with the modern age,[6] whereas Max Weber could still do so. Speculating boldly, Weber saw the international historical significance of the Reformation in the fact that the 'spirit of capitalism' derived from the Protestant ethic.[7]

But remarkably little is known about the *spirit* engendered by the Reformation. So long as Protestantism was regarded as the essential goal of Christianity (or in the secular variant, so long as liberty was regarded as the goal of human history), the Reformation could be explained as to some extent necessarily proceeding from its own nature; history was not the discipline that could or should help to cast light on these connections. Now that teleological interpretations of the world are no longer current, we may ask whether and how Reformation theology connects with its own time, the nature of which is very clearly revealed in its political constitution.

I will answer this question in three stages, indicating the constitutional development of the late Middle Ages (I), explaining its possible influence on the theology of the reformers (II) and trying to account for its presumed connection with the process whereby the Reformation became established (III).

I   Late Medieval Constitutional Development and Communal Spirit

German historians like to describe the constitutional change from the late Middle Ages to the modern period, between 1200 and 1500, as a shift of political authority from the Empire to the territories. If we understand more than that by the term 'constitution', seeing it as the institutionalized form of communal life and the organized distribution of political power, then the constitutional change was a dialectical game

6   Niklas Luhmann, *Funktion der Religion*, (Frankfurt am Main, 1977); for a particular reference, see p. 157. Cf. Hans-Christoph Rublack, 'Reformation und Moderne. Soziologische, theologische und historische Ansichten', in Hans R. Guggisberg and Gottfried G. Krodel (eds), *Die Reformation in Deutschland und Europa. Interpretationen und Debatten* (Archiv für Reformationsgeschichte, Sonderbd.), Göttingen, 1993, pp. 24–8).

7   Max Weber, 'Die protestantische Ethik und der Geist des Kapitalismus', in ibid., *Gesammelte Aufsätze zur Relgionssoziologie*, vol. 1, 6th edn (Tübingen, 1972), pp. 17–206. With different emphasis, see also Weber, 'Die protestantischen Sekten und der Geist des Kapitalismus', in *Gesammelte*, pp. 207–36. The present state of critical study of the 'Weber thesis' can be found in the contributions to Hartmut Lehmann and Guenther Roth (eds), *Weber's Protestant Ethic: Origins, Evidence, Contexts* (Washington, 1993), and Rublack, 'Reformation und Moderne'.

played not by the emperor and the princes, but by the nobility and communities. The late Middle Ages were politically shaped by the development of communities in the form of towns and villages.[8]

I Central Europe

This thesis derives support first from the statistics: there were fifty towns and cities in the Empire around the year 1200, and some 4000 in 1500. Around 1200 the appearance of the countryside was marked by widely dispersed hamlets and isolated farms, but by around 1500 there were tens of thousands of villages.

A common feature of towns and villages is that they called themselves by the same name: a *Gemeinde*, a commune or community. A town might be founded by a ruler's decree; a community was not. Like the village community, it was formed deliberately and by agreement. The statutes of Ulm in 1376 contain an entry stating that 'no one will tolerate or allow' acts of violence in the city 'against the ordinance and law of the community'. To ensure peace and good neighbourliness the craftsmen and noble patricians of Ulm joined together in a community and swore 'always to hold to the holy teaching . . . and to do all we can and may to ensure that rich and poor may live together in a community, according to the dictates of peace and friendship'.[9] The community was constituted in an oath taken by all the artisans and patricians of the city to devise regulations ensuring peace.[10] (Similarly, every peasant was bound by oath to keep the peace in his village.) The people of Ulm drew up a sworn document to specify and carry out these intentions, and it represents the first written constitution of the city, introducing the offices of mayor, the Greater Council, the Lesser Council and the community itself, and defining their functions.[11] Objectively, and seen in the

8   To cite evidence in support of this brief outline would take an excessive number of footnotes, so an abbreviated procedure may be justified in this section. For central Europe, I will mention as a general survey my study 'Kommunalismus. Begriffsbildung in heuristischer Absicht', in Peter Blickle (ed.), *Landgemeinde und Stadtgemeinde in Mitteleuropa* (Historische Zeitschrift, Beihefte, revised version, 13), Munich, 1991, pp. 5–38. For other European countries I will cite only the most important and most recent titles. However, the sources of all quotations will be given.

9   Carl Mollwo (ed.), *Das rote Buch der Stadt Ulm* (Württembergische Geschichtsquellen, vol. 8), Stuttgart, 1904, p. 24.

10   The statutes drawn up at this time are the original form of the civic charter of Ulm. See Mollwo, pp. 24–33.

11   Mollwo, pp. 258–64, 749, 776, 785. The ongoing character of the entire process is evident in the fact that twenty years passed between the first agreement on oath and the drawing up of the constitution itself.

context of the preceding late medieval social and political systems, which took government from above as both natural and exclusively reserved for the nobility, the community was something entirely new – and in the context of the organization of power wholly illegitimate.[12]

With the community came sophisticated political organizations with an aesthetic deriving from their logical and objective structures. These were the *Gemeindeversammlungen*, community assemblies, held annually in both urban and rural areas. They were representative organs of the community, and were known in towns as the *Rat* (town council) and in the country usually as the *Vierer* (the parish council 'of four'). The presiding officers were known respectively as the *Bürgermeister* (mayor) in a town, and the village equivalent was the *Ammann*. All these officers were approved by the community, generally through an electoral process, and they justified their policies by acting for the good of the community, as they had promised to do when they took the oath of office.

Community policy was principally expressed in the statutes, which could be drawn up by the community assemblies, or alternatively – and reasonably, in view of the communal mandate involved – by the town and parish councils. Thousands of clauses in the legal sources, both urban and rural, begin with such monotonously automatic formula as, 'And it is enacted by the citizens all in common', or 'And we have enacted it after due consideration, by common consent of the council and the community'.[13] Formally, the statutory law was a voluntary agreement ratified by those who introduced it. Materially, it was not the re-interpretation of an old law but the making of a new one. In this it followed the guidelines of utility and practical common sense,[14] and intro-

---

12   Max Weber, *Wirtschaft und Gesellschaft. Grundriss der verstehenden Soziologie*, 5th edn (Tübingen, 1972), pp. 749f. See also Eberhard Isenmann, *Die deutsche Stadt im Spätmittelalter 1250–1500. Stadtgestalt, Recht, Stadtregiment, Kirche, Gesellschaft, Wirtschaft* (Stuttgart, 1988), pp. 190ff, 207f.

13   Quotations from the charter of Leutkirch and Isny from Karl Otto Müller (ed.), *Oberschwäbische Stadtrechte*, vol. 1, *Die älteren Stadtrechte von Leutkirch und Isny* (Württembergische Rechtsquellen, vol. 18), Stuttgart, 1914, pp. 39 (no. 57 in the statutes) and 47 (no. 85).

14   The drawing up of community statutes resulted in close links with the law-courts. The courts, older in origin than the communites, were integrated with them first in order to check the formal legality of the statutes, and then to judge any infringement of them. They did so with varying degrees of success, performing better in towns than villages. The actual area of competence of the urban court of law coincided with the municipal juridical area, while village and law-court did not always coincide in the country. At the same time a rival area of jurisdiction deriving from the council developed from statutory activity in towns, and there may have been a similar development in village parish councils, although this subject has not yet been adequately studied. The legal proceedings of these new bodies were more

duced a process of rationalization into the juridical area.[15] In order to enforce it – not entirely easy, since it lacked the dignity of tradition – harsh penalties were imposed for transgressions, even including the *Bann*, expulsion from the community or outlawry.

The community statutes were legitimated by the principle of the *Gemeinnutz*, the common good. It was not just a usual but the exclusive basis. To avoid misunderstandings, it should be said that the common good was defined first by its having nothing to do with the *bonum commune* of political rhetoric in the theory of classical antiquity and its imitators.[16] Its instrumental function was to counter the *Herrennutz*, the good of the lord. Townspeople and villagers derived their authority from the old formula of the oath that swore 'to increase the lord's good and avert harm from him', but 'the community' or 'the commonweal' was substituted for 'the lord'. The *Bannwart* or warden of outlawry of St Alban in Basle, 'to be appointed annually around St Lawrence's Day by a provost and the community', had to swear in his oath of office 'to avert all harm from the whole community and promote its good', a point further emphasized by the repetition of the fact that he is to advance 'the common good'.[17] In 1381 the mayor, the council and all the citizens of the town of St Gallen were still swearing 'to promote the good and the pious devotions of lord Cun, abbot of the monastery of St Gallen and of his monastery, and to avert harm from him', but a generation later every citizen swore 'to promote the common good of the town of St Gallen and avert harm from it'.[18]

The common good was not just a rhetorical figure in propaganda, but had a firm ethical foundation: it served first to secure peace, and second

concise, avoiding the more expensive and formal proceedings of the old local and aristocratic courts. I mention the field of jurisdiction only to complete the list of communal institutions.

15 Here the late medieval community was far in advance of the territories, where local and police regulations followed on from preceding communal statutary laws and may simply have reflected them. It was on these regulations, often called *Polizei*, that the early modern state was constructed, from the fifteenth century in France, the sixteen century in Germany and the eighteenth century in Russia. Cf. Hans Maier, *Die ältere deutsche Staats-und Verwaltungslehre* (Munich, 1980), 2nd edn.

16 This interpretation is difficult to establish scientifically, and I will mention only that the statement is based on a systematic survey of just under 10,000 documentary records (from two separate bodies of sources, one from a town and one from an area under monastic rule). A study of the subject will shortly be published in the more extensive context of a monograph.

17 Rudolf Wackernagel et al. (eds), *Urkundenbuch der Stadt Basel*, 11 vols (Basle, 1890–1910), here vol. 8, p. 350, no. 441.

18 Quoted in Hermann Wartmann et al. (eds), *Urkundenbuch der Abtei Sanct Gallen*, 6 vols (Zurich and St Gall, 1863–1955), here vol. 4, p. 256, no. 1835, and p. 403, no. 2007.

to secure adequate subsistence. For 'the sake of peace and the common good',[19] as the citizens often put it, feuds and acts of violence were forbidden in towns, confederations of towns were created, and to that extent peace and the common good were related. At least in the area of Bavarian and Austrian jurisdiction, there was a tendency in the late Middle Ages to define subsistence by the term *Hausnotdurft*,[20] 'domestic need'. If carters and pack animals came to Kufstein to sell corn they were 'to sell it immediately at a proper price to any who wish for it and require it for their domestic needs'. Since the 'domestic needs' of the villagers were estimated at a higher rate than the pedlars' ' own needs', the legal precedents of Sarnthein gave community members the preemptive right to buy foodstuffs.[21] The necessity of securing subsistence for the household and its members came before any kind of trade, and before claims from the authorities for taxes, dues and services.

The common good was a concept challenging the lords outside the community and measured by the criterion of domestic need within it. The common good and domestic need were complementary, in that an economy which did not exceed the requirements of the household served the common good, and it was in the common good to provide for household needs. This was the system behind the management of common land and the regulation of local mills, smithies, bakeries, bathhouses and taverns, in fact the conduct of all the trades and handicrafts in the town.

As the common good related to domestic need on the economic level, so the community related to the household in general. This was not a matter of chance, since both must have become established entities at the same time. Before 1300 a house was still widely regarded as a movable asset,[22] consisting of little more than a few boards that could

19   Wartmann, p. 567f, no. 2167, and vol. 2, p. 617, no. 3580 (a selection of references).
20   The concept has been studied with reference to Bavarian material by Renate Blickle, 'Hausnotdurft. Ein Fundamentalrecht in der altständischen Ordnung Bayerns', in Günter Birtsch (ed.), *Grund- und Freiheitsrechte von der ständischen zur spätbürgerlichen Gesellschaft* (Veröffentlichungen zur Geschichte der Grund- und Freiheitsrechte, vol. 2), Göttingen, 1987, pp. 42–64. It also applies on other areas, and is taken up in more general terms by Hugues Neveux and Eva Österberg, 'Peasants' Norms and Values', in Peter Blickle (ed.), *Resistance, Representation and Community* (The Origins of the Modern State, vol. 4), Oxford, 1995.
21   Ignaz V. Zingerle and K. Theodor von Inama-Sternegg (eds), *Die Tirolischen Weisthümer*, vol. 1 (Österreichische Weisthümer, vol. 2), Vienna, 1875, p. 25, and Ignaz V. Zingerle and Josef Egger (eds), *Die Tirolischen Weisthümer*, vol. 4 (Österreichische Weisthümer, vol. 5), Vienna, 1888, p. 268.
22   The collections of juridical precedents provide plenty of material to support this assertion. Cf. Jacob Grimm (ed.), *Weisthümer*, 7 vols (Göttingen, 1840–78), on this point vol. 1, pp. 42, 45, 277; vol. 4, pp. 498, 512. See also Roger Sablonier, 'Das

be dismantled and loaded on a cart; only after 1300 did the building of solid houses on stone foundations with a sturdy half-timbered frame become more usual.[23] The internal structure of the community was based on its houses. Within their walls and the built-up area, towns and villages were divided into quarters (or *areae*) in which the houses were located. Since each house represented its own legal peace-keeping area – the offence of breaking the domestic peace is still in force today – all houses were at first regarded as equal, and in theory distinctions depending on the size of the household remained secondary. Each house was to be represented in the community assembly, and legally speaking the household was to some extent superior to the individual. To this day, households rather than the faithful are summoned to hourly devotions in the Valais on the day of prayer and repentance.[24] Since the master of the house was head of the household, and described as the *Hauswirt* or *Hausherr*, he went to the community assembly and sat in council chambers and law courts. The household was organized on the principle of *dominion* and thus followed older forms of the hierarchy of power; of its very nature the idea of dominion was foreign to the community. The councillors and mayors were authorities, not overlords.

The points outlined here, empirically supported by material from southern Germany, can be extended in all directions of the compass. The theory that the idea of the community marked the late Middle Ages finds support in the fact that it also occurs in the rest of Europe.

2 Europe

That fact immediately becomes obvious if we think of the associations called up by the mention of Italy in such a context. Beginning with the great Lombard communities, social systems organized in terms of dominion had been undermined in the whole of northern and central Italy, apart from a few isolated areas.[25] Community assemblies, com-

Dorf im Übergang vom Hoch- zum Spätmittelalter. Untersuchungen zum Wandel ländlicher Gemeinschaftsformen im ostschweizerischen Raum', in Lutz Fenske et al. (eds), *Institutionen, Kultur und Gesellschaft im Mittelalter. Festschrift für Josef Fleckenstein* (Sigmaringen, 1984), pp. 727–45.

23   Konrad Bedal, *Fachwerk in Franken* (Hof, 1980); Bedal, 'Der vollendete Anfang im Mittelalter – Unzeitgemässer Versuch einer Generalisierung', in Bedal (ed.), *Hausbau im Mittelalter III* (Sobernheim, 1988), pp. 9–29.

24   Arnold Niederer, *Alpine Alltagskultur zwischen Beharrung und Wandel. Ausgewählte Arbeiten aus den Jahren 1956 bis 1991*, (Berne, Stuttgart and Vienna, 1993) (pictorial section).

25   The literature on Italy is copious. In brief, I will mention the following: Giorgio Chittolini, *La formazione dello stato regionale e le istituzioni del contado. Secoli XIV e XV*,

munal organs of representation and communal statutary rights were typical features of the Italian late Middle Ages, not just in towns but also in the country, and from the Alps to Rome. In the middle of the fifteenth century, Italian lawyers involved in a legal dispute between some peasants and their noble over-lords gave it as their opinion that the peasants' claim to the right of free association was legitimate, and so therefore was the right to establish such associations by statute,[26] a ruling that lent communal structures some of the dignity of natural law. Against this background, the classical constitutional types of monarchy, aristocracy and democracy could be narrowed down to two alternatives: the *regimen regale*, unrestrained government by the king and the nobility, and *regimen politicum*, government restrained by the law. In practice, the system of government in towns was the *regimen politicum*, which also described itself as republican. It acquired forward-looking significance in the realm of political theory through its definition as *dominium plurium*, rule by the many or by most. In colloquial speech of the time it was called government *a comune* or *stato franco*. Thereafter, the republic served to counter the concept of princely government, entering the Italian and French languages as *repubblica* and *république*.[27]

La República and *la comunidad* were interchangeable terms in late medieval Spain. Around the middle of the fourteenth century a process of the conversion of villages and hamlets into towns began. In Castile alone, 5000 towns had been created by 1517.[28] As in Italy and Germany, these towns had their community assemblies, their elected

Turin, 1979; Carlo Fabri, *Statuti e riforme del commune di Terranuova 1487–1675. Una comunità del contado fiorentino attraverso le sue istitutzioni* (Biblioteca storici toscana, 25), Florence, 1989; John Kenneth Hyde, *Society and Politics in Medieval Italy. The Evolution of the Civil Life, 1000–1350* (London and Basingstoke, 1982), 3rd edn; Hagen Keller, ' "Kommune": Städtische Selbstregelung und mittelalterliche "Volksherrschaft" im Spiegel italienischer Wahlverfahren des 12–14. Jahrhunderts', in Gerd Althoff et al. (eds), *Person und Gemeinschaft im Mittelalter. Karl Schmid zum 65. Geburtstag* (Sigmaringen, 1988), pp. 573–616; Keller, 'Veränderungen des bäuerlichen Wirtschaftens und Lebens in Oberitalien während des 12. und 13. Jahrhunderts', in *FMSt* 25 (1991), pp. 340–72; Antonio Pini, *Città, Comuni e corporazioni nel medioevo italiano* (Bologna, 1986).
26   C. Storti Storchi, 'Betrachtungen zum Thema "Potestas condendi statuta" ', in Giorgio Chittolini and Dietmar Willoweit (eds), *Statuten, Städte und Territorien zwischen Mittelalter und Neuzeit in Italien und Deutschland* (Schriften des Italienisch-Deutschen Historischen Instituts in Trient, vol. 3), Bologna, 1991, pp. 251–70, esp. p. 269f.
27   Cf. Wolfgang Mager, article, 'Republik', in Otto Brunner et al. (eds), *Geschichtliche Grundbegriffe. Historisches Lexikon zur politisch-sozialen Sprache in Deutschland*, vol. 5 (Stuttgart, 1984), pp. 549–651, esp. pp. 582–86.
28   Helen Nader, *Liberty in Absolutist Spain. The Habsburg Sale of Towns, 1516–1700* (Baltimore and London, 1990).

councils and other organs of representation, and they had statutes drawn up by themselves. The Spanish called this process *liberar*, and it was carried out through petitions from the peasants to the king, who sold rural settlements the privilege of self-administration at an exorbitant price.

France, in brief, followed the Italian and Spanish example in the south of the country, while the north was more like Germany, although the French towns were older and the parishes were more significant in the formation of political communities.[29]

Parallel changes were taking place in Scandinavia at the same time. Around 1200 the upper social class of Viking chieftains and clan leaders lost power to the provincial authorities and the king. Thereafter, both the nobility and the church were weak and unimportant. 'Communal self-rule at the king's command' is the brief description of one Norwegian historian.[30] Communal self-rule entailed the administration of justice, taxation and local defence, and in principle (although there is still some obscurity about the details of the transitional process) it was based on the organization of a ship's crew, transferred from water to land. The Scandinavian hundred, the unit of division of the Scandinavian kingdoms of the late Middle Ages in the form of a legal and administrative area known as the *härad*, has been explained as equivalent to the crew of four ships, comprising four sets of twenty-four oarsmen each and four steersmen.[31]

There was no preceding theoretical design for community structures, and no political or Utopian ideals were involved; this comment is made

29   There is little controversy on these developments in French research. Cf. André Chédeville, 'De la cité à la ville, 1000–1150', in Georges Duby (ed.) *Histoire de la France urbaine*, vol. 2: *La ville médiévale des Carolingiens à la Renaissance* (Paris, 1980), pp. 28–181; Charles Petit-Dutaillis, *Les communes françaises. Caractéres et évolution des origines au XVIIIe siécle* (L'évolution de l'humanité, vol. 44), Paris, 1947; Jean Schneider, 'Les origines des chartes de franchises dans le Royaume de France (XIe–XIIe siécles)', in *Les libertés urbaines et rurales du XIe au XIVe siécle*. Colloque International, Spa, 5–8 October 1966 (Brussels, 1968), pp. 29–50.

30   Steiner Imsen, *Norsk bondekommunalisme*, Part 1: *Middelalderen* (Trondheim, 1990), p. 205.

31   Gerhard Haffström, 'Die altschwedische Hundertschaft', in *Die Anfänge der Landgemeinde und ihr Wesen* II (*VuF*, vol. 8), Sigmaringen, 1964, pp. 443–63. The latest research on legal and administrative history is set out by Pia Letto-Vanomo, 'Vom archaischen Gerichtsverfahren zum staatlichen Prozess. Bericht über zwei finnische Forschungsprojekte', in Heinz Mohnhaupt and Dieter Simon (eds), *Vorträge zur Justizforschung. Geschichte und Theorie*, vol. 2 (Rechtsprechung, Materialien und Studien, vol. 7), Frankfurt am Main, 1993, pp. 97–130, esp. pp. 114ff. Finally, the communal element was reinforced by the parish community authorities; cf. Peter Aronsson, 'Swedish Rural Society and Political Culture: The Eighteenth- and Nineteenth-Century Experience', in *Rural History* 3 (1992), pp. 41–57 (with detailed bibliographical information).

in the light of the development of Italian urban communities, and there is no reason to confine its application to towns or to Italy. Instead, the *comune* was 'a really new form of political association',[32] in which 'distrust of dominion and power became a guiding principle of its internal organization'.[33]

The commune replaced the rural hamlet, the soccage farm and other prevailing systems of noble (and ecclesiastical) rule in the Middle Ages. The nobility was weakened, at least where its rights to dominion were concerned, but it was very seldom entirely suppressed by the community.

3   Communal spirit

Communal spirit was expressed in the taking of political decisions by community assemblies and other representative institutions, often elected and at any rate ratified by the community, with the intention of ensuring peace and organizing communal life by the criterion of the common good. The community represented the whole body of its households. The representatives of those households united into their own legal and peace-keeping entities, and agreed on oath to form a community. With their oath before God, every member of the community – formally and legally, this meant every head of a household, and in terms of social rank every citizen and every peasant – swore to observe the statutes, promote peace and act for the common good.

II   The Responses of the Reformation

To my mind, the *communal spirit* that developed in Europe in the late Middle Ages provides the best explanation of the theology of the reformers (and hence of their ethics and politics), in so far – and this is an important proviso – as it can be deduced at all from concrete historical circumstances.

32   Hyde, *Society*, p. 48f.
33   Keller, 'Kommune', p. 575. Communities 'entered a world of ideas of order emanating from divine grace, while the hold of royal and princely government grew tighter. . . . The main aim of the many different kinds of communal constitution was to distinguish clearly between official functions undertaken in the service of the community and positions of power and personal influence, breaking through the nexus that had constituted the system up to that point.'

Basically, the theology of the Reformation developed from Martin Luther's very painful sense that he was never in a state of divine grace however strictly he observed his monastic vows, and although he zealously availed himself of the means of grace through the sacraments provided by the church, where there was a widespread understanding that God would give grace to those who made full and deliberate use of the opportunities offered to them through the divine creation: *Si homo facit, quod in se est, Deus dat gratiam.*[34] In Luther's experience, however, all that man could do of himself and of his own nature was nothing but sin. How will I be justified before God, asked man, how can God be gracious to me? Luther found an answer much simpler than those provided by elaborate and complicated scholastic theology. God justifies sinful man in so far as sinful man acknowledges God and believes in him. Faith is a prerequisite of grace; indeed, even the ability to believe is a kind of grace. Faith and grace are at the heart of Luther's *doctrine of justification*, which in turn is at the heart of his theology. Man can be both a sinner and justified – he is *simul iustus et peccator*. There is only one way to attain faith, through the *logos*, Christ, the word of God revealed in the gospel. Luther builds his theology on grace, faith and the scriptures.

Wherever Luther's doctrine of justification became religious practice it was bound to have devastating consequences for the Roman church. The necessity of the sacraments for salvation now seemed superfluous, and with it the position of the consecrated priests who administered them. The one thing necessary to salvation was the gospel, and it was *sui ipsius iterpres*; it interpreted itself to the faithful. Consequently there was no need for the Pope and the Councils to expound scripture.[35] Theoretically, the two main props upon which the church was founded were pulled from under it.

The Pope and the bishops, the priests and monks, the mass and good works, the ecclesiastical courts and ecclesiastical law all came under such pressure to prove themselves as had hardly ever been felt before in the history of Christianity.

Luther's doctrine of justification was shared, through experience or conviction, by the other Reformation theologians who are regarded as outstanding and particularly influential in Europe: Huldrych Zwingli in Zurich and Jean Calvin in Geneva.

---

34   Otto Hermann Pesch, *Theologie der Rechtfertigung bei Martin Luther und Thomas von Aquin. Versuch eines systematisch-theologischen Dialoges* (Walberger Studien der Albertus-Magnus-Akademie, vol. 4), Mainz, 1967, pp. 708–14.

35   This brief outline is based on many new attempts to describe the dividing line between the two theologies with some accuracy. Cf. also Martin Brecht, *Martin Luther*, vol. I (Stuttgart, 1981), p. 369f.

I   The community in Reformation theology

The new theology inevitably called for a new church. In 1523 Martin Luther published a treatise entitled: 'That a Christian assembly or community may have the right and power to judge of all teaching and to appoint, install and dismiss teachers, the grounds and cause proceeding from scripture.'[36] This was one of the first and most far-reaching concepts upon which the Reformation church was founded. 'Where nothing but the gospel is preached', there was the community.[37] Everyone (including the Pope and the bishops) had the right to teach, but what was taught would be decided by the community alone. Luther drew the logical conclusion: 'In order to judge of teaching, and to appoint or dismiss teachers and pastors, we must not turn to human law, old traditions, custom, usage, etc., God grant, whether such law be ordained by pope or emperor, by princes or bishops, whether half or the whole world has observed it, whether it has endured for one year or a thousand.'[38] In principle, any member of the community could be appointed to preach the gospel, since as a believer he 'has the word of God, and he is taught and anointed priest by God'.[39]

Both sets of arguments, one concerning the primacy of the community's interpretation of true doctrine, the other the priesthood of all believers, led to the conclusion that 'the community that has the gospel may and should choose and appoint from among its members one who is to teach the Word in their stead'.[40]

Both here and in many other earlier writings,[41] Luther based the structure of the church entirely on the community. In giving direct guidance to Christians no longer sure how to act towards bishops and prelates, princes and the nobility,[42] Luther leaves them in no doubt that

36   Text from Martin Luther, *Werke. Kritische Gesamtausgabe* (*Weimarer Ausgabe*, subsequently cited as WA), 60 vols, Weimar, 1883–1980, here vol. 11, pp. 401–16.
37   WA, p. 408.
38   WA, p. 408f.
39   WA, p.411.
40   WA, p.413.
41   In particular *Address to the Christian Nobility* of 1520 (Luther, WA, vol. 6, p. 408) and of 1523: 'Eyn Sermon am tag unsser frawen Liechtmess gethan zcu Wittemberg durch Doc: Marti: Luther M.D. 23' NA, vol. 12, pp. 420–6), and the treatise published in Latin and German, *De instituendis ministris ecclesiae* (NA, pp. 16–96).
42   The occasion for this treatise was a request from the community of Leisnig for information about the position of the pastor. Luther obviously gave the work a general character intentionally, as it contains no definite reference to Leisnig and conditions there.

the visible church in the form of the community has the right and duty to ignore ecclesiastical and secular law.[43]

2 The Community, communion and the law – Zwingli and Calvin

The other reformers[44] shared Luther's concept of the community in principle, but developed it in various different ways. Huldrych Zwingli[45] and Jean Calvin[46] considerably reinforced the idea of the community, first by granting it the power of the *Bann*, that is to say the right and duty of ensuring that no unworthy person took communion,[47] and second by bringing the sacrament of communion into the community itself. This is a central point of Reformation theology as a whole, since it was here that opinions differed. The two major Protestant denominations, the Lutheran and Reformed churches, developed from a different understanding of communion. The Reformed communion service does not claim any transubstantiation of bread and wine into the body and blood of Christ; it is a service of commemoration by the community, although conducted in such a way that the community pledges itself in the communion service to follow Jesus;[48] consequently adulterers, fornicators, drunkards, blasphemers and usurers must be excluded from it.[49] This idea was developed by Zwingli, and requires rather more detailed examination.

43 Unlike the theologian, the historian must and indeed should emphasize that Luther's remarks were by no means of a purely theoretical and speculative nature.
44 For a comparison between ideas of the community, principally those of Luther, Zwingli and Calvin, cf. Euan Cameron, *The European Reformation* (Oxford, 1991), pp. 145–55. For the further dissemination of such ideas among other theologians cf. the material compiled in Peter Blickle, *Gemeindereformation. Die Menschen des 16. Jahrhunderts auf dem Weg zum Heil*, Munich, 1985, pp. 138–42 (English version, *Communal Reformation. The Quest for Salvation in Sixteenth-Century Germany*, London, 1992).
45 The relevant passages are in Huldrich Zwingli, *Sämtliche Werke*, 14 vols (Corpus Reformatorum, vols 88–101), Berlin and Zurich, 1905–83, here vol. 1, p. 537f and vol. 3, p. 64. After 1524 if becomes particularly clear the 'the community shall choose the preacher [. . .]; for the community and none other will judge of his teaching' (vol. 3, p. 78).
46 See Willem Nijenhuis, article 'Calvin' in *Theologische Realenzyklopädie*, vol. 7 (Berlin and New York, 1981), pp. 584–6 (section on 'Ekklesiologie').
47 On the other hand the autonomy of the community is restricted again, at least by Zwingli, who thinks the advice 'of wise Christian prophets and evangelists' necessary for the appointment of the preacher. Zwingli, *Sämtliche Werke*, vol. 4, p.427.
48 'Is not the cup . . . we drink with words of thanks the community of the blood of Christ? Is not the bread we break the community of the body of Christ?' was Zwingli's translation of 1 Corinthians 10 (Zwingli, *Sämtliche Werke*, vol. 4 p. 860).
49 For Zwingli's understanding of communion, cf. Ulrich Gäbler, *Huldrych Zwingli. Eine Einführung in sein Leben und Werk* (Munich, 1983), pp. 118–25. I owe the fol-

At first, communion remained what it was in the Roman church, a *sacrament*. 'In this sacrament,' says Zwingli, 'man is united publicly with all believers',[50] as the *Eidgenossen* [the Swiss] have 'a pact with one another' that they periodically 'renew with an oath'.[51] Indeed, the *coniuratio*, the citizens' oath, was renewed twice a year on the 'day of swearing' in Zurich cathedral and in hundreds of communities. Communion was celebrated four times a year in Zurich, at Easter, Whitsun, Christmas and on the feast of a church's dedication. The 'day of swearing' was also a renewal of the act of *coniuratio* that had created the community. The analogous use of the words *sacrament* and *oath*, referring back to early Christianity when an oath was indeed a sacrament,[52] also implies a sanctification of the political community.[53] *Sacramentum* and *coniuratio*, communion and oath,[54] had a common focal point in the community. There was no sacrament outside it. Communion was not to be taken outside community ceremonies – for instance in the form of private communion, mass celebrated in the family or in a fraternity – and Calvin

lowing ideas to Heinrich R. Schmidt, 'Die Häretisierung des Zwinglianismus im Reich seit 1525', in Peter Blickle (ed.), *Zugänge zur bäuerlichen Reformation* (Bauer und Reformation, vol. 1), Zurich, 1987, pp. 219–36, esp. pp. 231–35.

50   Zwingli, *Sämtliche Werke*, vol., 3, p. 535.

51   Zwingli speaks of *Eidgenossen*, 'confederates' in the general and all-embracing sense of the people of Switzerland. However, 'confederates' were also the members (by virtue of their oath, *Eid*) of a political community.

52   Paolo Prodi, 'Der Eid in der europäischen Verfassungsgeschichte. Eine Einführung', in ibid/Prodi (ed.), *Glaube und Eid. Treueformeln, Glaubensbekenntnisse und Sozialdisziplinierung zwischen Mittelalter und Neuzeit*. (Schriften des Historischen Kollegs, Kolloquien, vol. 21), Munich, 1993, VII–XIX, here IX.

53   This question is not yet entirely answered, and can probably be properly answered only with theological authority. However, the connection is clear enough to Zwingli, 'Firstly, you must know,' he writes in the *Auslegung der Schlussreden* of 1523, 'that this word *sacramentum*, an old Latin word, does not mean what it is now used for [he is referring to the old believers, P.B.], but it is called sacrament, meaning really an oath. 'Zwingli, *Sämtliche Werke*, vol. 2, p. 120.

54   Ibid., vol. 6/1, p. 150: *Iusiurandum species religionis est; qui enim* **sacramentum** *praestat, ad summam religionis sese religat* (my emphasis; P.B.). I owe this observation to the work of André Holenstein, 'Seelenheil und Untertanenpflicht. Zur gesellschaftlichen Funktion und theoretischen Begründung des Eides in der ständischen Gesellschaft', in Peter Blickle (ed.). *Der fluch und der Eid. Die metaphysische Begründung gesellschaftlichen Zusammenlebens und politischer Ordnung in der ständischen Gesellschaft* (Zeitschrift für Historische Forschung, Beiheft 15), Berlin, 1993, pp. 11–63, here p. 24, note 34.

The legal aspects of the connection referred to here deserve re-examination and further study, since a refusal to take the community oath could lead to exacommunication (at least in French towns). Cf. Albert Vermeesch, *Essai sur les origines et la signification de la commune dans le Nord de la France (Xie et XIIe siécles* (Studies presented to the International Commission for the History of Representative and Parliamentary Institutions, vol. 30), Heule, 1966, p. 181.

condemns the displaying of the Host and the custom of keeping it and carrying it in procession as rank superstition.[55]

Argument by analogy from the political to the Christian community and vice versa may also explain how it was possible for Zwingli and Calvin to link the juridical activities of the state with *divine law*, as Zwingli frequently does. The justice of existing laws must be checked to see 'if it be of the same nature as the divine law, or against it'.[56] The *divine law* is love of one's neighbour *and* natural law; 'the two are one law'. Now and then Zwingli also calls this *divine justice*. 'The authorities' are 'appointed that they may act through divine justice in the matters closest to them'.[57] Calvin implicitly makes the same point in saying that it is the task of representatives of the state 'to watch over both tablets of the law'.[58]

3   The community and the household – Luther

Luther found it intolerable to mingle divine justice and secular justice, as this would have been a confusion of the Two Kingdoms, a merging of the gospel (evangelium) and the law (lex).'

Historically, every relationship involving dominion was the result of the Fall. *Politia autem ante peccatum nulla fuit, neque enim ea opus fuit*, said Luther in his lecture on Genesis 2.[59] The evil in man is a permanent threat to God's creation. Order and dominion are necessary to sustain creation. The first legally ordained relationship of dominion in this world is the government of the household by the father of the family.[60]

---

55   'D'une mesme source sont procedées les autres façons superstitieuses, comme de porter en pompe le Sacrament par les rues une fois l'an, et luy faire l'autre iour un tabernacle, et tout au long de l'année le garder en une armoire pour amuser là le peuple, comme si c'estoit Dieu.' Johannes Calvin, *Opera selecta*, ed. Petrus Barth, vol. 1, Munich, 1926, p. 522.
56   Zwingli, *Sämtliche Werke*, vol. 2, p. 329f. For the context, see also Arthur Rich, 'Zwingli als sozialpolitischer Denker', in *Zwingliana* 13 (1969–73), pp. 67–89 (especially on points where Zwingli differs from Luther), and Alfred Farner, *Die Lehre von Kirche und Staat bei Zwingli* (Tübingen, 1930), pp. 43–7.
57   Zwingli, *Sämtliche Werke*, vol. 2, p. 520.
58   Nijenhuis, article 'Calvin', p. 587.
59   And he continues, *Est enim politia remedium necessarium naturae corruptae.* Luther, WA, vol. 42, p. 79; complemented in WA vol. 30/1, p. 152. Cf., for this assessment, Reinhard Schwarz, 'Luthers Lehre von den drei Ständen und die drei Dimensionen der Ethik', in *Lutherjahrbuch* 45, 1978, pp. 15–34, and also Karl-Heinz zur Mühlen, article 'Luther II', in *Theologische Realenzyklopädie*, vol. 21 (Berlin and New York, 1991), pp. 530–67, here 557.
60   Aristotle himself was convinced that 'all relationships of dependency in the household . . . are to be related to the head of it, who is the leader of it and makes

All state hierarchies imitated the hierarchy of the family and the household. 'For all else flows from parental authority and then spreads.'[61] 'What a child owes its father and mother', Luther concludes, 'is also owed by all within the government of the house.' God is praised and man's own works come to fruition in such conduct. 'The same is also to be said of obedience to worldly authority,' Luther continues his analogy, 'which is all found (as I said) in the station of the father, and exerts very wide influence around it. For here we have not a single father, but as many fathers as there are freeholders, citizens or subjects. For through them (as if through our own parents) God maintains us and gives us nourishment, house and home, protection and security. Therefore, because they bear such names and titles with all honour as their highest prizes, we too owe them honour and great respect for the greatest treasure and most precious jewel on earth.'

Luther endows the patriarchal structures of the *household* with a paradigmatic character for any form of dominion,[62] and consequently he

it whole'. The Romans had the same idea in the image of the *pater familias*, but it was Luther who made this figure enduringly German and transformed him from *oikodespot* into the *Hausvater*, father of the household. See Otto Brunner, 'Das"ganze Haus" und die alteuropäische "Ökonomik"', in ibid., *Neue Wege der Verfassungs- und Sozialgeschichte* (Göttingen, 1980) 2nd end, pp. 103–27, here p. 112, particularly with reference to Luther's translation of Matthew 20: 1. (References could just as well be taken from Luther's *Large Catechism*.) According to Brunner, the German language had previously preferred the word *Wirt* to *Vater*, and called the head of the household the *Hauswirt* instead of the *Hausvater*.
61   Luther, WA, vol. 30/1, p. 152f, from which all the following quotations are taken. 'Therefore,' the text continues, 'menservants and maidservants must be sure that they are not only obedient to their masters and mistresses, but honour them as if they were their own fathers and mothers, and do all that they know is required of them, not from compulsion and reluctantly, but with joy and pleasure.' The family is quickly extended to the whole household, for the father of the household must 'also have the servants, both men and maids, under him in the government of the house. Therefore,' Luther continues, 'all who are called masters are in the position of parents, and from that position they must take the power and might of government.' He adds some etymological and semantic reflections on the word *Vater*, translates *pater familias* (and *mater familias*) by *Hausvater* (and *Hausmutter*), and praises the Romans for 'calling their princes and rulers [. . .] *patres patriae*, that is to say, fathers of the whole land', a dignity and honour which unfortunately, he adds, christians no longer concede to their authorities.
62   The idea of the three 'orders' ordained by God, comprising the office of priest, the state of marriage and the condition of authority, takes the parallels further. A detailed description of the state of marriage illustrates the relationships within the household: 'Thus anyone who is father or mother, who governs the household well and brings up children to serve God, does nothing but what is holy, sacred work, and this is a sacred order. And it is the same when children or servants obey their parents or their masters, for that too is nothing but holy work. . . . 'Luther, WA, vol. 26, p. 504f. The state of marriage is held up for particular approval, as the centre of the

can draw a parallel between the immaturity of children, who also need the caring attention of authority, and any kind of subject status. The relation between those above and those below is conveyed chiefly through the idea of *obedience*, obedience itself being interpreted as an act of love for one's neighbour. Luther preaches that obedience 'is as much as if you gave a naked man a cloak, or fed the hungry'.[63]

Luther developed the analogy with particular cogency in his *Large Catechism* of 1529. A more prominent position for the idea can hardly be imagined, both in view of the significance Luther thereby lends the question and the effect his attitude was bound to have.

Luther thus refers not just to the community but also to the household as a typical structural element in the community of the late Middle Ages, whereas there is more exclusive reference to the community alone in Zwingli and Calvin.

III   The Reformation as a Historical Process

Constitutional change in the late Middle Ages and the theology of the Reformation can therefore be related to each other in that the organization of the church, until now extremely hierarchical, conformed to the political community in its structure and areas of competence. Just as the assembly of the political community decided on its constitution, so the assembly of the church community decided on its religious confession; just as the political community chose its officers, so the church chose its pastors; and just as the political community periodically confirmed its existence by taking an oath, so the church community confirmed its identity through the sacrament of communion. The political and church communities were even in agreement on the disciplinary measure of the *Bann*. I am not making too much of the term 'community', for wherever the reformers' understanding of the church was put to the test of practice, the political community was ultimately its institutional setting, in Wittenberg, Zurich and Geneva alike.[64]

---

oeconomia. It is 'the most common and noblest condition, and so . . . it is found throughout the world'. Cf. zur Mühlen, article 'Luther', p. 558.

63   See Gunnar Hillerdal, 'Der Mensch unter Gottes Regiment, der Untertan und das Recht', in Gunter Wolf (ed.), *Luther und die Obrigkeit* (Wege der Forschung, vol. 85), Darmstadt, 1972, p. 24f.

64   There is no need to cite separate references for Zurich and Geneva, and similar findings have been made for Wittenberg by Stefan Oehmig. His studies are published in a volume on the procedings of a seminar, edited by him, for the Wittenberger Kolloquium of 1993.

Such links may be called speculative. If they are to be methodologi-
cally plausible in a historical context then they must be made empirically, through the record of actual events.

*I 'No duty to pay the tithe' – constitutional conflict in the imperial
town of Memmingen*

'There is no duty to pay the tithe on pain of mortal sin,' Christoph
Schappeler preached in the church of St Martin in Memmingen in
1523.[65] The response came at the time of the next harvest in the
summer of 1524, when peasants of the countryside belonging to Memmingen and some of the citizens of the town simultaneously refused to
pay tithes (consisting of every tenth sheaf of the corn harvest). Since
the hospital, one of the most important charitable institutions in the
town, was dependent on these tithes, the town council took measures
of remarkable severity against the offenders.[66] It forced payment of the
tithes by issuing stern threats of punishment.[67] One master baker,

65 Franz Ludwig Baumann (ed.), *Akten zur Geschichte des deutschen Bauernkrieges
aus Oberschwaben*, (Freiburg im Breisgau, 1877), p. 1. Schappeler claimed elsewhere
that the tithe, usually paid in the form of every tenth sheaf of corn at harvest, had
been misappropriated and went not to the priests but to knights and princes, towns
and corporations. The edited text is in Friedrich Braun (ed.), 'Drei Aktenstücke zur
Geschichte des Bauernkrieges', in *Bulletin für bayerische Kirchengeschichte* 3 (1890),
pp. 26–9. In fact the text is anonymous (for attribution and dating see Baumann,
pp. 29–32), but is ascribed to Schappeler by Braun. In my view Schappeler's author-
ship is also supported by his detailed reasoning on tithes in the Memmingen disputation; this text is in *Evangelisches Kirchenarchiv Kaufbeuren*, appendix 102/7, p. 47f.
The minutes of the Memmingen religious disputation are edited by Thomas Pfund-
ner, 'Das Memminger und Kaufbeurer Religionsgespräch von 1525', in *Memminger
Geschichtsblätter*, 1991–2, pp. 23–66, esp. pp. 33–42.
66 Hannes Lambacher, *Das Spital der Reichsstadt Memmingen. Geschichte einer Für-
sorgeanstalt, eines Herrschaftsträgers und wirtschaftlichen Grossbetriebes und dessen
Beitrag zur Entwicklung von Stadt und Umland* (Memminger Forschungen, vol. 1),
Memmingen, 1991, pp. 69ff. For a general comparative survey of the economic
importance of the tithe, see Christian Heimpel, *Die Entwicklung der Einnahmen and
Ausgaben des Heiliggeistspitals zu Biberach an der Riss von 1500 bis 1630* (Quellen und
Forschungen zur Agrargeschichte, vol. 15), Stuttgart, 1966, p. 21f; Ewald Gruber,
'Geschichte des Klosters Ochsenhausen. Von den Anfängen bis zum Ende des 16.
Jahrhunderts', Ph.D. dissertation (Tübingen, 1956), p. 116; Wolfgang von Hippel,
Die Bauernbefreiung im Königreich Württemberg, vol. 1 (Forschungen zur deutschen
Sozialgeschichte, vol. 1), Boppard am Rhein, 1977, pp. 209ff, 292.
67 Other important political considerations made it difficult for the council to
compromise: not only did parishes and hospitals in the town have a claim on the
tithes, so did monasteries and nobles outside it. The case was bound to attract unwel-
come attention elsewhere; according to the council records there was already 'an
outcry' to the effect that the people of Memmingen were 'the most disobedient and

however, obstinately refused, and was thrown into prison. As a result several hundred citizens spontaneously assembled outside the town hall,[68] formed a committee organized by guilds, and not only succeeded in getting the baker freed at once but pressed their complaints on the council: the gospel was to be preached in all the town churches 'without any human addition', and uniformity of belief was to be established by a disputation between old and new believers.[69]

Around the turn of the year the reforming movement in Memmingen peremptorily forced a binding decision on the whole town. In December 1524 Schappeler replaced the Roman liturgy at St Martin's church with an evangelical liturgy.[70] Christmas saw tumultuous scenes in the city's second parish church, the church of Our Lady. The Catholic priest would have been murdered in the sacristy if some of the town councillors had not used their authority to get him out of the church and take him into protective custody for the next few days.[71] The price

refractory in the Empire'. Stadtarchiv Memmingen (cited hereafter as StAM), 341/1, p. 3. (The archive has no page numbering; the numbers are mine.)

68 'It was very . . . riotous and agitated, and more and more people arrived, assembling in the market place to the number of several hundred,' according to a detailed account of 13 July 1524 by the town clerk, preserved in a draft version (StAM 341/1).

69 Among other things the committee demanded that 'the word of God and nothing but the word of God be preached clearly in public, without any human addition, not only in the parish church of St Martin but also in the church of Our Lady and other churches'. Offensive and derogatory remarks about the progressive preacher Schappeler, hitherto a common occurrence, would no longer be tolerated. Anyone 'who wishes or desires to dispute something with him, then let him do it, as our doctor the preacher often demands and has frequently requested, at the proper place and in such a way as is fitting', Barbara Kroemer, *Die Einführung der Reformation in Memmingen. Über die Bedeutung ihrer sozialen, wirtschaftlichen und politischen Folgen* (Memminger Geschichtsblätter 1980), Memmingen, 1981, p. 97. On 13 July the council had a vigorous and controversial discussion of the demands of the community committee on all these measures. There was no outright majority for a council decision. Six out of twelve guilds supported the committee.

70 Julius Miedel, 'Zur Memminger Reformationsgeschichte', in *Beiträge zur bayerischen Kirchengeschichte* 1 (1895), pp. 171–9, here p. 171.

71 'As soon I came down to St George's altar,' said the priest, Megerich, 'a great murmuring arose from the Lutherans, men and women, and then there was great uproar and turbulence. And they chased and drove me into the sacristy very roughly, calling all manner of insults, and shouted angrily, striking me with their fists on my head and shoulders, and kicking me in the side and the hips with their feet, throwing stones at me in the sacristy, and the stones cracked and broke the glass, pictures on the altars were smashed and the ampullas overthrown. The candles on the altar were snapped off and carried away. There were four to six of them doing this mischief and violence, and if Hanns Keller the mayor and six of the councillors had not come, I would have been murdered in the sacristy.' Miedel, p. 172. See the same source for the complicated history of the transmission of this story.

of his safety was the disputation that the community demanded, and it took place between New Year and Twelfth Night of 1525, attended by all the clergy of the town, its four doctors, all the town councillors, and 'one man out of every guild, representing them all, and chosen for that purpose by a free vote in every guild'.[72] The clergy of the Roman faith refused to enter into theological argument, and the adjudicating committee of councillors and guild representatives delivered the euphemistic verdict that 'the matter was thereby agreed'.

No more Roman Catholic rites were observed in the town; they were replaced by evangelical church rules. The clergy became guild members, were subject to taxation and required to take the citizens' oath. They could now be brought before secular courts, and preachers were appointed by agreement between the council and a guilds committee.[73]

2 'That you preach nothing to us but the Gospel and the Word of God' – the Reformation in the village of Wendelstein

Events similar to those in Memmingen and other towns were also occurring in the villages. Wendelstein in Franconia may serve as an example.[74]

Wendelstein was a typical south German village. The community chose the two village 'masters' and eight wardens at the community assemblies; it also administered community funds and organized local agriculture and security in the village.

Since 1464 the parish church of Wendelstein had been in the gift of its patron, the Margrave of Ansbach. The village was a very devout place, judging by the existence of a fraternity, the many endowments for the observation of anniversaries and days of remembrance, and a special endowment for an early matins, the income of which assured the priest of a standard of living suitable to his station. Two winged

72   Evangelisches Kirchenarchiv Kaufbeuren, appendix 102/7. See also StAM 341/5, 'Instrucion der disputaz halb', [2 January] 1525.
73   Martin Brecht, 'Der theologische Hintergrund der Zwölf Artikel der Bauernschaft in Schwaben von 1525. Christoph Schappelers und Sebastian Lotzers Beitrag zum Bauernkrieg', in *Zeitschrift für Kirchengeschichte* 85 (1974), pp. 174–208, here 184; Wolfgang Schlenck, *Die Reichsstadt Memmingen und die Reformation* (Memminger Geschichtsblätter 1968), Memmingen, 1969, pp. 44.
74   Rudolf Endres, 'Die Reformation im fränkischen Wendelstein', in Blickle (ed.), *Zugänge*, pp. 127–46. As far as I know this study by Endres is one of the very few comprehensive accounts of the introduction of the Reformation into a German village. Cf., for a parallel study, Peter Bierbrauer, 'Die Reformation in den Schaffhauser Gemeinden Hallau und Thayngen', in Blickle, *Zugänge*, pp. 21–53.
   The reason why fewer sources are cited for Wendelstein than Memmingen is that I have not taken the material from the archives myself.

altar-pieces of some size had been installed in the church just before the Reformation. The church property was administered by three provosts, elected annually by the parish community, meeting on Ascension Day in the parsonage.

By comparison with the piety of the villagers themselves, their pastoral care was not particularly good. The priest appointed in 1510, Hieronymus von Ansbach, neglected his duties so badly that his patron the Margrave had to make him resign. His successor Friedrich Santner, himself a native of Wendelstein, was very popular at first but soon found himself in financial difficulties. The pension paid to the priest who had resigned meant that Santner's income was below the sum provided by the matins endowment. He therefore introduced new surplice fees, so that part of the money for his officiating in church ceremonies was paid to himself, and cited an old land register the validity of which the community did not recognize. Over the years a futile quarrel between priest and community dragged on, brought before all kinds of different authorities but never reaching any conclusion. It ended up as a case pending in the ecclesiastical court at Eichstätt.

In this tense situation preachers from Nuremberg sometimes visited Wendelstein, held services of baptism in the German language in private houses, and made disparaging remarks about the mass. Those villagers who took an interest in the new and the sensational attended divine service in nearby Nuremberg.

The peasants of Wendelstein, like the citizens of towns, were now obviously demanding the preaching of the unadulterated gospel, for in 1523 they appointed a 'Christian preacher' whom they paid themselves by raising a levy. The talk in the village was now of 'schism'.[75] Violence was offered to the priest of the old faith, and he asked for a transfer. On 19 October 1524 Kaspar Krantz was installed as the new pastor by the district official in Schwabach. On this occasion the community representative made a speech which was printed as a pamphlet the same year and became famous. In it he informed Krantz that 'we will not recognize you as a lord, but only as a servant of the community, so that you are not to command us but we are to command you, and we require you accordingly to provide us faithfully with the Gospel and the unadulterated Word of God, nothing else, according to the truth (untainted and unsoiled by human doctrine)'.[76] He further informed Krantz that since

75   Endres, 'Wendelstein', p. 141.
76   Text in *Bulletin für bayerische Kirchengeschichte* 2 (1889), pp. 75–78, quotation p. 76. It is more easily accessible, but not quite complete, as printed in Günther Franz (ed.), *Quellen zur Geschichte des Bauernkrieges* (Ausgewählte Quellen zur deutschen Geschichte der Neuzeit, Freiherr vom Stein-Gedächtnisausgabe, vol. 2), Darmstadt, 1963, p. 315f., no. 97.

the benefice would provide an income suitable to his station, the community would no longer be liable for any other expenses 'such as offerings for souls, fees, and other such things, through which we have been led into expense'. There would be an end to the constant litigation too: Krantz was to bring any claims against the villagers in the local court, not the bishop's ecclesiastical court.

It could be said that the community was stipulating voluntary capitulation on the part of their pastor, thus claiming definitive authority over the church constitution in Wendelstein.

3   Reformation from within the community: some general conclusions

Memmingen and Wendelstein may be regarded as two typical examples of the way the Reformation was introduced into towns and villages.[77] The theological ideas of the Reformation are expressed in demands for the preaching of the unadulterated gospel, the election of pastors by the community, and the making of decisions on teaching by the community. In terms of ecclesiastical organization, it manifested itself in the wish for the pastor to live in his parish, for an inexpensive church, and for abolition of the ecclesiastical court or at least limitation of its authority.

The point of departure and centre of argument in the Reformation movement, without a doubt, was the preaching of the unadulterated gospel. The unadulterated gospel became as good as synonymous with the Reformation itself.[78] Townspeople and peasants say again and again

77   For urban areas, cf. Bernd Moeller, *Reichsstadt und Reformation*, revised new ed., Berlin, 1987 (with less emphasis than in the first edition on the importance of Zwingli in south German towns with their guild-based constitutions); Thomas A. Brady, Jr., 'In Search of the Godly City: The Domestication of Religion in the German Urban Reformation', in Ronnie Po-Chia Hsia (ed.), *The German People and the Reformation* (Ithaca, 1988), pp. 14–31; Heinrich Richard Schmidt, *Reichsstädte, Reich und Reformation. Korporative Religionspolitik 1521–1529/30* (Veröffentlichungen des Instituts für Europäische Geschichte Mainz, Abteilung für Abendländische Religionsgeschichte, vol. 122), Stuttgart, 1986. For rural areas, cf. Franziska Conrad, *Reformation in der bäuerlichen Gesellschaft. Zur Rezeption reformatorischer Theologie im Elsass* (Veröffentlichungen des Instituts für Europäische Geschichte Mainz, Abteilung für Abendländische Religionsgeschichte, vol. 116), Stuttgart, 1984; Christian Dietrich, *Die Stadt Zürich und ihre Landgemeinden während der Bauernunruhen von 1489 bis 1525*, Frankfurt am Main, 1985, pp. 125–203, and Peter Kamber, 'Bauern, Reformation und Revolten in Zürich', Ph.D. dissertation (MS), Berne, 1992; Peter Bierbrauer, *Die unterdrückte Reformation. Der Kampf der Tiroler um eine neue Kirche* (Bauer und Reformation, vol. 2), Zurich, 1993.
78   The town council of Basle stated that 'only the holy gospel and the teaching of God' was to be preached, adding that this subject area covered 'the four evangelists,

that they cannot achieve salvation without the preaching of the gospel. However, practical conclusions relating to ordinary life were increasingly being drawn from it. The concept of the unadulterated gospel called for the promotion of the common good and the practice of brotherly love, and to that extent it favoured egalitarian tendencies.[79] In this context it was also to be seen as a guide to the construction of political and legal order, thus acquiring the character of a law. Not even the Imperial Chamber Court (*Reichskammergericht*) – the most highly regarded authority among the law-courts of the Holy Roman Empire – was good enough now to settle arguments with the lords; the peasants were claiming that 'divine law . . . tells every station in life what should and should not be done'.[80] Finally, all civil and criminal law – in so far as it was not the law of the community but governed legal relations with the nobility and the church – was to be examined to see if it accorded with holy scripture.[81] Divine justice was to be expounded by theologians, in effect Reforming theologians. If an illuminating although imprecise modern comparison may be made, their function was that of judges in the German constitutional court of today. It is indicative of this approach that the list of theologians to be appointed as experts, drawn up by the peasants, was called the *Richterliste*, list of judges. It enumerates all the famous reformers: those of Wittenberg, headed by Martin Luther, the reformers of Zurich, led by Huldrych Zwingli and the reformers of Strasbourg with Matheus Zell at their head.[82]

Choice of pastors by the community itself ensured that their preaching would be in line with the scriptures, and soon it was being said throughout the land that 'it is our desire and our request, and the will and opinion of us all, that we may have the might and the power for a

St Paul, the prophets and the Bible, and *in summa* [. . .] the Old and New Testaments'. Emil Dürr and Paul Roth (eds), *Aktensammlung zur Geschichte der Basler Reformation in den Jahren 1519 bis Anfang 1534*, 4 vols, Basle, 1921–42, here vol. 1, p. 66f. There is a survey of the preaching mandates in German towns in Schmidt, *Reichsstädte*, pp. 122–8.

79   Cf. Frank Ganseuer, *Der Staat des 'gemeinen Mannes', Gattungstypologie und Programmatik des politischen Schrifttums von Reformation und Bauernkrieg* (Frankfurt am Main, 1985).

80   Emil Egli and Rudolf Schoch (eds), *Johann Kesslers Sabbata mit kleineren Schriften und Briefen* (St Gall, 1902), p. 175.

81   For instance in Mühlhausen in Thuringia, where preachers and the community committee known as the Achtmannen had established all the statutes of civic law, 'which, if they do not match the gospel, shall be set aside, and we shall consider how to proceed in difficult civic matters'. Quoted in Günther Franz, *Der deutsche Bauernkrieg* (Munich 1933), 1st edn, p. 421.

82   Several such lists were prepared. See Franz (ed.), *Quellen*, p. 149ff.

whole community to choose and select a pastor for ourselves'.[83] In cases of doubt, the community decided who actually did preach according to the scriptures.[84] Communal supervision of the clergy, replacing that of church patrons and the bishops, was also intended to ensure the residence of the pastor in his parish. The lay population was tired of pastors who held two or three benefices and seldom acted as spiritual advisers in the community, where poorly paid vicars represented them. The people were also opposed to the incorporation of their parishes with the monasteries, a practice that often meant divine service was carried out by priests who were also monks and lived in the monastic community, confining their parish duties to celebrating mass on Sunday. In the diocese of Augsburg this was the case in half of its 1000 parishes.[85]

Finally, the ecclesiastical court also came under strong pressure. Monastic and secular clerics could bring their claims to tithes and interest before the ecclesiastical court, which imposed not only financial penalties but excommunication and interdiction. Priests came within the jurisdiction of these courts, and thus did not have to appear before the legal institutions of towns or villages. Town councillors often complained that 'the priests here scorn, fail to observe and disdain the traditional edicts, statutes and laws we have made in our town concerning gaming, cards, long knives and other matters, which our citizens and inhabitants are bound to observe on pain of penalties, and thereby these priests give our people a reason to scorn our edict and laws, although they would do better to set a good example than cause discord in our community'.[86]

These references and quotations are all from the triangular area of northern Germany between Thuringia, Alsace and Austria. As a movement with deep roots in civic and rural society, however, the Reformation was by no means confined to this region. A brief glance at the rest of Europe will show that Scandinavia[87] owed the introduction of the

83 The reference is from the Twelve Articles; quoted from Peter Blickle, *Die Revolution von 1525* (Munich, 1993), 3rd edn, p. 322 (English version, *The Revolution of 1525*, London, 1992).
84 In Solothurn, for instance, the call went out for 'a whole area to meet together' and decide which confession to adopt. Quoted in Hans Haefliger, 'Die solothurnishen Volksanfragen vom Jahre 1529 über die konfessionelle Zugehörigkeit', in *Jahrbuch für Solothurnische Geschichte* 11 (1938), pp. 133–57, here p. 149.
85 Blickle, *Gemeindereformation*, p. 56.
86 Kroemer, *Memmingen*, p. 36. Three decades earlier the town was already asking the archbishop of Mainz 'to give us the liberty and permission to take those priests, clerics and other men of the cloth in our town, and outside it in the area around the church of Our Lady, who shamefully do ill and wrong, and having taken them to send them to your Grace' (op. cit.).
87 Its introduction into the duchies of Schleswig and Holstein and the kingdom of Sweden has recently been described as 'a purely princely Reformation with only

Reformation solely to the dynastic interests of its kings; there was almost no popular interest. In Spain[88] and large parts of Italy[89] the few attempts to introduce the Reformation were suppressed early and successfully by the Inquisition.[90] However, the Reformation was welcomed into the Netherlands,[91] Switzerland,[92] and above all France.

In France the first efforts to introduce reform came after 1520 in the diocese of Meaux,[93] soon setting off an intellectual discussion at court in Paris. The movement began among the more prosperous artisans, and after the 1540s spread in social terms to the urban lower classes and to peasants, and in terms of location to the Cevennes, the Dauphiné,

few, localised examples of real popular involvement'. Ole Peter Grell, 'Scandinavia', in Andrew Pettegree (ed.), *The Early Reformation in Europe* (Cambridge, 1992), pp. 94–119, here p. 97f. In Denmark, after *Herrendagen* to prepare the way in 1526, the Reformation was introduced through enormous pressure on the king's part in the parliament of 1536, and the church order of Bugenhagen established its form as Lutheran in 1537 (Pettegree, *The Early Reformation in Europe*, p. 111).

88   A. Gordon Kinder, 'Spain', in Pettegree (ed.), *The Early Reformation in Europe*, pp. 215–37.

89   Manfred E. Welti, *Kleine Geschichte der italienischen Reformation* (Schriften des Vereins für Reformationsgeschichte, vol. 193), Gütersloh, 1985, pp. 28–84 (with a survey of the development in individual Italian towns); Euan Cameron, 'Italy', in Pettegree (ed.), *The Early Reformation in Europe*, pp. 188–214. In Italy the Reformation first found adherents among the ecclesiastical and academic elites, then in noble circles, and only then in the towns, although even there it was based mainly in patrician circles. The Inquisition established itself in Italy in 1542 and expelled the comparatively small Reformation groups in several stages. Last to be obliged to leave the country, in 1601, were the Piedmontese, who had put their confession of Calvinism in writing.

90   Only in Piedmont, where heretical movements in the form of Waldensianism had already taken root, was there any longer-lasting connection between the Reformation and urban and rural society.

91   However, the Reformation made slow progress in the Netherlands because of persecution by the Spanish crown. Between 1523 and 1555, although 63 heretics were executed in the Walloon towns, 100 in Flanders, and 384 in the county of Holland, the Reformation remained in existence as an underground movement, particularly in the towns, where it was especially significant among the artisans. A comprehensive survey will be found in Alastair Duke, 'The Netherlands', in Pettegree (ed.), *Reformation in Europe*, pp. 142–65.

92   Except in the internal areas of Switzerland (the cantons of Uri, Schwyz, Unterwalden, Zug and Lucerne), the entire Swiss Confederation of the time became Protestant. Accounting for the special development of the internal Swiss cantons would take up too much space here; I intend to do so soon, in more detail, in an essay entitled 'Warum blieb die Innerschweiz katholisch?' to appear in 1995 in the proceedings of the Historischer Verein des Kantons Schwyz. Cf. Carl Pfaff, 'Pfarrei und Pfarreileben. Ein Beitrag zur spätmittelalterlichen Kirchengeschichte', in *Innerschweiz und frühe Eidgenossenschaft*, vol. 2 (Olten, 1991), pp. 203–81.

93   David Nicholls, 'France', in Pettegree (ed.), *Reformation in Europe*, pp. 120–41, here p. 123.

the south of France and Normandy.[94] Harsh persecution in Provençal villages in 1545 gave adherents of the Reformation the charisma of martyrdom, and eventually made the area 'a centre of French rural Calvinism'.[95] Pierre Chaunu thinks that responsibility for this development lay with the strength of the *pouvoir municipal* and its structural similarity to the towns of the Upper Rhine and Switzerland, and in that case it would be no coincidence that the diocese of Nîmes alone contained 172 parishes organized on the Genevan model. The south of France, as Roland Mousnier has said, could be described as 'une république protestante dans la monarchie française'.[96]

The movement taking place in thousands of European towns and villages in the early sixteenth century was unique, with neither precedent nor parallel. The process itself was far from chaotic, and there was certainly no 'wild growth of the Reformation' or 'stormy years of the Reformation', phrases that enjoyed a long period of popularity in German Reformation studies. In fact events followed the contours of the social constitution in which people were living, and can therefore be interpreted in constitutional terms. The *community as a constitutional instrument* introduced the Reformation when it selected pastors, decided on correct doctrine in disputations, and subjected priests to the jurisdiction

94   Henry Heller, *The Conquest of Poverty. The Calvinist Revolt in Sixteenth Century France*. (Studies in Medieval and Reformation Thought, vol. 35), Leiden, 1986, p. 234; Nicholls, 'France', p. 130.

95   Cameron, *Reformation*, p. 288. Cf. Menna Prestwich, 'Calvinism in France, 1559–1629', in ibid. (ed.), *International Calvinism 1541–1715* (Oxford, 1985), pp. 71–107, here p. 71. A detailed analysis of the persecutions may be found in Nicola Mary Sutherland, *The Huguenot Struggle for Recognition* (New Haven and London, 1980), pp. 10–61, esp. p. 37.

96   Roland Mousnier, 'La participation des gouvernés à l'activité des gouvernants dans la France du XVIe et du XVIIIe siécles', in *Schweizer Beiträge Zur Allgemeinen Geschichte*, 20, 1962–3, pp. 200–29. According to Mousnier, the Huguenots were treated by the king like 'un ordre du Royaume . . . les Protestants bénéficièrent d'une organisation religieuse analogue à celle du Clergé de France, d'une organisation de justice et de police . . . et même, dépassant les textes en pratique, d'une organisation politique et militaire, qui fit des Protestants plus qu'un ordre, une république protestante dans la monarchie française' (p. 214). The firmly established position of Calvinism in the south of France can be explained by the 'puissance du pouvoir municipal. Le *municipium* méridional s'est comporté comme un magistrat suisse ou rhénan.' Thus, summarizing recent French studies, Pierre Chaunu, *Eglise, culture et société. Essais sur Réforme et Contre-Réforme (1517–1620)*, Paris, 1981, p. 281f (including the statistical material). Accounts of French history which are more in the nature of reference books confirm that the sixteenth century was a high point of communal development. Cf. Jean Jacquart, 'Immobilisme et catastrophes', in Georges Duby and Armand Wallon (eds), *Histoire de la France rurale*, vol. 2, Paris, 1975, pp. 175–353, here p. 284. One the question of 'social geography', cf. Mark Greengrass, *The French Reformation* (Oxford, 1987), pp. 42–62.

of the local courts.[97] In Wendelstein this was obviously done through decisions taken by the community assembly; in Memmingen, a community committee featured in all the crucial phases of the process, from the quarrel over payment of tithes to the disputation.[98]

A church of a communal character had developed in connection with religious endowments long before Luther. Villages without their own parish churches often built chapels and endowed them out of community funds or by raising levies, so that a priest could be appointed to read mass daily and on occasion perform other liturgical ceremonies, such as baptism or giving the last sacraments to the dying. Where parishes were poorly provided for because the priest held several benefices, or because they were incorporated with monasteries, the communities often compensated with similar endowments. Endowment documents provided legal security: they specified that the priest must live locally, must not require special fees for this pastoral duties, his right of appeal to the ecclesiastical court was considerably restricted, and sometimes the content of his preaching was explicitly laid down. In short, a good many things were done that became general requirements in the Reformation and paved the way for it. The communities enforced their idea of the church through these endowments, and they could even take negligent priests to court. On Lake Constance, where quantifying data is available for a large region, a quarter of all priests were paid out of communal endowments before the Reformation.[99] These facts

97 Cameron, *Reformation*, points out such connections and sees them as a major factor in the establishment of the Reformation. 'The Reformation', runs one of his main theses, 'flattered its hearers by treating them as fit to hear and to judge the most arcane doctrines of the religious elite, and by portraying the layman as the true custodian of biblical truth' (Cameron, *Reformation*, p. 311; see also p. 420f).

98 The theory of the connection between community structures and the Reformation movement is one that I first put forward in some detail in Blickle, *Communal Revolution*. The breadth and depth of critical consideration of this theory is represented by Thomas A. Brady, Jr., 'From the Sacral Community to the Common Man: Reflections on German Reformation Studies', in *Central European History* 20 (1987), pp. 229–45, and Heinz Schilling, 'Die deutsche Gemeindereformation. Ein oberdeutsch-zwinglianisches Ereignis vor der "reformatorischen Wende" des Jahres 1525?', in *Zeitschrift für Historische Forschung* 14 (1987), pp. 325–32. I returned to the discussion with a view to elucidation in an essay: Peter Blickle, 'Eidgenossenschaften in reformatorischer Absicht oder: Wie begründet ist die Kritik an der "Gemeindereformation"?' in Guggisberg and Krodel (eds), *Reformation*, pp. 159–74, esp. 167–71.

99 Rosi Fuhrmann, *Kirche und Dorf. Religiöse Bedürfnisse und kirchliche Stiftung auf dem Lande vor der Reformation* (Quellen und Forschungen zur Agrargeschichte, vol. 40), Stuttgart, Jena and New York 1994; ibid., 'Dorfgemeinde und Pfründstiftung vor der Reformation. Kommunale Selbstbestimmungschancen zwischen Religion und Recht', in Peter Blickle and Johannes Kunisch (eds), *Kommunalisierung und Christianisierung. Voraussetzungen und Folgen der Reformation 1400–1600* (Zeitschrift

underline the opinion of a leading German legal historian who thirty years ago said, controversially, that 'the Reformation . . . merely recognized the fundamental legality of offshoots that the tree of the church had long been putting out, usually with great vigour, on the basis of the constitution and the popular piety of the late Middle Ages'.[100]

4   Complications and conclusions

The idea that the communal spirit can explain the Reformation gains support from the European perspective. It is more than coincidence that the Reformation developed in Wittenberg, Zurich and Geneva, in a German and French cultural context, and first found broad social acceptance there. In Italy, Spain and Scandinavia communities were indisputably recognized components in the theory and practice of late medieval policy;[101] in the Empire and in France they were not. King Ferdinand swept aside the claim of the imperial cities for the *ius reformandi* by arguing that 'like has no power over like', and the noble patricians in Augsburg were prompt to echo him, saying that cattle do not take cattle to pasture, nor do goats keep goats.[102] Communal government was denounced as something unnatural, and Emperor Charles V put this

für Historische Forschung, Beiheft 9), Berlin, 1989, pp. 77–112; Hans von Rütte, 'Von der spätmittelalterlichen Frömmigkeit zum reformierten Glauben. Kontinuität und Bruch in der Religionspraxis der Bauern', in *Itinera* 8, 1988, pp. 33–44 (with the quantifying data for the Lake Constance area); Bierbrauer, *Unterdrückte Reformation*, pp. 19–38.
100   Karl Siegfried Bader, *Dorfgenossenschaft und Dorfgemeinde* (Studien zur Rechtsgeschichte des mittelalterlichen Dorfes, vol. 2), Cologne and Graz, 1962, p. 183. for similar developments outside the German and Swiss area, cf. Clive Burgess and Beat Kümin, 'Penintential Bequests and Parish Regimes in late Medieval England', in *Journal of Ecclesiastical History*, 44 (1993), pp. 610–30.
101   Cf. notes 23–31 above. It can be said of Italy that the *signorie* had long been established by the time of the Reformation, and its example therefore could not take on the requisite elucidatory function. The objection is not unjustified. However, two points may explain why Italy can still be usefully incorporated in the present elucidatory theory: first, achievements of the communal phase such as the acquisition of statutory rights could not now be suppressed (cf. Giorgio Chittolini, 'Statuten und städtische Autonomie, Einleitung', in Chittolini and Willoweit (eds), *Statuten*, pp. 27–9, 33–7), and Mariarosa Cortesi, *Statuti rurali e statuti di valle* (Bergamo, 1983), p. 21. Secondly, Italy had obviously gone through the opportunities offered by communal order, and given that there was wide retention of the institutions already created, there was not necessarily any sense that the new political systems were debilitating.
102   These (and other) references in Eberhard Isenmann, 'Die Städtische Gemeinde im oberdeutsch-schweizerischen Raum (1300–1800)', in Blickle (ed.), *Landgemeinde* (as note 8), pp. 191–261, here 244f.

idea into political practice by re-establishing noble dominion in twenty-seven imperial cities through government by patricians. In France the crown was constantly intervening in the affairs of the autonomous towns, even in the late Middle Ages.[103]

The theoretical legitimation of the community theologically provided by the Reformation ensured its impact in Germany and France. The devout could not wish for a theory relying on higher dignities, and these people were devout.

The view that the communal spirit was responsible for the Reformation is also borne out by the difference between the confessions of the Reformation. Where the community played a major theological and ethical part, as in the thinking of Zwingli and Calvin, it did so against a background of the more strongly marked communal political culture of Zurich and Geneva. Luther's experience lay in the princely territorial state, or to use his own analogy in the dominion of the household, although he had spent his life in the privileged surroundings of monasteries and universities. The typically late medieval constitutional elements of community and household can be theoretically traced in these theological systems in various ways and in different sets of circumstances.[104]

IV Assessment

Leopold von Ranke stands at the beginning of historical study of the Reformation. He was convinced that it had been 'necessary to bring the hidden heart of religion out from the thousands of different chance disguises it had worn, and back into the light of day'.[105] To do that, in his view, was Martin Luther's achievement. Luther succeeded because 'the German nation . . . took on this great task'.[106] The nation meant the

103   Petit-dutaillis, *Commune françaises*, pp. 176–99.
104   For more on these connections see also Antony Black, 'Der Verborgene Ursprung der Theorie des Gesellschaftsvertrages: Die in der Entwicklung befindliche Sprache des Contractus und der Societas', in Prodi (ed.), *Glaube und Eid*, pp. 31–48. For the consequences of emphasis on the household in Protestantism, cf. Maier, *Staats- und Verwaltungslehre*, esp. 160 (central reference), and also Roland Mousnier, *Les institutions de la France sous la monarchie absolue*, vol. 1 (Paris, 1974), p. 74. On the consequences of the importance of the community see Heinrich Richard Schmidt, *Dorf und Religion. Reformierte Sittenzucht in Berner Landgemeinden der Frühen Neuzeit* (Quellen und Forschungen zur Agrargeschichte, vol. 41), Stuttgart, Jena and New York, 1995.
105   Leopold von Ranke, *Deutsche Geschichte im Zeitalter der Reformation*, 2 vols (*Sämmtliche Werke*, wols 1 and 2), 4th edn (Leipzig, 1867), here vol. 1, p. 165.
106   Ranke.

imperial princes and their subjects, 'whose inborn nature,' said Ranke, had 'a natural affinity . . . with the inner truth of Christianity'.[107] With the empirical resources available to historians, Ranke orchestrated the note first struck by Hegel, although achieving skilful alienation effects through intriguing enharmonic confusions.

Ranke's standards of reference in philosophical questions are those of a Lutheran,[108] in political questions they are basically Saxon,[109] and in theological matters they are those of Luther's late writings.[110] Franz Schnabel, expressing criticism with his usual elegance, suggests that on balance, 'nowhere . . . was Ranke's approximation to his ideal of objectivity more difficult than in his account of the German Reformation'.[111] Ranke's interpretation was long regarded as valid because of the positive foundation it provided for the present, and the academic political position of the Lutheran bourgeoisie in Germany. It was perceptibly echoed in Gerhard Ritter's studies of around 1940[112] and in reference books of the post-war period.[113]

Before the Leipzig demonstrations of 1989, the weight of history on the German political presence was expressed nowhere more strongly than on the occasion of the celebrations of Martin Luther's 500th birth-

107   Ranke, vol. 2, p. 343.
108   Ranke, according to Franz Schnabel, was 'convinced of the historical and human authority of the Lutheran movement: not only did autonomy of thought within the revealed truth of faith, as he saw it, correspond to the level of development that had been achieved in the west, but the nature of western Christianity had also paved the way for it.' Franz Schnabel, *Deutschlands geschichtliche Quellen und Darstellungen in der Neuzeit*, vol. 1: *Das Zeitalter der Reformation 1500–1550* (Stuttgart, 1931; repr. Darmstadt, 1972), p. 297f.
109   'It was obvious from his circle of interests that academically he adopted the viewpoint of *Saxon* policy . . .' Schnabel, p. 299.
110   'On religious matters, however, his account is dictated by the *conservative* spirit. He has undoubtedly glossed over the revolutionary force of the young Luther and the consequences of the new religious position.' Schnabel, p. 299.
111   Schnabel, p. 298f. For critical comment, with much material, see Walter Peter Fuchs, 'Ranke und Luther', in *Lutherjahrbuch* 45 (1978), pp. 80–100.
112   Gerhard Ritter, *Die Weltwirkung der Reformation*, 3rd edn (Darmstadt, 1969), pp. 9–15 (a work first published in 1938).
113   This is chiefly the case with respect to the concept of their structure. On the rather slight progress made in developing rival interpretations, cf. Heinrich Lutz, *Reformation und Gegenreformation*, (Oldenbourg Grundriss der Geschichte, vol. 10), Munich and Vienna, 1979, pp. 122–7. Interestingly, Lutz can add little to Schnabel's study of forty years earlier, *Deutschlands geschichtliche Quellen*. Among later interpretations, one particularly close to Ranke is by Volker Press, 'Reformatorische Bewegung und Reichsverfassung. Zum Durchbruch der Reformation – soziale, politische und religiöse Faktoren', in ibid. and Dieter Stievermann (eds), *Martin Luther. Probleme seiner Zeit* (Spätmittelalter und Frühe Neuzeit, vol. 16), Stuttgart, 1986, pp. 11–42, esp. pp. 11–14, 42.

day in 1983 – to return to our point of departure and conclude with it. They engendered a sense of community in both the German states that had not been expressed in forty years of partition, allowing at least a suspicion that the Reformation will still remain an important point of reference in the future for German history, or will become one again.

No one today would think it plausible – and Catholic Europe never did think it plausible – to interpret Protestantism and the nation state as exerting mutual influence on each other, and present them as the teleological culmination of European history. But to understand the Reformation as the theological answer to the communal spirit of the late Middle Ages makes a historical process of Protestantism, relieving it of a responsibility it cannot carry. It loses none of its character as a confession of faith, and its political and social influence is in no way diminished. In so far as Protestantism accepted communal traditions into its theology, impressing the mould of its ecclesiasticism on large areas of Europe for centuries – although Protestant enlistment of the communal spirit in its cause has not been studied in the areas of either political and social theory or of constitutional practice – the cultural significance of the Reformation for the present day calls for re-examination, both with the reference to Luther it demands and in the wider European perspective it deserves.

6

Pressures towards Confessionalization? Prolegomena to a Theory of the Confessional Age

Wolfgang Reinhard

Originally appeared as Wolfgang Reinhard, 'Zwang zur Konfessionalisierung? Prolegomena zu einer Theorie des konfessionellen Zeitalters'. *Zeitschrift für Historische Forschung*, 10 (1983), pp. 257–77.

Editor's Introduction

The ultimate impact of the Reformation cannot be assessed in purely religious terms. From the very outset of the movement the campaign to reform the church was necessarily associated with the social and political forces of the age. Indeed, the evangelical movement would not have survived without the support of the cities or without the favour of certain princes. Nor would Luther have found so rapid a following if his message had been lacking a social or political dimension. But the relationship between the reform movement and the secular world lasted long after Protestantism had become an established religion in Europe. As a consequence, any measure of the full impact of the Reformation must adopt a fairly broad range of analysis. Mindful of this, the historian Wolfgang Reinhard has developed the paradigm of confessionalization in an effort to come to terms with the problem. For confessionalization, an idea which refers to the growth of religious groups or 'confessions' in the sixteenth century, regards religion as central to the general constitution of early modern Europe. In this view, any religious change necessarily had an effect on the broader context of intellectual, cultural, social, and political relations. The evangelical movement did not just inspire a reform of the church, but affected all of early modern society, from the quality of primary education to the nature of rule. Moreover, it was not just in Lutheran lands where this occurred, but in Calvinist and Catholic regions as well. With confessionalization, the religious developments of the sixteenth century are thus understood as part of a broader process of change. And Catholicism, no less than Protestantism, participated in the process.

It might be easier to grasp what is meant by the term confessionalization if we examine the process in historical context. The German duchy of Württemberg became a Lutheran state in 1534 when duke Ulrich was restored to power and decided to introduce the Reformation. To this purpose, the duke summoned the reformer Johannes Brenz to the principality and drew up a Lutheran agenda. This was the first stage in the process of confessionalization as defined by Reinhard: a clear confession of the faith. In Württemberg, this was largely achieved with the drafting of the *Württemberg Church Order of 1536*, a Lutheran document, wherein the duke made it clear that he expected 'all of [his] preachers, pastors, and deacons to honour this without reservation, so that the aggravations of the weak and all kinds of loose talk might be prevented'. Even more theological definition followed with the *Great Church Ordinance of 1559*, which also provided the framework for the institutional church. In Württemberg, the Lutheran church evolved in a series of stages: the Reformation was first implemented through church visitations; superintendents then replaced the former diocesan officials; in 1553 a church consistory was established, a new superintendents' ordinance was issued, and a church treasury was created; and in 1559 the new church order set a final Lutheran stamp on the principality. And all of this was controlled by the duke of Württemberg. In effect, the church became an organ of state governance. The consistory, for example, was staffed by both secular and spiritual officials, with the mass of routine affairs left the ducal ministers and the doctrinal or pastoral matters left to the theologians. Using the church and its officials as yet another aspect of his rule, the duke was able to extend his range of power.

Confessionalization, as Reinhard describes it, views the Reformation as more than just one development among many in the early modern age. Religious division gave rise to an entirely new dynamic in the sixteenth century, with entirely new consequences. There was a unprecedented fusion of church and state, so much so that the powers of Europe began to determine public policy on the basis of faith. This development was most pronounced in the German lands, where the cities and territories of the realm, once loosely united under the banner of Empire, now divided amongst themselves. Political relations were henceforth determined by confessional sympathy: Lutheran powers, for example, might join together to meet the common threat presented by the Catholics and the Calvinists. In a similar fashion, domestic decisions were taken with religious convictions in mind. Ultimately, the entire political landscape was affected by this process of confessionalization. The continent of Europe, as a result, became divided over religion. Domestically, on the other hand, the process of confessionalization encouraged a degree of order and control rarely experienced in European history. The sovereign was now in command of both the church and the state; and what is more, as the church ordinances pronounced with regularity, God had placed him in office. The ruler now had a divine obligation to police the moral and spiritual welfare of his subjects. Theoretically, nothing was beyond the rule of state, neither the quality of public behaviour nor the character of private religious belief. And it is with this development in mind that Reinhard makes mention of Gerhard Oestreich's theory of social disciplining. For confessionalization, as much as any other development of the period, provided the state with greater control over the subject population.

Wolfgang Reinhard has developed the concept of confessionalization in an effort to come to terms with the full impact and meaning of the reform movements of the sixteenth century. Confessionalization is thus not a theory which can only be applied to the German territories or the Protestant Reformation. Reinhard's own research often prefers to draw on Catholic rather than Protestant examples in order to bear out his case, and the analysis has been applied to all of European history, not just the history of a single people or a single land. But the concept is particularly suited to an analysis of the Reformation as it developed in the German lands, where political division provided an ideal setting for the onset of confessional plurality.

Pressures towards Confessionalization? Prolegomena to a Theory of the Confessional Age

Wolfgang Reinhard

There is no particular need for me to justify this attempt to use the findings of two previous studies in ecclesiastical history[1] to cast further light on the development of the early modern political system. On the contrary: if I did not do so I would incur criticism for having paid too little attention to the political aspect in those studies, for in Europe of the sixteenth and seventeenth centuries, our subject here, ecclesiastical and political action still coincided if not entirely then to a considerable extent. Consequently, in answering the questions, 'When, how and why were large social groups in the form of the new churches created by "confessionalization"?', it becomes immediately obvious that political ambition at the time had little option but to take part in the process. The popular notion that the supra-confessional neutrality of the state power was a necessary or even sufficient condition for the further growth of that power will prove anachronistic: a retrospective projection of circumstances that prevailed at a later date. Instead, 'confessionalization' turns out to be an early phase of modern European state formation, a phase found with remarkable regularity.

This fact means that our general subject – 'Political opportunities in the Holy Roman Empire' – will not be directly addressed here, although it will appear all the more effective approached indirectly. I am not discussing the Empire itself, but the territories within it and the other 'states' of Europe. However, the 'confessionalization' of German territories sometimes does seem to differ from that of those other European 'states'; despite uniformity of substance, the particular circumstance of being part of the Empire makes itself incidentally felt. In this way, then, I am in fact taking our main subject into account: the general 'confessionalization' of these territories was not only fundamental to *politics in the Empire*, it also determined the sphere of action of *Imperial policy*.

1 W. Reinhard, 'Gegenreformation als Modernisierung? Prolegomena zu einer Theorie des konfessionellen Zeitalters', in *Archiv für Reformationsgeschichte* 68 (1977), pp. 226–251; ibid., 'Konfession und Konfessionalisierung in Europa', in W. Reinhard (ed.), *Bekenntnis und Geschichte* (Munich 1981), pp. 165–189. As I have been asked to summarize my thoughts on the subject so far, I hope I may be forgiven for quoting relatively frequently from my own works.

I am arguing with what, to a historian, is a disquietingly high degree of generalization, although I do not resort to formal sociological models here. However, when one is looking for the 'predominant tendencies' of a period the level of abstraction will inevitably be greater than in other studies. I do not mean to claim higher status for my work; I merely observe that in such a case partial falsification is easier but final falsification less likely than in others. I could easily cite examples contradicting many of my own general statements.[2] I think, however, that in the absence of proof to the contrary such cases may be regarded as deviations from the 'normal course' of events, deviations which require and are capable of a special explanation.[3] I hope to show that there was indeed such a 'normal course' of events, and that it was rather different from what has previously been widely assumed.

A prerequisite for my theses here is the revision of traditional scholarly ideas which have long ceased to pass unchallenged, and of their traditional division of history into periods, which has moulded society's awareness of history in general and is thus prejudicial to research.[4]

Thesis 1: Parallels between the 'Reformation' and the 'Counter-Reformation'[5]

The idea that the Reformation and the Counter-Reformation were irreconcilable opposites and consecutive historical phases can no longer be supported. It now seems more accurate to distinguish between a relatively short-lived 'evangelical movement' which does, however, represent the culmination of two centuries of efforts to introduce reform, and a process of 'confessionalization' lasting around another two centuries, beginning as early as the 1520s and

2 For instance, see J.-M. Valentin (ed.), *Gegenreformation und Literatur. Beiträge zur interdisziplinären Erforschung der katholischen Reformbewegung* (Amsterdam, 1979); after a number of articles in this volume confirming the sympathy felt in the Catholic principalities for Counter-Reformation literature one suddenly comes (pp. 271–98) upon an essay by E. M. Szarota on 'Boleslaus der Kühne und der Hl. Stanislaus auf den Bühnen des 17. Jahrhunderts', illustrating the glorification on stage of ecclesiastical resistance to princely autocracy.

3 In the exceptional cases cited in note 2, for instance, the plays were still intellectually rooted in the monarch-making phase of Catholic political theory; two-thirds of the dramas studied, moreover, were from Poland, a special case politically, and two derived from the Benedictine order, which tended to be less enthusiastic in support of the Counter-Reformation.

4 Today, for instance, the idea that 1789 is the epoch-making date in French history is rightly questioned; the idea goes back to the ideology of the revolutionaries, and has become established in the archives.

5 When no new sources are quoted, all examples cited and extensive discussion of them are to be found in W. Reinhard, 'Gegenreformation'.

coming to an end in the early eighteenth century. The important point is that the process occurred to a great and to some extent chronologically parallel degree in all three confessional areas: Calvinism, Catholicism and Lutheranism.

Both parts of that dialectical pair of opposites, the 'middle-class and progressive Reformation' and the 'feudal and reactionary Counter-Reformation', need correction. The 'modernity' of the 'Reformation', once so readily cited, has long been in doubt, or at least the concept has been considerably restricted by precise statements of what it actually means. Recently it has also been discovered that in many ways the 'Counter-Reformation' was more 'modern' than was previously thought (and often still is). Not only do the forward-looking features of both Reformation and Counter-Reformation often correspond, they were also linked by a common past in the shape of two hundred years of attempts to reform the church. As a Catholic, Hubert Jedin may have felt some partisan satisfaction in establishing that reforms in the old church preceded the Protestant Reformation,[6] but there is no reason to suppose that Pierre Chaunu, a Protestant, felt the same in simply classifying the 'Reformation' and the 'Counter-Reformation' as the second and third in a series of *réformes.*[7]

The pressure of population in the 'crowded world', followed by the economic crises and catastrophic plagues of the fourteenth century, the growing importance of towns with the consequent rise of the money economy and education of the laity, to sum up the elements involved: increasing social division of labour and the complexity of differentiated lifestyles now that large numbers of people were living together, severe crises in the political and ecclesiastical system, in particular schisms and the extensive failure of the reforming councils to which they gave rise, and finally new trends in intellectual life that were at least partially connected with these other phenomena, even if we do not know exactly how – all this led to more and more attempts between the thirteenth and sixteenth centuries to reform the church and the secular world.

From today's viewpoint, then, the supposedly irreconcilable opposites of the 'Reformation' and the 'Counter-Reformation' seem closer than ever in origin and character. None the less, the early 'evangelical movement' does occupy a special position in this context, entailing as it did

6   H. Jedin, *Katholische Reformation oder Gegenreformation? Ein Versuch zur Klärung der Begriffe nebst einer Jubiläumsbetrachtung über das Trienter Konzil* (Lucerne, 1948).
7   P. Chaunu, *Les temps réformes, Histoire religieuse et système de civilisation, La crise de la chrétienté, L'éclatement 1250–1550* (Paris, 1975). Cf. also S. Ozment, *The Age of Reform 1250–1550. An Intellectual and Religious History of Late Medieval and Reformation Europe* (New Haven and London, 1980).

unusually energetic innovation and modernizing tendencies. However, that was not the end of it. Once the princes took a hand in the 1520s and the 'Reformation' began to be organized by secular authorites, then for all the innovations one cannot help detecting conservativism in the measures adopted, and an approach to the behaviour of the opposite side.[8] The *Confessio Augustana* itself, marking the start of evangelical confessionalization, was careful to dissociate itself from 'the left', the radical currents in the evangelical movement, and made a deliberate approach to the forces of the old church.[9] And anyone hoping to trace the principle of progress found in radical Calvinism in more conservative Lutheranism will discover that the Reformed church too was overwhelmingly introduced into the Empire under princely authority, with the consequences one might expect. Although Calvinism, on the other hand, developed autonomously and in the context of political opposition in western Europe, it was as the result of historical contingency, not an expression of its alleged 'nature': Calvin's political doctrines and correspondence leave no room for doubt on that point.

In fact studying the history of political ideas to find the origins of the sovereignty of the people and the right to resist will show how little such developments depend on the supposed qualities of any particular confession, and on the other hand how important the political circumstances involved always were. The justification of resistance derived from a crisis in the usually rather conservative Lutheran confession; Calvinistic monarch-making was followed by the Catholic variety when the cause of the old church seemed to be endangered by the monarchy, until both confessions went over to supporting absolutism as soon as it became a guarantee of their confessional rights. Consequently we find both supporters of 'the sovereignty of the people' and absolutist theoreticians among the Jesuits, and neither friends

---

8 The term 'evangelical movement(s)' to describe the open-ended situation up to about 1525, in contrast to the 'Reformation' established by the authorities, has recently enjoyed new popularity, particularly in a remarkable article by H.-J. Goertz, 'Aufstand gegen den Priester. Antiklerikalismus und reformatorische Bewegungen', in P. Blickle (ed.), *Bauer, Reich und Reformation, Festschrift für Günther Franz* (Stuttgart, 1982), pp. 182–209. This does not of course imply a revival of the idea of the 'alleged end of the Lutheran Reformation as a spontaneous popular movement', refuted by F. Lau in 1959 and more recently in W. Hubatsch (ed.), *Wirkungen der deutschen Reformation bis 1555* (Wege der Forschung 203), Darmstadt, 1967, pp. 68–100. Today we know more about both the emergence of apparently 'spontaneous' movements and the complicated interaction between mass feeling and the authorities.
9 Cf. W. Reinhard, 'Das Augsburger Bekenntnis im politischen Zusammenhang', in H. Jesse (ed), *Das Augsburger Bekenntnis in drei Jahrhunderten* (Weissenhorn, 1980), pp. 32–50.

nor foes of the order lack evidence to cite in support of their own interests.[10]

The Jesuit order, still rightly regarded as one of the most important exponents of the new Catholicism, is a particularly good example of modernity in the supposedly 'reactionary Counter-Reformation'. Compared to the traditional monastic orders, the Society of Jesus was positively revolutionary; not for nothing were their opponents such conservative churchmen as Carafa, later Pope Paul IV.[11] And it was no coincidence that attempts to found a parallel order of Jesuit nuns failed; it would have been intolerable to see the ecclesiastical emancipation of women added to the innovations introduced by the male Jesuits. The founding of a *new* order in the shape of the Jesuits was startling in itself; previously there had been, at the most, reforms of the old orders. The elitist recruitment policy of the Jesuits was new, and so was the extremely careful training they gave, in which spiritual exercises occupied a central position. Although the content of those exercises may have been anything but 'modern', the institution itself was one of fascinating modernity in three ways. First, the internalization of the group's central values was planned and organized with considerable psychological acuity. Second, the process concentrated on individuals in an entirely new way. Third, individual internalization made it possible to dispense with traditional forms of monastic community life such as choral prayer and seclusion, and allowed the Jesuits unrestricted activity in the world. It is not surprising that such an order was particularly famous for its schools, and significantly enough there are parallels here with evangelical achievements, which have led to accusations of 'plagiarism'.

If we add to all this the sometimes disquietingly modern economic organization of the Jesuits, we come to an area – the economy – where the reactionary character of early modern Catholicism also seemed to be established beyond doubt. In the matter of credit Reformation doctrine may have been more honest, but despite occasional attacks of rigour the casuistry of the old faith could deal just as well with financial transactions; perhaps even better, since Catholicism was more elastic. The papacy itself had been the major financial power in the Middle Ages and remained one of the most important borrowers, with a financial system superior to any western European and German parallels. Today the increasing economic backwardness of Catholic southern Europe is

10   Cf. H. Fenske, D. Mertens, W. Reinhard and K. Rosen, *Geschichte der politischen Ideen von Homer bis zur Gegenwart* (Königstein, 1981), pp. 225–47.
11   Cf., finally, P. A. Quinn, 'Ignatius von Loyola and Gian Pietro Carafa: Catholic Reformers at Odds', in *Catholic Historic Review* 67 (1981), pp. 386–400.

not blamed on the Counter-Reformation but on genuine economic factors, such as an altered structure of demand and different production costs.

The undisputed theological oppositions, then, were by no means expressed in practical life in the form of consistent structural divergencies between the large religious communities. On the contrary: one might venture to say that irreconcilable theological positions actually led to the development of largely similar answers to problems, particularly the fundamental problem of ensuring confessional identity, on the basis of a common tradition and the actual situation. Thus closely related processes of discrimination and discipline among the adherents of the various religious tendencies led to the formation of confessions: large, new, self-contained groups. Confessionalization began with the evangelical visitations of the 1520s and various inadequate measures taken at the same time by Catholicism,[12] and ended with the forcible establishment of confessional homogeneity in France in 1685, the guaranteeing of the Protestant character of the English monarchy between 1688 and 1707, and the expulsion of the Salzburg Protestants in 1731.[13] It has long been recognized that confessionalization in the Empire by no means ended in 1648.[14]

Thesis 2:   The methodical establishment of large new groups[15]

The self-contained nature of the large new group called a 'confession' was achieved in Calvinism, Catholicism and Lutheranism by the following methods:

1   A return to clear theoretical ideas;
2   The dissemination and establishment of new standards;

12   In particular the Mühlberg reforming convention of 1522 and the Regensburg 'Reformation' of 1524; cf. G. Pfeilschifter (ed.), *Acta Reformationis Catholicae*, vol. 1 (Münster, 1959). This work does not deal so extensively with the term 'confessionalization' as does W. Eberhard, *Konfessionsbildung und Stände in Böhmen 1478–1530* (Munich 1981), but confines itself to the 'post-Reformation' period when activity by the secular authorities predominated.
13   Cf. F. Ortner, *Reformation, katholische Reform und Gegenreformation im Erzstift Salzburg* (Salzburg and Munich, 1981), emphasizing (perhaps over-emphasizing) the political background.
14   Cf. H. Jedin. 'Die Reichskirche der Schönbornzeit', in H. Jedin (ed.), *Kirche des Glaubens, Kirche der Geschichte*, vol. 1 (Freiburg, 1966), pp. 455–68; M. Becker-Huberti, *Die tridentinische Reform im Bistum Münster unter Fürstbischof Christoph Bernhard von Galen (1650–1678)* (Münster, 1978).
15   Where no new sources are cited, all examples and more extensive discussion of them are to be found in W. Reinhard, 'Konfession'.

3   *Propaganda, and the taking of measures against counter-propaganda;*
4   *Internalization of the new order through education and training;*
5   *The disciplining of adherents (in the narrower sense);*
6   *The practice of ritual;*
7   *The influencing of language.*

I shall try to give a brief account of these different methods and the variations on them.

1   The clarity of firm convictions and the stern pleasure of taking practical decisions could be acquired as basics only if a desire for pacification and compromise were regarded as an obstacle to be overcome. This was achieved theoretically with the construction of firm confessions of faith; hence the key function of the *confessio* at this time. In addition, the meaning of the term 'confession' was extended in the process of 'confessionalization': from denoting a personal act of confession, it became a term for the organization consisting of those who confessed to the faith. However, the positive achievement of establishing confessions of faith did not mean all was won, particularly in the religious confusion prevalent in the Empire; a negative achievement, the eradication of confessional obscurities, was also required. A typical example is the lay chalice, the receiving of communion in both forms, an issue not of theology but of church discipline. In view of the apparently small theological risk involved, it had been permitted in Jülich-Cleve and Bavaria, but soon turned out to be a vehicle of the new faith, and so although the practice had only just been authorized in Bavaria, it was immediately suppressed again.
2   The clarification of religious positions was less of a deciding factor than the subsequent dissemination and institutional establishment of the new norms. People in positions of authority – theologians, pastors, teachers, doctors and midwives, and sometimes the secular authorities – were examined and bound to maintain the new standards; with increasing frequency, they had to take an actual oath. As for the institutions, the hierarchical apparatus of the old church proved less of a help than a hindrance because of its unwieldy nature and initially unsuitable personnel. After the Council of Trent, however, spiritual and institutional innovations were introduced, and in the longer term ensured the survival of the old church, now regenerated as a confession. The decisions of the Council and the Popes were put into practice by nuncios working together, not always harmoniously, with new orders of the stamp of the Jesuits. Provincial and diocesan synods to be held regularly served the promulgation and specification of new norms; the

Milan of Carlo Borromeo was the most successful example. Missions spread the new spirit among the people. As well as the nuncios, another method of control was the regular visits paid by bishops to Rome to make their reports. The churches of the Reformation themselves developed no similarly rigid organization; consequently the new standards here – and not only here – were frequently carried out with the aid of the political apparatus of a city or a principality.

3   Propaganda and censorship went hand in hand, and were based on the deliberate extension of book printing.[16] The theology of controversy was suited to the needs of the confessional struggle. Group norms were to be reinforced and the errors of adversaries denounced by constant repetition. In addition there were forms of indoctrination more suited to ordinary people: catechisms, sermons and sacred music, and in Catholicism plays as well as such cult forms as processions, pilgrimages, and the veneration of relics and the saints.[17] Censors made sure that no incorrect ideas were allowed in. The Roman and Spanish indexes of prohibited books are the best known examples of censorship, but it was also expressly encouraged by the Lutheran Formula of Concord and was practised in Calvinism.

4   All the measures mentioned, however, were only preliminaries to the internalization of the new norms in the process of socialization: ultimately, that was the deciding factor. Every confession expanded and controlled its educational facilities so as to convey 'correct' ideas to younger generations in the group. The many school regulations published place religious education and religious exercises, with the control

16   Bavaria even had a large organization for the distribution of spiritual writings free of charge, the 'Güldene Almose', run by the Jesuits with princely support from 1614–1773, and apparently imitated in Augsburg-Dillingen, Constance, Lucerne, Würzburg, Cologne, Graz and Vienna. Cf. D. Breuer, 'Besonderheiten der Zweisprachigkeit im katholischen Oberdeutschland während des 17. Jahrhunderts', in Valentin, *Gegenreformation*, p. 148. Cf. in this connection L. Baldacchini, *Bibliografia delle stampe populari religiose del XVI – XVII secolo*, Bibliotheche Vaticana, Alessandrina, Estense, Florence, 1980. I have not been able to consult R. Kastner, *Geistlicher Rauffhandel. Form und Funktion der illustrierten Flugblätter zum Reformationsjubiläum 1617 in ihrem historischen und publizistischen Kontext* (Frankfurt and Berne, 1982). The political dimension of a propaganda campaign in the Reformed churches was already perceptible in England under Henry VIII; cf. G. R. Elton, *Policy and Police. The Enforcement of the Reformation in the Age of Thomas Cromwell* (Cambridge, 1972), pp. 171–266.

17   Cf. the various contributions to Valentin, *Gegenreformation*, and D.-R. Moser, *Verkündigung durch Volksgesang. Studien zur Liedpropaganda und -katechese der Gegenreformation* (Berlin and Munich, 1981), which makes it clear that the sacred 'folksong' was far from being 'spontaneous' but instead was the product of deliberate religious propaganda, and as such was moulded by the specific theological directives of the orders concerned.

of moral and religious conduct, at the centre of their concern.[18] Most
striking of all, however, is the founding of many new educational institutions at this period. The rapid spread of Jesuit colleges in Europe
helped to maintain Catholic elites.[19] Even more important, however, was
the training of reliable teachers to spread doctrine; for this purpose
Catholic priests' seminaries were founded, as well as additional central
training institutes in Rome such as the Collegium Germanicum.[20] In
the evangelical churches, Wittenberg had almost spontaneously
become the centre of education, but was then superseded by Geneva,
where the training of future generations of preachers to cover the whole
of Europe was systematically organized. Subsequently many universities were founded, to prevent members of the local group from going
abroad to be educated and to attract outstanding minds in conformity
with the system. In the Empire and the Netherlands in the confessional
age, twelve Catholic, twelve Lutheran and eight Reformed universities
were founded, and five more Reformed universities in Switzerland
alone.[21]

5   Besides educational policy, however, there were other disciplinary
procedures available to create a confessionally homogeneous group.
First of all, minorities were expelled, from the Italian Protestants of the
sixteenth century to the Salzburg Protestants of the eighteenth century.
Then the outside contacts of the group were cut off, and it was limited
to internal contacts, a process that reinforced and went hand in hand
with the deliberate fostering of hostility to 'others'. The central instru-

18   On Evangelical Germany, besides an older work by G. Mertz, *Das Schulwesen
der deutschen Reformation* (Heidelberg, 1902), see among others H. A. Stempel,
Melanchthons pädagogisches Wirken (Bielefeld, 1979), although Stempel emphasizes
the scholarly more than the political aspects; also G. Strauss, *Luther's House of
Learning. Indoctrination of the Young in the German Reformation* (Baltimore, 1978),
although Strauss's findings for the case of Strasbourg have been refuted by J. M.
Kittelson, 'Successes and Failures in the German Reformation: The Report from
Strasbourg', in *Archiv für Reformationsgeschichte* 73 (1982), pp. 153–75. According
to Kittelson, the effect of ecclesiastical and educational efforts to discipline pupils
was greater than supposed by Strauss.
19   Cf. G. P. Brizzi (ed.), *La 'Ratio Studiorum', Modelli culturali e pratiche educative dei
Gesuiti in Italia tra Cinque e Seicento* (Rome, 1981).
20   Cf. P. Schmidt, *Das Collegium Germanicum in Rom und die Germaniker in der
nachtridentinischen Kirchengeschichte* (Library of the German Historical Institute,
Rome), (Tübingen, 1983).
21   On this point see among others K. Hengst, *Jesuiten an Universitäten und Jesuite-
nuniversitäten* (Munich, 1981), on Ingolstadt, Cologne, Trier, Mainz, Würzburg,
Freiburg, Erfurt and Heidelberg on the one hand, and Dillingen, Paderborn, Mol-
sheim Münster, Osnabrück and Bamberg on the other. See also U. Im Hof, *Formen
der Sozialdisziplinierung in der reformierten Schweiz vom 16. bis zum 18. Jahrhundert*,
Ms., 1981.

ment of discipline, however, was the visitation, when individual communities and institutions were subjected to rigorous examination; in contrast to earlier times, precise records of the visitations were kept. Where there was no superior authority, as in the autonomous Reformed communities, the presbytery or consistory of pastors and elders acted as a functional equivalent, and had indeed been founded expressly for purposes of religious and moral supervision. In fact social control by the local community itself may have been even more effective than control by the Spanish Inquisition or the Bavarian 'police'.

6 In view of their importance for the coherence of the group, rituals also had to be subject to discipline, initially exercised through checks on participation. Lists of communicants were kept, and registers of baptisms, marriages and funerals, not for statistical purposes but to control life in the confession. Furthermore, rites that might serve as the distinguishing marks of a confession were deliberately encouraged or suppressed. In the Catholic church the lay chalice was regarded as heretical,[22] while the cult of the sacraments, the saints and holy pictures was seen as the quintessence of Catholicism. In the evangelical churches the removal of holy pictures, with rejection of the remants of the old liturgy of the mass and exorcism in the baptism service were salient features of the transition from Lutheranism to Calvinism. Finally, the initially disconcerting observation that discussions of faith, quite usual even in the confessional period, survived because they had actually become a ritual – a ritual of self-validation – is symptomatic of the way in which the fronts had hardened.[23] For reasons of discrimination, even confessionally neutral achievements by other confessions were rejected: the papal reform of the calendar of 1582 was not acceptable to evangelicals in the Empire until 1699.[24]

7 Finally, the desire for confessional identity extended to language and its regulation in conformity with the group – a subject into which little

22 In the Vatican Archive, Sec. Brev. 460, 43, there is a papal dispensation of 1610 permitting the admission to a knightly order of a candidate 'non obstante quod eius mater sub utraque specie communicet'.
23 Cf. in particular J. Tazbir, 'Die Religionsgespräche in Polen', in G. Müller (ed.), *Die Religionsgespräche der Reformationszeit* (Gütersloh, 1980), pp. 127–43, and other contributions to this volume.
24 Cf. F. Kaltenbrunner, *Beiträge zur Geschichte der Gregorianischen Kalenderreform* (Vienna, 1880); ibid., 'Der Augsburger Kalenderstreit', in *Mitteilungen des österreichischen Instituts für Geschichtsforschung* I (1880), pp. 497–540; F. Stieve, *Der Kalenderstreit des 16. Jahrhunderts in Deutschland* (K. Bay. Ak. d. W., Abh. Bd. 15/3), Munich, 1880, pp. 1–98; H. Gutzwiller, 'Die Einführung des Gregorianischen Kalenders in der Eidgenossenschaft in konfessioneller, volkskundlicher, staatsrechtlicher und wirtschaftspolitischer Schau', in *Zeitschrift für schweizerische Kirchengeschichte* 72 (1978), pp. 54–73.

research has yet been done. In Geneva people's first names were subject to confessional regulations. The traditional predominance of New Testament names was maintained, but certain names of saints and other typically Catholic first names were forbidden, and the well-known increase in the use of Old Testament names came in. Among Catholics, however, the old custom of choosing saints' names was established by law in 1566.

Regardless of theological opposition and the different instruments employed by different confessions, the process of confessionalization went ahead with remarkable uniformity and simultaneity. It is also noticeable that it involved a good deal of participation by the secular authorities, and indeed many of the most effective measures could never have been introduced without authoritative secular cooperation. Confessionalization was by no means in state hands only in Lutheran areas; it was the same in Calvinistic areas, although such an idea theoretically ran counter to the autonomous constitutions of the churches, and in the Catholic area, where in theory there was no lack of ecclesiastical organization to justify state intervention. The pioneering role of leading ecclesiastical groups cannot of course be denied – for instance, the strict self-discipline of such autonomous sects as the Hutterites[25] was closely related and characteristic of the period.[26] But the efforts towards confessionalization already made by noble elites[27] had a political dimension,[28] even if they were carried out in conflict with the 'power of the state' – or perhaps for that very reason. If we turn to the confessional policies of urban oligarchies, for instance in Switzerland,[29] there is an unmistakable similarity to measures undertaken by princely authorities.[30] There were times when a tolerant religious policy was in the

25   Cf. J. Runzo, 'Hutterite Communal Discipline, 1529–1565', in *Archiv für Reformationsgeschichte* 71 (1980), pp. 160–79, and on the present situation W. S. F. Pickering, 'Hutterites and Problems of Persistence and Social Control in Religious Communities', in *Archives de sciences sociales des religions* 22 (1977), pp. 75–92.

26   Cf. H. Lehmann, *Das Zeitalter des Absolutismus. Gottesgnadentum und Kriegsnot* (Stuttgart, 1980).

27   G. Heiss, 'Konfession, Politik und Erziehung. Die Landschaftsschulen in den nieder- und innerösterreichischen Ländern vor dem Dreissigjährigen Krieg', in *Bildung, Politik und Gesellschaft* (Wiener Beiträge zur Geschichte der Neuzeit 5), Vienna, 1978, pp. 13–83.

28   Cf. Eberhard, *Konfessionsbildung*.

29   Cf. Im Hof, *Sozialdisziplinierung*.

30   A. Endress, 'Phasen der Konfessionsbildung – Aufgezeigt am Beispiel der Reichsstadt Wimpfen im Zeitraum von 1523–1635', in H. Rabe, H. Molitor and H.-C. Rublack (eds), *Festgabe für E. W. Zeeden* (Münster, 1976), pp. 289–326; Endress establishes the fact that the end product of the process was government of the churches by the secular authority.

interests of leading civic groups, as with the council of the imperial city of Augsburg[31] or the 'Regents' of the Netherlands.[32] However, tolerant communities were politically weak in the sixteenth and seventeenth centuries; the emergent modern state required confessional intolerance as a prerequisite for the development of its power.

Thesis 3: Confessionalization in the service of political growth

If the emergent 'modern state' clearly encouraged confessionalization, the reason lay in three crucial advantages it thereby gained for its further development:

1 *Reinforcement of its national or territorial identity, both at home and abroad;*
2 *Control over the church as a powerful rival of the new state power, and not least over church property as an important means of power;*
3 *Discipline and homogenization of its subjects, for 'confessionalization' was the first phase of what Gerhard Oestreich has called the absolutist 'imposition of social discipline'.[33] It was therefore necessary for the politically ambitious to pursue a policy of confessionalization.*

1   After the general late medieval process of differentiation described above, both the European 'Corpus Christianum' and the Empire disintegrated into a multiplicity of churches, states and territories. However, the mere fact of their multiplicity brought these new structures under the pressure of competition, not least in justifying their existence. The process of differentiation did not initially reflect the present state of affairs, where autonomous sub-systems of 'politics', 'religion', 'the economy' and so forth are found side by side and it is usual for an individual to be affiliated to more than one of them; instead, the new sub-systems maintained the claim to totality of the old, all-embracing system, and membership of one excluded membership of any other. In other words, the religious concept of the time extended to politics, and conversely the political concept extended to the church and religion. The early modern state could thus not develop entirely independently of the confessional issue, but only on the basis of 'a fundamental consensus

31   Cf. F. Roth, *Augsburgs Reformationsgeschichte*, 4 vols (Munich, 1901–11), *passim*.
32   Cf. E. Hassinger, 'Wirtschaftliche Motive und Argumente für religiöse Duldsamkeit im 16. und 17. Jahrhundert', in E. W. Zeeden (ed.), *Gegenreformation* (*Wege der Forschung* 311), Darmstadt, 1973, pp. 332–56.
33   G. Oestreich, 'Strukturprobleme des europäischen Absolutismus', in ibid., *Geist und Gestalt des frühmodernen Staates* (Berlin, 1969), pp. 179–97.

on religion, the church and culture embracing the authority and its subjects alike'.[34]

Consequently Catholicism in Portugal,[35] Spain[36] and after some hesitation also in France[37] became as much a constituent part of national political identity as Protestantism in England, a country that today still sometimes promotes its image as a 'Protestant nation'.[38] Significantly, confessional uncertainty was not settled in Sweden until national identity seemed threatened by the succession to the throne of the Polish Sigismund Vasa. Only then, in 1593, did the Swedes accept the *Confessio Augustana*; in 1595 the Catholic national shrine of Vadstena was closed and Catholics were forbidden in the country.[39]

Recourse to confessionalism was almost more important to the territories of the Empire, for they had no national legitimate basis for political independence. The confession as a means of political demarcation is a particularly interesting phenomenon where even the dynastic factor was absent, in rival lines of the same house in Saxony and Hesse, and in the case of the Wittelsbachs of Bavaria and the Palatinate. Can it be historical coincidence that confessional conflicts regularly took place in these very areas, between different branches of the same dynasties? Even territories of the same confession used to discriminate between their national churches in terms of organization, worship and some-

34   H. Schilling, *Konfessionskonflikt und Staatsbildung. Eine Fallstudie über das Verhältnis von religiösem und sozialem Wandel in der Frühneuzeit am Beispiel der Grafschaft Lippe* (Gütersloh, 1981), p. 34.

35   Cf. Luis de Camões, *Os Lusiadas* VII, 14.

36   Cf. F. López de Gomara, *Historia General de las Indias* (Biblioteca de autores españoles Vol. 22), Madrid, 1877, repr. 1946, p. 156; dedication to Emperor Charles V, 1552. In this context, on the significance of the political and deliberate integration of the inquisition into state and nation cf., for instance, H. Kamen, *The Spanish Inquisition* (London, 1965), and B. Benassar, 'L'Inquisition espagnole au service de l'état', in *Histoire* (1979), pp. 35–46.

37   Although today we may seek the roots of the modern idea of the state and of ideological tolerance in the Huguenot Wars, the majority of the French upper classes of the early modern period certainly saw their political identity in the unity of faith and the kingdom as finally established by Louis XIV. Cf. R. Klienmann, 'Changing Interpretations of the Edict of Nantes: The Administrative Aspect, 1643–1661', in *French Historical Studies* 4 (1978), pp. 541–71.

38   Cf. C. Z. Wiener, 'The Beleaguered Isle. A Study of Elizabethan and Early Jacobean Anti-Catholicism', in *Past and Present* 51 (1971), pp. 27–62; or W. Haller, *Foxe's Book of Martyrs and the Elect Nation* (London, 1963); or J. P. Kenyon, *The Popish Plot* (London, 1972).

39   Cf. P. G. Lindhardt, *Skandinavische Kirchengeschichte seit dem 16. Jahrhundert* (Die Kirche in ihrer Geschichte 3/M 3), Göttingen, 1982, p. 281f; G. Schwaiger, *Die Reformation in den nordischen Ländern* (Munich, 1962), p. 142f; O. Garstein, *Rome and the Counter-Reformation in Scandinavia until the Establishment of the Congregatio de Propaganda Fide in 1622*, vol. 2: 1583–1622 (Oslo, 1980).

times doctrine.[40] Catholic princes had few such opportunities, but they tried to do the same by setting up 'national bishoprics'.

Early confessional demarcation in Switzerland, reaching a temporary conclusion as early as the Kappel Peace of 1531, is also extremely typical. Thereafter, confessionalization was almost established. Obviously early territorialization made early confessionalization possible,[41] just as confessionalization, conversely, reinforced the drawing of territorial boundaries.

The exclusion of hostile influences was the negative basis of new political and religious identity. Besides the notorious restrictions on mobility[42] and the marriages of subjects, fears of loyalty to foreign powers loomed large. John Locke still saw Catholicism as a danger because Catholics owed obedience to a foreign prince, the Pope.[43] The concept of the papacy as a state among other states, encountered here as elsewhere, is extremely typical of the ideas of the time.[44] In the Empire, the equivalent was the efforts of Brandenburg 'territorialism' to keep the archbishop of Cologne, who bore responsibility for Cleves, away from the city at all costs.[45]

40 Schilling, *Konfessionskonflikt*, p. 367.

41 P. Stadler, *Eidgenossenschaft und Reformation*, Lecture at the Historisches Kolleg, Munich, September 1982, in H. Angermeier's colloquium *Säkulare Aspekte der deutschen Geschichte im 16. Jahrhundert*; see also esp. E. Walder, 'Reformation und moderner Staat', in *Archiv des historischen Vereins des Kantons Bern* 64/65 (1980), pp. 441–583.

42 Cf. J. Stoye, 'Reisende Engländer im Europa des 17. Jahrhunderts und ihre Reisemotive', in A. Maczak and H. J. Teuteberg (eds), *Reiseberichte als Quellen europäischer Kulturgeschichte* (Wolfenbüttel, 1982), pp. 131–33.

43 J. Locke, *Epistola de tolerantia* (London, 1689).

44 Cf. P. Prodi, *Il sovrano pontefice. Un corpo e due anime: la monarchia papale nella prima età moderna* (Bologna, 1982).

45 Cf. D. Coenen, *Die katholische Kirche am Niederrhein von der Reformation bis zum Beginn des 18. Jahrhunderts* (Münster, 1965); M. Lackner, *Die Kirchenpolitik des Grossen Kurfürsten* (Witten, 1973); and K. Deppermann, 'Die Kirchenpolitik der Grossen Kurfürsten', in *Pietismus und Neuzeit* 6 (1981), pp. 99–114. In general, see G. Heinrich, 'Brandenburg II', in *Theologische Realenzyklopädie*, vol. 7, Berlin, 1981, pp. 111–28. It cannot be said that there was any early policy of tolerance that had far-reaching consequences for the rise of Brandenburg-Prussia. Apart from the tolerance (for economic reasons) of Jewish, Baptist and Socinian minorities, this was a case of coming to terms with the multi-confessionality of a motley array of ruling powers; for legal as well as political reasons, the principle *cuius regio eius religio* could not be applied. Consequently it was necessary to have peace between adherents of the Reformed and Lutheran churches, although whenever possible the Reformed church was given preference. Catholics were tolerated only reluctantly in the west, and were subject to all the rigours of territorialism. The 'soldier king' convinced himself personally of the 'true belief' of the emigrants who arrived from Salzburg: see G. Florey, 'Die "Grosse Emigration"', in *Reformation. Protestanten in Salzburg*, exhibition at Schloss Goldegg 1981, p. 105.

However, political identity was not created merely negatively, by demarcation from opponents, but also positively through consistent internal confessionalization. The process by no means primarily involved using the faith as an instrument to political ends. Even the political religion of a Machiavelli or a Rousseau[46] should not be confused with cynical modern strategies for manipulating voters. In the preface to the *Bavaria sancta* published for Duke Maximilian in 1615–28, the Jesuit Matthäus Rader writes:[47]

> Cities, boroughs, markets, districts, villages, fields, woods, mountains and valleys live and breathe the old Catholic religion in Bavaria . . . for the whole area is nothing but religion, and appears to be a single community church of the people.

'Tota regio nil nisi religio' is more than a wordplay on the phrase 'cuius regio eius religio': it describes a programme largely realized by Maximilian's 'ecclesiastical police government'.[48] and in the long term led to considerable internalization.[49]

2 'Your princely Grace shall be our Pope and Emperor,' wrote the peasants of Balhorn to Philip of Hesse as early as 1523.[50] The new sacral-

46 Reinhard, *Geschichte der politischen Ideen*, pp. 207, 290.

47 From P. B. Steiner, 'Der gottselige Fürst und die Konfessionalisierung Altbayerns', in H. Glaser (ed.), *Um Glauben und Reich. Kurfürst Maximilian I. Beiträge zur Bayerischen Geschichte und Kunst 1573–1657* (Wittelsbach und Bayern, vol. 2/1), Munich, 1980, p. 252f.

48 A classic text is F. Stieve, *Das kirchliche Polizeiregiment in Baiern unter Maximilian I 1595–1651* (Munich, 1876). As an important source, see *Landrecht/Policey: Gerichts- Malefitz und andere Ordnungen Der Fürstenthumben Obern und Nidern Bayrn* (Munich, 1616), esp. pp. 562–72 and 683–710. The Bavarian police regulations concerned also contain interesting remarks on schools on pp. 583–85. 'Our governments', the passage runs, have to be concerned with them, for 'not only is Christian discipline and the honour of God thereby promoted / but youth is brought up in awe and discipline/ for the good of the common fatherland.' A prerequisite, of course, is strict 'state control'. To this end Maximilian was at first particularly anxious to see a drastic decrease in the number of elementary schools; cf. D. Breuer, 'Besonderheiten der Zweisprachigkeit', pp. 155–57. Cf. also L. Westenrieder, 'Versuch einer Geschichte der baierischen Generalien in Hinsicht auf die Polizeygegenstände. Vom Jahr 1500 bis 1700', in ibid., *Beyträge zur vaterländischen Historie, Geographie, Statistik etc.* 8 (1806), pp. 280–392.

49 See H.. Rössler, in 'Warum Bayern katholisch blieb. Eine Strukturanalyse der evangelischen Bewegung im Bistum Freising 1520–1570', in *Beiträge zur altbayerischen Kirchengeschichte* 33 (1981), pp. 91–108. Rössler studies the evangelical movement to counter-check the theory that the conservative Catholicism of Bavaria was not a product of a popular nature, but instead involved discipline by the secular authority.

50 W. Heinemeyer, *Die Territorien zwischen Reichstradition, Staatlichkeit und politischen Interessen*, paper given at the Angermeier colloquium, *Säkulare Aspekte*.

ization of politics, going hand in hand with confessionalization, meant a functional increase for the emergent modern state power. Theoretically and practically, the church became an integral part of the state, and in practice that was the case for the Catholic almost as much as for the evangelical church. Although the Duke of Bavaria, unlike the Elector of Saxony, had no say on doctrinal matters, the 'Spiritual Council' in Munich remained structurally and functionally related to the Saxon Upper Consistory and the Palatinate Church Council.[51] When Thomas Hobbes says that ecclesiastical eminences are part of the power of the state, and every prince is both ruler and teacher of his subjects, but the power of the Pope remains confined to his own principality, the church state,[52] he is not aggressively anticipating a theory but giving a plain description of political facts. In line with these ideas, the electorate of Saxony ensured that the installation of evangelical bishops foreseen in the *Confessio Augustana* was not carried out.[53]

In Catholic areas the church retained its autonomous institutions and elites. Conflicts between 'church' and 'state' therefore accompanied the expansion of state power. Significantly, this was true even of the ecclesiastical state, where the 'state' hierarchy, in fact consisting of clerics, stood up to the 'ecclesiastical' authority just as much as in other territories, even as the reforming principles on the autonomy of bishops proposed by the Council of Trent and energetically pursued elsewhere fell by the wayside.[54] Moreover, Ferdinand of Wittelsbach, in his capacity as prince-bishop of Münster, carried the day for the ecclesiastical authority over the subordinate foundation belonging to the diocese of Osnabrück by virtue of his princely *cura religionis*.[55] Only attempts to ensure control over local territorial churches by eradicating the imperial church and setting up local bishoprics were usually thwarted by

---

51   Cf. D. Albrecht in *Handbuch der Bayerischen Geschichte* vol. 3 (Munich, 1969), pp. 51, 583; I. Höss, 'Humanismus und Reformation', in *Geschichte Thüringens*, vol. 3. Cologne and Graz, 1967; H. Reller, *Vorreformatorische und reformatorische Kirchenverfassung im Fürstentum Braunschweig-Wolfenbüttel* (Göttingen, 1959); V. Press, *Calvinismus und Territorialstaat. Regierung und Zentralbehörden der Kurpfalz 1559–1619* (Stuttgart, 1970); also, on the Bavarian pattern imitated in Baden, H. Steigelmann (ed.), *Der Geistliche Rat zu Baden-Baden und seine Protokolle 1577–1584* (Stuttgart, 1962); for the Wittelsbach area under ecclesiastical rule on the Lower Rhine, see among others H. Immenkötter, *Die Protokolle des Geistlichen Rats in Münster* (Münster, 1972).
52   Thomas Hobbes, *Leviathan* (London, 1651), ch. 42.
53   Cf. I. Höss, 'Episcopus Evangelicus. Versuche mit dem Bischofsamt im deutschen Luthertum des 16. Jahrhunderts', in E. Iserloh (ed.), *Confessio Augustana und Confutatio* (Münster, 1980), pp. 499–516.
54   Prodi, *Il sovrano pontefice*, pp. 249–93.
55   Immenkötter, *Die Protokolle des Geistlichen Rats*, p. 19.

Rome, even in Bavaria.[56] The imperial church system with its ecclesiastical principalities proved an obstacle to the expansion of territorial states, as comparison with western and southern Europe shows, for the kings of France and Spain, like most of the Italian princes[57] and republics, had ensured extensive control over their provincial churches and in some cases had even introduced a new organization, particularly in the Spanish Netherlands.[58]

Princely rule of the church did not have to be as ecclesiastically dysfunctional as it proved in France. The 'Catholic kings' introduced ecclesiastical reform to Spain[59] just as the dukes did later in Bavaria.[60] From the political viewpoint, there was no difference between this process and the introduction of the 'Reformation' by evangelical princes, particularly as long as there was a general feeling that it was not a case of founding a new 'church' but of purging the old one. However, even purely religious initiatives in policies of confessionalization had a political dimension. The Wettins, the ruling house of Saxony, used church visitations to make their political claims to power,[61] and in Bavaria even Catholic worship could be put to the service of the mediatization of the many monastic intermediate powers. The rise of the Marian cult propagated by the Jesuits and mendicant orders with 'state' encouragement was at the expense of the cults of traditional local saints venerated by monasteries. The *Patrona Bavariae* supplanted the patron saint who had held sway locally, just as the duke superseded local rule itself.[62]

To be safe from competition, the churches had to pay a high price to their princely rulers, not only through the loss of their autonomous rights but also literally, by transferring estates and revenues. It had been

56   Cf. H. Rankl, *Das vorreformatorische landesherrliche Kirchenregiment in Bayern, 1378–1526* (Munich, 1971), pp. 94f, 107f; D. Albrecht, *Handbuch der Bayerischen Geschichte*, p. 630.

57   Cf., for instance, recently, A Erba, *La chiesa sabauda tra cinque e seicento. Ortodossia tridentina, gallicanesimo savoiardo e assolutismo ducale (1580–1630)* (Rome, 1979).

58   M. Dierickx, *De oprichting der nieuwe bisdommen in de Nederlande onder Filips II 1559–70* (Antwerp, 1950); ibid. (ed.), *Documents inédits sur l'érection des nouveaux diocèses aux Pays-Bas 1521–1570*, 3 vols (Brussels, 1960–62).

59   Cf. esp. Tarsicio de Azcona, 'Reforma del episcopado y del clero de España en tiempo de los reyes catolicos y de Carlos V (1475–1558)', in *Historia de la Iglesia en España*, vol. 3/1 (Madrid, 1980), pp. 115–210.

60   Cf. D. Albrecht, *Handbuch der Bayerischen Geschichte*, pp. 626–56, and E. Metzger, *Leonhard von Eck (1480–1550), Wegbereiter und Begründer des frühabsolutischen Bayern* (Munich, 1980), pp. 73–128, and for the sake of continuity Rankl, *Das vorreformatorische landesherrliche Kirchenregiment*.

61   Höss, 'Humanismus und Reformation', p. 87.

62   Cf. esp. H. Hörger, *Kirche, Dorfreligion und bäuerliche Gesellschaft* (Munich, 1978).

possible to alienate church property even before the Reformation.[63] Extensive partial expropriations in the Catholic regions matched the many instances of Protestant secularization.[64] The French crown had financed the Huguenot Wars by the sale of church property,[65] and churchmen were exempt from taxation only in canonical theory. In practice the sovereign taxed the ecclesiastical state,[66] and the duke of Bavaria[67] taxed Bavarian clerics, just as the Spanish crown[68] and the French crown[69] did.

3   State rule of the church in general and abolition of the privileges of the clergy in particular were important steps towards evening out the status of all subjects. In this the Reformation did give considerable stimulus to the growth of the modern state. However, Catholics could already be seen employing their own means of closing the gap, up to and including the prince-abbot of Fulda who established absolutism in

63   Cf. on the case of Württemberg: F.-K. Ingelfinger, *Die religiös-kirchlichen Verhältnisse im heutigen Württemberg am Vorabend der Reformation* (Stuttgart, 1939); W. Schöntag, 'Die Aufhebung der Stifte und Häuser der Brüder vom gemeinsamen Leben in Württemberg. Ein Vorbote der Reformation', in *Zeitschrift für Württembergische Landesgeschichte* 38 (1979), pp. 82–96; W. Bofinger, 'Kirche und werdender Territorialstaat. Eine Untersuchung zur Kirchenreform Herzog Ulrichs von Württemberg', in *Blätter für Württembergische Kirchengeschichte* 65 (1965), pp. 75–149; W.-U. Deetjen, *Studien zur württembergischen Kirchenordnung Herzog Ulrichs (1534–1550)* (Stuttgart, 1981); H.-W. Krumwiede, 'Reformation und Kirchenregiment in Württemberg', in *Blätter für württembergische Kirchengeschichte* 68/69 (1968/69), pp. 81–111; H.-M. Maurer, 'Herzog Christoph als Landesherr', in ibid., pp. 112–38.

64   The term 'secularization', however, was avoided in favour of the contemporary term 'sequestration', to maintain the legal fiction that this state of affairs was only temporary. In fact, the property was transferred to the ownership of the princes, and was by no means used solely for 'pious' purposes. Cf. E. G. Franz, 'Die hessischen Klöster und ihre Konvente in der Reformation', in *Hessisches Jahrbuch für Landesgeschichte* 19 (1969), pp. 147–233; H.-M. Kühn, *Die Einziehung des geistlichen Gutes im albertinischen Sachsen 1539–1553* (Cologne and Graz, 1966); R. H. Seitz, 'Staats- und Klostergutsverkäufe zur Tilgung der pfalz-neuburgischen Landesschulden in den Jahren 1544–1557', in *Neuburger Kollektaneenblat* 133 (1980), pp. 61–79.

65   According to earlier studies by I. Cloulas, and more recently C. Michaud, 'Les aliénations du temporel ecclésiastique dans la seconde moitié du XVIe siècle. Quelques problèmes de méthode', in *Revue d'histoire de l'église de France* 67 (1981), pp. 61–82.

66   Prodi, *Il sovrano pontefice*.

67   Albrecht, *Handbuch der Bayerischen Geschichte*, p. 630.

68   Tarsicio de Azcona, 'Reforma del episcopado y del clero de España'.

69   A recent study is by I. Mieck, *Die Entstehung des modernen Frankreich 1450–1610* (Stuttgart, 1982), p. 216f. Cf. also W. Reinhard, 'Glaube, Geld, Diplomatie. Die Rahmenbedingungen des Religiongesprächs von Poissy im Herbst 1561', in Müller, *Die Religionsgespräche der Reformationszeit*, pp. 89–116.

his territory at the end of the seventeenth century, basing his actions on the authority ascribed to him by the rule of St Benedict.[70]

It is in this context that the modernization of church administration by the Reformation should be seen. The Council of Trent did the same for the old church.[71] The evangelical 'superintendent' might appear to derive his title from a translation of the Catholic term 'episkopos' (= overseer),[72] but none the less, like the later French 'Intendant', he was a modern official of the 'commissar' type,[73] and no longer held any benefice. According to Elton,[74] the early stages of the English 'Reformation' under Henry VIII could be seen simply as part of an administrative reform – so long as we do not apply modern ideas to the process. The Catholic church overcame the pre-modern society of privilege by concentrating the discipline of the faithful in the priest and the bishop, and filling any gaps with the new marriage law and the keeping of registers. All confessions made written administrative records and laid down an abundance of detailed regulations. Bureaucracy was on its way. The apparatus of church and state worked together to discipline their subjects.

> Of all laws there is none more favourable to princes than the Christian law, for it makes not only the bodies and goods of those they rule subject to them . . . but also their souls and consciences, and binds not only hands but also thoughts and feelings.

Thus Giovanni Botero, writing in 1589.[75] And in 1653 Dietrich Reinkingk wrote:[76]

70   K. Wittstadt, *Placidus von Droste, Fürstabt von Fulda 1678–1700* (Fulda, 1963).
71   On this subject, briefly, see W. Reinhard, 'Die Verwaltung der Kirche', in *Deutsche Verwaltungsgeschichte*, Stuttgart, 1983, vol. 1 (six vols in total, 1983–88).
72   Höss, 'Humanismus und Reformation', p. 86.
73   Cf. O. Hintze, 'Der Commissarius und seine Bedeutung in der allgemeinen Verwaltungsgeschichte (1910)', in ibid., *Staat und Verfassung* (Göttingen, 1970), 3rd edn, pp. 242–74.
74   Cf. G. R. Elton, *The Tudor Revolution in Government* (Cambridge, 1953); G. R. Elton, *Policy and Police*.
75   'Tra tutte le leggi non ve n'è alcuna piú favorevole a prencipi che la cristiana, perché questa sottomette loro non solamente i corpi e le facoltà de sudditi . . . ma gli animi ancora e le conscienze, e lega non solamente le mani, ma gli affetti ancora ed i pensieri.' From G. Botero, *Della ragion di Stato*, ed. L. Firpo (Turin, 1948), p. 137.
76   D. Reinkingk, *Biblische Policey* (Frankfurt, 1653); quoted here from the Frankfurt edition of 1681, pp. 14, 35.

Religio and *ratio status* both begin with an R, and the greatest *arcanum republicarum* is in these two, more particularly when a new domain and a new rule are to be stabilized . . . Religion in a land and a *republica* binds and links together the minds of subjects among themselves and against those above them all the more strongly, and maintains faith the better . . .

The early modern secular authorities could thus expect that it would pay off politically to regulate the religious and moral lives of their subjects in every intimate detail, controlling them through officials, informers and spies;[77] it would pay off not just in terms of political stability, but through political gains. For while purely political expansion of the princely power must in the nature of things encounter vigorous resistance from those who formerly held power and their subjects, in some circumstances it was easier to make gains with the approval of their subjects, through ecclesiastical innovations given legitimate status by religion.[78] The participation of the estates in the introduction of the Reformation into Sweden, England and German territories represented the most striking triumph of this strategy, which in a more subtle form also constituted the basis of the actual confessional disciplinary process. Resistance to measures which were justified by their importance to the eternal salvation of the subject concerned[79] not only meant resistance to authority and the public order of things: the longer it went on the less it could be reconciled with a man's own conscience. Incidentally, this state of affairs provides an answer to the latent contradiction set out in Gerhard Oestreich's well-known study:[80] how is absolute 'social disciplining' possible when the 'state' disposes of the requisite administrative apparatus only to an inadequate degree, and local autonomies make it harder for subjects to be directly influenced through central offices? It is still not clear how far Prussia was actually affected by the many measures its 'soldier king' introduced.[81] In my view the church filled the gap. It provided its own apparatus and made the consensus of those affected possible. In this way, then, 'confessionalization' became the first phase of 'social discipline'.

77 Cf. esp. Stieve, *Das kirchliche Polizeiregiment in Baiern*.
78 Cf. Schilling, *Konfessionskonflikt*, p. 366.
79 The prince also shared responsibility for his subjects' eternal salvation; cf. among others J. E. Estes, 'Church Order and the Christian Magistrate according to Johannes Brenz', in *Archiv für Reformationsgeschichte* 59 (1968), pp. 5–24; also, in general, M. Raeff, 'The Well-Ordered Police State and the Development of Modernity in Seventeenth- and Eighteenth-Century Europe: An Attempt at a Comparative Approach', in *American Historical Review* 80 (1975), pp. 1221–43.
80 G. Oestreich, 'Strukturprobleme des europäischen Absolutismus'.
81 G. Oestreich, *Friedrich Wilhelm I., Preussischer Absolutismus, Merkantilismus, Militarismus* (Göttingen, 1977).

As mentioned above, in assessing the confessional policies of the emergent modern state the modern historian must be careful to avoid the mistake of simply viewing the entire process as an instrument. As early as 1600 Traiano Boccalini wrote that the Reformation was nothing but a skilful device of German princes to assert their own power against the Emperor, and to this end they had allowed the ambitious professor Martin Luther to appeal to the lower instincts of the populace, thereafter using the movement thus created for their own purposes.[82] However, this was certainly only a half-truth. Even a witness as unsuspecting of blind idealism as Thomas Hobbes bases princely rule of the church not on the sovereign's interests but on his conscience.[83] More historically interesting is the *manner* in which the 'Christian king' contrived to serve his own interest *while* following the dictates of his conscience.

For politics in the confessional period in general, and the sphere of action of politics in the Empire in particular, significant consequences do emerge from this appeal to the conscience of leading political figures, and it is to be taken seriously. Not only did confession become the nucleus of political crystallization, so that the confessional link was a constituent part of the estates of the Empire, not only did the formation of political fronts in the Empire almost automatically correspond to connections with the various European confessions, but most important of all, confessionalization drastically impaired the ability to make political compromises, and it could be won back only in the course of a painful learning process.

82   H. Jedin, 'Religion und Staatsräson. Ein Dialog Traijano Boccalinis über die deutsche Glaubensspaltung', in ibid., *Kirche des Glaubens, Kirche der Geschichte*, vol. 1 (Freiburg, 1966), pp. 271–85.
83   Thomas Hobbes, *Leviathan*, ch. 42.

7

The Reformation and the Modern Age

Richard van Dülmen

Originally appeared as Richard van Dülmen, 'Reformation und Neuzeit. Ein Versuch'. Zeitschrift für Historische Forschung, 14 (1987), pp. 1–25.

Editor's Introduction

The Reformation has long been associated with the dawn of the modern age. A strong tradition of European history thinks of the sixteenth century, the century of Reformation, as marking the transitional stage from the medieval era to modern times. In the conventional view, it was the point of division between the intellectual stagnation, religious superstition, and political primitivism of the 'dark ages' and the dynamic progressive and enlightened age that was to follow. The modern age, as scholarship would have it, was clearly a post-Reformation phenomenon.

The association of the Reformation with modernity, as Richard van Dülmen illustrates, has lost none of its power today. Indeed, many of the traits which we hold to be favourable or desirable (and thus modern) can trace their roots back to the century of confessional division. Modernity, in a sense, was born of historical necessity. In the German lands of the Holy Roman Empire, for instance, the sheer fact of religious pluralism forced certain changes on the social and political relations of the age. The Empire, once a Catholic union, was now comprised of distinct confessional states. This necessarily gave rise to a new religious awareness, a realization that there was more than one standard of Christian belief. The Europe of today, modern Europe, comprised of nations with their own political agendas and their own distinct sense of identity, found its footing during this age. And it was not just the framework of international political relations that was altered by the Reformation. Internally, the reform campaigns inspired a process of confessionalization (as discussed in the contribution by Wolfgang Reinhard). Religion set its stamp on the state. Again, this was a process which had a major effect on the German lands. In the Lutheran and Reformed territories (and in Catholic territories as well, though less dramatically), the church fell under the control of the state. It was now the explicit aim of the ruling elite to integrate both the church and the norms of the faith into the evolving system of rule, and this gave rise to an institutional revolution. The state was staffed by trained officials, secular and spiritual alike, and government became much more professional. Like many powers of the modern age, the confessional state sought unity, precision, and political order, as well as singularity in both form and ideas.

Today scholars speak of the theory of modernization, an idea born of nineteenth-century sociology and academic Marxism. In general, proponents of the theory think of historical development in economic terms. There has been a historical trend, they claim, one that is both predictable and prone to certain uniform patterns and structures, toward the industrial development and sophisticated institutions of the modern age. Here, once again, many of the institutional developments considered in a theory of this kind have their roots in the Reformation. Van Dülmen speaks of the separation of church and state, for instance. This might seem a paradox, given that one of the main legacies of the Reformation was the Lutheran state church; but the difference was that now there were clear boundaries between the spiritual and the secular realms. The confusion of powers, so common in the Middle Ages, was replaced by two distinct and separate spheres of competence. Church officials no longer meddled in rule as they had done in the medieval past; while religion – and that meant forms of worship and matters of doctrine – was left to the higher clergy. A similar process occurred in the educational institutions, where the medieval notion of the schools being a religious reserve was replaced by a broader, more modern idea of mass education. Schools grew in size and number, while the quality of teaching improved. Moreover, education was no longer just the preserve of the church and its officials, but a training ground for the officials who would staff the offices of the state. There was a general turn away from the spiritual to the secular world, a process historians sometimes refer to as secularization. Religious values were not abandoned, but they slowly waned in daily importance as people pursued secular ideals. And this not only affected the structure and function of the state; even at the level of the household or the parish the process of secularization made itself felt. Van Dülmen describes the affect this shift of values had on both the household and the workplace, and how these changes prepared the ground for the development of later centuries.

Throughout the discussion van Dülmen is speaking of the relationship between the *Protestant* Reformation and the modern age. The Reformation is just one of a number of factors and developments which gave shape to modern times, but an essential and necessary component. And this does not just hold true for nations and institutions. Without the Reformation and its stress on the Word of God, it is difficult to imagine the modern individual and the modern virtues of intellectual honesty and moral responsibility. For Protestantism concentrated on the text; it now became an act of worship to read. Of course, there were still limits to what might be believed, but each individual was encouraged to understand the Word of God on his or her own terms, and each individual was thereby forced to develop a social and religious conscience. The result, as van Dülmen reveals, was a culture which expected its citizens to be literate, intelligent, rational, hard-working, and morally responsible, for these are the highest values of church, state, and society. They are also the basic expectations of the modern age.

The Reformation and the Modern Age

Richard van Dülmen

The Reformation has always been regarded as a development of universal historical importance.[1] No differences of academic opinion exist on that point, although individual historians, students of ecclesiastical history and sociologists of religion do place the emphasis in different places,[2] often contenting themselves with more or less lapidary statements. However, although attention has been paid to many aspects of the Reformation, particularly in the anniversary celebrations of recent years, its contribution to the development of the modern period has not yet been the subject of extensive study.[3] Since the major works by Ernst Troeltsch[4]

---

1 In general, from the historian's viewpoint, see among others H. Rückert, 'Die geistesgeschichtliche Einordnung der Reformation', in *Zeitschrift für Theologie und Kirche* 52 (1955), pp. 43–64; K. Brandi, *Deutsche Geschichte im Zeitalter der Reformation und Gegenreformation* (Darmstadt, 1960³), pp. 11ff; K. Bosl, 'Die Reformation. Versuch einer Bestimmung ihres historischen Ortes und ihrer Funktion in Gesellschaft und Kultur Europas', in *Zeitschrift für Bayerische Landesgeschichte* 31 (1963), pp. 104–23; M. Steinmetz, 'Die nationale Bedeutung der Reformation', in L. Stern and M. Steinmetz (eds), *450 Jahre Reformation* (Berlin, 1967), pp. 44–57; G. Ritter, 'Das 16. Jahrhundert als weltgeschichtliche Epoche', in ibid., *Die Weltwirkung der Reformation* (Darmstadt, 1969³), pp. 9–31; G. R. Elton, *Reformation Europe 1517–1559* (London, 1963); R. Wohlfeil (ed.), *Reformation oder frühbürgerliche Revolution* (Munich, 1972); H. A. Oberman, 'Reformation: Epoche oder Episode', in *Archiv für Reformationsgeschichte* 68 (1977), pp. 56–109; and finally P. Blickle, *Die Reformation im Reich* (Stuttgart, 1982), p. 9 ('The Reformation is regarded as an event of epoch-making significance. The traditional division into periods of international history, in which the Reformation marks the beginning of the modern period, is the clearest expression of this concept.') On the present state of the discussion, see H. Lutz, *Reformation und Gegenreformation* (Munich and Vienna, 1979), pp. 122ff; S. Skalweit, *Der Beginn der Neuzeit. Epochengrenze und Epochenbegriff* (Darmstadt, 1982), pp. 76–122.
2 Only the sociology of religion deals with the issue systematically; historians tend to concentrate on the subject as it relates to national history, while ecclesiastical historians dwell on the significance of the Reformation in church history.
3 Only Oberman's contribution to the subject in 'Reformation' is worth mentioning here.
4 E. Troeltsch, *Die Bedeutung des Protestantismus für die Entstehung der modernen Welt* (1906, Munich, 1924²); ibid., 'Luther, der Protestantismus und die moderne Welt', in *Gesammelte Schriften IV* (Aalen, 1966), pp. 202–54. In his approach to the issue Troeltsch concentrates exclusively on Protestantism, taking the Reformation as his subject solely in that aspect.

and Max Weber,[5] at least, no new attempt at synthesis or interpretation has been made with the energy the subject deserves, although it should be a central concern of history never to lose sight of the Reformation as a whole and the part it played in the historical process. Indeed, study of the effects of the Reformation on the emergence of the modern world is a major issue in historical investigation of the early modern age.[6]

The question can no longer, of course, be answered by the methods and approaches of the late nineteenth century, any more than it can be denied that the reformulation of Troeltsch and Weber's discussion of the modern period still provides intellectual stimulus, although the findings of more recent detailed research should not be neglected. If we return to the 'old' discussion in the following pages, we must not forget that other issues have since been raised and invalidate many of the more cut-and-dried answers to the old question.[7] We are not, therefore, resuming the well-known discussion as if nothing had changed our awareness in

---

5   M. Weber, *Die protestantische Ethik*, 2 vols (Hamburg, 1972–73²). (This collection contains all his important writings on the subject.)
6   On the complex of ideas as a whole: for the development of the modern world in general cf. among others R. Koselleck (ed.), *Studien zum Beginn der modernen Welt* (Stuttgart, 1977); also ibid., *Vergangene Zukunft. Zur Semantik geschichtlicher Zeiten* (Frankfurt, 1979); on problems of the early modern period cf. R. van Dülmen, 'Formierung der europäischen Gesellschaft in der Frühen Neuzeit', in *Geschichte und Gesellschaft* 7 (1981), pp. 5–41; ibid., *Entstehung des frühneuzeitlichen Europas 1550–1648* (Frankfurt, 1982), pp. 256ff. Weber's positions are reflected by C. Seyfarth, *Protestantismus und gesellschaftliche Entwicklung. Zur Reformulierung eines Problems*, and by R. Döbert, 'Die evolutionäre Bedeutung der Reformation', in C. Seyfarth and W. M. Sprondel (eds), *Religion und gesellschaftliche Entwicklung. Studien zur Protestantismus-Kapitalismus-These Max Webers* (Frankfurt, 1973), pp. 338–66 and 303–12 respectively; S. N. Eisenstadt, *Tradition, Wandel und Modernität* (Frankfurt, 1979), pp. 236–52; W. Schluchter, *Die Entwicklung des okzidentalen Rationalismus. Eine Analyse von Max Webers Gesellschaftsgeschichte* (Tübingen, 1979), pp. 204–55 ('Das historische Erklärungsproblem: Die Rolle der Reformation im Übergang zur Moderne'); J. Habermas, *Theorie des kommunikativen Handelns*, vol. 1: *Handlungsrationalität und gesellschaftliche Rationalisierung* (Frankfurt, 1981), pp. 299–331 ('Modernisierung als gesellschaftliche Rationalisierung: Die Rolle der protestantischen Ethik'). A recent well-balanced account is W. Pannenberg, 'Reformation und Neuzeit', in *Troeltsch-Studien*, vol. 3: *Protestantismus und Neuzeit* (Gütersloh, 1984), pp. 21–34.
7   Concentration on issues of social history has introduced great differentiation into research work. See among others H. Schilling, 'Religion und Gesellschaft in der calvinistischen Republik der Vereinigten Niederlande. "Öffentlichkeitskirche" und Säkularisation; Ehe und Hebammenwesen; Presbyterium und politische Partizipation', in *Kirche und gesellschaftlicher Wandel in deutschen und niederländischen Städten der werdenden Neuzeit* (= *Städteforschung*, A/10), Cologne and Vienna, 1980, pp. 197–250, esp. p. 198f; ibid., *Konfessionskonflikt und Staatsbildung. Eine Fallstudie über das Verhältnis von religiösem und sozialem Wandel in der Frühneuzeit am Beispiel der Grafschaft Lippe* (Gütersloh, 1981), p. 20ff.

.

the meantime; we are reformulating the question. Another point to emphasize is that in studying the connection between the Reformation and the advent of the modern era, the Reformation is not seen as the 'essential' dividing line between the Middle Ages and modernity, nor is it hailed as already embodying modern freedom, rationality and morality. New areas of freedom certainly emerged during the Reformation, but so did new strategies of suppression. Moreover, the Reformation, meaning the Reformation as a whole comprising the Lutheran, Calvinist and other movements,[8] represents only one force among many in the genesis of the modern age. However, the nature of the Reformation's relation to the state political and socio-economic forces of a particular contemporary period must remain an open question.[9] In any case, we are not returning to a view of the modern world as deriving chiefly from the Reformation and making causal connections, but nor are political or economic processes to be raised to the status of the real dynamic forces of history.[10]

The Reformation was a 'universal phenomenon', and the advent of modernity cannot be imagined without it. In this context, however, much as one may wish to provide adequate information, it is impossible to take account of all the impulses, stimuli and developments involved. Instead, we will concentrate on analysing the chief influences and effects of the Reformation, those that can be more or less definitely

8   Chronologically, this means studying the whole sixteenth and part of the early seventeenth century and concentrating on what is in common to all Reformation movements: the ways in which they distinguished themselves from both late medieval and Tridentine Catholicism, and the way in which each became socially and politically relevant. There are certainly difficulties involved, but it may be pointed out that both Catholic and Evangelical contemporary witnesses always saw the Reformation as a unit; its entire spectrum reaches from the German Reformation to the English Revolution.

9   Cf., among other, M. Walzer, *The Revolution of the Saints. A Study in the Origins of Radical Politics* (London, 1966); G. Swanson, *Religion and Regime. A Sociological Account of the Reformation* (Ann Arbor, 1968). To trace the 'process of transformation' could be an important area of Reformation studies. Ideas leading further may be found in Schilling, 'Religion und Gesellschaft in der calvinistischen Republik der Vereinigten Niederlande'. I speak deliberately of 'forces', not of 'elective affinities' in the Weberian sense.

10   A possible line of enquiry is described by van Dülmen, 'Formierung der europäischen Gesellschaft in der Frühen Neuzeit'. On the function of religion in modern times, cf. H. R. Kippenberg, 'Wege zu einer historischen Religionssoziologie', in *Verkündigung und Forschung* 1971, pp. 54–82; R. van Dülmen, 'Religionsgeschichte in der Historischen Sozialforschung', in *Geschichte und Gesellschaft* 6 (1980), pp. 36–59; ibid., 'History of Religion as Social Science', in *Telos* 58 (1983–4), pp. 20–29. Out of the abundant literature on the subject. I shall have to confine myself in the following notes chiefly to the most important German-language sources, and dispense with citing details in full.

ascribed to it in connection with the rise of early modernity, by studying three linked questions: (1) What was the importance of the Reformation in the development of religious and Christian awareness in the modern churches, as authorities in a process of socialization central to modern society?; (2) What part did the Reformation play in the creation of the modern state, modern education, the family and the world of work? and (3) How did the Reformation affect people's ordinary consciousness and conduct in modern society?

I

As a socio-cultural phenomenon, the Reformation not only brought an end to the existence and universality of the medieval church; in concentrating on religious subjectivity and the formation of new confessional churches it also redetermined the relationship of religion to society and to the world of daily life, redefining the content and boundaries of the religious and spiritual, political and social, and moral and ethical order. The idea of 'religion' as a 'spiritual' phenomenon outside the secular order of things first emerges in the Reformation, although it could be defined in various ways.

1 We now see the Reformation as linked to the rise of an ecclesiastical pluralism never previously known or indeed imaginable. A universal church that had long been able to integrate many different religious movements broke up into several alternative, distinct and mutually exclusive ecclesiastical systems.[11] This was not really a case of ecclesiastical schism (although for a long time Catholics in particular regarded the Reformation churches as schismatic and condemned them for it) for under the pressure of the emergent Reformation and its far-reaching effects, the Catholic church itself was transformed after the Council of Trent into a confessional church comparable to the Protestant churches.[12] The universality of the Catholic church as a community of

11 E. W. Zeeden, 'Grundlagen und Wege der Konfessionsbildung in Deutschland im Zeitalter der Glaubenskämpfe', in *Historische Zeitschrift* 185 (1958), pp. 249–99; ibid., *Die Entstehung der Konfessionen. Grundlagen und Formen der Konfessionsbildung im Zeitalter der Glaubenskämpfe* (Munich and Vienna, 1965); P. T. Lang, 'Konfessionsbildung als Forschungsfeld', in *Historisches Jahrbuch* 100 (1980), pp. 479–93; F. Petri (ed.), *Kirche und gesellschaftlicher Wandel in deutschen und niederländischen Städten der werdenden Neuzeit* (Cologne and Vienna, 1980).
12 G. Schreiber (ed.), *Das Weltkonzil von Trient*, 2 vols (Freiburg, 1951); E. W. Zeeden (ed.), *Gegenreformation* (Darmstadt, 1973); W. Reinhard, 'Gegenreformation als Modernisierung? Prolegomena zu einer Theorie des konfessionellen Zeitalters', in *Archiv für Reformationsgeschichte* 68 (1977), pp. 226–52.

worship embracing social life as a whole was questioned, and a number of very different ecclesiastical systems and religious communions appeared, holding different ideas about their faith and making different social and religious demands. Although it was not originally so intended – we know that neither Luther nor Zwingli nor Calvin wanted to found a new church, but on the contrary long maintained that Christianity was a single entity – under the pressure of state and political interests, social forces and circumstances, and not least because of the extraordinarily uncompromising attitude of the Roman Catholic church, an ecclesiastical pluralism developed that led to the formation of the great independent Lutheran, Reformed and Anglican churches, at the same time allowing a great many more or less well-organized religious communities of Nonconformists to come into being during the Reformation.[13]

Widely as the structure of the new churches varied, they all had three fundamental characteristics. The hierarchical church dominated by a 'consecrated' priestly caste was replaced by a lay church, in which a clerical class set apart from other men did soon reappear, its existence justified mainly by its knowledge, but where laymen – including the local ruler – exercised a new function, having a say in the life and organization of the church.[14] The fact that this development was more marked in the Calvinist churches than in Lutheranism does not invalidate the basic structure. The new churches no longer saw themselves as religious communities of worship. Instead of religious ceremonies and rituals the content of which the old church could and did define only vaguely, the scriptures now became the focal point of religious and ecclesiastical life.[15] In principle, every believer had access to them, although that did not exclude the possibility that the new, theologically trained clerics, under pressure from alternative exegetical possibilities, might wish their own interpretation to have a monopoly. Nor did reference to scripture as a guideline exclude the reintroduction

13   Especially the Anabaptists; cf. C. P. Clasen, *Anabaptism. A Social History 1525–1618* (Ithaca and London, 1972); H. J. Goertz (ed.), *Umstrittenes Täufertum 1525–1975. Neue Forschungen* (Göttingen, 1975). In general, cf. B. R. Wilson (ed.), *Patterns of Sectarianism* (London, 1967); C. Hill, *The World Turned Upside Down. Radical Ideas during the English Revolution* (New York, 1976³).

14   W. Rochler, *Martin Luther und die Reformation als Laienbewegung* (Wiesbaden, 1981); J. Bohateč, *Calvins Lehre von Staat und Kirche* (Breslau, 1937), among other works. Cf. also H. Schilling, 'Calvinistische Presbyterien in Städten der Frühneuzeit – eine kirchliche Alternativform zur bürgerlichen Repräsentation?', in W. Ehbrecht (ed.), *Städtische Führungsgruppen und Gemeinde in der werdenden Neuzeit* (Cologne and Vienna, 1980), pp. 385–444.

15   Among others, see R. Schäfer, *Bibelauslegung in der Geschichte der Kirche* (Gütersloh, 1980).

of ritual, but the scriptural principle remained a central constituent. A church embracing life as a whole, with the entire broad spectrum of human interests, was eventually replaced by a system that felt itself responsible only, or primarily, for directly religious, ecclesiastical and moral concerns,[16] even though many new religious communions reverted to making comprehensive claims for themselves or even assumed a theocratic character. There was never any actual proposal to separate church and state, but for the first time religious ideas and ecclesiastical practices were clearly distinct from the sphere of purely social and political life,[17] as witness the withdrawal of churchmen from public politics.

2   Extensive religious confessionalization went hand in hand with the rise of the new ecclesiastical system.[18] Every new church had a different understanding of itself, and made very different demands on its members, but the pressure exerted by the new churches and religious communions, including Tridentine Catholicism, was remarkably similar everywhere, differing only in the degree of its intensity. Confessionalization meant principally that the faith of a church came to be interpreted according to a creed or confession set down in writing and increasingly under the control of theologically trained clerics. Hardly any sixteenth-century church did not have extensive regulations printed governing its faith and forms of worship. These regulations were regarded as standards for training the clergy and educating the people. Henceforward the individual member of a church was distinguished chiefly by an explicit confession of faith, although many theologians had misgivings on this point. Among the less educated, in religious as well as other matters, confessionalization brought about a considerable expansion of educational institutions and the spread of ecclesiastical and biblical knowledge even to the common folk, while at the same time society was purged of all kinds of magical and superstitious ideas and alternative, aberrant doctrines, that is to say, erroneous teachings were

16   Among others, see W. Koehler, *Zürcher Ehegericht und Genfer Konsistorium*, 2 vols (Leipzig, 1932, 1942); Schilling, 'Religion und Gesellschaft in der calvinistischen Republik der Vereinigten Niederlande'.
17   K. Eder, *Die Kirche im Zeitalter des konfessionellen Absolutismus 1555–1648* (Freiburg, 1949); H.-W. Krumwiede, *Zur Entstehung des landesherrlichen Kirchenregimentes in Kursachsen und Braunschweig-Wolfenbüttel* (Göttingen, 1967); H. Lehmann, *Das Zeitalter des Absolutismus. Gottesgnadentum und Kriegsnot* (Stuttgart and elsewhere, 1980).
18   Zeeden, *Die Entstehung der Konfessionen*; Lang, *Konfessionsbildung*; B. Vogler, 'Die Ausbildung des Konfessionsbewusstseins in den pfälzischen Territorien zwischen 1555 und 1619', in H. Rabe et al. (eds), *Festgabe für Ernst-Walter Zeeden* (Münster, 1976), pp. 281–8; Schilling, *Konfessionskonflikt und Staatsbildung*; van Dülmen, *Entstehung des frühneuzeitlichen Europas*, p. 270ff.

precisely defined and condemned.[19] For the first time, and for large sectors of the population, an attempt to achieve purity of doctrine in which almost all churchmen participated by preaching and writing defined such matters as church membership, but at the same time condemned all who deviated as enemies of society. The Anabaptist movement was most affected, like other evangelical separatist groups, but so was crypto-Calvinism in the Lutheran area and Protestantism in Catholic territories.[20]

Confessionalization also established the individual's Christian and moral norms, which took their guidelines from the scriptures and the new confessions of faith. For the first time, the churches began to issue public definitions of what was to be believed and of the devout life that would be pleasing to God in accordance with the faith.[21] Of course the process took different forms in different churches and religious communities, independently of the fact that the major religious communions, whose existence was assured, were usually less strict than the small ones, particularly when the latter were under social pressure and threatened with persecution. The Lutherans were less inclined to intervene with rules and regulations, while Calvinism wanted to change mankind almost entirely.[22] In principle, even the new Catholicism was no longer indifferent to the manner of a Christian's life, not just in church-going or answering the requirements of the church but in his conduct to his fellow men and the morality of his public life. The idea of subjection to radical Christian precepts had existed earlier, but mainly for those who devoted themselves to the monastic life. With the Reformation, however, Christian standards of life were enjoined upon all Christians, although they did not imply the acquisition of any particu-

19   See esp. C. Ginzburg, *Der Käse und die Würmer. Die Welt eines Müllers um 1600* (Frankfurt, 1979); English, tr. John and Anne Tedeschi, *The Cheese and the Worms* (London, 1982); R. Muchembled, *Kultur des Volkes – Kultur der Eliten. Die Geschichte einer erfolgreichen Verdrängung* (Stuttgart, 1982); R. van Dülmen, 'Volksfrömmigkeit und konfessionelles Christentum', in *Geschichte und Gesellschaft* (Sonderheft, 1986), pp. 14–30.

20   See among others Goertz (ed.), *Umstrittenes Täufertum*; R. van Dülmen, *Reformation als Revolution. Soziale Bewegung und religiöser Radikalismus in der deutschen Reformation* (Munich, 1977); T. Klein, *Der Kampf um die Zweite Reformation in Kursachsen 1586–1591* (Cologne and Graz, 1962); J. Bossy, *The English Catholic Community, 1570–1850* (New York and Oxford, 1976).

21   This is particularly clear in the visitations; cf. E. W. Zeeden and H. Molitor (eds), *Die Visitation im Dienst der kirchlichen Reform* (Münster, 1977²). An exemplary work providing a wealth of material is B. Vogler, *Vie religieuse en Pays Rhenan dans la seconde moitié du XVIᵉ siècle (1556–1619)*, 3 vols (Lille, 1974).

22   M. Weber, 'Die protestantische Ethik und der Geist des Kapitalismus', in *Die protestantische Ethik*; also W. F. Dankbaar, *Calvin, sein Weg und sein Werk* (Neunkirchen, 1966²).

lar merit or the attainment of eternal salvation. Only faith as defined by
a church made its members true believers. The confession of sins and
ecclesiastical discipline, preaching and teaching were all at the service
of that faith. Consequently, religious practices were not the prime factor
in church membership, which came through acknowledgement of the
Word – by now important even in Catholicism, and entailing the obligation to live a moral life.[23] Although Lutherans might admire the moral
rigour of Anabaptists or Jesuits, while Catholics valued the moral standards of Protestants, orientation by doctrine was not affected.

3   With the Reformation, and despite the rigid conditions of inclusion
in the new religious communions, a man's subjective faith, his 'internal' religious attitude, came to occupy the centre of religious and ecclesiastical life for the first time.[24] Although the idea was put forward
with varying degrees of radicalism – and here the free church Nonconformists and to some extent Calvinism were more logical than
Lutheranism, which organized itself along ecclesiastical or state lines –
yet all the new evangelical communities freed individual Christians both
from their dependence on the spiritual mediation of the clergy and from
ritual observation of the sacraments, thus opening up the way of immediate communication with God to all believers. The old mediating function of the church and its saints was retained only in Catholicism,
although Catholicism also affirmed the value of subjectivity. The Reformation referred Christians fundamentally to God, to whom alone they
owed faith, grace and justification. The certainty of faith was independent of social status or a man's degree of religious enlightenment,
although it was admitted that educated people and the clergy had a
certain advantage. In principle, therefore, all Christians had the same
religious opportunities, and at the same time, within the religious and
ecclesiastical regulations, they had independence and a degree of self-
determination that in no way contradicted church membership – to
some extent church membership was seen as a prerequisite for freedom
of decision – but no longer allowed an individual's faith to be primarily
defined by it. This did not mean that he was an autonomous 'early bour-

23   H. Leube, *Die Reformidee in der deutschen lutherischen Kirche zur Zeit der Orthodoxie* (Leipzig, 1924); ibid., *Calvinismus und Luthertum im Zeitalter der Orthodoxie*
(Aalen, 1966²); C. Hill, *Puritanism and Revolution* (London, 1969); A. Lang, *Puri-
tanismus und Pietismus* (Darmstadt, 1972²); P. Warmbrunn, *Zwei Konfessionen in
einer Stadt. Das Zusammenleben von Katholiken und Protestanten in den paritätischen
Reichsstädten* (Wiesbaden, 1983).
24   On these ideas see W. Dilthey, *Weltanschauung und Analyse des Menschen seit
Renaissance und Reformation* (Leipzig and Berlin, 1921); E. Troeltsch, *Aufsätze zur
Geistesgeschichte und Religionssoziologie* (= Gesammelte Schriften IV) (Aalen, 1966²);
H. Bornkann, *Mystik, Spiritualismus und die Anfänge des Pietismus im Luthertum*
(Giessen, 1926).

geois' in the Enlightenment sense, and there was no sudden change in ideas of political autonomy and self-determination during the Reformation period, even in the thinking of Thomas Müntzer,[25] although the beginning of such a change can perhaps be seen in English sects of the seventeenth century.[26] For the first time, however, independence and self-determination became factors liberating man not only from religious and ecclesiastical but also from social and political traditions.[27] The idea of religious and political 'immediacy' implied what for the society of the time was a high degree of autonomy and freedom from the existing order. In principle, this concept opened up social opportunities, but it also made very heavy demands on mankind, since no religious practices or good works could now intervene between man and almighty God. It was easier for an independent elite to accept such ideas than for the dependent common folk, and easier for socially disorientated groups than for 'normal' members of an urban or village community. Since, in addition, there was no certainty of salvation, religious autonomy entailed psychological risks, and the resulting fears of damnation could lead people back into a new kind of dependency.

Everyone now had to fend for himself, and here we find the basic reasons why the institution of church discipline found increasing approval as a social or spiritual aid. Although the devout Christian's assumption of responsibility for himself in the Reformation was interrupted once again by confessionalization and the forging of new links to the state or the political community, yet in principle anyway the certainty, unshakability and traditionally all-inclusive nature of the old religious order were broken in the Reformation, making it possible for a kind of self-determination and self-reflection to develop that would soon also be able to break the religious mould, or at least the ecclesiastical mould, as witness the example of England, where political revolution and religious self-determination were very closely linked indeed.[28]

25 H.-J. Goertz, *Innere und äussere Ordnung in der Theologie Thomas Müntzers* (Leiden, 1967); T. Nipperdey, 'Theologie und Revolution bei Thomas Müntzer,' in ibid., *Reformation, Revolution, Utopie. Studien zum 16. Jahrhundert* (Göttingen, 1975), pp. 38–84.

26 E. Troeltsch, *Die Soziallehren der christlichen Kirchen und Gruppen* (= *Gesammelte Schriften*, I), Tübingen, 1912, p. 794ff; C. Webster (ed.), *The Intellectual Revolution of the Seventeenth Century* (London and Boston, 1975).

27 For instance among the Levellers in England; cf. B. Manning (ed.), *Politics, Religion and the English Civil War* (London, 1973); H.-C. Schröder, 'Die Levellers und das Problem der Republik in der Englischen Revolution', in *Geschichte und Gesellschaft* 10 (1984), pp. 461–97.

28 C. Hill, *God's Englishman: Oliver Cromwell and the English Revolution* (New York, 1970); B. S. Capp, *The Fifth Monarchy Men. A Study in Seventeenth-Century English Millenarianism* (London, 1972).

4   Finally, faith that could be set down in writing and concentration on the individual's own belief created the first prerequisites for religious tolerance.[29] Although the Reformation claimed total loyalty and gave rise to acts of violence against people who thought differently, while some reformers actively suppressed rival doctrines and opinions, as Protestantism gained ground its ideas of faith meant that it could not treat dissenters as Roman Catholicism did. It was part of the new understanding of an evangelical faith to recognize no secular power in the religious area, and not to subordinate spiritual and religious matters to any secular force. This attitude did not rule out opposing tendencies, but Protestant authors were prominent among the earliest champions of religious tolerance. However, not only did separation of the sacred and the secular create important prerequisites for the idea of tolerance, ultimately the very idea of the 'free' and voluntary confession of faith prohibited the suppression of those who thought otherwise, although neither party abandoned its confessional claim to the absolute truth, and hardly any community united by a confession failed to exclude dissenters. The dictates of political reason, which saw it necessary to pacify the confessional world, beginning with the Augsburg Religious Peace and reaching a culmination in the Peace of Westphalia, led to the necessity for an understanding of a faith that was based on scripture and Christian freedom and took the beliefs of individuals seriously. That necessity did not lead, however, straight to religious tolerance any more than it propagated ideas of a supra-confessional Christian church: the prime concern was to refrain from violence in arguments about confessional faith. Naturally enough marginal religious groups, first in Germany, then in Holland and finally in England, made speedier progress here than Calvinism and above all Lutheranism. For small Nonconformist groups, tolerance was the basic premise of survival, and they advocated the separation of church and state. In general, however, 'religious' tolerance was more prevalent in Protestantism than in Catholicism, and finally political freedom of opinion too was achieved earlier in Protestant countries.

The rise of church pluralism, the confessionalization of religion, the emergence of religious subjectivity and the formation of ideas of tolerance were effects of the Reformation that left a deep mark on the society of the early modern period. However, other social and political powers were also involved in making them genuine constituent factors in the process whereby the modern world developed.

29   In general, cf. J. Lecler, *Geschichte der Religionsfreiheit im Zeitalter der Reformation*, 2 vols (Stuttgart, 1965); G. Güldner, *Das Toleranz-Problem in den Niederlanden im Ausgang des 16. Jahrhunderts* (Lübeck and Hamburg, 1968); H. Lutz (ed.), *Zur Geschichte der Toleranz und Religionsfreiheit* (Darmstadt, 1977).

II

The Reformation took place at a time of political and social change of which it was to some extent the expression, and in its own turn it had a strong influence on the consequences and outcome of those changes. The specific form taken by the state, the development of education and culture, the structure of the family and the re-evaluation of the world of work in the early modern period cannot be understood without the Reformation and early Protestantism.

1   The early modern state, either in its absolutist and authoritarian or in its estatist and libertarian form, was not a product of the Reformation, but the Reformation did leave a particular mark on the shape it took, and that is not just true of Holland and England. Three groups of ideas must be studied here. Theoretically, the evangelical churches – like Catholicism – had always striven to use the power of the state authorities as an instrument to promote their interests, or indeed as a means of extending ecclesiastical claims, but on the basis of their experience of secular intervention most Reformation forces supported separation of the sacred order from the secular order. To be free of secular intervention, the churches were to withdraw from all secular areas – ranging from the political sphere itself to charitable work for the poor – and conversely if the states were to be independent from ecclesiastical opposition they must keep out of all strictly religious matters, such as the conduct of divine service and pronouncements on doctrine. These ideas promoted both the de-politicization and indeed spiritualization of the Protestant church and the de-sacralization and secularization of the state.[30] In any case the Reformation strengthened state authority: there are classic examples in the German territories, Sweden and England. Although the Protestant churches wished to be free of state patronage, their own lack of hierarchical structure, in the Lutheran and the Calvinist churches alike, meant that they all depended on protection by the secular authorities. Since this situation suited the desire of the state not to tolerate any other autonomous order beside itself, while on the other hand not dispensing with the churches as stabilizing forces for national

---

30   See esp. E. W. Böckenförde, 'Die Entstehung des Staates als Vorgang der Säkularisation', in *Säkularisation und Utopie. Ebracher Studien, Ernst Forsthoff zum 65. Geburtstag* (Stuttgart, 1967), pp. 75–94; K. Blaschke, 'Wechselwirkung zwischen der Reformation und dem Aufbau des Territorialstaates', in *Der Staat* 9 (1970), pp. 347–64; G. Benecke, *Society and Politics in Germany 1500–1750* (London and Toronto, 1974); Schilling, *Konfessionskonflikt und Staatsbildung*, E. Hinrichs, *Einführung in die Geschichte der Frühen Neuzeit* (Munich, 1980), p. 178ff.

or territorial unity, the churches had to subordinate themselves to authoritarian state interests in such a way that they themselves became quasi-state institutions, or joined other institutions in a composite state organization.[31]

The emergent state church was thus not a product of the power interests of the secular state, but many Reformation ideas went into that state, and gave considerable support to state efforts at integration. Lutheranism in particular, but Calvinism too and not least Anglicanism, had to accept subordination to the state to reinforce their own interests. Only the free church religious communities, themselves in danger of suppression or abolition, steered clear of all integrating policies. Finally, Reformation forces were also involved in the formation of the early modern state in helping to determine whether the late medieval territorial state would become an absolutist state or a libertarian and estatist one.[32] The churches and confessions by no means remained neutral in the conflicts between the estates and the princes of the sixteenth and seventeen centuries which were of such importance for the future state structure of Europe. All the evangelical churches were certainly in favour of the authorities holding a clear balance of power, for without it their own existence would be endangered. However, it is revealing that the Reformation movement as a whole ultimately promoted libertarian, even republican and anti-absolutist powers more strongly than did Roman Catholicism, which seldom gave the estates more support than the princes. There are obvious examples in Austria and France. The anti-absolutist powers of the estates worked very closely with the reformed churches, in particular Calvinism, and neither the Dutch war of liberation nor the English Revolution can be understood without religious and confessional disputes. It was no coincidence, then, that the first libertarian democratic states came into being in Protestant areas, on the basis of the separation of church from state and the foundation of state power on natural rights.

31   See among others O. Hintze, 'Die Epochen des evangelischen Kirchenregiments in Preussen', in ibid., *Gesammelte Abhandlungen*, vol. 3 (Göttingen, 1967[2]), pp. 56–96; K. Holl, 'Luther und das landesherrliche Kirchenregiment', in ibid., *Gesammelte Aufsätze zur Kirchengeschichte*, vol. 1 (Tübingen 1927[5]), pp. 326–87; Krumwiede, *Zur Entstehung des landesherrlichen Kirchenregimentes in Kursachsen und Braunschweig-Wolfenbüttel*.
32   H. Sturmberger, *Georg Erasmus Tschernembl. Religion, Libertät und Widerstand* (Graz and Cologne, 1953); E. Hinrichs, *Fürstenlehre und politisches Handeln im Frankreich Heinrichs IV* (Göttingen, 1969); C. Hinrichs, *Preussentum und Pietismus. Der Pietismus in Brandenburg-Preussen als religiös-soziale Bewegung* (Göttingen, 1971); Manning, *Politics*; J. L. Price, *Culture and Society in the Dutch Republic during the 17th Century* (London, 1974); H. Vahle, 'Calvinismus und Demokratie im Spiegel der Forschung', in *Archiv für Reformationsgeschichte* 66 (1975), pp. 182–212.

2   There is no doubt that the early modern urban bourgeoisie, like the early modern state, had interests of its own in the expansion of intermediate and higher education. Humanist endeavours had shown the way, but education would not have flourished as we know it did in the sixteenth century without the support it received from the entire Reformation movement.[33] Even Catholicism was now obliged to encourage an educational system of its own, and was soon competing in the educational field with the Protestants.[34] The popular educational movement of the early seventeenth century, however, spread only in Germany and England.[35] The Catholic church concentrated chiefly on higher education. After the second half of the sixteenth century most schools in Protestant areas in fact soon came under the control of state institutions or at least state forces, in line with growing Protestant tendencies towards secularization; however, the expansion of elementary education was quite important to the forces of Reformation, since the general concentration on the scriptures made literacy a priority even for the lower classes. If the new faith was to be realized, preaching the Word from the Bible was not enough: individual Christians must be able to read the Bible for themselves. Literacy became a mark of Protestantism; England was the most obviously successful country in this respect. However, Protestants were soon no longer satisfied with educating people to read and write; children must also be brought up to live a Christian life.

The Christianizing of the world, an aim acknowledged by Protestantism as a whole despite its abstention from intervention in the secular order, was in essence a matter of education. Education soon came to be more important in the Catholic church as well, but there it never became instrumental in bringing the faith to the lower classes of society in particular. A convinced Protestant could only be someone who could read the Bible and above all, in so far as he was able, could understand church doctrine, which called for a long

---

33   Hinrichs, *Einführung*, p. 100ff; H. Hermelink and S. A. Kaehler, *Die Philipps-Universität zu Marburg 1527–1927* (Marburg, 1927); A. Schindling, *Humanistische Hochschule und freie Reichsstadt, Gymnasium und Akademie in Strassburg 1538–1621* (Wiesbaden, 1977); P. Baumgart and N. Hammerstein (eds), *Beiträge zu Problemen deutscher Universitätsgründungen der frühen Neuzeit* (Bremen and Wolfenbüttel, 1978). There is no comprehensive study of the subject.
34   The Jesuit schools in particular deserve mention. See J. W. Donohue, *Jesuit Education. An Essay on the Foundations of its Idea* (New York, 1963).
35   K. Schaller, *Die Pädagogik des Joh. Amos Comenius und die Anfänge des pädagogischen Realismus im 17. Jahrhundert* (Heidelberg, 1962); L. Stone, 'The Educational Revolution in England 1560–1640', in *Past and Present* 28 (1964), pp. 41–80; R. Engelsing, *Analphabetentum und Lektüre. Zur Sozialgeschichte des Lesens in Deutschland zwischen feudaler und industrieller Gesellschaft* (Stuttgart, 1973); R. Chartier et al., *L'éducation en France du XVIe au XVIIIe siècle* (Paris, 1976).

process of assimilation. Unfathomable as God was in the Protestant tradition, and strictly as all new forms of spreading the Word distinguished between faith and knowledge, faith being removed from any form of knowledge – the old sceptical attitudes to metaphysical speculation were still maintained – in practice faith was essentially a matter of thought and reflection. This concept, despite the acceptance of a number of mystical ideas, was supported in an ultimately plain form of divine service where the Word was always the focal point.[36] The Word of God was intended to encourage the believer's spiritual and religious adaptability, an aim promoted by the greater emphasis on education. It did not yet encourage any obvious secularization of teaching and education in the content of what was taught or the institutions themselves, for although Protestantism set store by knowledge and culture – and important as they had now become to the laity as well – in Protestant circles they were still essentially servants of faith and Christian virtue, and Calvinism proved no less rigid on this point than Lutheranism.

3   Marriage and family life had become to a great extent secularized in Protestantism.[37] However, though the sacramental character of marriage was questioned, that did not by any means indicate that the structure of family life was left to the household itself or to the authorities. Indeed, the family moved to the centre of social interest in all Protestant churches, particularly those of the Puritans, since it was seen as the nucleus of the Christian community, a place where Christian life was practised and the father of the household acted as Christ's representative. If the churches were to Christianize the world by bringing up children in the Christian faith and the Christian way of life, they must begin with families. The Protestant household was to act as an example.

The development of the bourgeois family does not go as far back as the Reformation, but certain modern trends did receive considerable support from Protestantism, particularly in its Puritan form.[38] Attempts

36   In general see P. Graff, *Geschichte der Auflösung der alten gottesdienstlichen Formen in der evangelischen Kirche Deutschlands bis zum Eintritt der Aufklärung und des Rationalismus* (Göttingen, 1921); W. Nagel, *Geschichte des christlichen Gottesdienstes* (Berlin, 1962); R. W. Scribner, 'Ritual and Popular Religion in Catholic Germany at the Time of the Reformation', in *Journal of Ecclesiastical History* 35 (1984), pp. 47–77.

37   H. Dietrich, *Das protestantische Eherecht in Deutschland bis zur Mitte des 17. Jahrhunderts* (Munich, 1970); A. Niebergall, *Die Geschichte der evangelischen Trauung in Hessen* (Göttingen, 1972).

38   L. L. Schüding, *Die puritanische Familie in literar-soziologischer Sicht* (Berne and Munich, 1964); L. Stone, *The Family, Sex and Marriage in England 1500–1800* (London, 1977). An important recent work is P. Zschunke, *Konfession und Alltag in Oppenheim. Beiträge zur Geschichte von Bevölkerung und Gesellschaft einer gemischt-konfessionellen Kleinstadt in der frühen Neuzeit* (Wiesbaden, 1984).

were made to exert moral influence on family relationships by preaching in church, teaching, and the social controls of ecclesiastical discipline. There were three central areas of concern. All varieties of Protestantism reinforced the traditional patriarchal power of the head of the household: the father of the family was regarded as not only its legal but also its spiritual and religious head, so that henceforward disobedience on the part of his children and even his wife was not just an offence to the good order of the household but to some extent a 'sin' against God. A new respectful attitude towards the father of the family from other members of the household was called for, but the head of the household himself must also be exemplary in his dealing with his subjects. Although this meant that his wife had no independence, but was wholly a part of the household, with a clearly defined role in it, greater value was assigned to her in evangelical culture, for the father of the family was supposed to treat her as his moral equal and not just a labour force. Consequently, he was no longer permitted to use violence against her, and indeed he was regarded as sharing the responsibility for his wife's moral behaviour. The converse was also true. For her part, the wife represented Christian order in the family and cared for the children's Christian education. The disciplinary authorities of the church thus did not examine the problems and difficulties of heads of households alone but also those of their wives, whose concerns they took just as seriously. For the first time the moral and religious responsibility for each other of all members of the household was a characteristic of relationships within marriage and the family. Finally, Protestantism deliberately placed control over children in the hands of their parents. They no longer grew up 'free', left to their own devices.[39] Their education at home became the responsibility of their parents; on the one hand children were bound to strict obedience, not just to guarantee the order of the domestic community but to honour Christian order that was based on obedience to authority and god, and on the other hand parents were bound to watch over both the physical and the spiritual wellbeing of their children and take proper account of their individual wishes, a point particularly evident in marriage policy. If parental authority were to be preserved, the child must be taken seriously as an individual.

In the introduction of ideas of morality into family relationships by the Protestant church, making the family the central place of religious and spiritual instruction, the Reformation revalued family life consider-

---

39 P. Aries, *Geschichte der Kindheit* (Munich, 1975); L. Stone, 'The Rise of the Nuclear Family in Early Modern England. The Patriarchal Stage', in C. E. Rosenberg (ed.), *The Family in History* (Philadelphia, 1975); N. Z. Davis, 'Ghosts, Kin and Progeny: Some Features of Family Life in Early Modern France', in *Daedalus* 106 (1977); L. De Mause (ed.), *Hört ihr die Kinder weinen?* (Frankfurt, 1977).

ably, although often at the cost of free self-determination in the individual's life.

4   Above all human work, including physical labour, underwent moral and social re-evaluation. Idleness had always been condemned in Christian ethics, and work regarded as the true task of man, but only the Reformation freed work from the taint of inferiority and sinfulness, raising it to the status of everyone's chief duty.[40] Even in ascetic versions of Protestantism, however, there was as yet none of the modern ethos of professionalism and profit-orientated capitalism, although constant secular activity went on even in particularly religious circles. Protestant morality did not sanction secular activity for its own sake: activity that did not serve to combat vice or build a Christian order. However, by evaluating the secular order positively and putting it on a par with spiritual and religious concerns, practical secular activities took on an equal value. Moreover, work and the exercise of a profession now became part of everyone's Christian life and actions, and could serve to honour God. Concrete secular work thus acquired a role unknown in earlier Christianity, where the contemplative life had always been regarded as superior.[41] Work thus became the 'secular' mark of a Christian, whereas idleness and begging – even for religious reasons, indeed particularly for religious reasons – were discredited as being not just unworthy but immoral and un-Christian.

This was the beginning of an important development, and one that made a crucial mark on the social consciousness of early modern society. People began to assess others by the quality of their work, and to consider poverty and idleness obstacles to a Christian life.[42] The civic and state authorities certainly shared this view of poverty and idleness on pragmatic grounds, but the world of this new morality cannot be

40   On the problem of poverty, work and idleness in early modern times, see G. Uhldorn, *Die christliche Liebestätigkeit* (Stuttgart, 1895[2]); T. Fischer, *Städtische Armut und Armenfürsorge im 15. und 16. Jahrhundert. Sozialgeschichtliche Untersuchungen am Beispiel der Städte Basel, Freiburg und Strassburg* (Göttingen, 1979); G. Sachsse and F. Tennstedt, *Geschichte der Armenfürsorge in Deutschland vom Spätmittelalter bis zum 1. Weltkrieg* (Stuttgart, 1980); T. Fischer, 'Der Beginn frühmoderner Sozialpolitik in den deutschen Städten des 16. Jahrhunderts', in *Jahrbuch der Sozialarbeit* 4 (1982), pp. 46–68; R. Jütte, *Obrigkeitliche Armenfürsorge in deutschen Reichsstädten der Frühen Neuzeit. Städtisches Armenwesen in Frankfurt am Main und Köln* (Cologne and Vienna, 1984).

41   The principle of *ora et labora* did make the superiority of the contemplative life a relative matter, but no particular Catholic incentive encouraged people to fill life with work in a positive way.

42   The first and sole purpose of work was certainly to prevent idleness and sin, but also to make a contribution to community life, although not for personal satisfaction.

understood without the commitment of the churches and their religious and moral struggle.

In the long term at least, the result was increasing discrimination against social borderline groups, beginning at the end of the sixteenth century and affecting the poor or those who were not integrated into society. At the same time, pressure was thereby increased for the churches and the Protestant states to remove the causes of beggary and poverty – not through the institution of charitable donations any more, but by an institutionalization of poverty which could ultimately be supported only by the secular authorities. The first workhouses were Protestant institutions.[43] With the re-evaluation of work and secular activity in general, the Reformation as a whole created important prerequisites for a modern professional ethos and in general prepared the way for self-realization through work, although few inroads were made into the problem of poverty. However, since only the active and industrious received social approval and could have positive expectations of life beyond the grave, Protestantism introduced an intensive campaign against poverty and in support of new 'industries', although it also discriminated against poverty in a way unknown to Catholicism. Catholicism too was soon propagating similar principles, but work and poverty were fundamentally different experiences in, for instance, England and Spain.

III

The Reformation was far from being a phenomenon concerned only with the subjective faith and piety of individuals, or one that was merely a matter of ecclesiastical and secular public institutions. Without effecting any profoundly revolutionary changes in human conduct and community life, the Reformation did in the long term exert considerable influence on everyday structures of thought and conduct. Above all, by encouraging 'rational' communication in public life, the moral awareness of responsibility, a plain and practical piety and 'civilized' everyday behaviour, it favoured the development of modern forms of behaviour and structures of communication. The Reformation differs from the open culture of the Enlightenment, however, in being of a uniformly religious character.

1   The Reformation eradicated ritual and sacramental forms of piety with some rigour. Catholic cults were replaced by an evangelical divine

43   Sachsse and Tennstedt, *Armenfürsorge*, pp. 112f; C. Lis and H. Soly, *Poverty and Capitalism in pre-industrial Europe, 1350–1850* (Hassocks, 1979).

service with its concentration on the Word. The reading of scripture and explanatory preaching were at the heart of religious devotion. Not all ritual religious practices were abandoned, but since Christ was the one central intermediary of grace and justification, the Word of God gradually became the exclusive guideline for human faith and life. Emphasis on the Word ultimately meant verbal, non-sensual communication, and a new factor thus entered the world of religious and social experience in the early modern period. Incomprehensible as God was agreed to be, faith implied an understanding of 'pure' doctrine, spiritual wrestling and an intellectual confrontation with it.[44] The philosophical rationalism of the seventeenth century was not a product of the Reformation, even in its Christian forms. But the ability to hold a 'reasonable' conversation on issues of faith or have a 'rational' view of the truths of faith – in a secular as well as a sacred connection – were strongly encouraged by the Reformation. Calvinism encouraged this more than Lutheranism, but it was a general conviction, and not just within an intellectual elite. By way of contrast, according to the Council of Trent and in the intellectual and confessional disputes of Catholicism with the Reformation, in principle a Catholic needed no religious knowledge for his salvation, need make no spiritual effort, and finally did not need to know the Bible or be able to follow a sermon. The simple evangelical often did not understand his pastor either, but he was obliged to make the effort to do so.[45]

With the Reformation an understanding of the Gospel, not mere acceptance and symbolic ritual assimilation of the truths of salvation but their intellectual absorption, did at least become a prerequisite and component of faith. Although man thus entered into verbal communication with God through the preaching of the Word, that did not mean that the assembly of all Christians, the community life of the church, was unimportant. On the contrary: although the pastors themselves could not be intermediaries providing salvation, although private devotions were encouraged and religious reflection and prayer outside the church itself were supposed to be part of the religious practice of Protestants, so that the church community itself was not the essential constituent of religious life, divine service in the congregation remained at the heart of religious and ecclesiastical practice. However – and here

44   R. Wohlfeil, *Einführung in die Geschichte der deutschen Reformation* (Munich, 1982), p. 123ff; H. Oberman, *Werden und Wertung der Reformation. Vom Wegestreit zum Glaubenskampf* (Tübingen, 1979²). Teaching and religious discussions emphasize this point.
45   The visitations provide ample confirmation: see among others B. Vogler, 'Die Entstehung der protestantischen Volksfrömmigkeit in der rheinischen Pfalz zwischen 1555 und 1619', in *Archiv für Reformationsgeschichte* 72 (1981), pp. 159–95.

was the crucial point – it was not an act celebrated by a priest in which the rite of worship, rather than the congregation, was the centre of the ritual. It was now a religious memorial celebration, in which each individual saw himself as a member of an assembled Christian community.[46] Whereas before the Reformation a believer could win merit according to his needs and find aid for every problem in the church, the religious advantages offered by the evangelical community were reduced solely to the central aim of religious instruction and moral edification through the scripture, which called for much effort by the pastor and required his purposeful interest in all community members. These were important prerequisites in a community based on the Word alone. The reduction of religious practice to verbal communication was certainly more marked in free church and Puritan circles than in Lutheranism; we may think, for instance, of religious life in Holland and England.[47] In principle, however, and in contrast to Catholicism, religious and verbal communication always took precedence over symbolic ritual. A ceremonial act of worship that could be interpreted in many ways, satisfying all possible religious needs, was replaced by a form of service based on the Word of God, binding all community members together in the same way. Thus spiritual adaptability and intellectual interests were encouraged even outside the educated elite, and the early Enlightenment conformed far more to Protestant than to Catholic interests.

2   The Reformation encouraged verbal communication outside the needs of everyday life. It also fostered a subjective sense of responsibility and thus promoted moral conduct in line with a conscience that was no longer controlled by the church but must be developed by the individual human being.[48] The idea of personal responsibility had long existed, but only with the coming of the Protestant ethic did it become everyone's duty to deal consciously with moral situations. The removal of all mediating authorities between God and man, and man's new inability to draw on particular means of acquiring grace (for instance, through the performance of religious practices), forced all individual Christians to come to terms with themselves

46   For this reason the moral link between community members was closer, engendering obsessions, particularly among the excitably religious.
47   Schilling, 'Religion und Gesellschaft in der calvinistischen Republik der Vereinigten Niederlande'; ibid., 'Der Aufstand der Niederlande: Bürgerliche Revolution oder Elitekonflikt?', in Geschichte und Gesellschaft (Sonderheft 2, 1976), pp. 177–231; Webster, The Intellectual Revolution; Price, Culture and Society; Hill, God's Englishman.
48   K. Duchrow, Christenheit und Weltverantwortung, Traditionsgeschichte und systematische Struktur der Zweireichelehre (Stuttgart, 1970); J. Baur et al., Die Verantwortung der Kirche in der Gesellschaft (Stuttgart, 1973).

and their God. Of course the Christian was to trust God and act in God's name, but taking personal responsibility for his own actions for the first time meant facing the world with a sense of full accountability.[49] This, ultimately, was the real meaning of the exhortation to Christianize the world: it was to be restructured in line with Christianity. Again, this is a factor most evident in Puritan Protestantism, and it is also present in Pietism.

The new religious subjectivity, an awareness of oneself and one's own abilities, did not exclude responsibility for public conduct in the family and at work. On the contrary: it was in his public commitment and the face he deliberately turned to the world that the Protestant bore witness to the truth of the Christian faith. The churches gave support to the faithful, encouraged them to be active and even prescribed detailed patterns of behaviour, but every Christian had to take his own final decision on his faith and his social and political conduct. The old sense of safety and relief provided by an abundance of rituals, both ecclesiastical and non-ecclesiastical, was gone. Man's duty towards his own conscience made demands that could ultimately be satisfied only by someone with the necessary abilities and in possession of the prerequisites for free self-determination. In general, this challenge appealed more to the new elites than the common people, and to stand out in estatist society through its public assumption of responsibility became the mark of a new elite. If subjective responsibility and conscience clearly became points of reference in social and political activity, despite all material influences, then the Reformation had given the first widely effective incentive to moral and political action, an appeal to all mankind to show responsibility while in this world. It became almost a commandment of ascetic Protestantism not to adopt the principle of letting the world run according to traditional rules and institutions, but instead to use moral action in practice to guide the course of events. The estates of the time found themselves most threatened in this point; early bourgeois attitudes found their justification in part in the Protestant ethic.[50]

3   While as far as we are aware, pre-Reformation religious practice and secular activity were barely separable, the Reformation divided the secular from the religious and ecclesiastical area for the first time. Conversely, 'religion' was purged and liberated from all 'worldliness'. This division, which implied a new definition of religion and the world – and

---

49   R. van Dülmen, *Die Utopie einer christlichen Gesellschaft. Joh. Val. Andreae* (Stuttgart, 1978).
50   The great extent to which early Enlightenment commitment grew from Protestant roots is pointed out in W. Martens, *Die Botschaft der Tugend. Die Aufklärung im Spiegel der deutschen Moralischen Wochenschriften* (Stuttgart, 1971).

of the spiritual and secular orders, of faith and reason – was of considerable importance, affecting not only community life in the church itself, but the secular lives of rulers and the daily lives of simple folk, touching on funeral rites and the routine of work alike. Two areas where this became particularly relevant deserve special mention. First, religion and work, that is to say religious interests and activities and secular opinions and business, were divided in such a way that religion became detached from the world, untouched by secular concerns, a pure matter of the mind, while the world of work, now free of religious significance and religious standards, became a purely economic and social sphere of action, and no longer needed the blessing of the church.[51] In concrete terms this development was evident in many working customs that were not actually abolished but no longer had any connection with the church. That did not prevent the real sense of religious life from being seen in 'secular' labour, but the interpretation was a new one. Secondly, Christian religion and 'heathen' superstition were separated in such a way that the magical practices formerly connected with Catholic forms of worship might still be tolerated outside the church as part of the secular world – although they were often in fact condemned as anti-Christian – but they were utterly rejected and eradicated from the religious area, being seen as superstition taking concrete shape in the churches.[52] Religion and 'magic' – which in the Protestant view included the Catholic cult of the sacraments – were mutually exclusive, although it cannot be denied that 'the Word' often became a substitute for rituals in Protestantism.[53]

In this the Reformation broke with the long amalgamation of Christian, magical and heathen practices as they existed in pre-Reformation Catholicism, permeating and regulating the whole of religious and social life. Instead, the Reformation de-mystified the world, answering a growing need for rational explanations in secular life. It is true that the rigid separation of magic and religion, which purged the Christian faith of all magical practices, was more evident in Calvinism and Puritanism than in Lutheranism, as inter-confessional discussion of the sacraments clearly shows, but in principle opposition to magic was one of the core

---

51 On this point see in general K.-S. Kramer, *Volksleben im Hochstift Bamberg und im Fürstentum Coburg (1500–1800)*, Würzburg, 1967; ibid., 'Protestantisches in der Volkskultur Frankens', in *Hessische Blätter für Volkskunde* 60 (1969), pp. 77–92; Vogler, 'Protestantische Volksfrömmigkeit'.
52 See van Dülmen, 'Volksfrömmigkeit'.
53 On the discussion of religon and magic, cf. L. Petzold (ed.), *Magie und Religion. Beiträge zu einer Theorie der Magie* (Darmstadt, 1978); also M. Mauss, 'Entwurf einer allgemeinen Theorie der Magie', in ibid., *Soziologie und Anthropologie* I (Munich 1974), pp. 43–179.

ideas of all Reformation tendencies.[54] Ultimately this opposition affected the traditional understanding of faith even more than the removal of the cult of saints and intercession and the practice of church blessings, for it presupposed a new understanding of both God and the world. Fundamental as the new division was for the development of the modern era, it also gave rise to the process of de-sacralization that brought about an increasing contrast between the religious way of thought – turning away from the world – and an obsession with work that turned towards the world.

4   Finally, one more point must be mentioned. It too resulted from the clear-cut division between what was sacred and what was secular, but it derived chiefly from the moral secular responsibility of the Protestant. Deliberately realizing his faith in a different way within the world, that is to say, regulating secular activities by Christian standards, meant not just acting responsibly but submitting to a morality not governed by worldly precepts. Without turning his back on the world, he sought to prove himself in the struggle against his passions, his physical nature and his idleness. The morality of the Reformation did indeed become integrated into society in a disciplinary process that found support in social forces, but Protestantism was the driving force at first. It aimed at four areas: most important of all was to counter intemperance in daily conduct in the matter of eating, drinking, and clothing oneself, and in celebrations and sexuality. Intemperate passions must be suppressed; physical and sensual needs and desires were subjected to Christian reason.[55] It was also necessary to bring people up, by force if need be, to habits of regular work, industry and order, not just as a means of defence against idleness, begging and thus vice, but in order to realize their Christian natures. And a 'clean' environment must be created, not merely as a condition of life without sickness and epidemic disease, but to make dignified living possible. Purity of the soul included cleanliness of the

54   Pioneering works are K. Thomas, *Religion and the Decline of Magic. Studies in popular beliefs in sixteenth and seventeenth-century England* (London, 1971); Muchembled, *Kultur des Volkes*; C. Ginzburg, 'Volksbrauch. Magie und Religion', in R. Romano et al. (eds), *Die Gleichzeitigkeit des Ungleichzeitigen. Fünf Studien zur Geschichte Italiens* (Frankfurt, 1980).

55   L. C. Eisenbart, *Kleiderordnungen der deutschen Städte zwischen 1350 und 1700. Ein Beitrag zur Kulturgeschichte des deutschen Bürgertums* (Göttingen, 1962); P. Münch (ed.), *Ordnung, Fleiss und Sparsamkeit. Texte und Dokumente zur Entstehung der 'bürgerlichen Tugend'* (Munich, 1984); N. Schindler, 'Karneval, Kirche und die verkehrte Welt. Zur Funktion der Lachkultur im 16. Jahrhundert', in *Jahrbuch für Volkskunde* (1984), pp. 9–57; J. H. Flandrin, *Familien, Soziologie, Ökonomie und Sexualität* (Berlin, 1978); J. Solé, *Liebe in der westlichen Kultur* (Berlin, 1976).

body.[56] Hygiene was not a problem explicitly tackled by the Reformation, but the Reformation did create the important conditions in which it could develop. Finally, every Christian was to have an education, or at least learn to read and write, not only so as to read the scriptures but to assert himself in the world as a Christian conversant with the major doctrines. Although grace and salvation could not be won by these endeavours to structure life, nor were they a basic part of the faith, it became increasingly unthinkable – and not just to theologians and pastors – that anyone who was, for instance, a drunkard, lazy, dirty and uneducated could also be a Protestant believer. A true Christian who bore witness to Christianity and his church was a chaste, industrious, clean and educated person. It was some time before the churches understood that to a great extent this ideal could be realized only in the upper social classes, so that ascetic Protestantism could not embrace wide social strata.[57] This image of a 'reasonable' evangelical Christian was by no means, of course, identical with that of a man of the Enlightenment, but the Reformation and its evangelical churches had as much influence as courtly society on the development of the 'civilized man' who ordered his life by reason rather than tradition, and whose passions were subjected to proper conduct.

The Reformation as a whole left profound traces behind it, affecting daily life as well as religion and the world of public politics. Its effects were extremely diverse and ambivalent; they destroyed old ways of life and founded new ones, they supported ideas of freedom and created new kinds of dependence. The Reformation encouraged a rational way of life but also suppressed vital elements. It may not have been the dividing line between the Middle Ages and the modern era, in so far as we can speak of such a thing, but without the Reformation and Protestantism it is impossible to understand certain vital modern developments. Different circumstances made the potential for rationalization stronger in Calvinism and Puritanism than in moderate Lutheranism, but Lutheranism too shook off tradition. No one single image of Protestantism exists, but unlike Catholicism, both before the Reformation and to some extent also after the Council of Trent, all the new evangelical

---

56   C. Webster, *The Great Instauration. Science, Medicine and Reform 1626–1680* (New York, 1975); J. Goudsblom, 'Zivilisation, Ansteckungsangst und Hygiene. Betrachtungen über einen Aspekt des europäischen Zivilisationsprozesses', in P. Gleichmann et al. (eds), *Materialien zu Norbert Elias' Zivilisationstheorie* (Frankfurt, 1979), pp. 215–253.
57   This does not exclude the independent contribution of Catholicism. Cf. Reinhard, 'Gegenreformation als Modernisierung?'; J. Bossy, 'The Counter-Reformation and the People of Catholic Europe', in *Past and Present* 47 (1970), pp. 51–70.

religious communities, alone or in collaboration with secular forces, consciously or unconsciously (for what the Reformation intended is often different from what it actually did), achieved the following: (1) the separation of religion from the secular order, meaning, despite the rise of established state churches, a 'de-secularization' of religion; (2) a revaluation of the secular order, including the world of work, although this de-sacralization did not by any means exclude theocratic or re-sacralizing tendencies; (3) support for free political organizations, although patriarchal structures also received much support; and (4) the subjection of all social relations to morality, although with emphasis on the religious responsibility of the individual. Important preconditions for the development of the modern world were thus created. Although they were at the same time socially relevant, concrete, and ushered in social change, that fact was not solely due to the Reformation or Protestantism. The effects of the Reformation were part of the process whereby modern society developed, and it gave a powerful impetus to the 'modernization' of Europe.

8

Success and Failure in the German Reformation

Gerald Strauss

Originally appeared as Gerald Strauss, 'Success and Failure in the German Reformation', *Past and Present*, 67 (1975), pp. 30–63.

Editor's Introduction

A religion based on the word presupposes a basic education – or at the least the ability to read simple prose. Luther realized this at the very outset of the movement, and he was careful to stress the need for more Latin and German schools. He recognized that the faith could only take root if the young received a proper Christian education. 'For it is a grave and important matter,' he wrote in his tract *To the Councilmen of all Cities in Germany that they Establish and Maintain Christian Schools* (1524), 'and one of which is of vital concern both to Christ and the world at large, that we take steps to help the youth.' In response, the evangelical authorities turned to the foundation wealth once reserved for Catholic worship and used it to reform the schooling systems. New school orders were published, new standards were created, and new schools were built. Nuremberg, for instance, founded a new *Gymnasium*, and the city even had Philip Melanchthon draw up a curriculum for the institution. In the principality of Hesse, landgrave Philip envisioned a reform of the educational system as early as 1526, calling for the establishment of German schools in all the cities and villages in his territory. Numerous other evangelical powers, both territories and cities, followed suit.

In addition to formal education, the reformers also turned to the catechism as a way of implanting the faith. Catechisms were small, cheap, lightweight booklets containing the main tenets of the faith, and they proved essential to the evangelical movement. 'For among us the catechism has come back into use,' wrote Luther, 'I mean the Lord's Prayer, the Apostles' Creed, the Ten Commandments, penance and baptism, prayer, the cross, living and dying . . .' Luther himself wrote two catechisms for general use, as did hundreds of other reformers in Germany. But the catechism, no less than the theological tract, was composed of words on a page, and the Protestant authorities had to make sure that the faithful could understand it. Once again the importance of education was paramount.

Gerald Strauss believes that the historian can assess the success or failure of the educational initiative. In suggesting this, he is in a sense repeating the opinion of the reformers themselves, for they too believed that the process of learning (the catechism sessions, the classroom rote) could be measured in real terms. This was, after all, one of the main functions of the Protestant visitation process: the purpose was to determine whether the Reformation had made an impact on the religious understanding of parish population, the young in particular. With this concern in mind the reformers revived the visitation process, and used it to great advantage. The first Lutheran visitation took place in Electoral Saxony. Melanchthon penned a tract entitled *Instruction of the Visitors to the Pastors in the Electorate of Saxony* (1528) which spelled out what was required of the clergy and the subject population, while Luther provided a justification for the undertaking in the preface. The Elector Frederick, he wrote, in the absence of any action from the bishops, and 'out of Christian love . . . and for the benefit and welfare of all the wretched Christians in his lands,' had thought it necessary to implement a visitation. The Lutheran principality of Brandenburg-Ansbach also held a visitation in 1528, Hesse introduced its own in 1533, Pomerania in 1535, and Brandenburg in 1540. By the end of the century, annual visitations were common throughout the German lands (whether Lutheran, Calvinist, and indeed Catholic as well). The visitation committee, which was usually comprised of both secular and spiritual officials, assembled the results of the parish-to-parish progress and forwarded an abstract to the appropriate institutions. Gathered together, these visitation abstracts (or returns) then allowed the authorities to draft a picture of the state of religion in the territory.

For the most part, Strauss is basing his evaluation on the contents of the visitation returns. The returns are an ideal source for this type of investigation, for they survey the results of the visitation process, and thus speak directly to the question of success and failure. Moreover, given the thoroughness of the visitation process itself, there is an abundance of material at hand. Early visitations tended to concentrate on the basic requirements of the church. As the Reformation church became more secure in the Empire, however, the range of inquiry broadened. Visitors were empowered to watch over the physical condition of the church (tithe collection, the fabric of the church, local economic conditions). The demands placed on the clergy grew in number, while the expectations increased. The *Visitation Instructions* (1560) of the city of Nuremberg, for instance, looked into what the pastors read, the frequency of catechism lessons, the frequency of communion, the quality of social relations in the parish, the quality of religious understanding in the parish, and the private life of the clergy. By the later decades of the century, this type of survey was also regularly extended to the parishioners. The *Church Ordinance of Saxony* (1580) commissioned the visitors to probe deeply into parish affairs. The visitors investigated the quality of public worship, the educational standards of the parish, the nature of social activities, such as drinking, dancing, or communal assemblies (all of which were forbidden), the general level of religious understanding, and the moral character of the parishioners and parish life in general. If a village or a congregation did not measure up, the visitors referred the problems to the central authorities.

There is a danger, as Strauss is aware, of taking these visitation returns at face value. Given the expectations of the reformers, it is hardly surprising that they were able to find fault with the parishioners. It is also difficult to determine the truth of the returns, for the visitors may have overlooked some facts (for better or worse) to serve their own agenda. Equally, we should not assume that the testimony of the local clergy or the parishioners was given without some distortion. This source material must be viewed with a critical eye. Nevertheless, despite all of their failings, the visitation returns remain one of the most important sources of information for our understanding of the Reformation. Used in the appropriate manner, the paperwork generated by the visitation process offers a very vivid picture of the successes and the failures of long-term religious reform.

Success and Failure in the German Reformation

Gerald Strauss

A hundred and thirty years ago the catholic historian and church politician Ignaz von Döllinger scored a polemical point by using the Protestant reformers' own words to prove his contention that the evangelical movement in Germany had *failed* in its *objectives*. The first of Döllinger's three volumes on the Lutheran Reformation consists almost entirely of quotations from eighteen reformers, led by Luther and Melanchthon, who speak of their defeat in explicit terms and vivid language. No change for the better had occurred in the hearts and minds of men. On the contrary, they said, all was worse now than it had been under Rome. Melanchthon's deep pessimism became evident as early as 1525. A decade or so later Luther began to vent his despair in increasingly gloomy outpourings of his bitter disappointment over public indifference to the Gospel and the absence of any visible effects of his work on the thoughts and lives of his fellow Germans. Assembled in Döllinger's book these utterances make a powerful argument for his case against the Reformation.[1]

Many of Döllinger's quotations turn up again in Johannes Janssen's *History of the German People at the Close of the Middle Ages*, where they help substantiate Janssen's contention that social and intellectual conditions quickly deteriorated in Germany on the introduction of the Lutheran heresy.[2] Janssen's book found a wide response which could not fail to provoke reaction from the Protestant camp. The most prolific of Lutheran spokesmen, Wilhelm Walther, began to reply in 1884;[3] in 1906 he published *For Luther Against Rome*, a systematic apology in

---

1 Johann Joseph Ignaz von Döllinger, *Die Reformation, ihre Entwicklung und ihre Wirkungen im Umfange des lutherischen Bekenntnisses*, i (Regensburg, 1846), pp. 1–408. Passages from Luther: ibid., pp. 284–348. Döllinger's list is indiscriminate; it includes Erasmus as well as Luther, also radical dissenters such as Franck and Schwenkfeld.

2 Johannes Janssen, *History of the German People at the Close of the Middle Ages*, trans. A. M. Christie, 16 vols (London, 1896–1910). See generally iii, pp. 363–70, on Luther's complaints about decline; vii, pp. 141–3, on Melanchthon's despair. Cf. also Janssen's *An meine Kritiker* (Freiburg i. B., 1882), p. 122.

3 Walther published a series of pamphlets entitled *Luther im neuesten römischen Gericht* in the Schriften des Vereins für Reformationsgeschichte, nos. 7 (Halle, 1884), 13 (Halle, 1886), 31 (Halle, 1890), 35 (Halle, 1892).

answer to Catholic allegations.[4] Walther rejects many of the passages quoted by Janssen and Döllinger as inaccurate or taken out of context. Others, particularly Luther's own, he acknowledges as genuine but tries to explain away. In any case, he argues, beside each despairing utterance can be set a passage in which Luther asserts confidently that the Gospel had wrought a beneficial change among men.[5]

There is little satisfaction nowadays in making one's way through these wordy and contentious volumes. Janssen's one-sidedness now appears evident on nearly every page. For his part, Walther – the author, incidentally, of a ferocious tract of the First World War entitled *Germany's Sword Consecrated by Luther*[6] – writes throughout in a strident tone which neither gives nor asks mercy. Today this aggressive bickering leaves one with a sinking feeling of energies wasted and talents misapplied. Is there anything to be gained from opening once again the question of whether the Reformation is a success story or the tale of a failure? Let us see.

I

I shall beg for the moment the question of what constitutes 'success' in the Reformation. Let us first recognize it as a fact that most of the leading participants in the Lutheran movement during its first half century or so came to believe that they had been defeated. Given their resolutely pessimistic view of human nature any other conclusion would, perhaps, have been surprising. All the same, the chorus of disenchantment conveys a distinct sense of tragedy. Luther himself foresaw the demise of the evangelical movement, and his loyal followers did not fail to point to his prediction as the legitimation of their own disillusionment. Johann Aurifaber, who edited Luther's 'Table Talk' in 1566, concluded that '[Luther's] teachings have grown and prospered up to our own time, but from now on they will decrease and fall, having completed their appointed course'.[7] Luther had anticipated this outcome, Aurifaber said. He knew that 'God's word has seldom tarried in one place longer than forty years', a prophecy sadly come true, 'for [Luther's] teachings are now everywhere despised, and so many men

4   Wilhelm Walther, *Für Luther wider Rom: Handbuch der Apologetik Luthers und der Reformation*... (Halle, 1906). Walther presents arguments against Heinrich Denifle, as well as against Janssen.
5   Ibid., pp. 716–21, for these arguments and passages.
6   W. Walther, *Deutschlands Schwert durch Luther geweiht* (Leipzig, 1914).
7   Aurifaber's preface is reprinted in *Dr. Martin Luthers sämtliche Schriften*, ed. Johann Georg Walch, xxii (Halle, 1743), pp. 40–54; the passage quoted here is on p. 50.

have lost interest in them that his very name is held in contempt'.[8] Aurifaber – and other loyal Lutherans – pointed to sectarianism as the chief symptom of this decline. But even more disturbing was the general indifference to Scripture, especially when it occurred 'in Germany, a country blessed above all others with the pure word of the Gospel'.[9] The ingratitude of men! 'Good things that come to us are soon forgotten in this world, and no one gives thanks for what he possesses.' Who remembers nowadays, Aurifaber asks, what life was like in the time of struggle against Rome?

> We ought to look back fifty years and recall how gruesome, how frightful and pitiful had been the state of religion and church government then. We were all in a dungeon under the pope. But who remembers this today? Young people know nothing about it, and their parents have forgotten it too![10]

It will be useful to remind ourselves at this point that speculations of a cosmic nature must have coloured this pessimistic assessment of the course of the Reformation. Men who had read Daniel and Revelation, who studied the stars and contemplated the senility of nature as they anticipated the approaching end of the world knew what to expect from their own time.[11] Nonetheless the many expressions of discontent[12] make a poignant contrast to the assertive optimism of the movement's early years when Luther could write exultantly of the reformation he had inaugurated: 'I declare, I have made a reformation which will make the popes' ears ring and hearts burst'; and of 'the substantial benefit,

8   Ibid., p. 51. Aurifaber's entire preface is drenched in a mood of bitter disillusionment, saved from cynicism only by his conviction that the events he witnesses are evidence of the imminent end of the world.
9   Andreas Musculus, *Vom Himmel und der Hellen* . . . (Frankfurt an der Oder, 1559), fo. aii[v].
10   Aurifaber, p. 50. For a popular version of these sentiments, see 'Pasquillus zwischen einem Bair und Sachsen', c. 1556, printed in August Hartmann (ed.), *Historische Volkslieder und Zeitgedichte*, i (Munich, 1907), no. 8.
11   For a very good example of this, see Justus Jonas, *Das siebend Capitel Danielis* . . . (Wittenberg, 1529), especially fo. B[v], where the images of Daniel 7 are applied to the advancing Turkish empire and this, in turn, is seen as a punishment of Christians, especially Lutherans, who do not heed the Gospel.
12   A sampling of these: Wenceslaus Linck, preface to Leonhard Culman's *Ein christlich teutsch spil, wie ein Sünder zur buss bekert wird* (Nuremberg, 1539), in Julius Tittmann (ed.), *Schauspiele aus dem 16. Jahrhundert* (Leipzig, 1868), p. 110; Veit Dietrich, *Kinder-Postilla* (Nuremberg, 1549), fos. 44[r]–45[v]; Musculus, fo. Aii[v]; Caspar Huberinus, *Spiegel der geistlichen Hauszucht* (Frankfurt am Main, 1569), fos. cxix[r], ccxliii[v]; Simon Musaeus, *Catechismus* . . . (Frankfurt am Main, 1571), fo. 2[v].

peace and virtue it has brought to those who have accepted it'.[13] Against detractors, who at that time were still mostly in the Roman camp, he declared that 'hardly one of them is willing to acknowledge the good which the Gospel has accomplished not only in the individual conscience, but also in public affairs and in the quality of family and household life'.[14] It was generally agreed that the year 1530 marked the zenith of the Lutheran movement in Germany.[15] Thirty years later its fortunes had begun to decline. Politicians were taking over, 'the jurists and courtiers who now control our churches and pulpits'.[16] Evidently the spirit had gone out of the evangelical revival in Germany.

II

It has not usually been noticed that much of the reformers' early optimism rested on their conviction that they had found a way to implant evangelical Christianity in the minds of their fellow men, particularly in the minds of the young, who represented the movement's best hope of survival. Religious instruction would root the principles of the faith in the impressionable minds and malleable characters of children and adolescents, with beneficial results inevitably to follow when the new generation came to adulthood. In 1528 Luther apparently felt that this effort, just begun, was succeeding. Expanding on the proud claim (mentioned in the preceding paragraph) that he had accomplished a true reformation, he asserts that

> nowadays a girl or boy of fifteen knows more about Christian doctrine than did all the theologians of the great universities in the old days. For among us the catechism has come back into use: I mean the Lord's Prayer, the Apostle's Creed, the Ten Commandments and all that one should know about penance, baptism, prayer, the cross, how to live and how to die, and the sacrament of the altar, also about marriage, civil obedience, the duties of father and mother, wife and children, father and son, master and servant. In short, I have established the right order and a good conscience for all estates in society, so that each will know how to live and to

13   Luther in his preface to Stephan Klingebeil's *Von Priester Ehe* (Wittenberg, 1528): *D. Martin Luthers Werke. Kritische Gesamtausgabe* (Weimar, 1883–   ) (hereafter *Luthers Werke*), xxvi, p. 530.
14   From his lectures on the Song of Songs, given 1530–1, published in 1539 by Veit Dietrich: *Luthers Werke*, xxxi (2), p. 613.
15   This is said by Aurifaber, p. 50.
16   Ibid., p. 49.

serve God in his appointed rôle. And to those who have accepted it, my reformation has brought not a little benefit, peace and virtue.[17]

Luther's own catechisms, in preparation since 1523, were ready in 1529.[18] Proving almost at once their merit as instruments for training pastors and for instructing the young and the ignorant, they generated countless emulation.[19] In 1530 Luther took stock of his accomplishments. Writing to the Elector of Saxony, he boasted that

> there is no other land in the world to compare with Your Electoral Grace's territories for excellent pastors and preachers. Nowhere else do they teach so piously and purely and help maintain such serene peace among men. Our tender youth, girls as well as boys, are now so well taught in catechism and Scripture that my heart grows warm as I observe young children praying more devoutly, believing more firmly, and discoursing more eloquently on God and Christ than, in the old days, all the learned monks and doctors.[20]

The accuracy of this description is open to question; Luther was trying to encourage the Elector at a difficult moment. But Luther here illustrates the enormous trust placed by the early reformers in the educational – more properly indoctrinational – undertaking on which they were then embarking. According to what they knew about the young and the problems of teaching them (and what they knew they had, of course, read in books) there was every reason to expect good results from a soundly conceived pedagogy energetically applied in institutions established for that purpose. A vast literature on the education of children, dating back to pagan and Christian antiquity and tended as a living tradition by pedagogical writers throughout the centuries, supplied reformers with a body of theoretical evidence to show that all but a very few were capable of learning and that the learning process – providing it began early in the child's life, was pursued methodically, limited its aims to individual talents, and employed appropriate methods – was bound

17　See n. 13 above.
18　Cf. Georg Buchwald, *Die Entstehung der Katechismen Luthers . . .* (Leipzig, 1894).
19　The only comprehensive attempt to survey the stupendous number of Lutheran catechisms produced in Germany in the sixteenth century was made by Johann Michael Reu, *Quellen zur Geschichte des kirchlichen Unterrichts in der evangelischen Kirche Deutschlands zwischen 1530 und 1600*, part 1, *Quellen zur Geschichte des Katechismus-Unterrichts*, 5 vols (Gütersloh, 1904–24).
20　Luther to Elector John of Saxony, 20 May 1530: *Luthers Werke, Briefwechsel* (hereafter *Br.*), v, no. 1572.

to produce lasting results.[21] That the older generations were too far gone in ignorance and corruption was a matter of general agreement among reformers. 'Let them go to the devil', said Luther.[22] 'Instead,' said Johann Agricola, 'let us with God's help try it with children'.[23] The future evidently rested upon the young. 'I believe with all my heart,' said a Lutheran pedagogue, 'that this is our only hope for restoring corrupt Christendom'.[24]

This only hope could lead to some drastic experiments. Preachers in Strassburg, outraged at the deplorable conditions they had found in the city and in despair over the indifference of parents to pulpit admonitions to send children to school, proposed to the council that they city's young be declared to 'belong to God and the religious and civic community and not to their parents' so that they could then be conscripted to their appointed lessons.[25] The date was 1547 and hopes for an immediate and whole-hearted response to the Gospel had already been dimmed. Twenty years earlier, discussions about Christian education were not yet muted by fears of failure. By 1528 reformers had worked out a compromise solution to the dilemma inherent in the contradiction between their theological conviction that education leading to faith was an impossibility, and their recognition that at a worldly level training in religious and civic duties was not only possible, but necessary.[26] For the able – those suited by intellect and character to be pastors, teachers, lawyers, and so on – Latin schools (traditional institutions, but reformed and restaffed) would be established. Ordinary youngsters would receive religious instruction in catechism classes and a modicum of useful learning in 'German schools' to be raised in a way not yet determined from their

---

21   I examine the pedagogical literature and its impact on Lutheran educational thought and policies in 'The State of Pedagogical Theory *c.* 1500: What Protestant Reformers Knew about Education', since published as Gerald Strauss, 'The State of Pedagogical Theory *c.* 1530: What Protestant Reformers Knew about Education', in Lawrence Stone (ed.), *Schooling and Society. Studies in the History of Education* (London, 1976), pp. 69–94.

22   Luther to Elector John, 22 Nov. 1526: *Luthers Werke, Br.*, no. 1052 (iv, p. 133).

23   Johann Agricola, *Hundert und dreissig gemeiner Fragestücke für die jungen kinder* . . . (Wittenberg, 1528), fo. Aii^v.

24   Johann Bader, *Ein Gesprächbüchlein vom Anfangk Lebens, mit dem jungen Volk zu Landaw* (Landau, 1526), quoted in J. P. Gelbert, *Magister Johann Baders Leben und Schriften* (Neustadt, 1968), p. 123.

25   Strasbourg, Archives de la ville, Archive St. Thomas 84, carton 48, fo. 188^v. The council rejected the proposal, preferring to rely on persuasion.

26   On Luther's complex views regarding the limits and possibilities of education, see Ivar Asheim, *Glaube und Erziehung bei Luther* (Heidelberg, 1961), esp. pp. 88ff. Also Edgar Reimers, *Recht und Grenzen einer Berufung auf Luther in den neueren Bemühungen um eine evangelische Erziehung* (Weinheim, 1958).

present condition as private and local enterprises.[27] In 1524, the date of his tract *To the Councillors of all the Cities in Germany*, Luther abandoned for all practical purposes his earlier notion that fundamental Christian concepts of religion and citizenship could be taught in the home. As late as 1523 he had recommended as a model (*eyn gemeyn exempel*) the constitution of the town of Leisnig, according to which each householder was obliged to teach the Bible to his children and domestic servants.[28] But results of this procedure were disappointing.[29] By the later 1520s everybody knew that parents were not doing the job of giving a Christian upbringing to their children. This was not for lack of exhortations to do so, nor of assurances that in principle the home was the ideal place for Christian nurture and instruction.[30] But it was no secret that little or no Christian teaching was actually taking place in the home.[31]

The upshot of such painful reflections was that reformers willingly collaborated with political authorities in drafting school ordinances setting up educational systems in cities and territories wherever Lutheranism had become the established religion.[32] As is well known, these school ordinances, which are nearly always integral parts of comprehensive ecclesiastical constitutions, laid down detailed and explicit regulations covering teaching, curriculum and conduct. Specific rules

27   I deal with the objectives of Lutheran education in 'Reformation and Pedagogy: Educational Thought and Practice in the Lutheran Reformation', in Charles Trinkaus and Heiko A. Oberman (eds), *The Pursuit of Holiness. Papers from the University of Michigan Conference* (Leiden, 1974), pp. 272–93.
28   *Luthers Werke*, xii, p. 11.
29   Luther noted shrewdly that 'discipline taught in the home seeks to teach the child by encouraging him to utilize his own experience (*eygen erfarung*). But before this can bring results, we are a hundred times dead.' *An die Ratsherren aller Städte deutsches Lands* (Wittenberg, 1524): *Luthers Werke*, xv, p. 45.
30   Asheim quotes passages in which Luther urges parents to take on the Christian training of their children. See also Bugenhagen's letter to the city council of Hamburg: Johann Bugenhagen, *Von dem christlichen Glauben und rechten guten Werken* . . . (Wittenberg, 1525; Nuremberg, 1527 edn.), p. 245. See also Justus Menius, *An die hochgeborne Fürstin, Frau Sibilla Hertzogin zu Sachsen, Oeconomia christiana* . . . (Wittenberg, 1529), fo. H iv[v]. The best synopsis of Luther's own view of the parental office is found in his explication of the Fourth Commandment in the Larger Catechism of 1529: *Luthers Werke*, xxx (1), pp. 156ff. Asheim discusses the inconsistencies arising from Luther's recommendation of two possible courses of action, education in the home and education in schools. In the course of the sixteenth century a large *Hausväter-Literatur* sprang up, designed to train and assist householders in their responsibility to their children's upbringing.
31   E.g. Veit Dietrich's statement in *Kinder-Postilla*, fo. 44[r–v].
32   For a chronological list of school ordinances established in the sixteenth century, see Georg Mertz, *Das Schulwesen der deutschen Reformation* (Heidelberg, 1902), pp. 162–5. The texts of most *Schulordnungen* may be found in Reinhold Vormbaum, *Die evangelischen Schulordnungen des 16. Jahrhunderts* (Gütersloh, 1860).

were framed in statements of general purpose placing education in the grand design of a religious and political reformation of state, society and individual. The state being in nearly all instances the moving force behind the establishment of new schools and the reform of old ones, political ends came inevitably to be fused with religious objectives. Religious leaders, for their part, were gratified to know that the state was always prepared to intervene should pulpit persuasion fail to convince the faithful that schooling was necessary and good. School systems established in these circumstances could hardly fail to be 'instruments of magisterial education', as they have rightly been called.[33] To the extent possible in an age of very imperfect centralization, educational procedures were made uniform and subject to enforcement. Municipal and territorial school authorities, composed of secular and ecclesiastical officials working jointly, wrote curricula, selected books, drew up lesson plans, appointed teachers, and controlled the enterprise by means of inspections and examinations. Apart from taking leading roles in the drafting of school ordinances, reformers gave their formal blessing to the dominant role of the state in educational (and of course ecclesiastical) matters. Luther reminded the Elector in 1526 that 'as supreme guardian of our youth (*oberster furmund der iugent*)' he had every right to force cities and towns to employ part of their wealth to build schools.[34] Elsewhere rulers and magistrates were addressed as 'fathers of our youth' and granted the sweeping regulatory powers implied in this description of the nature and scope of their authority.[35]

By far the most promising instrument for religious and moral instruction was the catechism. Lutherans took justified pride in their development of the catechism as a means of teaching the elements of the faith to the young and simple, claiming its reintroduction into Christian practice as a distinctly Protestant contribution.[36] No other method seemed as suitable to the purpose.[37] Its aims were clearly stated in a memoran-

---

33 Wilhelm Maurer, *Der junge Melanchthon* (Göttingen, 1967–9), p. 463.
34 Luther to Elector John, 22 Nov. 1526: *Luthers Werke, Br.*, no. 1052 (iv, p. 134).
35 In the Gengenbach *Kirchenordnung*: E.-W. Kohls (ed.), *Evangelische Bewegung und Kirchenordnung. Studien und Quellen zur Reformationsgeschichte der Reichsstadt Gengenbach* (Karlsruhe, 1966), p. 35.
36 Cf. Melanchthon's assertion in Article 8 of the *Apology of the Augsburg Confession*: 'Among our adversaries children receive no catechism instruction whatever'. The most convenient reference to the Latin text and its English translation is: *Concordia Triglotta: The Symbolical Books of the Evangelical Lutheran Church* (St. Louis, 1921), pp. 324 (Latin) and 325 (English).
37 This point is made too frequently for citation. One example: Johann Spangenberg, *Des kleinen Catechismi . . . kurtzer Begriff* (Wittenberg, 1541), repr. in Reu, *Quellen . . . Katechismus-Unterrichts*, ii (2), pp. 285–98: Nothing is as dear to God as pious, obedient, God-fearing children 'and it is certain that no other ways or means

dum prepared in 1531 by a group of Nuremberg theologians while that city's council was considering the establishment of public catechism lessons as a matter of policy:

> Catechism is Christian instruction for children. By this we do not mean only that such instruction should be given to children alone, but that all Christians must from the age of childhood learn and understand the catechism. 'Catechism' comes from the word 'echo', which means reflected sound, for in catechism lessons we teach by saying aloud a sentence or two which the learner then repeats in the manner of the reverberation of the human voice in a great hall or in a forest. And this speaking out loud and repetition is to be kept up until the children can recite the entire catechism word for word without missing a syllable.[38]

The question-and-answer form adopted by Luther for his Shorter Catechism of 1529[39] proved ideal for purposes of rudimentary indoctrination and was never seriously challenged. For the sake of simplicity and orthodoxy authorities also stressed the need to keep always to the same text, to make no additions and attempt no innovations in content or wording. This, too, goes back to Luther's warning that young minds are easily confused by diversity.[40] In the course of time uniformity became a kind of fetish. In actual fact, however, there existed such a bewildering profusion of different catechisms in Lutheran Germany that a recent student of the subject can seriously suggest that 'something like every third pastor drew up a substantial catechism of his own'.[41] No figures

exist for training children to piety and obedience than through the catechism'. A popular rhyme ran: 'Der Catechismus Luther klein/Das höchste Buch auf Erden,/das fast die ganze Schrift so fein/in kurtze summ zu lernen (Luther's Shorter Catechism is the best book on earth, for it gives us the sum of all Scripture so that we can learn it with ease)'. Quoted in Friedrich Hahn, *Die evangelische Unterweisung in den Schulen des 16. Jahrhunderts* (Heidelberg, 1957), p. 66. There were, of course, several catechisms in circulation before Luther's. On these, see Ernst-Wilhelm Kohls, *Evangelische Katechismen der Reformationszeit vor und neben Luthers kleinem Katechismus* (Texte zur Kirchen- und Theologiegeschichte, pt. 16, Gütersloh, 1971), pp. 7–11. For an up-to-date bibliography on Lutheran catechism instruction, see ibid., pp. 12–20. The older literature on all aspects of catechisms is cited in C. A. G. von Zezschwitz, *System der christlichen Katechetik*, 2 vols (Leipzig, 1863–74).

38 Quoted in Klaus Leder, *Kirche und Jugend in Nürnberg und seinem Landgebiet 1400 bis 1800* (Einzelarbeiten aus der Kirchengeschichte Bayerns, lii, Neustadt an der Aisch, 1973), p. 54.

39 Zezschwitz, ii (2), p. 36, argues that Luther got the idea from visitation examinations. But he also shows earlier uses of question-and-answer materials in popular devotional and confessional literature: ibid., ii (2), chaps. i–ii.

40 In *Der kleine Katechismus für die gemeinen Pfarrherren und Prediger* (Wittenberg, 1529): *Luthers Werke*, xxx (1), p. 268.

41 Kohls (ed.), *Evangelische Bewegung und Kirchenordnung*.

are given, and the estimate is almost certainly exaggerated. But a glance through the far from complete collection of sixteenth-century catechisms in Johann Michael Reu's voluminous compilation[42] is likely to stun the reader with the sheer number of catechisms in circulation. At least until the general acceptance of the Formula of Concord in 1577–88 catechisms multiplied at a prodigious rate, the printed ones which have survived representing only a fraction of manuscript copies actually in use.[43]

It was a long time before control through territorial visitations reduced this profusion to something like the desired uniformity. In the meantime, however, catechism teaching was taking root, at least to the extent of making instruction mandatory in parish schools and churches as an obligation imposed by ecclesiastical constitutions.[44] For Latin scholars, particularly students in the upper forms, catechisms offered theologically demanding material to be learned and expounded. But for the common folk and the very young, contents and format of catechetical indoctrination were for the most part exceedingly simple. In rural areas, that is to say for the preponderance of the population, the sexton – called *Küster* in the north and *Messner* in the south, normally a rural artisan by trade – was responsible for catechism teaching. His emphasis was on plainness of instruction. Little was expected of common folk in the way of comprehension. But in cities, and in the hands of able preachers catechisms could offer substantial food for thought. Some played rather heavy-handedly on the consciousness of inherited sin, evidently attempting to use induced sensations of shame and guilt as a means of exerting social control;[45] others made light of

---

42   Reu.

43   I have seen few surviving MS. copies. No doubt these cheaply produced and flimsily bound booklets were read to pieces. Kohls (ed.), p. 35, quotes a statement to this effect by the preachers who produced the catechism for the city of Gengenbach. Even the printed catechisms do not survive in abundance. They too were used up, and their small format made them easy to lose.

44   All *Kirchenordnungen* required this. For texts of these, see Emil Sehling (ed.), *Die evangelischen Kirchenordnungen des 16. Jahrhunderts*: vols. i–v (Leipzig, 1902); continued under the auspices of the Institut für evangelisches Kirchenrecht der evangelischen Kirche in Deutschland zu Göttingen, vols. vi (1955–7)–xiv (1969).

45   Most notably Andreas Osiander's influential *Catechismus oder Kinder-Predig, wie die in meiner gnädigen Herrn Marggraven zu Brandenburg und eines ehrbaren Raths der Stadt Nürnberg Oberkeiten und Gebieten allenthalben gepredigt werden* (Nuremberg, 1533): repr. in Reu, i (1), pp. 462–564. Osiander's catechism, intended as a commentary on Luther's, was also introduced to Weissenburg (1533), Dinkelsbühl (1534) and elsewhere. On some of the political implications of Osiander's emphasis on sin, see my article 'Protestant Dogma and City Government: The Case of Nuremberg', *Past and Present*, no. 36 (Apr. 1967), pp. 38–58.

this.[46] Some catechisms confined themselves to basic religious instruction. Many others tried also to inculcate civic virtues and discipline. The Fourth Commandment generally served as the point of departure for disquisitions on social obligations and behaviour, while the Seventh – thou shalt not steal – often provided occasion for explicit affirmations of the right to property and to the rewards of one's labour.[47] Some catechisms were intended for use in the classroom, others for instruction in church. A few were turned into primers. Luther's Shorter Catechism usually served as the source for these.

If all this failed to produce results, it was not for lack of conviction, nor of methodical effort on the part of the reformers and their schoolmasters. Teaching techniques in the early sixteenth century rested on certain generally held assumptions about the workings of the mind and the responses of the learner. A large body of received knowledge, dating back to classical and Christian antiquity and absorbed into the educational writings of the middle ages and the Renaissance down to Erasmus's comprehensive *de pueris instituendis* of 1529, assured sixteenth-century pedagogues that, given minimum natural endowment on the part of the child, successful teaching was almost entirely a matter of practice and discipline.[48] The generally accepted model of the mind described the learning process as an essentially mechanical activity in which facts were stored in the memory for later recall, much as a scholar used the information, tags and sentences he had entered under appropriate categories in his commonplace book.[49] To the sixteenth-century pedagogue the mind was an efficient engine with discrete parts and a tidy division of operations. Outstandingly endowed talents (*ingenia*) were few, but nearly every human being was believed able to

46 The best example I have seen of an approach emphasizing the sinner's ability to overcome his base inclinations through acceptance of the faith is Andreas Musculus's *Catechismus, Kinderpredig, wie die in Marggrävischer zu Brandenburgk und der Stadt Nürnberg Oberkeiten und Gebieten gepredigt werden* (Frankfurt an der Oder, 1566).

47 A good example for the Fourth Commandment: Thomas Lindner, *Catechismus . . . vor die evangelische Kirchen und Schulen zu Ravensburg . . .* (Ravensburg, 1546; repr. in E.-W. Kohls, *Die evangelischen Katechismen von Ravensburg . . . Ein Beitrag zur oberdeutschen Katechismusgeschichte* [Stuttgart, 1963]), pp. 53ff. For the Seventh: Caspar Huberinus, *Der Catechismus. . . . Allen frommen Hausvättern sehr nutzlich . . .* (Augsburg, 1543), fos. Mviii^r–Nv^r.

48 Erasmus, *de pueris instituendis*, critical edn. by J. C. Margolin, *Opera Omnia Desiderii Erasmi*, i (2) (Amsterdam, 1971), pp. 46–7. For a discussion of the history of pedagogical literature and its influence on the educational thought of the Reformation, see my article cited in n. 21 above.

49 This analogy was made explicitly by Rudolf Agricola, *de formando studio*, written in 1484, first published in Basel in 1518; I use the Freiburg, 1539 edn. The reference is to pp. 75–90.

absorb and retain enough knowledge to allow him to be a useful member of church and society. To make him learn what he needed to know, pedagogues concentrated on practice and discipline (*exercitatio*) as the means of implanting knowledge, habits and values. Plutarch's old story about Lycurgus's experiment with the two dogs, one highly bred, the other a mongrel but carefully drilled, was repeated by nearly every modern educational writer. Since it was the trained dog in the test who performed better than the well-born but untaught animal, the story was taken to demonstrate that 'nature can do much, but instruction is superior because it can do more'.[50] Education was mainly training, and every child could be coached in right ideas, sound purposes and good habits, assuming only that the intellectual and moral conditioning process was begun in infancy[51] and was maintained throughout childhood and adolescence as a methodical and relentless programme of habituation.

No other word turns up as frequently in the school ordinances and visitation articles of the Reformation as 'habituation' (*Gewöhnung, consuetudo, usus*). Plutarch was usually quoted on this point: 'Moral virtue is habit long continued.'[52] Formed early in life, habits are fixed in maturity and become second nature. *Consuetudo est quasi altera natura.*[53] This implicit reliance on the powers of habituation to effect a permanent conditioning of thoughts, values and habits goes a long way toward explaining the universal trust placed in catechism drill with its repetition of memorized questions and answers and its incessant, often lifelong reiteration.[54] Thus when the dukes of Saxony declared in 1574 that 'young people will not comprehend our teachings unless they are first accustomed to the practice of explicit repetition',[55] they were asserting

---

50   'Efficax res est natura, sed hanc vincit efficacior institutio': Erasmus, p. 29. Plutarch, *de liberis educandis*, 4 (cf. n. 52 below).

51   This is the main and pervasive argument of Erasmus's *de pueris instituendis*.

52   *De liberis educandis*, 3A. Plutarch is probably not the author of this treatise, but it was throughout the middle ages and early modern period attributed to him. Many Latin translations of the work circulated, including one by Guarino da Verona. The Latin of the quoted phrase usually ran 'cum mores . . . nihil sint quam assuefactio diuturna': *Plutarchi . . . moralia*, trans. Guilielmus Xylander (Basel, 1572), p. 4.

53   This same point, that the adult person is the product of mental and moral habits acquired in early life, is made emphatically by Thomas More, *Utopia*, bk. ii: *The Complete Works of St. Thomas More*, iv. ed. Edward Surtz, S. J., and J. H. Hexter (New Haven, 1965), p. 228.

54   On constant repetition, cf. e.g. Caspar Huberinus, *Vierzig kurtze Predig uber den gantzen Catechismum . . .* (Nuremberg, 1550), fo. iiii[r–v]: catechism teachers should do nothing other than 'take up one piece after another in the Catechism; and when you have finished with it and preached it all the way through, start again from the beginning, and this you are to make a constant, eternal custom (*in stetem ewigen brauch*)'.

55   'Dan die iugent fast die lehre nicht, so sie nicht zu ausdrücklichem nachsprechen gewehnet wird . . .'. From the *Instructions-Artikel* for the 1574 visitation

the only pedagogical principle then thought capable of assuring success in their endeavours to create the conditions for a general reform in society.

III

Let us sum up. As we see the educational ideas and practices of early Lutheranism from the vantage point of institutions, curricula, instructional materials and methods, we can understand the original trust placed by the reformers in the promise of their movement. Where so much legislation had generated so many schools, where able pedagogues and theologians had written so many useful teaching books, where such general agreement existed on the right techniques for imparting knowledge, and where political and ecclesiastical authorities were so eager to demonstrate their interest in the whole enterprise, it would appear that learning was bound to take place and that evangelical principles could not fail to come to permeate personal and social life.[56]

This confidence, and the enterprises on which it rested, suggest, it seems to me, a fair criterion for judging the success of the reformers' labours. Did their pedagogical effort bring about the anticipated results? Were men improved in some way as a consequence of the new education? Was society made better by the edifying instruction pressed upon the young? Had the adult population in Lutheran territories acquired some basic religious knowledge by the end of the sixteenth century? Had anything changed in the consciences and minds of men as a result of the Reformation?

I think that we do have in this point a means of assaying the success of the Reformation, using – it should be emphasized – as our touchstone the reformers' own criteria, which were of course not political but religious and moral. They are surely the criteria by which they themselves would have wished to be judged. We cannot do them an historical injustice by making them our own. If we agree that this is so, we can now proceed to an examination of the results of the Lutheran enterprise in mass education.

in Electoral Saxony, printed in Karl Pallas (ed.), *Die Registraturen der Kirchenvisitationen im ehemals sächsischen Kurkreise* (Geschichtsquellen der Provinz Sachsen, xl–xli, Halle, 1906–14), xli (Allgeneiner Teil), p. 91.

56 One example of an expression of this confidence: in Leipzig in 1539 Lutheran church officials recognized existing opposition to their religion among the people, but thought it would prevail only 'until our doctrines have been implanted and rooted (*bis die lere eingepflantzt, eingewurzelt*) among the people and have won them over to a common and peaceful understanding'. Stadtarchiv Leipzig. Tit. VII B.2.

Fortunately we have in our grasp a suitable instrument for studying these results, for measuring them, and for judging their relation to the reformers' original purposes. Our instrument is the church visitation and the written record surviving in visitation protocols. Great quantities of these documents are extant; most still repose unprinted in the archives although some have been published.[57] Visitation protocols make absolutely splendid sources for the social historian, but they have never really been scrutinized from this point of view.[58] Scholars interested in rural work and life, in folk customs and belief, in the prevalence of witchcraft, in attitudes to family, property, the village community, near and distant ecclesiastical and political authorities, the work ethic and the enjoyment of leisure, and so on, will find in the visitation records of the Reformation era enough material to engage them for years.

As is well known, the Lutheran reformers revived what they considered an ancient apostolic practice of periodic inspections of Christian life and manners in parish congregations. The political circumstances under which the Reformation was established strengthened the already firmly rooted medieval custom of associating secular and ecclesiastical authorities in the planning and execution of visitations. Luther's appeal in 1525 to Elector John to inaugurate such a visitation in Electoral Saxony, and Melanchthon's *Instruction of Visitors to the Pastors* of 1528 (with a vigorous preface by Luther) provided the programme for all subsequent territorial and municipal visitations.[59] Their purposes were, at the beginning, to discover conditions which the introduction of the Reformation was intended to correct; subsequently to investigate the population and its ecclesiastical and secular leaders in order to determine how firmly the – by now officially defined and established – Reformation was taking root.[60] It was the appalling general ignorance

---

57   A convenient guide to the published and unpublished visitation records is Ernst Walter Zeeden and Hansgeorg Molitor (eds), *Die Visitation im Dienst der kirchlichen Reform* (Münster, 1967).

58   The editors of most of the published visitation materials were impelled either by purely local historical concerns or by an interest in the administrative and financial history of churches and monasteries. For a general history of visitations in one territory, see C. A. H. Burckhardt, *Geschichte der sächsischen Kirchen- und Schulvisitationen von 1524 bis 1545* (Leipzig, 1879).

59   P. Melanchthon, *Unterricht der Visitatorn an die Pfarhern ym Kurfursten-thum zu Sachssen* (Wittenberg, 1528): *Luthers Werke*, xxvi, pp. 195–240. The 1528 visitation in Electoral Saxony is a model in every respect, including the documentary record. For the amazingly full and orderly protocols, see Staatsarchiv Weimar, Registrande I, nos. 1ff.

60   'We see a great need for conscientious inspectors so visit the parishes from time to time, in order to investigate the doctrines and habits of pastors and the Christian

of religion revealed in the Saxon visitation of 1527–9 that prompted Luther to write his two catechisms. On many other substantive and procedural matters, too, the church visitations of the sixteenth century proved fruitful.

It is easy to see why the visitation scheme appealed to governments strongly committed to bureaucratic procedures: it offered excellent opportunities for supervision and control. Visitors themselves were given little freedom of action. Everything they were to say and do was precisely laid down for them in the *formula visitationis* issued by the authority mandating the visitation.[61] Interrogation formularies were drawn up, very long ones in some cases, with explicit, probing questions entering deeply into all areas of public and private life. Visitors were told exactly whom to interrogate: local officials (pastors, sextons, schoolmasters, mayors, councillors and so on), a stated number of private citizens including men and women in several age groups, children and adolescents, male and female servants, country people and towndwellers. The deep-seated distrust of human nature which was then the hallmark of the governing mentality prompted authorities to oblige visitors to press parishioners for information critical of their clergymen and other officials, as well as of their neighbours. In gathering this information visitors could make little distinction between fact and rumour, and it does not seem to have disturbed them that their insistent prodding about public and private derelictions was bound to undermine respect for those local dignitaries whose authority they wished to strengthen. All respondents were urged to tell on each other. In Saxony every cleric was asked: 'Can you report anything suspicious about the teachings of your colleagues?'[62] If a pastor was known to frequent the tavern, the locals were encouraged to describe his drinking habits. Recorded answers to such questions were often explicit enough to allow us to satisfy our curiosity about popular life at the village, hamlet and town level.

Armed with their questionnaire, visitors appeared at pre-announced places to which the official visitation mandate had summoned local worthies and citizens. Respondents were examined one at a time and their replies written down on makeshift pads formed by folding a folio sheet or two in four along its long side. These pamphlets, called *Kladden* (from

understanding and moral improvement of the common people . . .': Staatsarchiv Bamberg, c7/X, no. 1, fo. 91^r.
61   A good description of the surviving documentation of Protestant visitations is found in Pallas (ed.), xli (Allgemeiner Teil), pp. 199–232: 'Das urkundliche Material'.
62   Ibid., p. 142. Also in Bavaria: Bayerisches Hauptstaatsarchiv München: Hochstift Literalien Passau 83, XI, fo. 16^r.

kladderen, to scrawl or jot) hold the raw data of the visitations. Few of them survive. Respondents' replies were numbered to correspond to the questions in the questionnaire; thus visitors could simply write 'Custor: Ad 1, affirmat; ad 2, negat; ad 3 . . .' – perhaps a lengthy response in German or Latin. The requisite number of individuals having been interrogated, the visitors moved on to the next place. Their tour completed, they retired to make clean copies of the collected information. One clean copy was despatched to the consistory, or whatever the central office of the territorial church organization was called; another went to the secretariat of the territorial ruler. The latter copy was confirmed by receiving the ruler's seal and became the official protocol of the visitation. Normally it is these protocols that survive in the archives. In making use of them the historian must, of course, remember that visitors may occasionally have altered data in accordance with what they wished their superiors to know, or with what they thought the latter might prefer to hear. It is not clear, however, whether visitors would have wanted to make local conditions appear to be better than they found them, or worse. An argument might be made for either of these temptations. My guess is that attempts on the part of visitors to aggravate or gloss over the largely unpleasant information they had gathered tend to cancel each other out, and that the visitation protocols cast an accurate reflection of conditions as they were.

Ecclesiastical and political authorities took the information received with the utmost seriousness. Protocols were closely examined and discussed in the synods and consistories charged with supervision of religious life. Summaries of these discussions, with indications of action to be taken, were noted on the left-hand side of each protocol page which had been left blank for this purpose.[63] These notes were then turned by secretaries into official instructions to superintendents, pastors, mayors, bailiffs, informing them of what was to be done. The territorial ruler's or magistrate's authority was, of course, behind these instructions. Like the visitation procedures themselves, these instructions ignored the line between public and private affairs. A village couple's habitual bickering, the failure of certain parents to make their children attend catechism, blasphemous language overheard in someone's home, a farmer's failure to lay by enough grain for the winter – such matters were as disquieting to the authorities as a pastor's or schoolmaster's flagrant incompetence. Visitors cultivated an air of benign *bonhomie* to encourage people

---

63   This custom was taken over from the method of drafting official letters, where the left-hand half of the page was allowed to remain blank for additions and corrections. I describe a typical documentary situation. Bureaucratic customs differed from region to region.

to open their hearts to them,[64] while skilful questioning nearly always enabled them to check and double-check on a complaint or a piece of gossip. These procedures left officials confident that they had at hand accurate information on which to base decisions, not only on the correction of individual abuses, but also on the matter of a general reform of moral and social conditions in the land.

General reform was clearly the overriding purpose of these visitations. Most mandates announce this purpose explicitly as the objective to be attained. In Württemberg for example, in 1557, the visitation was undertaken to accomplish 'the imposition of good government and discipline, but first and foremost the planting among our people of God's saving Word'.[65] In order to discover how broadly and deeply God's Word was in fact being planted among the population, every visitation instruction contained questions intended to test the religious knowledge and moral conduct of parishioners old and young. Most questions were taken directly from the territorial catechism, and respondents' replies allowed authorities to determine how well and how soundly people were being instructed. Thorough visitations – and by no means all visitations were thorough; they varied considerably from time to time and place to place – began by testing the local pastor on his religious knowledge and on his effectiveness as a preacher. In the duchy of Braunschweig-Grubenhagen, for instance, the Reformation had been established in 1532 and an Ecclesiastical Constitution promulgated in 1544; but a visitation undertaken in 1579 revealed generally unsatisfactory conditions among the town and country population. Church authorities thereupon examined all pastors in order to determine where the fault lay. Pastors were asked, first, what they had been studying during the preceding year (independent study was made an obligation for all clerics by Luther himself and by the first Saxon Visitation of 1528). Here are a few answers and follow-up questions, taken directly from the protocol:

> Genesis. How many chapters? Fifty. What subject is treated in the first chapter? Creation. Do you find reference to Christ in this chapter? Yes, for there is mention of Almightly God and His Word. . . . In which chapter do

---

64 'Let them [the visitors] take particular care that they and their assistants do nothing to cause distress to anyone. Those who are to be examined, be they spiritual or secular, should be encouraged to open their hearts and reveal their thoughts. This they will never do if they are given offence'. Bayerisches Hauptstaatsarchiv München: Hochstift Literalien Regensburg 34, fo. 7^{r-v}.
65 '. . . zu anrichtung guter pollicey und äusserlicher zucht, zuvorderst aber pflantzung Göttlichs heilmachendes worts . . .'. From the *Visitations-Ordnung* for the duchy of Württemberg, 1557: Württembergisches Hauptstaatsarchiv Stuttgart, A63, B21, fo. 1^r.

we read 'Abraham believed in the Lord and he counted it to him for righteousness'? Chapter fifteen.

[Another pastor]: Says he has read Genesis but remembers little of it. Says he took notes. Did not suspect he would be asked about it. Responded very poorly.

[Another]: In John 16, Jesus says: 'I leave the world.' How, then, can he be in the Sacrament? Responded: Visibly Jesus left the world, but invisibly he has remained. For he also says: 'I am with you until the end of the world.' *Recte respondit.*[66]

Other questions related to preparation of sermons and the response of auditors, to the number of parishioners regularly attending communion and catechism instruction, and to suspected reasons for the deplorable moral standards found to prevail in the population.[67] Similarly, a general visitation held in Electoral Saxony in 1578 began with seventy-four questions put to pastor, sexton and schoolmaster. Many questions related to catechism instruction. 'Do servants and children go regularly to catechism?' 'Who [meaning what is the name of anyone who] fails to attend catechism lessons and examinations?' 'Is the catechism being read in school and are all pupils regularly examined?'[68] School curricula and teaching practices were also investigated. 'Visitors are instructed,' the Mandate said, 'to inquire into what is being taught in elementary schools in our towns and cities, especially whether children are well instructed in the principles of religion and what lessons they are given to learn'.[69]

Following the examination of pastors, visitors turned to the general public. The Visitation Mandates ordered them to examine 'the common people' in their knowledge of the catechism, but this did not always prove possible if time was short. In our example from Saxony in 1578 it was therefore decided to concentrate the questioning on children. In each parish a certain number of children were put through their paces. Where poor performance pointed to the failure of parents to compel their children's attendance at catechism lessons, the former's 'insubordination' was reported to ducal authorities.[70] In Strassburg – to take a rare example of an urban visitation – visitors ordered parishioners to appear in church on a Sunday afternoon with their children, to whom

66 Printed in Friedrich Spanuth (ed.), 'Die Herzberger Synoden und Kirchengerichte von 1582 bis 1588', *Jahrbuch der Gesellschaft für niedersächsische Kirchengeschichte*, liv (1956), pp. 24–5.
67 Ibid., pp. 25–46.
68 Pallas (ed.), *Registraturen der Kirchenvisitationen*, xli (Allgemeiner Teil), pp. 142ff., questions 8, 16, 56.
69 *Instruktions-Artikel* for the visitation of 1574: ibid., p. 95.
70 Ibid., pp. 92–6.

it was first to be explained 'in the friendliest and most patient manner', why it was that they were being examined that day. 'Then the visitor goes among the children,' the instructions continue, 'asks the pastor about the forms into which they have been divided and what each group has learned, and then selects from each form several boys and girls to recite in a clear and loud voice, and before the entire congregation, what they have learned from the catechism'.[71]

Such examinations took place at regular intervals in nearly all German territories, Protestant and Catholic, secular and spiritual. There can be no doubt that they produced comprehensive and elaborately detailed evidence on which to base considered judgements concerning the effectiveness of religious edicts, ecclesiastical constitutions, school ordinances, and previous visitations. By examining the evidence, we, like the governments of the Reformation era, can arrive at an independent opinion of what had been accomplished in the realm of religious and moral teaching. In fact we are more fortunate than sixteenth-century authorities, for while their knowledge was necessarily limited to the regional scope of their documents, we can see the whole picture.

It should be said at this point that our evidence is somewhat deficient in one important respect: it offers us little solid information on the state of religious knowledge in the larger cities. Visitations were not very well received in urban parishes. Territorial dignitaries found clergy and parishioners resentful of interference from above, and uncooperative to the point of sullenness. The general result of this was that authorities abandoned attempts to inspect cities through parish visitations. In Strassburg, for instance, Johann Marbach, the successor of Bucer, persuaded the council in 1554 to decree annual visitations of all city parishes. But he generated such opposition from the clergy that the visitation had to be cancelled in the following year, and none was undertaken again.[72] Owing to a similar situation in Saxony, the Visitation Instructions of 1578 stipulated that in the cities only domestic servants and children were to be examined, while in smaller towns, hamlets, and villages 'the old as well as the young' faced the test.[73] The city of Magdeburg refused to admit visitors. So did Leipzig.[74] Exemption of urban

71   From a comprehensive memorandum written by Johann Marbach to the Strassburg council in 1533 on the virtues of visitations: Strasbourg, Archives de la ville, Archive St. Thomas 45, carton 21, 1, pp. 478–9.
72   Johann Adam, *Evangelische Kirchengeschichte der Stadt Strassburg* (Strassburg, 1922), pp. 318–20.
73   Pallas (ed.), xli (Allgemeiner Teil), p. 136.
74   The visitation protocol for the archbishopric of Magdeburg for 1563 notes laconically: 'The old city of Magdeburg refused to submit to visitation (Alte Stadt

parishes did not, of course, mean that rural churches in the territory under the control of the city escaped visitation. Visitations were as frequent and thorough in urban domains as in princely ones. It is the city population itself which remains just outside the light cast by the visitation documents.

Let us now look at the evidence gathered by territorial visitations from the 1530s to the end of the sixteenth century. Needless to say, what is presented here for purposes of demonstration is but a tiny sampling taken from a huge mass of documentation. I must ask the reader to place his trust in my judgement: I have selected only such instances as could be multiplied hundredfold.

When the Electoral Saxon visitors informed Duke John Frederick in 1535 that the common people, following the bad example of nobles and burghers, 'hold in many places of your realm the servants of God's Word in contempt',[75] the duke might well have reflected that seven years – the period since the first territorial visitation in Saxony – had not been enough time for the Gospel to be firmly implanted or for a new generation of effective pastors to be trained.[76] Unfortunately the visitations of 1574 and 1577 showed that conditions had not changed forty years later.[77] As before, pastors and sextons everywhere complained of poor church attendance and poorer attendance still of catechism sermons. 'You'll find more of them out fishing than at service', said the visitors. Those who do come to church walk out as the pastor begins his sermon. Parents withhold their children from catechism classes and refuse to pay school fees. Domestic servants leave their jobs rather than let themselves be sent to service. No wonder that blasphemy, fornication, adultery,

Magdeburg hat sich der visitation nicht unterwerfen wollen)': Staats-archiv Magdeburg, Rep. A12, Generalia, no. 2434, fo. 1ʳ. For Leipzig: Stadtarchiv Leipzig, Tit. VII B. 3, fos. 160ᵛ–161ʳ.

75   *Schreiben der Visitatoren in Chursachsen über die mancherlei Unrichtigkeit, Gebrächen und Mängel,* in Pallas (ed.), xli (Allgemeiner Teil), p. 30.

76   The qualities and conditions of Lutheran pastors in Ernestine Saxony and Thuringia are examined in Susan Karant-Nunn, *Luthers' Pastors: The Reformation in the Ernestine Countryside* (Philadelphia, 1976). See also Bernhard Klaus, 'Soziale Herkunft und theologische Bildung lutherischer Pfarrer der reformatorischen Frühzeit', *Zeitschrift für Kirchengeschichte,* lxxx, no. 1 (1969), pp. 22–49. Klaus's assertion that the educational and theological level of the average clergyman rose significantly during the sixteenth century (pp. 48–9) is not borne out by the evidence.

77   The following information is taken from the visitations of 1574 to the end of the century. For the Saxon visitation of 1555, see Wilhelm Schmidt, *Die Kirchen- und Schulvisitation im sächsischen Kurkreise vom Jahre 1555,* pt. 1, *Die kirchlichen und sittlichen Zustände . . .* (Schriften des Vereins für Reformationsgeschichte, year xxiv [1], no. 90, Halle, 1906). This is a summary description of the protocols. Conditions in 1555 were no better than they had been twenty years earlier.

drunkenness and gambling abounded. Admonitions and threats are useless, the pastors note. We warn them, reports one, 'but they answer "why pray? The Turk and the Pope are not after us"!'[78] Churches are half empty while taverns are full. Sunday work, though forbidden, is openly carried on. At Seegrehna a pastor testified in 1577 that he often quits his church without having preached the catechism because not a soul has turned up to hear him.[79] In Grasso, a village in the administrative district of Schweinitz, only twenty out of 150 parishioners regularly attend church. Many don't know their prayers.[80] Children perform poorly in catechism exams.[81] They are being raised – the superintendent summarizes elsewhere – 'like the dumb beasts of the field, without an inkling of the word of God'.[82] Several reasons are suggested for this disgraceful state of affairs: the obtuseness of the population, addiction to drink and fornication so deep-seated that no preacher can hope to change it, the peasant's habitual tight-fistedness (when a child is sent to parish school his parents usually remove him before the end of the quarter to avoid having to pay the fee[83]), above all a deplorable lack of concern with religion, indeed with the state of their own souls.

Territorial rulers tried to counteract this lack of interest, but they could think only of using instruments which had already failed them: stricter mandates, longer sets of instructions to visitors, more systematic methods of inspection,[84] a six-stage method of dealing with offenders, from 'fatherly admonitions in private' to the full ban proclaimed by the synod.[85] But these steps did not help. Visitations in Electoral Saxony continued to prove that even late in the seventeenth century no change had taken place. Matters stood no better in the region of Saxony belonging to the princes of Coburg. Visitations there in 1577 and 1589 brought to light a deplorable general disrespect for the church and its mission. Nothing seemed to avail against widespread absenteeism from divine service and catechism sermons. Nor could pleas or threats prevent congregations from stampeding out of church the moment the pastor began his sermon. Groups of men continued to gather in the churchyard to drink brandy and sing bawdy songs while service was being conducted inside. Malicious gossip spread through parishes touching pastors and other clerics. And there was near-universal blas-

---

78   Pallas, *Registraturen der Kirchenvisitationen*, xli (1), p. 129.
79   Ibid., p. 160.
80   Ibid., xli (3), p. 580 (the year is 1602).
81   E.g. 1578, parish Kleinrössen: ibid., p. 591.
82   Ibid., p. 93.
83   Ibid., xli (5), p. 120.
84   Ibid., xli (Allgemeiner Teil), pp. 136–7.
85   Ibid., pp. 148–9.

pheming, widespread sorcery, wife-beating and neglect of children, general refusal to fulfil congregational obligations, and so on.[86] Again and again it was said plaintively that warnings, threats, even exemplary punishments brought no result.[87] In some villages one could not find even a single person who knew the Ten Commandments.[88]

Visitations in the duchy of Brandenburg told the same story. Pastors in the villages and hamlets belonging to the bishopric of Magdeburg were discovered in 1584 to 'have such a poor memory that they can't retain one passage from the Bible, in fact, most seem never to have looked at it at all'.[89] These were not exceptional cases: 'many of them are like this,' a visitor's note explains, 'the register shows it plainly'.[90] Of course the flock was no better than its shepherds. 'A great crudeness is among these people. Few of them can pray . . .'.[91] 'We could not find three people here who knew the whole catechism. Some could not recite even one section from it.'[92] In one village the pastor confused the three persons of the Trinity.[93] His parishioners knew nothing at all. Things were not so dismal everywhere. A hard-working minister, a good school made all the difference. But even where the Brandenburg visitors could coax the words of the catechism from a few children and adults, how much of it was understood? In 1583 officials inspected villages 'in which twenty, thirty, forty even fifty peasants could recite the whole catechism, piece by piece'. But when a random group of men was invited to explain what it all meant, the result was disheartening. 'We asked them how they understood each of the Ten Commandments, but we found many who could give no answer at all, who could not even say against which commandment a given sin offended. Moreover none of them thought it a sin to get dead drunk and to curse, using the name of God.'[94] Visitors often found it difficult to persuade people to let themselves be examined. 'No one wants to answer our questions. Therefore we must assume that they don't know their catechism . . .'.[95] 'Many say they have forgotten it long ago.'[96] It is unnecessary to add that the visitors found everywhere

86   This sampling of abuses is taken from a detailed description of such conditions in Saxony-Coburg in 1589: Staatsarchiv Coburg, B 2492–3.
87   Ibid., B 2468, fo. 47^r.
88   From 1569 visitation in Albertine Saxony: Staatsarchiv Weimar, Reg. I, i, no. 29, fo. 264^v.
89   Staatsarchiv Magdeburg, Rep. A2. no. 511, fo. 209^r.
90   Ibid., fo. 211^v.
91   Ibid., Rep. A12, Generalia, no. 2435, fo. 141^r.
92   Ibid., no. 2436, fo. 40^r.
93   Ibid., fo. 39^r.
94   Ibid., Rep. A2, no. 511, fos. 105^v–9^v.
95   Ibid., Rep. A12, Generalia, no. 2445, fo. 160^r.
96   Ibid., fo. 165^v.

evidence of prodigious drinking, horrible blasphemy, whoring, witch-craft and soothsaying, and widespread contempt for the clergy. The words chosen by the Brandenburg consistory to describe the situation: 'a wild, disorderly, Cyclopic life',[97] would seem to err on the side of moderation.

It was possible, of course to find in regional and local circumstances the explanations for such behaviour. In some places Catholicism and Lutheranism had succeeded each other for a while with every change of ruler. The innumerable religious controversies dividing and inflaming Protestants against each other are likely to have contributed to the common man's religious confusion. Wars, natural catastrophes, epidemic diseases took their toll.[98] Relics of feudal obligations imposed labour service on some groups of peasants even on Sundays.[99] Chaotic social conditions in some regions made people reluctant to leave their homes on Sunday for fear of robbery.[100] The authorities knew all this, and no doubt considered it in their policies. But *tout comprendre* did not persuade them *tout pardonner*. In the matter of religion they could brook no compromise. A 'horrible epicureanism' pervaded the land.[101] The records of their deliberations, the tone of their directives and mandates, show a deep dismay at deteriorating religious and moral circumstances and a nagging sense of frustration over the failure of corrective measures.

Frequent changes of religion may go some way toward explaining the unsatisfactory conditions discovered in the Brunswick duchies of Lower Saxony (*Niedersachsen*),[102] but they could not, in the eyes of the author-

97   Ibid., no. 2545, fo. 2^{r-v}.

98   In the hamlet and parish of Wahrenbrück in Electoral Saxony the 1577 visitation noted that while the parish had 1127 communicants, only 12 boys attended school. This is so, the visitors remarked, because most pupils had been carried away by the plague during the previous year. Pallas (ed.), *Registraturen der Kirchenvisitationen*, xli (5), p. 170.

99   E.g. Electoral Saxon visitation of 1577, parish of Dolien: peasants when questioned about staying away from catechism instruction on Sunday afternoons testified that they were obliged to do forced labour (*Frondienst*) at that time. Ibid., xli (1), p. 116. In 1585 Margrave Joachim Friedrich of Brandenburg urged that peasants be let off on Sunday to hear the word of God 'because even cattle and draught oxen are allowed to rest on the Lord's day': Staatsarchiv Magdeburg, Rep. A12, Generalia, no. 2442, fo. 98^v.

100   In 1577 some Saxon peasants said it was not safe to go to church because roaming *Landsknechte*, counting on empty houses on Sundays, stole people's pigs and chickens: Pallas (ed.), xli (1), fo. 116.

101   Staatsarchiv Weimar, Reg. I, i, no. 45, fo. 71^r.

102   On this subject and its confusing geographical, political and dynastic ramifications, see Johannes Meyer, *Kirchengeschichte Niedersachsens* (Göttingen, 1939).

ities, condone them. The duchy of Wolfenbüttel had been made Protestant during occupation by the Schmalkaldic League in 1542, re-Catholicized in the late 1540s, and turned Lutheran again by Duke Julius in 1568. A visitation of the duchy that year revealed incredible ignorance on all points of religion even on the part of the clergy. In the administrative district of Bockenem not one of the fourteen pastors examined could name the parts of the New Testament. No one knew the books of the Old Testament.[103] A decade later no improvements were noted, though every effort had been made. Visitation procedures in the duchy of Wolfenbüttel were thorough and methodical. Visitors interrogated pastors and other clerical staff, inspected their books and investigated their private lives, asked leading questions about conditions in the parish, and examined heads of households with their wives, children and servants.[104] But the information compiled in the visitors' protocols has the familiar ring of general hopelessness. People stay away from service, at most two or three souls turn up for weekday catechism sermons, no children come to catechism class 'and it is a pity to see the poor sexton stand there, all by himself in the empty church'. No amount of pastoral admonition could persuade parishioners to cease their week-long drinking orgies. The visitors summarize:

It is the greatest and most widespread complaint of all pastors hereabouts that people do not go to church on Sundays. . . . Nothing helps; they will not come. And the same obstinacy exists on weekdays when the catechism is preached. Only a small part of the population attends these sermons so that pastors face near-empty churches. . . . No wonder, then, that the people respond miserably in catechism examinations. Even if one finds a man or a woman who remembers the words [of the catechism], ask him who Christ is, or what sin is, and he won't be able to give you an answer.[105]

Not everywhere was the picture quite so dark. In the district of Salzliebenhall most children could recite their catechism pretty well in 1583.[106] But in Waldenburg in 1586, when,

103   The visitation records are published in Friedrich Spanuth, 'Quellen zur Durchführung der Reformation im Braunschweig-Wolfenbüttelschen Lande, 1551 bis 1568', *Zeitschrift der Gesellschaft für niedersächsische Kirchengeschichte*, xlii (1937), pp. 241–88; the reference is to p. 284.
104   Wolters (ed.), 'Die Kirchenvisitation der Aufbauzeit (1520–1600) im vormaligen Herzogtum Braunschweig-Wolfenbüttel', pt. 1, ibid., xliii (1938), pp. 206ff.
105   This passage and the preceding remarks relate to Barum, visited in 1572, 1575, 1577 and 1579: ibid., pp. 206–26.
106   Ibid., pp. 226–32.

after the hymn had been sung and the congregation admonished to answer all questions to the best of everyone's ability, [the visitors] asked the people to repeat something from the previous Sunday's Gospel reading, they found not a single person among the grown-ups or the young who remembered as much as a word of it.[107]

Here too, however, the children could repeat their catechism. Four years later the parish of Liebe in the same district of Salzliebenhall could not produce even one parishioner to answer the question 'who is our redeemer?' When the visitors turned in indignation on the pastor he vigorously denied blame for this unbelievable piece of ignorance. It's the people's fault, he said. They don't go to church. And where else were they to learn their religion?[108]

Even allowing for the religious shifts in Wolfenbüttel in the middle of the century, which older people would still recall in the 1590s, it is difficult to account for such abysmal ignorance except as the consequence of monumental public lack of interest in religion, at least in the doctrines of the established creed. Although Duke Julius took energetic measures to improve religious and practical teaching in his duchy, his best efforts failed in the face of such lack of concern. In the duchy of Grubenhagen, where the Reformation had been introduced in 1532 and institutionalized by the Ecclesiastical Ordinance of 1544, visitations in 1579 and 1580 tell the same sad story. Indeed, Superintendent Johann Schellhammer, who had charge of them, was moved to wonder whether 'visitations themselves will not in the end become an object of mockery among the people'.[109] Schellhammer reports that churches are largely empty on Sundays, that no one can be found who knows the catechism (one man, he says, could recite the Lord's Prayer in Latin, but when asked to explain it he hadn't an idea of what it meant) and nothing could be done to persuade or compel them to go to catechism sermons. Everywhere he found 'that people over eighteen years of age are embarrassed to memorize the catechism and cannot be made to attend the lessons'. The superintendent concludes with the usual recital of depravities among the common people: drunkenness, gambling, adultery and fornication, widespread witchcraft and sorcery – this latter practice very difficult to prove 'because they won't tell on each other'.[110] In the 1580s and in 1610 the basic situation had not changed, though a few parishes

107   Ibid., pp. 233–4.
108   Wolters (ed.), pt. 3, ibid., xlviii (1950), p. 84.
109   Friedrich Spanuth, 'Die Grubenhagensche Kirchenvisitation von 1579 durch Superintendent Schellhammer', *Jahrbuch der Gesellschaft für niedersächsische Kirchengeschichte*, lii (1954), p. 106.
110   Ibid., pp. 113–17.

exhibited exceptions to the general rule.[111] Children could sometimes say their catechism tolerably well, but the pity of it was that 'by the time they have grown up they have forgotten it all. In cases where we know that a certain child learned his catechism years ago, we discovered that by the time he becomes an adult he remembers not a word of it'.[112]

In the duchy of Kalenberg, where Catholicism had been re-established in 1543 and Lutheranism in 1568, the situation was so terrible[113] that Duke Julius of Wolfenbüttel, who inherited the territory in 1584, ordered an exhaustive inquisition of all clerics to see what might be done. The protocols of the sessions with each of the duchy's pastors are dramatic documents. None of them was let off the hook if his answers were vague or evasive. Only the totally ignorant were dismissed without further questioning. Others were pressed hard on troublesome theological subjects, especially the Trinity: 'Which person of the Trinity assumed human form?' 'The Father.' 'Is it the Father, then, who died for us?' Long silence, then 'no'. 'Prove that three persons are one.' No reply. Original sin: few pastors were able to explain this adequately. Mortal sin: 'Is it mortal sin if a man gets dead drunk?' 'Yes, for God has forbidden it.' And free will: most pastors knew that the answer to this should be no, but they could prove nothing and were reduced to utter confusion by probing questioning.[114] While turning the pages of these protocols in the archive, I was moved to sympathy as I felt the wretched men squirm under the onslaught of questions of considerable theological complexity and, in the case of poor respondents, distinctly unfriendly tone. The ordeal to which they were being put seemed ludicrously incommensurate with the rudimentary pastoral duties these men had to perform among people who could remember no more than one or two of the Ten Commandments and barely knew the words of the Lord's Prayer.

Even where the church was organizationally and financially in good shape the religious attitudes among the public were often deplorable. In the duchy of Lauenburg, for example, visitors described a sound and smoothly functioning ecclesiastical apparatus. But the reports on moral conditions and the admonitions contained in the visitation recesses reveal outright disrespect for the church among the population. In

---

111   Spanuth (ed.), 'Die Herzberger Synoden und Kirchengerichte von 1582 bis 1588' ibid., liv (1956), pp. 35ff.; 'Die Generalvisitation in Grubenhagen von 1617', ibid., liii (1955), pp. 49ff.

112   From visitation in Kalenberg-Göttingen 1646. Printed in Karl Kayser (ed.), 'Die Generalvisitation des D. Gesenius im Fürstentum Göttingen 1646 und 1652', ibid., xi (1906), p. 201.

113   As revealed in the visitation of 1583: Hauptstaatsarchiv Hannover, Hann. 83, IV.

114   The entire protocol is ibid., no. 101. The examinations took place in 1588.

Gronau in 1581 'the congregation behaved shockingly, refusing to answer a single question so that the examiner had to break off the visitation'.[115] An attempt to explain such insolence by the presence of 'Anabaptists' in the community[116] carries little conviction when one reads of the universal drinking, whoring and other abominations detailed in the protocols. Conditions in this duchy show how little even the most determined governments could do against lack of religious interest. In the end the authorities contented themselves with the weak recommendation that every parent should 'as much as he is able ' send his children to school or to catechism lessons.[117] No wonder that the visitation of 1614 registered no change in the dismal situation.

It needs to be stressed that the scenes depicted here are not the whole picture. Well endowed and expertly staffed Latin schools in towns and cities turned out soundly trained pupils. Visiting such institutions evidently gave officials much pleasure.[118] Village schools, too, were found on occasion to be functioning effectively.[119] As might be expected, the situation varied enormously from region to region. The point is, however, that while elite institutions produced able ministers, and while children and youngsters acquired in an occasional local school the rudiments of a religious education, very little of this transferred itself to the general adult population on whose everyday lives and thoughts the formal religion, Catholic or Protestant, seems to have made little impact. No sociologically revealing pattern – as, for example, between rich and poor – emerges from the records. Thus, in the county of Oldenburg the catalogue of ignorance and other outrages compiled during the visitation of 1609 did not vary between the ill- and the well-favoured agricultural sections of the land. Identical conditions prevailed in the Geest, where the soil was sandy and the population lived hand-to-mouth, and the Marsch, where farms were prosperous. In both sections of the county churches were largely empty, the catechism was ignored, and according to the visitors everyone led a scandalously godless life. In each place there were some exceptions. But the rule was the generally pre-

---

115   Landesarchiv Schleswig-Holstein, Abteilung 218: Lauenburgisches Konsistorium Ratzeburg, no. 653, fo. 78ʳ.
116   Ibid., no. 654, fo. 119ᵛ.
117   Ibid., fo. 43ʳ⁻ᵛ.
118   For example, the visitations of schools in the towns of Grund, Lauental, Wildemann and Zellerfeld: Landeskirchliches Archiv Braunschweig, Voges 1926.
119   For example in Württemberg: Staatsarchiv Stuttgart, A281, B 46ff. (visitations of the duchy at the end of the sixteenth century). Each sexton or other person with teaching duties is characterized in these documents. See also Eugen Schmid, Geschichte des Volksschulwesens in Altwürttemberg (Stuttgart, 1927).

vailing obtuseness.[120] Church officials never ceased to be scandalized by this. The superintendent of the district of Wiesbaden (in the county of Nassau-Wiesbaden) reported in 1619 that in many places no more than fifteen or so out of 170 householders went to church.[121] Among those who attend, he goes on, 'there is such snoring that I could not believe my ears when I heard it. The moment these people sit down, they put their heads on their arms and straight away they go to sleep'.[122] They could not of course answer any of the questions put to them. In one village the visitor discovered that sons and daughters of peasant householders were taking employment in Catholic regions for no other reason than to escape the Sunday catechism classes – 'so as to be free to dance all the day'.[123] Children were found who could say the catechism, 'but among the older youngsters, who no longer attend classes, there is the greatest ignorance you can imagine!'[124]

Matters stood no better in the territories of independent cities where means of surveillance, control and correction were more efficient. The Strassburg territorial visitation of 1554 – which collected detailed data while the urban visitation of the same year elicited practically no information about the city population – revealed that people avoided church-going, especially on Sunday afternoons when they ought to have studied the catechism (rural pastors complained that city-dwellers walking in the country on fine Sunday afternoons were setting a corrupting example), that one could compel little girls to go to catechism lessons, but boys ran off to hide in the vineyards, and that nothing was being done to divest the people of 'their native crude and sullen ways'.[125] Though an occasional improvement is registered in the course of the following years, the later sixteenth century showed no general rise in religious knowledge and morality. In 1560 visitors acknowledged that even where the catechism was being taught, 'as soon as boys and girls begin to grow into adulthood they turn from it as though it is beneath them to know it, and what they studied as children with such effort and diligence, they now forget in a moment's time'. And this, the visitors add, at a stage of life – they mean adolescence – 'when it is most neces-

---

120   Niedersächsisches Staatsarchiv Oldenburg, Bestand 73, II, pp. 170ff. (for Geest), pp. 124ff. (for Marsch). See ibid., fos. 12^r–21^v for an exception, the parish of Stolhamme.
121   Hessisches Hauptstaatsarchiv Wiesbaden, Abt. 137 Xa, no. 1, fo. 19^r.
122   Ibid., fo. 72^r.
123   Ibid., fo. 11^r. This was in 1594.
124   Ibid., Abt. 340, no. 1605a, fo. 174^r.
125   Strasbourg, Archives de la Ville, Archive, St. Thomas 45, carton 21, 1, fos. 535ff.

sary for them to know the catechism'.[126] In 1598 a visitor noted plaintively that 'as far as the catechism is concerned, things seem to go downhill from year to year'.[127] What he meant was that he could not get correct answers out of children and grown-ups, and where someone did know the words by rote, 'ask him what does *Evangelium* mean in German, what is a sacrament, what do we mean by New Testament, and you will get the most ignorant, absurd, ridiculous replies you have ever heard'.[128] Council decrees deploring and correcting year after year the same misdemeanours, abuses and nuisances tell the same story.[129]

Scholars familiar with the history of Strassburg might argue that this city never cared sufficiently about the instruction of its general public. Educational concerns were limited almost exclusively to ensuring an uninterrupted flow of trained personnel into the clerical and other learned professions. In Nuremberg, on the other hand, where the council gave more attention than in Strassburg to rural schools and catechism lessons, the outcome as far as the general population was concerned was no different. In 1560–1 Nuremberg visitors complained of irresponsible parents who could not be persuaded to send children to school or sermons.[130] In 1626 we hear of grown men who could give no answer to such a question as 'on what day of the year did our Lord die?' and of adolescents who had forgotten every one of the Ten Commandments.[131] The city of Ulm boasted an excellent gymnasium and a network of council-supervised German schools. But the countryside offered the same dim picture for inspection. Early visitations in 1532, 1535, 1543 and 1556 revealed stubborn resistance on the part of the Catholic country population to the imposition of the new creed; we hear of people kneeling before the stumps of sawn-off wayside crosses and shrines. But even at the end of the sixteenth century visitation protocols record near-total ignorance of religious matters. Although the Ulm catechism had been adopted as early as 1528 and had later been made mandatory in the city's entire territory, pastors reported that few of their parishioners knew even the words of the Lord's Prayer. Village school-teachers agreed when asked by the visitors that the fault lay with parents who could not care less whether their children received instruction or not.[132] In the city of Rothenburg visitors sent by Margrave Fred-

126   Ibid., fos. 737 and 760.
127   Ibid., fo. 668.
128   Ibid., carton 21, 2, fos. 415–16.
129   E.g. ibid., carton 48, fo. 576: a decree of 1573 outlawing everything complained of in former years back to the 1530s.
130   Staatsarchiv Nürnberg, Kirchen und Ortschaften auf dem Lande, fos. 451–4.
131   Quoted in Leder, *Kirche und Jugend in Nürnberg*, pp. 162–3.
132   Stadtarchiv Ulm, A 9063, I, fo. 131. The date is 1605.

erick of Brandenburg found in the 1550s that hardly anyone had learned his catechism;[133] despite repeated edicts to the contrary no change had occurred by 1618 when it was once again discovered that 'neither grown-ups nor children know a word of the catechism'.[134] In Hamburg visitors to the country discovered 'unbelievable wickedness and contempt for preaching, for the holy sacraments, the Commandments, and for sacred songs',[135] along with complaints about everyone being late for church, 'making indecent gestures at members of the congregation who wish to join in singing the hymns', even bringing dogs to church 'so that due to the loud barking the service is disturbed and occasionally even interrupted'.[136] Late in the seventeenth century we can read the same stories and complaints: Nearly everyone is ignorant of the main points of religion. Many people 'can't pray'. Children are kept out of school and from the catechism. At best they know it by rote, and few examiners ever bother to ask them to explain what it means. The plaintive note of one despairing visitor can stand as a general conclusion: 'Pastors are doing all they can. If people would only go to church!'[137]

IV

The evidence of the visitations speaks for itself; no comments are needed. Lutheranism had not succeeded in making an impact on the population at large. Early hopes for a renewal of religious and moral life in society were not fulfilled. Experiments in mass indoctrination were stillborn or turned out not to work. The Gospel had not been implanted in the hearts and minds of men. An attitude of utter indifference prevailed toward the established religion, its teachings, its sacraments and its ministers.

To say this is not to argue that there were among Lutherans in Germany no men and women of serious, sincere and informed piety. Our evidence is inconclusive for the larger cities where we would expect to find such people. We ought surely to suppose that things stood brighter there for religion than in the hamlets and villages of the countryside. If not, who was it who responded to the beautiful hymns of the Lutheran service? What would explain the loss of religious conviction by

133　Staatsarchiv Nürnberg, Reichsstadt Rothenburg Akten 2089.
134　Ibid., 2096, fo. 83ᵛ.
135　This quotation is from the visitation of Amt Bergedorf in 1581: Staatsarchiv Hamburg, Cl VII. Lit. Hd., no. 8, vol. ic, fasc. 1.
136　Ibid. For an identical complaint about dogs in church, see Hessisches Hauptstaatsarchiv Wiesbaden, Abt. 137 Xa, no. 1, fos. 72–4.
137　Landeskirchliches Archiv Braunschweig, Voges 1924.

descendants of the guild members of Ulm whose names we can still read on the voting lists of 1530 where they recorded their overwhelming support of the Lutheran cause?[138] What could have choked the religious spirit of the grandchildren of Nuremberg burghers who had crowded St. Sebald's and St. Lawrence's churches to hear the sermons of Dominicus Schleupner and Andreas Osiander?[139] Cities had abler pastors, more and better schools, and more effective means of control over conduct. But even if we assume, as I think we should, that city people went to church, paid attention to sermons, made their children learn the catechism, gave support to schools, and were responsive to the emotional appeals of their religion, we cannot tell much about their understanding of the faith they professed, nor about the ways in which this understanding affected their lives. The documents contain enough complaints from theologians and preachers to suggest that city people were no paragons of piety. Simon Musaeus, the orthodox Lutheran administrator and polemicist, mentions an encounter with a cloth-merchant during a visitation in the 1560s. Having failed in his attempt to elicit from the man a recollection of the previous Sunday's sermon, Musaeus inquired about the price of a bolt of cloth a year ago. To this the merchant gave a precise answer. Why was it, Musaeus wanted to know, that he could remember wool prices for a year and forget a Christian sermon within a week?

> To which the man replied that these are two entirely different matters. 'Wool is my business,' he said. 'I must think about it day and night, because that is how I make my living. As for the sermon and the catechism – I don't worry much about them'.

'Is this not horrible blindness?' Musaeus exclaims. 'But that is how they all are!'[140] Despite obligatory drills in catechism and repetitious preaching on the articles of the creed, religious comprehension in cities is likely to have been much more shallow than the kind of understanding for which the reformers had worked and hoped in the years before 1530 when public enthusiasm for their cause ran so high. The exact nature of the faith of the urban citizenry has not yet been analysed. Much work can still be done on this subject, the sources of which remain to be exploited by students of *mentalités collectives*.

138   Julius Endriss, *Die Abstimmung der Ulmer Bürgerschaft im November 1530* (Ulm, 1931).
139   See my *Nuremberg in the Sixteenth Century* (New York, 1966), ch. iv.
140   Simon Musaeus, *Catechismus. Examen mit kurzen Fragen und Antwort ...* (Frankfurt am Main, 1571), fo. 3^r. For a more sweeping judgement on the behaviour of burghers in Leipzig, see the visitation protocol in Stadtarchiv Leipzig, Tit. VII B. 3, fos. 59ff.

A fully coherent explanation of the phenomena described in this article would require more space than is available here. A few factors may however be suggested. It should first be noted again that the reporting procedures of sixteenth-century visitations differed among themselves. Some visitations gathered information on the basis of a 'soft' questionnaire, and these would naturally fail to turn up the explicit data about the state of religious knowledge and behaviour compiled by visitations in other lands where 'hard' techniques of investigative questioning were employed. Our general picture is therefore bound to be uneven. Generally speaking, however, the more exhaustive the questions, the more disheartening the information brought to light. It also stands to reason that geographic and economic factors must have operated in the obvious way: isolated and poor parishes were more likely to persist in ignorance than well-to-do places in touch with urban culture. Still, as I have tried to show, the evidence does not suggest that religion was taken more seriously by the comfortable than by the poor. Occasionally an effective pastor or school-teacher could overcome the general laxness, but the protocols, which are not self-serving in this respect, make it clear that the absence of tangible Christianity among the people was not usually due to lack of pastoral effort. The interminable theological polemics of the time must have had a deadening effect on people's religious interest. On the other hand there is also a strong possibility that visitation protocols occasionally confound religious indifference with confessional opposition to politically enforced creeds: Catholic to Protestant and vice versa, Zwinglian to Lutheran, and so on. One gets the impression that the most knowledgeable, serious and courageous Lutherans were to be found in hostile environments such as northern Bavaria under the rigorously Catholic regimes of Albrecht V and Wilhelm V.[141] In this as in so many other instances, strength of conviction seemed born of adversity. Where people had learned to adjust to the routine of officially sanctioned orthodoxy, on the other hand, their religious interest seems to have diminished. One might also take notice of the Marxist view that the lack of religious concern must have been the inevitable reaction of 'progressive' groups to the collapse of the peasant rebellion and the suppression of urban independence movements. But I have found little in the documents to support this interpretation of religious indifference as a conscious withdrawal by the disaffected.

141   This assertion is based on analysis of ample documentation in Bavarian archives. E.g. Bayerisches Hauptstaatsarchiv München: Staatsverwaltung 2784, fos. 189–97, 272 a–m: lists of persons in Ingolstadt and Wasserburg willing to be expelled rather than abandon their religious practices; ibid., 2786, fos. 141–8, 155–9: lists of persons unwilling to conform to the Religious Edict of 1571.

One other point seems worth making here. The evidence of the visitation protocols supports the view – much emphasized in recent years – that the operative religion of country folk, and perhaps of many city-dwellers as well, had much less to do with the doctrines of established Christianity than with the spells chants, signs and paraphernalia of ancient magic lore and wizardry, the cult of which flourished unaffected by the imposition of new or old denominational creeds.[142] To call the persistence of these magic practices a 'counter culture' to the official culture of Christianity[143] is perhaps an overreaction to our belated discovery of this fact of popular life. But there can be little doubt that magic cults held the trust and engaged the interest of the majority of the populace at a time when the official religion as preached from pulpits and taught in catechisms became increasingly abstract, dogmatic and detached from the concerns of ordinary life.

Ecclesiastical officials knew that this was so. Lutheran theologians never stopped warning against the plague of soothsayers.[144] Visitors had standing instructions to probe for evidence of conjuring, wise women and cunning men, the evil eye, witchcraft, fortune-telling, spells and curses. Although it proved difficult to extract solid information from the people (interestingly enough, villagers did not often tell on each other and accusations are rare) the clergy usually knew and told enough to convince officials that they had a problem on their hands. Magic was pervasive and deep-seated in popular culture. One example will have to suffice here for the mass of evidence suggesting the penetration of popular culture by magic practices. It comes from the visitations of the administrative district of Wiesbaden, in the county of Nassau-Wiesbaden, in 1594. According to the visitors' report:

The use of spells (*das Segensprechen*) is so widespread among the people here that not a man or woman begins, undertakes, does or refrains from

---

142   See Keith Thomas, *Religion and the Decline of Magic* (London and New York, 1971); Alan Macfarlane, *Witchcraft in Tudor and Stuart England* (London and New York, 1970); H. C. Erik Midelfort, *Witch Hunting in Southwestern Germany 1562–1684* (Stanford, Cal., 1972); Friedrich Merzbacher, *Die Hexenprozesse in Franken* (Munich, 1970). For a good *Forschungsbericht*, see E. William Monter, 'The Historiography of European Witchcraft: Progress and Prospects', *Jl. Interdisciplinary History*, ii (1972), pp. 435–51.

143   Lawrence Stone, 'The Disenchantment of the World' (a review of several books on magic and witchcraft, including the volumes by Thomas and Macfarlane cited in the preceding note), *New York Rev. of Books*, xvii (9) (2 Dec. 1971), pp. 18, 24.

144   E.g. Huberinus, *Spiegel der geistlichen Hauszucht . . .* , fos. ccxlv–vi; Christoph Vischer, *Auslegung der Fünf Heubtstück des heiligen Catechismi* (Schmalkalden, 1573), fo. cii^v.

doing anything . . . without employing some particular blessing, incantation, spell, or other such heathenish means. To wit: in pangs of childbirth, when a babe is taken up or put down (so that no evil enchantment may befall him [*damit es nit bezaubert werde*]) . . . when cattle are driven into the fields, or are lost, etc., when windows are shut against the night, etc. . . . Whenever an article has been mislaid and cannot be found, when someone feels sickly or a cow acts queer, they run at once to the soothsayer (*warsager*) to ask who has stolen it or put a bad spell on it, and to fetch some charm to use against the enchanter. . . . Daily experience with these people shows that there is no measure or limit to the use of these supersititious spells, both among those who cast them, and among those who ask them to be cast, believing thereby to keep their lives and property from coming to harm. All the people hereabouts engage in superstitious practices with familiar and unfamiliar words, names, and rhymes, especially with the name of God, the Holy Trinity, certain angels, the Virgin Mary, the twelve Apostles, the Three Kings, numerous saints, the wounds of Christ, his seven words on the Cross, verses from the New Testament. . . . These are spoken secretly or openly, they are written on scraps of paper, swallowed (*eingeben*) or worn as charms. They also make strange signs, crosses, gestures; they do things with herbs, roots, branches of special trees; they have their particular days, hours and places for everything, and in all their deeds and words they make much use of the number three. And all this is done to work harm on others or to do good, to make things better or worse, to bring good or bad luck to their fellow men.[145]

Sixteenth-century theologians could not understand this. But to us, looking back, it should not appear astonishing that these ancient practices touched the lives of ordinary people much more intimately than the distant religion of the Consistory and the Formula of Concord. The deep current of popular life whence they arose was beyond the preacher's appeal and the visitor's power to compel. The permissive beliefs of medieval Catholicism had absorbed these practices and allowed them to proliferate;[146] but this accommodating milieu was now abolished. Hostile religious authorities showed themselves unbendingly intolerant of deeply ingrained folkways. The persistence of occult practices in popular life is therefore certainly a cause, as well as a symptom, of the failure of Lutheranism to accomplish the general elevation of moral life on which the most fervent hopes of the early reformers had been set.

145   Hessisches Hauptstaatsarchiv Wiesbaden, Abt. 137, no. 1, fo. 9ʳ.
146   The fusion of Catholic with ancient magic practices emerges clearly from the documents. An excellent example is the passage just quoted from the visitors' report on Wiesbaden in 1594.

9

The Reformation, Popular Magic, and the 'Disenchantment of the World'

Robert W. Scribner

Originally appeared as Robert W. Scribner, 'The Reformation, Popular Magic, and the "Disenchantment of the World"', *Journal of Interdisciplinary History*, 23 (1993), pp. 475–94.

Editor's Introduction

Religious culture on the eve of the Reformation embraced more than just the approved rites and rituals of the Catholic church. Historians have long recognized that there were many dimensions to the faith, both in practice and understanding. It has become a relative commonplace to speak of the differences between popular religion, the religion of the ordinary parishioners, and elite or official religion, religion as defined by the church and its institutions. Of course, there are problems with a model of this kind, for it tends to over-simplify things. Many of the religious practices we might think of as popular had themselves developed out of official Catholic practice. Equally, many of the rites sanctioned and endorsed by the Catholic church had long passed into popular culture. In a sense, the meaning of the phrase 'popular religion' became easier to define with the Reformation movement, for the evangelicals not only wanted to do away with all religious practices that were not sanctioned or regulated by the church. The reformers also wanted to cleanse the parishes of the residues of Catholic belief, for Catholicism, in their eyes, was based on idolatry and superstition.

The Protestant objection to both popular religion and medieval Catholicism, as Robert W. Scribner observes, was grounded in a new understanding of the divine. There was nothing the believer could actively undertake to gain the knowledge or the grace of God. 'All sacred action flowed one-way,' is how Scribner words it in his contribution, 'from the divine to the human, and even salvation was but a recognition in the human heart of a grace apparently arbitrarily given by God.' That is why the evangelicals condemned both the cult of the saints and the monastic orders, for there could be no intermediary between the believer and Christ. Nor could the powers of the divine be manipulated by the faithful (clergy or laity), which meant that the reformers rejected the traditional understanding of the sacraments and the sacramentals. In the medieval Catholic church, the sacraments were visible signs of God's invisible grace; they contributed to salvation, and their effect was automatic (they worked, as the theologians would term it, ex opere operato – effective by virtue of the rite itself). Sacramentals, in contrast, were not thought to be necessary for salvation; they were objects associated with forms of piety (water, salt, candles), and they derived their powers from the act of consecration. (In the words of the theologians, sacramentals did not work automatically, but rather ex opere operantis – dependent on the disposition of the handler.) The Reformation took issue with both the sacraments and the sacramentals. Ultimately, the number of sacraments was reduced from the seven of the Catholic church to the two of the Protestant faith (baptism and the Eucharist). Sacramentals were rejected outright; and it soon became a priority of the Reformation church to root out the magical and 'superstitious' beliefs associated with the sacraments and the sacramentals of medieval Catholicism.

As Scribner illustrates in his contribution, the Protestant reform of popular religion encountered considerable resistance. The parishioners were reluctant to give up their traditional religious culture. Throughout the sixteenth century and beyond, the Protestant authorities lamented the lack of progress that had been made in the reform of popular beliefs. The magical or 'sacramental' world-view seemed as widespread and as popular as it had been in the medieval age. The visitation returns offer countless examples of the use of remedies and spells, blessings, charms, ritual and ceremonies, many of which had been practiced since the days of medieval Catholicism. Parishioners still treated baptismal water and salt as if they were sacramentals endowed with divine power, for example, and blessed church bells were still rung to ward off danger. The Protestant pastor Rudolf Gwerb took note of such local beliefs in his *Account of the Superstitious and Forbidden Blessing of Humans and Livestock* (1646). Gwerb recorded numerous instances when his parishioners turned to forms of magic such as blessings, spell, ointments as well as the 'papist blessings' of the medieval age. Moreover, Gwerb also made reference to forms of popular religion that seemed to be Protestant in inspiration. This is a point

Scribner makes in his contribution. In place of the use of images or recourse to the saints, the Protestant parishioners turned to the Word of God in order to work magic. Passages and verse from Scripture were held to have sacral powers, as were the books themselves. This was a type of popular religion born of a Protestant environment, but in essence these objects were viewed no differently than the former Catholic sacramentals.

Scribner's central point, however, is not that traditional religious practices in the German parishes survived the Protestant Reformation. Scribner is suggesting that the common estimation of Protestantism as a religion which desacralized or 'disenchanted' the world of popular belief is false. The idea of disenchantment has a long pedigree, and it found its most influential formulation in the work of Max Weber, who wrote in his work *The Sociology of Religion* (which appeared in English translation in 1963) that there was an absence of 'magical sacramental grace' in ascetic Protestantism. The result, in Weber's view, was the evolution of a religion based on an 'ethically rationalized pattern of life'. The faithful became more rational and grounded in the world of experience, 'particularly where such a religion also devalues the priestly grace of penance and sacrament in favour of the exclusive importance of the personal relationship to god'. In the hands of later scholars, Weber's thesis has led to the assumption that Protestantism took the magic out of popular religion. But the truth, as Scribner suggests in his contribution, was much more complex, though no less the legacy of the Reformation.

The Reformation, Popular Magic, and the 'Disenchantment of the World'

Robert W. Scribner

For most college-educated people, one of the two or three things they commonly know about the Reformation is that it contributed, alongside the Enlightenment, to a process of secularization, often understood as the rationalization of modern thought-modes by the 'disenchantment of the world', the elimination of magic from human action and behaviour. This did not mean the repudiation of religious belief, but a separation of 'magic' from 'religion' in early modern Europe. The distinction between religion and magic had been blurred in the pre-Reformation church; indeed, for convinced Protestants the central act of medieval Christian worship, the Mass, with its doctrine of the transubstantiated Eucharist, had at its heart a form of magic. The Reformation removed this ambiguity by taking the 'magical' elements out of Christian religion, eliminating the ideas that religious rituals had any automatic efficacy, that material objects could be endowed with any sort of sacred power, and that human actions could have any supernatural effect.[1] Religion was thus freed of 'superstitious' notions about the workings of the world and became a matter of internal conviction, enabling the rational human action characteristic of modernity.

The focus of this article is popular magic, which may certainly be used as a touchstone for judging the extent and manner in which the Reformation redefined the nature of religion. However, the problem is complicated because our modern view of the Reformation rests essentially on the ways in which it was constructed in the nineteenth century out of the characteristic intellectual concerns of that age (nationalism, scientific rationalism, and a preoccupation with evolutionary models of development). The Enlightenment and post-Enlightenment thought first

---

1 Richard van Dülmen, *Religion und Gesellschaft. Beiträge zu einer Religionsgeschichte der Neuzeit* (Frankfurt am Main, 1989), 10–35, 204–214. The term 'Entzauberung der Welt" is derived from Max Weber, who saw it as a "great historic process in the development of religions . . . which . . . came here to its logical conclusion', Weber (trans. Talcott Parsons), *The Protestant Ethic and the Spirit of Capitalism* (New York, 1958), p. 105.
  The best summary of the argument about the Reformation taking the 'magical' out of Christian religion is Keith Thomas, *Religion and the Decline of Magic* (Harmondsworth, 1971), pp. 27–89. Weber (trans. Ephraim Fischoff), *The Sociology of Religion* (London, 1965), pp. 151–2, also held the Mass to be a form of magic.

positioned the Reformation as part of a long-term process of rationalization and secularization, whereas post-Enlightenment thought-modes failed to understand the essential characteristics of medieval Christianity, especially the medieval notion of the sacramental. The view that the Reformation was a logical stage on the road to modernization is now seen as problematic, as is the conventional wisdom of how it changed the notion of the sacred. In order to understand the relationship of 'religion' to 'magic' both before and after the Reformation, a good deal of rethinking is required.[2] Thus, it is necessary to begin with the relationship of magic to pre-Reformation Christianity before we can go on to appreciate the problem magic posed for both Protestantism and Catholicism alike.

Let us begin with a definition of magic, which can be understood in the words of Flint as 'the exercise of a preternatural control over nature by human beings, with the assistance of forces more powerful than they'. Religion, by contrast, is the recognition by human beings of a supernatural power on whom they are dependent, to whom they show deference and are obligated. On the face of it we have a clear-cut distinction between religion and magic: on the one hand, human dependence on, and deference toward, the divine; on the other, human attempts to appropriate divine power and apply it instrumentally. Yet the contrast is not so simple when the reality of religion as a historical phenomenon is considered. Late-medieval European religion was complex and varied, and to grasp its totality we must be aware of its multidimensionality. There are at least seven major features of medieval European religion to consider. It was simultaneously soteriological, functional, pastoral and concerned with piety, as well as having irre-

---

2   For the developing historiography of the Reformation, see A. Geoffrey Dickens and John M. Tonkin, *The Reformation in Historical Thought* (Oxford, 1985). This impressive pioneering work is very sketchy on the interpretative currents in nineteenth-century Germany, but adequately reveals how the Enlightenment changed historical understanding of the Reformation.
    A rethinking of the problem of the relationship of 'religion' to 'magic' is indicated in Scribner, 'The Impact of the Reformation on Daily Life', in *Mensch und Objekt im Mittelalter und in der frühen Neuzeit: Leben-Alltag-Kultur* (Vienna, 1990), 316–43 [Österreichische Akademie der Wissenschaften, phil.-hist. Klasse, Sitzungsberichte, DLXVIII]. See also Scribner, 'Symbolising Boundaries: Defining Social Space in the Daily Life of Early Modern Germany', in Gertrud Blaschitz, Helmut Hundsbichler, Gerhard Jaritz, Elisabeth Vavra (eds), *Symbole des Alltags. Alltag der Symbole. Festschrift für Harry Kühnel zum 65. Geburtstag* (Graz, 1992), 821–41. It is worth noting that this rethinking process began with Thomas, *Religion and the Decline of Magic*, a work which might have led to a reconceptualization of the Reformation's understanding of religion had less attention been devoted on his discussion of witchcraft.

ducible social, political and economic dimensions. Only the first four will be mentioned here as most relevant to our theme.[3]

Medieval European religion was 'soteriological' in that it offered an understanding of, and a means toward, human salvation focused on the saving death and resurrection of Christ as revealed in the Bible, and, in particular, redemption from sin and its consequences for humans both individually and collectively. It was 'functional' in that it gave meaning to daily life by marking out religiously the key stages in the human life cycle and in the cyclical rhythms of the seasons, thus providing a form of cosmic order for human existence. Its 'pastoral' role was to offer consolation amid the anxieties of daily life and to provide a means of reconciliation for human frailty. The concern with 'piety' refers to a consistent state or attitude about the religious meaning of life, expressed in actions symbolizing dependence upon and preoccupation with the divine, perhaps better signified by the word 'godliness'.

It was in the functional aspect of medieval religion that the line between religion and magic could become blurred. Religion functioned as a means of order in daily life because it was predicated on the assumption that all creation depended for its well-being on the sustaining power of the divine. Irregularities and discontinuities in the material world were understood either as a form of breakdown of this cosmic order or as a result of sacred power operating upon the world. Sacred power could entail the operation of either beneficient or malign supernatural forces, the divine and the angelic or the demonic. All manifestations of the sacred – whether in persons, places or events – also entailed manifestations of sacred power and therefore the possibility of access to it. Saints, their bodies, their relics and the places in which they were active; other holy places and charismatic centers; and moments of intense ritual significance all offered possibilities of sacred power manifesting itself. It was a power to which all persons sought access in their attempts to deal with the exigencies of the human condition – sickness, dearth, climatic variation, threats to human and

3   Valerie I. J. Flint, *The Rise of Magic in Early Medieval Europe* (Oxford, 1991), 3. Adapted from the definition of religion in Stanley J. Tambiah, *Magic, Science, Religion and the Scope of Rationality* (Cambridge, 1990), 4, although Tambiah's own favored definition might do as well: 'a special awareness of the transcendent, and the acts of symbolic communication that attempt to realize that awareness and live by its promptings', 6. For the ways in which religion is socially stratified and its political and economic features, see Robert W. Scribner, 'The Reformation and the Religion of the Common People', in Hans R. Guggisberg and Gottfried G. Krodel (eds), *Die Reformation in Deutschland und Europa: Interpretationen und Debatten* (Göttingen, 1993), pp. 221–41.

animal reproduction, fear and anxiety and the breakdown of human relationships.[4]

The medieval church, as the institutionalized form of the organized community of believers, found itself under a twofold pressure. Its sacramental system, slowly developed over the course of several centuries of Christian practice, was primarily soteriological. Sacraments involved ritual actions which effected in the supernatural sphere that which they symbolized by their signifying performances in the natural: thus, the cleansing and purifying symbolic action of water in baptism brought about the purification of the soul from sin. But sacraments were also targeted on the whole person – body, soul and spirit – so that they were seen as offering consolation, succour, and nourishment for the body as well as the soul. Sacramental action thus had inner-worldly as well as transcendental efficacy. This was one field in which any firm lines between religion and magic could become blurred, but we can only appreciate the full complexity of the problem if we highlight another feature of sacramental action, the way in which it dealt with the demonic and the diabolical.

Christianity's view of the human need for salvation stressed the action of a perverted form of the supernatural in bringing about sin and human corruption from a preternatural state, personified in the shape of the Devil. The Devil represented and occasioned spiritual, moral, social and material disorder in the natural world, and the sacramental system was primarily (soteriologically) directed at reversing the effects of his actions and offering future protection against them. Sacraments thus had a multiple efficacy – providing a means to salvation, offering succour for body, soul and spirit, and serving as protection against the temptations of the Devil. The Devil could, of course, work effects in the natural world, albeit only on divine sufferance, although theological opinion throughout the medieval and early modern period was divided as to whether these effects were real or imaginary. Be that as it may, the blurring of boundaries between religion and magic also extended along a second axis, the means through which one dealt with the this-worldly effects of the diabolical. The twofold problem for the church was, first, how to balance the soteriological with the functional and pastoral aspects of its sacraments; second, how to define the ways in which they could be employed to combat the wiles of the Devil. The problem was made the more complex

4 I outlined some of these ideas in a preliminary way in *Popular Culture and Popular Movements in Reformation Germany* (London, 1987), 1–17, relying on concepts drawn from Mircea Eliade, *Patterns in Comparative Religion* (New York, 1958), 1–3.

by the medieval understanding that the sacraments' soteriological efficacy was automatic (*ex opere operato*); extending this notion to the other features of a sacrament would have brought it perilously close to a form of 'magic'.

The difficulty became yet more intricate with the development of the practices known as 'sacramentals'. In part, sacramentals were no more than ritual blessings of certain elements or objects used in liturgical action, a means of consecrating them to sacred use; for example, the water and salt used in the baptismal ceremony or the altar on which the Mass was performed. But they also involved an act of exorcism by means of which harmful spirits were expelled from these elements or objects. This aspect may have arisen from a Christianizing attempt to incorporate pagan amulets as non-Christian peoples were converted: the demonic beings from which they were believed to gain their efficacy were ordered to depart in the name of God as Creator, the Trinity, and Christ as Lord of the world, and they were then blessed so that Christians could use them without harm. Indeed, many of the blessed items used as expressions of piety by medieval Christians had this character. However, by the later middle ages, sacramentals involved the exorcism and blessing of a wide range of objects, the efficacy of which was held to be analogous to that of the sacraments. The differences in efficacy were nonetheless crucial. Sacraments were primarily soteriological and only secondarily pastoral and consolatory, whereas the pastoral and consolatory aspects predominated in the sacramentals, which *could* be an aid to salvation insofar as they were used in the right way and with the right frame of mind (*ex opere operantis*).

There were three ways in which sacramentals could slide over into the field of magic: the element of exorcism could be taken to impart apotropaic significance to them, the blessing or consecration could be seen to impart a sacred power, and their primarily this-worldly orientation could lead to their instrumental application. Moreover, the official distinction between efficacy *ex opere operato* and *ex opere operantis* was commonly ignored, and sacramentals in popular practice were regarded as though they were automatically effective. Finally, these items fell more easily than the sacraments outside the control of the institutional church, since they became a matter of daily use by laypeople, rather than being (as the sacraments were) under the control of the institutional church in the person of the clergy. Sacramentals were enormously popular and it was widespread demand which led to the mushrooming of such blessed objects throughout the later middle ages and into the post-Reformation period (indeed, up to the present day). They, above all else, have earned the designation of 'the magic of the late-medieval church' and attracted the scorn and hostility of the Protestant reformers of the sixteenth century.[5]

One further matter must be considered before we can claim to have mapped, even in crude outline, the problem magic posed for religion in pre-Reformation Christianity. Throughout the European middle ages there also existed a range of beliefs and cultural practices that could more properly be labeled 'magic' to which the institutionalized church was, in theory at least, unambiguously hostile. These included divination, astrology, magical medicine, love magic, the invocation of demons and the dead, and other forms of the 'magical arts'. Many of these beliefs and practices predated Christianity, some may have been dressed in Christian garb – possibly the result of attempts at Christianization – such as certain types of binding and loosing spells and a whole complex of spells and charms in the form of magical blessings. All involved the instrumental application of sacred power in ways the church regarded as 'superstitious', that is, as a form of false belief. As Flint has recently shown, the dialogue between the church and the magical arts in the early middle ages was as much a matter of creative assimilation and acculturation as it was of unremitting rejection, and it may be that this two-pronged strategy continued throughout the high and later middle ages as well. One strategy of rejection that had worked well in combatting non-Christian religion was that of demonization, accusing pagan gods of being no more than servants of the Devil, that great begetter of disorder in the world. From the fifth century it was applied to magic by John Cassian in attributing the effects and efficacy of magic to demons, identified from Old Testament sources as those who fell with Lucifer. The choice presented to Christians was between sanctity and magic, the former enabling them to subdue demonic malice, the latter to invoke it, in which case one was consorting with demons.[6] Thus, any distinction between beneficent and malefic sorcery disappeared, and all magic involved subordination to the Devil.

A consistent policy of demonization would have done much to keep a firm boundary between religion and magic, but this was not always

---

5 The classic (and still unsurpassed) work on sacramentals is Adolf Franz, *Die kirchlichen Benediktionen im deutschen Mittelalter* (Freiburg im Breisgau, 1909), 2 v. For their widespread importance, see the references in Scribner, *Popular Culture and Popular Movements*, 361. For their designation as the magic of the medieval church, Thomas, *Religion and the Decline of Magic*, 27–57.

6 Flint, *The Rise of Magic*, 21, 393–407. We still lack a thorough modern investigation of popular magic in the later middle ages, but see Richard Kieckhefer, *Magic in the Middle Ages* (Cambridge, 1990), 56–94, for a useful sketch. He stresses patterns of prohibition, condemnation, and prosecution without considering the question of acculturation and assimilation, 176–200.

possible in practice, since it would have ruled out Christianizing strategies. The most important area of the latter strategy was that of curing and healing charms. The persistence of non-Christian magical healing practices led monks, as exemplars of sanctity and so as wielders of sacred power, to adopt Christianized forms of healing charms in which the names of Christ or other Christian figures replaced those of pagan gods. Healing thus became a result of Christian prayer which, if not merely dependent on the power of the cross as the most potent Christian symbol, could be accompanied by magico-medical healing techniques, the success of which could be made dependent on the invocation of Christian forms of sacred power. The ambiguity between prayer and the magical use of a spell or charm remained built into such Christianized forms, especially when they escaped the control of the monastic milieu and became the stock in trade of popular healers, cunning folk, sorcerers, and ultimately, of lay people. Thus, a third axis of ambiguity was created between religion and magic, along which ranged acceptable Christian practices based on notions like the healing power of prayer; mistaken or misguided 'superstitious' invocation of Christ, the Trinity, and other Christian sacred persons; and being deceived into collaborating with the Devil.

This very crude sketch enables us to see why those approaching pre-Reformation religion through post-Enlightenment thought-modes failed to understand essential characteristics of medieval Christianity and popular magic or the troubled relationship between the two. What difference did the Reformation make to this complex and subtle structure of sacrality? The radical point of departure associated with Martin Luther and (even more radically) Ulrych Zwingli resided in their understanding of the absolute sovereignty and otherness of God, so that it was impossible for human beings to gain any knowledge of the divine by merely created means. This viewpoint destroyed the basis for sacraments and sacramentals, indeed for any kind of ritual by means of which this-worldly symbolic action could have any transcendental efficacy. All sacred action flowed one-way, from the divine to the human, and even salvation was but a recognition in the human heart of a grace apparently arbitrarily given by God. Even pastoral-pedagogical means, such as devotional images, were held by the most extreme exponents of this position (such as Zwingli and Andreas Bodenstein von Carlstadt), to so distract Christians from this relationship of faith that they were condemned as idolatry.[7]

---

7   See the discussion on this point by Carlos M. N. Eire, *War against the Idols: The Reformation of Worship from Erasmus to Calvin* (Cambridge, 1986), 54–104, 197–233.

The consequence was in no sense, however, a desacralization of the world; quite the contrary. Luther had a powerful belief in the presence and activity of the Devil in the world, and believed that his age had finally unmasked the Devil's main agent, the Antichrist, the diabolical antithesis of Christ as Savior. He held his age to be the one in which the last great confrontation between Christ and Antichrist, between God and the Devil, was to be fought. It was an age witnessing a great outpouring of the Holy Spirit, guiding the world toward its providential culmination in the Last Days. Luther's thought was thus apocalyptic and eschatological, rather than desacralizing. Indeed, it can be said that the Word of God became for him the overwhelming sacramental experience, the sole means through which created humanity could come to knowledge of the divine. The world of Luther and the Reformation was a world of highly charged sacrality, in which all secular events, social, political and economic, could have cosmic significance. The same was true of the second generation of reform, associated with Calvin and the followers of the 'reformed religion', whose characteristic belief above all else was that Lutherans and Lutheranism had made too many compromises with the Antichrist by accepting that some matters were indifferent in the great cosmic struggle. Far from further desacralizing the world, Calvin and the reformed religion intensified to an even higher degree the cosmic struggle between the divine and the diabolical.

It is also incorrect to argue that the Reformation created an antiritual form of religion which dispensed with sacred time, places, persons, or things. After initial attempts to abolish or reform life cycle rituals, many, such as churching and confirmation, reappeared in modified form, even within the Reformed tradition. The attempt of the first generation of reformers to dispense with consecration or blessing as a means of setting sacred objects aside from the profane world proved futile. Throughout the sixteenth century and into the seventeenth, evangelical forms of consecration reemerged and multiplied, and were applied to a wide variety of objects: church foundation stones, new or restored churches, pulpits, fonts, organs, altars, bells, cemeteries, and even, in Saxony in 1719, a confessional box. Care was always taken to insist that such consecrations in no way imparted any form of sacred power, as under Catholicism. Nonetheless, popular belief insisted in treating such objects as if they were as sacralized as their Catholic equivalent, for example, church bells which were held to protect against storms and lightning. Memory of the power of Catholic sacramentals was long and proved difficult to eradicate, not least those practices associated with the power of the Eucharist, such as blessed bread, used like St. Agatha's bread to repel fire. Where Protestant pastors refused to accommodate lay demands for such sacrally potent objects, their parishioners were quite willing to go to Catholic priests for them. Pilgrimage sites, and the healing water sometimes associated with them, persisted in many Protestant territories into the seventeenth and eighteenth centuries.[8]

This was no matter of mere survivalism, the ignorant response of half-protestanized people incapable of understanding that sacred power no longer existed in a profane world. Protestant belief did not hold that the sacred did not intrude into the secular world, simply that it did not do so at human behest and could not automatically be commanded. Thus, there was no contradiction in regarding the Word of God as the most potent manifestation of the sacred in the world and so regarding the Bible as an especially sacred and potent object. By extension, this was also held of hymnals, prayerbooks, and catechisms, for they too embodied and expressed God's sacred Word. We can certainly speak of a distinctive Protestant form of sacramentalism, albeit one far weaker than its Catholic counterpart.

Nonetheless, the Reformation, both in its first and second generations, could be said to have drawn a firmer line between magic and religion by its changed understanding of the sacraments, and its repudiation of Catholic sacramentals. The profusion of blessed objects (salt, water, palms, herbs, and so forth) that so often gave sacred meaning to the daily life of pre-Reformation Christians did largely disappear from the lives of those of evangelical belief. Yet this did not remove the popular desire for some kind of instrumental application of sacred power to deal with the exigencies of daily life, and Protestants often turned to distinctively 'Protestant' remedies, using Bibles, hymnals, and prayer books for their healing and protective power. Indeed, their sacred character was even attested to by the belief that they were incombustible, a quality associated with the sacred power of sainthood in Catholic belief (and which was transferred to Luther as the quintessential Protestant saint). Some Protestants may have drawn the line at accepting the apotropaic power of blessed weather bells, but the no less apotropaic form of the 'hail-sermon' grew up as a Protestant custom, replacing the former eucharist procession through the fields to invoke divine protection over ripening crops.[9]

A further consequence of Protestant belief to which we must call attention before we can fully appreciate the problem posed for it by

8   See the discussion in Scribner, 'Impact of the Reformation', 323–40.
9   See Regine Grübe-Verhoeven, *Zauberei und Frömmigkeit*, Volksleben 13 (Tubingen, 1966), 11–57, on incombustibility, 48; also Scribner, *Popular Culture and Popular Movements*, 323–353, on incombustible bibles, 330–331. Heinze-Dieter Kittsteiner, 'Das Gewissen im Gewitter', *Jahrbuch für Volkskunde* (1987), 7–26, discusses the 'Hagelpredigt' as a form of Protestant protective magic.

popular magic concerns what I have called the 'moralized universe'. Alongside belief in a sacramental world, pre-Reformation religion also believed that certain human actions could provoke supernatural intervention in the natural world, either as a sign or a punishment. For example, the birth of deformed children or animals was often understood in this way, either as punishment for human sin (for example, a monk fornicating with a nun) or as a warning of impending divine wrath. Moral deviance, both individual and collective, was reflected in natural deformity, perhaps through belief in the links of microcosm and macrocosm, but more likely through a perception of a natural order influenced, via the supernatural, by the quality of human moral action. A stock late-medieval version of this causal nexus involved the belief that lepers had incurred the disease because of some sin committed by their parents, or that whole communities were at risk because of heresy in their midst. In summer 1523 the flooding of the Elbe and the destruction of crops was blamed by Saxon farmers on the activities of Luther and his cronies: God had afflicted the land because they had eaten meat in Lent.[10]

Protestant belief in a sacralized but weakly, rather than strongly, sacramental universe enabled this causal nexus to come more forcefully to the fore, especially since it accorded with belief in the sovereignty of God over the world. Indeed, the early evangelical movements had made ready polemical use of the notion by highlighting the way in which opponents of the Gospel sometimes appeared to be struck down by divine intervention, doubtless a reply to Catholic readiness to claim divine intervention in support of their own cause. It was applied with less polemical intent in the argument that those who used prohibited magical conjurations would become poor in consequence of divine punishment. However, Protestants significantly broadened the notion by insisting that the material consequences of moral failures were not simply confined to deviants and marginal groups, but were applicable to the failings of the population at large. It was summed up as early as 1530 by Johann Oldendorp, the Rostock city syndic who argued that if God's Word were ignored, it would lead to hunger, confusion, and ruin, but if it were observed, all streets and houses would be full of grain and money. This moral nexus became a constituent part of Protestant disciplinary ordinances aimed at moral improvement: failure to observe God's (and the prince's) laws would lead to dearth, hunger, crop failure,

10 Report of the Polish diplomat Johannes Dantiscus, traveling to Wittenberg in August 1523, in Inge B. Müller-Blessing, 'Johannes Dantiscus von Hofen. Ein Diplomat und Bischof zwischen Humanismus und Reformation', *Zeitschrift für die Geschichte und Altertumskunde Ermlands*, XXXI/XXXII (1967/68), 149–150.

war, plague, pestilence, and other punishments which God would visit on the earth and its people.[11]

The Protestant elaboration of the moralized universe had the effect of increasing anxiety among those it affected. Deprived of the protective means inherent in the Catholic sacramental system, Protestants found themselves prey to anxiety that was hardly allayed by invoking the Protestant doctrine of providence. Indeed, anxiety may even have been increased by awareness of the omnipresence of a sacred order in and among the secular. I do not mean just the activity of God, his Word and his Spirit, or of the Devil. Protestant belief allowed for a whole range of supernatural beings to be active in the world, especially angels, demons, and various kinds of spirits, such as those of the revenant dead. Their activity was accepted as possible not so much because it was experienced but because such beings were mentioned in the Bible, although there was a tendency to trace many such phenomena back to the "tricks of the Devil". Indeed, it seemed to many observers as though the Devil and demonic spirits had become wilder and more incalculable, attested by the remarkable efflorescence of Protestant demonology, which by the second half of the sixteenth century attained the level of an obsession.[12] However, Protestants found themselves deprived of ritual and sacramental ways of dealing with the activities of such beings, and official Protestantism was never quite sure what to make of ghosts, poltergeists, visions, prophecies, miracles, and, above all, demonic possession. The traffic between the supernatural and the natural worlds had perhaps become one-way, but the boundaries between sacred and secular remained highly porous and the seepage of the one into the other was highly unpredictable, incalculable, and even dangerous. It was for this

11   A typical Catholic tale of divine retribution concerned a pregnant weaver's wife in Magdeburg who demanded to be given communion under both kinds in 1524 and subsequently suffered a stillbirth. See 'Die Historia des Möllenvogtes Sebastian Langhans, 1524–25', *Chroniken der duetschen Städten* (Leipzig, 1899), XXXVII, 157. See Rudolf Gwerb, *Bericht von dem aberglaubigen und verbottenen Leuth-und Vych besegnen* (Zurich, 1646), 199–207; for the claims "Segner sind arm," 203, and "Segner erhalten schmale Vieh," 207. Johann Oldendorp, *Von Rathschlagen. Wie man gute Policey und Ordnung in Stadten und Landen erhalten möge* (Rostock 1597, facsimile ed., Glashütten im Taunus, 1971), the High German translation of the Low German original edition of 1530, 55–56. See, e.g., Duke Ulrich of Württemberg's mandate of 1547, Hauptstaatsarchiv Stuttgart A38, Bü. 12.

12   See the discussion of the *Teufelsbücher* by Rainer Alsheimer, 'Katalog protestantischer Teufelserzählungen,' in Wolfgang Brückner (ed.), *Volkserzählung und Reformation. Ein Handbuch zur Tradierung und Funktion von Erzählstoffen und Erzählliteratur im Protestantismus* (Berlin, 1974), 415–519; also H. C. Erik Midelfort, 'The Devil and the German People: Reflections on the Popularity of Demon Possession in Sixteenth-Century Germany', in Steven Ozment (ed.), *Religion and Culture in the Renaissance and Reformation* (Kirksville, Mo., 1989), 99–119.

reason that Protestants were tempted to turn to Catholic means of protection and also to forms of popular magic.

Protestantism thus experienced problems along two of the axes of ambiguity we have identified for pre-Reformation belief: inner-worldly efficacy of sacred action, and the activities of the diabolical/demonic. The same was also true along the third axis – the 'magical' power of prayer. As we might expect, practitioners of magic continued to ply their trade despite the implementation of religious reformation in any given territory. Indeed, we might well surmise that they received a double boost: the competition provided by the 'magic of the medieval church' was in great part removed, while the anxiety about how to deal with the exigencies of daily life was often intensified rather than lessened. In the absence of a Protestant rite of exorcism, practitioners of magic who were able to deal with demonic possession or with poltergeists found themselves virtually in a position to monopolize the market.[13] Indeed, they were able not only to survive under a Protestant dispensation but even to prosper, and they defied all attempts to eradicate them from the sixteenth to the eighteenth century and beyond. Practitioners of magic covered a wide range in early modern Germany, from purveyors of spells and charms (*Segner, Segenssprecher*), soothsayers and diviners (*Wahrsager, Wahrsagerinnen*), cunning men and women (*weise Männer, weise Frauen*), shepherds and herdsmen, specialists such as swine and cattle doctors (*Schwein und Viehartzet*), and those who practiced occasional sorcery based on acquired or inherited knowledge. Such persons, men and women, were approached for a variety of reasons: to perform counter-magic against bewitchment, to divine lost or stolen objects, to discover the cause of human and animal illness, to heal, to protect, and to cast spells of various kinds, whether against human or demonic ill will, or simply to guard against disaster.

In the 1540s it was clear to Protestant commentators that popular magic of this kind was a different phenomenon from Catholic sacramental magic and posed a quite different problem. Johann Spreter, a Württemberg pastor, in 1543 distinguished between two kinds of magic, that 'on the right side' and that 'on the left side'. The first was that practiced by the papist church in the traditional form of the sacramentals; the second involved the use of 'good or evil words' together with characters or objects through which the users believed 'creatures

---

13 It was probably coincidental and at best opportunistic that in 1529, at the point where the Elector of Saxony was actively reforming Catholic cult and doctrine in his territories, a woman exorcist approached him with the request that she be allowed to practice her art professionally, i.e. as a recognized trade, Carl A. H. Burckhardt, *Geschichte der sächsischen Kirchen-und Schulvisitationen 1524–49* (Leipzig, 1879), 87.

might be protected or changed'. The distinction was adopted in 1566 by Conrad Platz, a preacher in Biberach, in attacking the activities of a local exorcist (*Teufelsbanner*), although it was clear by then that 'magic on the left side' was causing far more trouble than that 'on the right side'. By the seventeenth and eighteenth centuries, popular magic was being discussed wholly within the framework of Protestant belief, but as false Protestant belief.[14]

Recourse to blessings, spells and charms caused the most difficulty for the attempts of official Protestantism, usually in the person of concerned pastors such as Spreter or Platz, to deal with forms of popular magic. If we recount the arguments offered by Platz in 1566, we can appreciate the nature of the problem. He called attention to the important role that words played in conjurations, spells and charms. These words were of three kinds: good, bad, and neutral. The 'bad' involved invoking the Devil; the 'neutral' consisted of saying words, harmless enough in themselves, in conjunction with certain 'superstitious practices' which turned them to misuse. Platz gave as examples the saying of words at certain times when it was hoped they would be especially efficacious such as reciting the names of the Trinity and making the sign of the cross in certain ritual contexts; and narrative spells said over wounds to effect healing. The 'good' words were words found in Scripture but which were misused for magical spells. Platz specifically mentioned the names of God, the Trinity, and Christ's five wounds, the inscription INRI above the cross of Christ, the first chapter of John, the Pater Noster, and the Ave Maria. These were used magically as spoken or written words, sometimes in conjunction with herbs and sometimes as amulets. Whatever their form, Platz asserted, they all involve 'magic' because the users put their trust in the power of words and ignore God as our only helper. As such they infringed the first and second commandments.[15]

It is worthy of note that Platz cited formulas and practices that were common in Catholic magical usage, and many of the forms of charms or spells used by Protestants certainly were adaptations of older Catholic versions. However, they seem to have been 'reformed' for evangelical use by removing references to Mary and the saints, and retaining the names

---

14   Johann Spreter, *Ein kurtzer Bericht, was von den abgötterischen Sägen [und] Beschweren zuhalten . . .* (Basel, 1543), Aiii; Conrad Wolfgang Platz, *Kurtzer, nottwendiger und Wollgegrundter bericht, auch Christentliche vermanung, von der Grewlichen, in aller Welt gebreuchlichen Zauberey, Sünd dem zauberischen Beschowren und Segenssprechen, Predigtweys gethon* (n.p., 1566). See the more detailed discussion in Scribner, 'Magic and the Formation of Protestant Popular Culture in Germany', forthcoming.

15   Platz, *Kurtzer, nottwendiger . . . Bericht*, B6^r–C4^r.

of God, Christ, or the Trinity; or else they used prayers found in Scripture such as the Pater Noster and the Ave Maria. Indeed, the Pater Noster, along with the sign of the cross and its invocation of the Trinity, were held by Catholic and Protestant alike to be formulas of great magical potency which found continual usage throughout the medieval and early modern period.[16] Platz listed, in order to refute them, various arguments advanced by those who used such spells and charms, but in so doing revealed how far such 'scripturally-based' spells and charms had come to constitute what was, in effect, a Protestant form of magic.

These are nothing but good words, their defenders claimed, which speak only of God, and what is done in God's name must surely be proper and good; one should use the means provided by God, who has blessed all things on earth; one prays and calls upon God with such words, so why should one not use them for blessings and incantations? It cannot be wrong to invoke the name of the Trinity when this is done by the words of the sacraments, for example, baptizing in the name of the Trinity or using the words of consecration in the communion. Moreover, the words spoken from the pulpit during a sermon have their efficacy and such words should also be efficacious in blessings; God expelled the Devil and worked miracles through the spoken word, and this same practice was allowed to the Apostles.

All of these arguments conformed to a typically evangelical understanding of the importance of God's Word as the most potent form of sacrality, and were not easy to refute, although Platz did his best to dispose of them. He insisted that such things must be founded in the Word of God and should be commanded by God: thus, words used in the sacraments are done only at God's command. The preacher speaking God's Word does so as his instrument and the efficacy of the Word in this case is not that of the spoken word but of the Word working in the heart, nor is it worked by the preacher of his own power but as a tool of God. Spells and charms even using such good words are not means provided by God; there is no command to do so in the Bible and magic is expressly prohibited there in several places. Moreover, the words used in such spells are mere human words of the spellcaster and these do not constitute a form of blessing, but rather an impious incantation.[17]

Platz may have had the better theological argument, but continued recourse not only to spells and charms but also to much the same 'evangelical' arguments over many subsequent generations shows that his

16 On the Pater Noster, Ludwig Strackerjan, *Aberglauben und Sagen aus dem Herzogtum Oldenburg* (Oldenburg, 1909), I, 2, 77, 120, 290; Carl Seyfarth, *Aberglauben und Zauberei in der Volksmedizin Sachsens* (Leipzig, 1913), 138.
17 Platz, *Kurtzer, nottwendiger . . . Bericht*, C6ᵛ–G7ᵛ.

refutations were held to be unconvincing. During the seventeenth century similar and somewhat more refined justifications of popular magic as wholly consistent with Protestant belief were still to be found, one of which involved a creative adaptation of the Protestant doctrine of adiaphora.[18] What may have counted more was the argument that experience showed that the spells actually worked. The retort of Platz and other pastors confronted with this claim was that this apparent success was a deception and was only possible through the work of the Devil. Thus, for Protestantism there was also a penumbra of ambiguity between religion and magic along the third axis, and when faced with the most intractable challenge thrown up by this ambiguity, that of the apparent efficacy of 'magical prayer', one resorted to the same strategy of demonization used in the pre-Reformation church.

If we were to lay a Protestant template on that formed by our three axes of Catholic belief, we would find one nestling inside the other like a pair of angle brackets. The relationship of Protestant to Catholic was a matter of degree, since the same axes were involved for both confessions in the three-dimensional relationship between religion and magic. Indeed, if individuals were positioned in the religio-magical space thus formed, many Protestants would be found at points not too far removed from Catholics. Protestantism was as caught up as Catholicism in the same dilemmas about the instrumental application of sacred power to secular life because it was positioned in the same force-field of sacrality. For this reason, Protestants experienced the same difficulties as Catholics when accusations of maleficent magic (and sometimes even of 'white' magic) were laid in ways that turned them into accusations of witchcraft. The possibility of consorting with, and becoming implicated in, demonic activity was as real for Protestants as for Catholics. Thus, the puzzle of how a massive witchcraze could apprently arise in a period said to usher in the dawn of 'modern rationality', a puzzle which Trevor-Roper saw as an 'intellectual challenge' and which caused Tambiah to raise a quizzical eyebrow, rests on a false dilemma.[19] There was no inconsistency between Protestant thought-modes and a mentality that accepted diabolical efficacy in the world.

This is not to say that we could not find in Protestantism elements pointing in the direction mapped by those who see the Reformation as

18   Gwerb, *Bericht von dem aberglaubigen . . . besegnen*, 265–6, had to repudiate the argument that the use of magical blessings was not expressly forbidden in the Bible, and that this was therefore permissible. At the end of the seventeenth century, Georg Christoph Zimmermann, a Franconian pastor, was also confronted with similar justifications, see the discussion in Scribner, 'Magic and the Formation of Protestant Popular Culture'.

19   Tambiah, *Magic, Science, Religion*, 47.

the first stage in the 'disenchantment of the world', as the first step on the road to modernity. The question of the typicality of such elements remains a major point on which the thesis could be criticized, although this is too large a subject to pursue here. The explanation for the apparent plausibility of the thesis resides less in the nature of the Reformation of the sixteenth century and more in its historiography. Historical understanding of exactly what 'the Reformation' had been about and what it produced developed through many stages and phases, although the view of the subsequent two centuries emphasized its potently sacred character: the Reformation was part of a great divine intervention in the world, part of God's ultimate plan for creation and humanity. It was the Enlightenment that first interpreted the Reformation as part of a long-term process of rationalization and secularization, an interpretation further reworked by the historiography of the nineteenth century until it constructed our modern view of the Reformation.[20]

The paradigm of a secularizing and rationalizing Reformation has influenced many overarching interpretations of the ways in which the religion of Protestants contributed to long-term historical development, foremost among them that of Max Weber, who injected the notion of the 'disenchantment of the world' into historical discussion. We may take Weber as a prime example of the ways in which nineteenth-century concerns were projected onto historical understanding of religion in the Reformation. Weber wrote from a background of nineteenth-century liberalism, claiming that he was himself 'religiously unmusical'. Many of the concepts he applied to the Reformation were arbitrary, if creative, adaptations of terms used in other, rather different contexts. The concept of 'charisma' was rationalized from the strictly theological usage of the church historian Rudolf Sohm, that of the 'disenchantment of the world' from Schiller's poetic usage. The notion of the 'Protestant ethic' was an insight Weber arrived as less from historical research and more from observations of nineteenth-century Protestant behaviour, which he then projected backwards in time in a classic example of the 'regressive method'. The further assumption that an adequate understanding of 'Protestantism' was achieved by focusing primarily on the theology of the main reformers, was a crucial next step, so that he did not have to confront the problem of the actual historicity of Protestantism, or the untidiness of the phenomenon as it was put into practice. It was sufficient to find examples to illustrate his ideal typical construction, drawn (as has often been remarked) rather indiscrimi-

20 Dickens and Tonkin, *Reformation in Historical Thought*, 7–89, 119–49; E. W. Zeeden, *Martin Luther und die Reformation im Urteil des deutschen Luthertums* (Freiburg im Breisgau, 1950, 1952), 2 v.

nately from several way stations along the road from Luther to Weber's own day.[21]

Whatever we may think of the sociological status of Weber's insights about the Reformation – and I must concede that I have always found them heuristically rewarding – I do not think that the thesis about the 'disenchantment of the world' will any longer pass muster as a historically accurate description. It has certainly inspired many contemporary treatments of how the Reformation relates to the process of 'modernization', not least the current interest among historians of the sixteenth century in social processes such as 'confessionalization', social discipline and the 'civilizing process' (alongside Norbert Elias and Michel Foucault, both of whom worked with the classic nineteenth-century paradigm of the Reformation). None of these interpretations, however, deal with, or show any understanding of, the nature of popular Protestantism.

I do not think it possible at this stage to offer an alternative vision of how the 'decline of magic' and associated developments came about (in many ways, they involve processes still in train). Thomas offered a number of useful conjectures over two decades ago, but his suggestions have yet to be properly explored in the English context, much less in that of Germany. Moreover, the discussion has yet to take cognizance of the possibility that processes of secularization and desacralization may not be as closely tied to the development of Protestantism as has been assumed. It is interesting that Acquaviva, writing from a Catholic tradition, is able to provide a nuanced and perceptive analysis of such religious and social phenomena without, at any point, mentioning Protestantism or the Reformation.[22]

21   H. H. Gerth and C. Wright Mills, *From Max Weber. Essays in Sociology* (London, 1974), 25, 51–52. This projection is apparent from the opening pages of *The Protestant Ethic*, 35–46, where Weber ponders on contemporary religious affiliation and social stratification, the more so when we realize that this question had been 'very much in the air' around 1900, along with theorizing on the role of Protestantism in the industrial revolution, Wolfgang J. Mommsen, *The Age of Bureaucracy: Perspectives on the Political Sociology of Max Weber* (New York, 1974), 100. Weber then embarked, according to Mommsen, 102, on his research on the sociology of world religions in order to corroborate *ex negativo* his findings on the 'Protestant ethic'. For the 'regressive method', Peter Burke, *Popular Culture in Early Modern Europe* (London, 1978), 77–87. Curiously, the very rich footnotes to the final version of *The Protestant Ethic* often reflect a more highly developed awareness of historical complexity than the main text. One is reminded by them how far the 'final' work was the product of almost two decades of thought on the problem in which some of Weber's later insights, for example those on the importance of Protestant sects, were more rewarding than his initial thoughts on the subject.

22   Thomas, *Religion and the Decline of Magic*, 767–800; Sabino S. Acquaviva (trans. Patricia Lipscombe), *The Decline of the Sacred in Industrial Society* (1966; rev. edn, Oxford, 1979).

To explore the role of Protestantism in such processes, it is first necessary to construct a new understanding of the Reformation of the sixteenth century which takes account of those dissonant elements which falsify the paradigm that has been hitherto accepted, and then to write a new history of Protestantism which includes the religious experience and practice of ordinary believers, with all of their contradictions and misunderstandings. From the progress made so far on this task, I suspect that we would discover that Protestantism was as much a part of the problem as the self-evident solution to it; not a prime mover, but as subject as any other confession to secularization and desacralization, whatever set these processes in motion and whatever forms, stages, and modes of development they passed through.[23] Some aspects of Protestantism doubtless encouraged some Protestants to recognize a world purged of magic, whereas other militated against it. It may also turn out that the 'disenchantment of the world' played a marginal role in both the developing history of Protestantism and in advance toward 'the modern world'. This, however, is a story which still awaits its careful analyst.

23   Exemplary for the kind of sensitive and nuanced study needed is C. Scott Dixon, *The Reformation and Rural Society. The Parishes of Brandenburg-Ansbach-Kulmbach 1528–1603* (Cambridge, 1996). It is illuminating that Protestantism and the Reformation feature only marginally in the reflections offered on such processes by Charles Tilly, *Big Structures, Large Processes, Huge Comparisons* (New York, 1984). Tilly presents a cogent argument for purging historical discourse of the 'pernicious postulates' of the nineteenth century before we can begin to understand the nature of long-term historical change.

Index